Québec

a tale of love

Québec

a tale of love

Laurier L. LaPierre

PENGUIN

VIKING

VIKING

Published by the Penguin Group

Penguin Books Canada Ltd, 10 Alcorn Avenue, Toronto, Ontario, Canada M4V 3B2

Penguin Books Ltd, 27 Wrights Lane, London W8 5TZ, England

Penguin Putnam Inc., 375 Hudson Street, New York, New York 10014, U.S.A.

Penguin Books Australia Ltd, Ringwood, Victoria, Australia

Penguin Books (NZ) Ltd, cnr Rosedale and Airborne Roads, Albany,
Auckland 1310, New Zealand

Penguin Books Ltd, Registered Offices: Harmondsworth, Middlesex, England

First published 2001

1 3 5 7 9 10 8 6 4 2

Author representation: Westwood Creative Artists
94 Harbord Street, Toronto, Ontario M5S 1G6

Grateful acknowledgement is made for permission to reprint excerpts from
the following copyrighted works:

"Efficiency," from *Social Notes II, 1935,* reprinted with the permission of William
Toye, literary executor for the estate of F.R. Scott.

Memoirs by René Lévesque, translated by Philip Stratford. Used by permission,
McClelland & Stewart, Ltd. *The Canadian Publishers.*

Printed and bound in Canada on acid free paper ∞

Canadian Cataloguing in Publication Data
LaPierre, Laurier L., 1929–
Québec : a tale of love

ISBN 0-670-87864-2

1. Quebec (Province) – History. I. Title.
FC2911.L357 2001   971.4   C00-932481-X
F1052.95.L37 2001

Visit Penguin Canada's website at **www.penguin.ca.**

For Alex:
She saw the darkness and chose the light as she allowed me to sing to her;
and for Dominic and Laura; Cary and Thomas; Paige and Georgia

Contents

Introduction

❧

I belong to a people who have been living on the land of Canada since the beginning of the 17th century. Between 1635 and the end of that century, these people fashioned for themselves a country that stretched from Hudson Bay to the Gulf of Mexico and from the Atlantic Ocean to the foot of the Rockies. In the process they became a people apart from the French from whom they had sprung. In other words, by the end of the 17th century, the *nation canadienne*—the nation to which I belong—was created. "It seems we are different nations," my friend de Bougainville admitted during his passage among us as an officer in the Seven Years War.

I take pride in that!

What you are about to read is anathema to many. But that doesn't make it less real. There is only one nation in Canada: the Canadian nation—*la nation canadienne*. Within that nation, all the others co-exist. It's a paradox, yes. However, if you remember that Canadians and Canadiens have fashioned one country out of many domains—coastlines and mountains, grasslands and tundra, lake and river valleys, and a massive rocky shield—the paradox becomes more understandable, even acceptable.

This land has shaped us; for like the land, we are a people destined to live in the midst of diversity. In that process of living, we become one. That doesn't mean that we are all the same. Wilfrid Laurier put it rather well in Toronto on December 10, 1886, and it was reported in *The Globe*:

> We are Canadians. Below the island of Montréal the water that comes from the north, the Ottawa, unites with the waters that come from the Western lakes; but uniting they do not mix. There they run parallel, separate, distinguishable, and yet are one stream, flowing within the same banks, the mighty St. Lawrence, rolling on towards the sea. . . . A perfect image of our nation.

Like him, we, Canadians and Canadiens, find the fullness of our being in living together. Apart we are insignificant.

Therefore, the *nation canadienne* that my ancestors created out of the seven thousand or so immigrants who came from France in the 17th and 18th centuries now co-exists within the nation of Canada. Our country consists of one people who have come from all over the planet and who express their being of this country in English and in French. (A reminder: the French language is not limited in its living to the territory of Québec and the National Capital Region of Canada. The French language exists, by right of citizenship, across our land. Today those who argue otherwise are, in my view, engaging in diatribes. In doing so, they weaken Canada, just like their "ancestors" did throughout our history.)

My earliest known ancestor here, Sergeant Pierre Denys, arrived in Canada from Gascogny in the last quarter of the 17th century. Little is known about him, except that on October 8, 1687, he married Marie Godin, a widow with one child. He died on September 18, 1727, in the village of Saint-Laurent on the Île d'Orléans, having sired nine children between 1688 and 1705. No doubt, his sons were explorers and coureurs de bois, farmers and priests. No doubt, his daughters married men like him, tilled the soil, had many children, and waited for their men to return from hunting, trapping, and exploring. No doubt, the blood and the sweat—and probably the tears—of those he sired nourished the soil of my country.

One of his grandsons, Pierre Denys, added "*dit* Lapierre" to his name—at least he was married as such in 1758. After that, the Denys disappeared, and my ancestors were known simply as Lapierre. I, part of the ninth generation since Sergeant Denys, changed the spelling to LaPierre.

What we, the Lapierres or LaPierres, and the many others who surround us, have done with his legacy is the subject of this book. I take pride in that!

Pierre Denys—*dit* Lapierre—came to Canada, but he lived in the territory that, since 1867, has been known as Québec. Québec is a Montagnais word that means "the narrowing of the river." Another story is that some of the sailors who came with Jacques Cartier in 1536, when noticing the tall cape around which the city of Québec is now built, exclaimed, "Quel-bec!" (What a beek!) A good story.

Québec, like many places in Canada, has its own distinct inheritance. It offers a different way of life, another sense of purpose, an instrument to better define Canada. But Québec is a place that is in—and of—Canada.

Unfortunately, Canadians and Canadiens have not always acted as if we took that as a given. It's a pity; because if we had, we would have avoided much pain as we lived the summons of our destiny to the fullest.

Four hundred and sixty years have passed since the first Europeans sailed the St. Lawrence River to the present city of Québec. Since then, the geography and the size of what is now called the Province of Québec have changed dramatically. From that first contact with the Aboriginal people until roughly the end of the 18th century, the territory governed by the authorities living in the town of Québec was enormous, encompassing as it did all the lands north and south, east and west, stretching from the Atlantic Ocean to the foot of the Rockies and from the Arctic Ocean to the Gulf of Mexico.

Over the centuries much has occurred to reduce the territory of Québec. Yet, today, at over one million and a half square kilometres, it is the largest of the Canadian provinces and the second most populous, with 80 percent of its population being French-speaking. The Hudson Strait borders it in the north, Labrador and the Gulf of St. Lawrence in the east, New Brunswick and the

United States in the south, and Hudson Bay and Ontario in the west. The Canadian Shield, that massive rock, covers nine-tenths of the province. It's a rich, beautiful, and promising land!

From the earliest time of Native settlement and of the arrival of my people from France, the St. Lawrence River (La Rivière du Canada, as the Aboriginals called it) is key to the tale of Canada.

This river flows from Lake Ontario, through the famed Thousand Islands, then travels over a thousand kilometres to the Gulf of St. Lawrence. En route, it passes by Montréal, Québec City, the rugged land of the North Shore and the plains to the south. Its tributaries are also part of the history of Canada: the Ottawa River, the Saguenay, the Manicouagan, the St. Maurice, and the Richelieu. From these rivers, the explorers, the settlers, and the searchers for a better way of life penetrated the core of North America.

Unlike the land of Canada, which is an old land, the St. Lawrence is young, barely ten thousand years old. The receding glaciers gashed it out of the earth. Since then, it has been the main axis of our country and its defining characteristic.

There cannot be just one history of Canada, particularly one created in central Canada. But that doesn't mean we don't have a national history. We do. Our national history, though, is the sum total of our diversity and of the parts that make up Canada. In other words, we are one people with a common history but our diversity in populations and geography has compelled us to live Canada in different ways.

So, I invite you to read this history in the spirit that I've written it—as a tale of love. You see, I love Québec as passionately as I love Canada. Both are the same to me.

Of course, my critics will say—as they have so often in the past—that I exaggerate and that my facts and interpretation are wobbly. Forget the critics. I dismiss them for the simple reason that, like the Bourbons of France, they have forgotten nothing and learned nothing.

Exaggeration is the natural consequence of passion. And what I lack in erudition, I make up for in imagination. After all, history is 99 percent imagination.

I should alert you, right at the start, that spirits from the past visit me—or I am transported to them—or I meet them on the Net. Everywhere I go, I engage in dialogue with them. I've been an interviewer all my life, so why should I not use my trade to illuminate the elements of my inheritance?

During my seven decades, I have found Canada to be magic, and the living in it and of it demands the making of miracles. Making it work is the greatest miracle of all.

I have often travelled the length and breadth of my country. I can attest that it's a land of incredible beauty, that it contains a people of remarkable worth, that its political, social, cultural, and economic order is one of the best in the world, and that it's a gift to live here.

Québec's good fortune is to be a part of it all. That's what my ancestor wanted. And that is what it shall be.

I hope this tale of love measures up to the expectations that Québec holds for those who accept her as she is.

Enjoy.

Laurier L. LaPierre, O.C.
Ottawa in the National Capital Region of my country

Part one

The People of
la rivière du Canada

I

The First to Come

*W*hen glaciers still covered most of Canada, a people entered our country via Alaska into the Yukon Territory, their ancestors having crossed the land-bridge of Beringia, now sunk into the sea. They came our way because the large fur-bearing animals they hunted and lived off had migrated to our land. In time, the ice receded and a couloir appeared between the Rockies and Coast Mountains. Most animals went south as did many early Aboriginals, but some remained in the land of the North. During the next several thousand years, the Aboriginals' descendants migrated in various directions in search of food and living conditions that appealed to them. In time they came to occupy self-governing and recognised territories on which they built their villages and acquired a way of life centred on the bounties of the land and the deities beyond.

The St. Lawrence lowlands have been occupied for thousands of years. Five hundred years or so before contact with the white man, these lands were inhabited by a people whom archaeologists and other experts call the St.

Lawrence Iroquois, who, no doubt, displaced those who were there before them. Living in well-defined "towns" like Stadacona (Québec), Achelacy (near Trois-Rivières), and Hochelaga (Montréal), they were mostly an agricultural people, growing corn, pumpkins, beans and tobacco, and hunting and fishing. They controlled the entire St. Lawrence River.

Others, of course, also occupied the land that was to become the Québec of today: the Mi'kmaqs, the Montagnais, the Algonquins, the Abenakis, the Crees and Naskapis. They traded and fought each other for dominance and favourable trading partnerships with the Portuguese, the Spanish, the English and, as far as the tale of Québec is concerned, the French.

Many of the First Nations who lived in what is now the territory of Québec came into contact with European civilisation early in the 16th century. However, there may have been earlier contacts. Iberian explorers, Carthaginian merchants, Israelites, Hindus, Romans, and many others may have "discovered" North America long before the Christian era. In the 5th or 6th century, an Irish monk, St. Brendan, may have come as well. He was searching for the *paradisum terrestre* (the Promised Land of the Saints). Close to half a century later, Leif Ericsson, a Norse mariner, sailed from Greenland to Vinland (in Newfoundland or Nova Scotia). However, it was Thorfinnr Thordarsson, the husband of Leif's widow, who left us evidence of that group's passage and dwelling among us at L'Anse aux Meadows.

Between 1000 A.D. and the arrival of Bristol fishermen (who are said to have discovered the great wealth of the Grand Banks off Newfoundland in the 1480s), no one else appears to have visited us from Europe.

Changes that significantly transformed the face of Europe by the last quarter of the 15th century brought the French to Québec. By that time, kingdoms had consolidated around powerful monarchs and dynasties, giving rise to nationalism and parallel rivalries. Newly fashioned kings limited the power of their aristocracies and came to depend on the skills and wealth of the rising middle class (the bourgeoisie). In time, the kings and princes challenged the hegemony of the medieval Church. To round out this picture, the long period of the exchange of goods between Asia and Europe ended with the fall of Constantinople to the Turks in 1453. A new route to the fabled East was needed.

In pursuit of that, Christopher Columbus (1492) and others discovered and acquired the Americas in the first quarter of the 16th century; Portuguese navigator Vasco da Gama managed to reach Callicut, India, in 1498; and Ferdinand Magellan circumnavigated the world in 1522. But it was John Cabot (or Giovanni Caboto, an Italian working for England's king, Henry VII) who came to what is now called Newfoundland in 1497.

Added to this activity, men from western Europe fished the Grand Banks off Newfoundland and became rich—including the English, then the Portuguese, then the French, represented by the Normans and the Bretons. It was the latter who paved the way for the French invasion of Canada, with their extensive fishing in the Strait of Belle Isle and off the coasts of Cape Breton Island and of Nova Scotia.

Forty years after Columbus's attempt to find Cathay, the Portuguese found a route, albeit a long one, around the Cape of Good Hope, the Spaniards one far to the south of the American hemisphere, and the English had begun their feverish search along North America's east coast. Could the French have remained far behind?

François I, king of France, didn't think so. Curious to find out if there was a way west between northern Florida and Cape Breton that had escaped his royal rivals, he hired an Italian, Giovanni da Verrazzano, to find the Sea of China two years after Magellan's voyage. Verrazzano failed, but in 1532, at a time when the king was in great need of money to pay for his wars against Charles V, the Holy Roman Emperor, Jean Le Veneur de Tilliers, bishop of Saint-Malo and abbot of Mont-Saint-Michel reawakened his royal interest. François I commissioned Jacques Cartier, a pilot and map-maker, who was said to have sailed with Verrazzano, to find both the route to Asia and the riches of the new world.

On April 20, 1534, Cartier sailed out of Saint-Malo with two ships and sixty-one men. Arriving in Newfoundland on May 10, he reached the Gaspé Peninsula in the Gulf of St. Lawrence in the middle of July.

And so—at least for us, the descendants of French Europeans—the tale begins.

The Europe that Jacques Cartier brought with him was technologically superior to the world he was about to visit. He had cannons and hand-held guns plus an arsenal of swords and other traditional weapons. He sailed ships equipped with navigational instruments, many sails and decks; and these were, in effect, sailing forts that afforded much security from attack. He knew that the America he would explore was inhabited. He came prepared.

Jacques Cartier, the first explorer of the Gulf of St. Lawrence, the discoverer of the St. Lawrence River, and the commander of the settlement of Charlesbourg-Royal (Cap-Rouge), was born in Saint-Malo in 1491. He was one of the best pilots and cartographers France ever produced. He was, as well, not without courage. On the other hand, he was certain—like most Europeans of his time—that his culture, civilisation, religion, and political system made him and his men superior to those who weren't like them. And he approached the Natives of our country with those sentiments firmly implanted, viewing the North American peoples as belonging to inferior cultures and civilisations. Above all, they were pagans. It was, therefore, appropriate—and a blessing in disguise—to steal from them, to use and abuse them, and even to kidnap them.

The Natives Cartier encountered possessed primitive weapons (in the face of the French firepower). Native tools were nothing compared to those the French used and sometimes gave as presents. And the glass beads, to the Natives, were crystals arising out of the earth, gifts of the gods. Where then had Cartier come from? From the land of the Spirits! And so, the Europeans were supernatural beings who lived on floating islands guided by white clouds (sails). French cannons and guns spewed forth thunder and lightning as punishment from the gods and the metal instruments and beads were the gifts of the Great Spirit.

What is remarkable in all of this is how quickly the supernatural disappeared—and the "inferiors" began to determine the intentions of the newcomers.

⚜

Mascou is my friend—my imaginary Native-spirit companion. He has been with me since the early days of my acquaintance with my country. When I was a child, I used to play with him in the attic of my parents' house. Of course, I played the part of the

Jesuit bent on converting him. He resisted constantly. As I grew up, I gave up trying, and we have remained friends. He still leads where I fear to go. Using few words and fewer gestures, he speaks at length about what matters to him and to his people—and to me and my people.

Mascou has been everywhere on the land we share together. Yet he claims no particular territory; "It's all mine," he once said. As well, he admits of being of no particular nation or tribe. "Everyone is in me!" he insists. He's therefore at home with whoever he is. Together, we've often journeyed throughout this vast territory that is ours.

I now hear a familiar noise behind me. It's Mascou, with a tall, skinny, brownish man in his early twenties with black hair and small inquisitive black eyes. They carry a canoe between them.

Mascou introduces me to his companion. He is Domagaya, a Mohawk prince of Canada.

I know, of course, who Domagaya is.

His duty done, Mascou disappears. Domagaya and I launch the canoe into the St. Lawrence. As we embark, he says in French, "I do not trust your people." I know why. We both row. He seems surprised at that.

"Mascou has taught me well," I say with a grin of satisfaction. Without uttering another word, we proceed across the river to the embankment of what is now the Gaspé Peninsula. I spend the time reconstructing, in my mind, Cartier's first encounter with Domagaya's people.

⚜

Jacques Cartier's first voyage to Canada, in 1534, took him to Cape Dégrat (Cap-Dégrat) at the very northern tip of Newfoundland. From there, he entered the Strait of Belle Isle on May 27, thirty-seven days after his departure from France. Hugging the western coast of Newfoundland from Rich Point to Cap à l'Anguille, not far from the southwestern tip of the island, he didn't like what he saw. He described the terrain as "la terre que Dieu donna à Cain" (the land God gave to Cain), filled as it was with "horrible and ill-shapen stones" without even a shovelful of dirt. On that barren land, on June 12, he saw his first Natives. He found them well-shaped and built but "farouches et sauvages" (fierce and savage). Their hair was closely tied to their heads and decorated with feathers. They dressed in furs and painted their faces a reddish colour. They were the Beothuks. European cod fishermen and the Mi'kmaqs, who lived mostly in what are now the Maritime provinces, managed to exterminate these Native peoples by 1829.

A few days after seeing the Beothuks, Cartier turned southwest. Had he continued due south for a few more kilometres, Cartier would have discovered that Newfoundland is indeed an island.

On June 24, he was at what is now called Prince Edward Island. What he saw thereafter was no longer the land of Cain. At the beginning of July, he entered the Baie des Chaleurs, which he hoped was a passage to the Asian Sea. So hopeful was he that he called the tip of it Cap d'Espérance (now Pointe Miscou). In that area, as well, he encountered and traded with the Mi'kmaqs who were accustomed to sell furs to the European fisherman.

After he discovered that the Baie des Chaleurs contained no passage to Asia, he sailed northward and, on July 14, he entered the Baie de Gaspé. It was there that Cartier met Domagaya's people.

⚜

Still in our canoe but facing the exact spot where he accosted Cartier, Domagaya begins to speak. "I am Domagaya, a prince of Canada. My father, Donnacona, is the King of Canada and the Lord of Ajoasta, Sitadin, Thoagahen, Stadacona, Deganonda, Thegnignouda, Thegadechoalla, Tequenonday, Tella, Stagoahen, Agouchonda, and Hochelay. We live in his capital, Stadacona, several days journey from here. Every summer, our people come to this place, Honguedo, to fish. We trusted your Monsieur Cartier. We offered him gifts. We danced and sang for him." He steadies the canoe before adding: "In return for our courtesies, he abused us."

"By planting a cross? It certainly infuriated your father."

"We knew the meaning of such acts. He was claiming our territory for himself, his god, and his king. My father rebuked him."

"But Cartier didn't take down his cross. Instead, he . . ."

Domagaya doesn't let me finish. Quite upset, he stands up in the canoe and says in a loud voice: "This land and the waters around it are part of my father's territory. This land is ours." He sits down and with sadness adds: "Your Monsieur Cartier had no right to take possession of our land. We went to his ship to speak with him, but he fooled us, capturing our canoe and dragging us on board. He parlayed my father in allowing him to take my younger brother, Taignoagny, and me to France and promising him to bring us back the following year. Unwilling to be impolite and disrespectful, my father agreed. He told us secretly to learn all we could of the ways of the invaders so that we could help our people. In return for the captivity of his sons, your Monsieur Cartier offered him an axe."

"You sailed for France the next day!"

"Yes. We journeyed not too far from the entrance of the great river that takes us to our home. Your Monsieur Cartier missed it, and I didn't point it out to him. We sailed north and then across a dangerous ocean to arrive at his home, Saint-Malo. My brother and I spoke French by then. None of the others on board our ship bothered learning our language."

"What did you do in France?"

"We met his king and brought greetings to him from my father, the king of Canada. We told his king and his court about our great river along the shores of which we have built our houses. We also talked to him at length about the kingdom that lay west and north of us and which was filled with gold and other metals. My father, we said, had travelled there."

Before I can ask if he feels he has betrayed his people, he looks around and says simply, "We wanted to return home!"

With few words, he tells me how he spent the months between

September 1534 and May 1535, when he and his brother sailed back to Stadacona with Cartier: "We lived in your Monsieur Cartier's village. I refused to be baptised." And with that he becomes silent again.

⚜

Cartier's second voyage was more perilous than his first. He had three ships at his disposal: the *Grande Hermine*, the *Petite Hermine*, and the *Émérillon*, with a 110 men on board, including Domagaya and Taignoagny. His mission was to pursue his explorations of distant lands beyond Newfoundland. Two months after his departure from Saint-Malo, and after a difficult crossing, he was back near the Gaspé Peninsula. From there on, both brothers helped him to find his bearings.

"Non!": Anticosti was not a peninsula, as Cartier stubbornly insisted it was, but an island; "Non!": Cartier's ships weren't in a bay but in a gulf (a fact Cartier finally accepted by giving it the name of Saint-Laurent); "Oui!": a large and long river emptied into the Gulf; "Oui!": a two-day journey on the river would take the capitaine and pilote to the outskirts of the Kingdom of the Saguenay they had talked about in France; and "Oui!": if they continued on the river, Cartier would reach another kingdom, the Kingdom of Canada and the town, Stadacona, in which lived their father and their people. "This river is the road to Canada—la Rivière du Canada," they told him. When he hesitated, Domagaya added: "It will even take you to Hochelaga from where you can also reach the Kingdom of the Saguenay." The river "went so far" that no man had ever been able to travel to the end of it.

With some trepidation Cartier accepted their arguments and followed their instructions. On the way to Donnacona's kingdom, Cartier's ship entered the Saguenay River, where the brothers met with some relatives who were on a fishing expedition. Cartier, eager to get to Canada and from there to Hochelaga, didn't explore the Saguenay River.

On September 7 his ships arrived at a group of fourteen islands, which was the beginning of the Kingdom of Canada. Domagaya and Taignoagny re-united with their kin on the shores of the Île d'Orléans, and the next day their father came to welcome them. There was much feasting, dancing and rejoicing. It was the first time since their kidnapping that the brothers could eat corn and smoke tobacco.

Without asking the permission of his hosts, Cartier set up his camp on a river he called Sainte-Croix (St. Charles River). From there he could see the Cap aux Diamants on which stood Stadacona, the town of the king of Canada. Stadacona, which means "standing rock," consisted of huts, with no enclosure to protect them. Cartier judged the land, which was filled with large and beautiful trees, to be fertile, productive and well looked after. However, he didn't spend a long time admiring the beauty and determining the value of his surroundings. His principal preoccupation was to reach Hochelaga (Montréal) as quickly as possible. But Donnacona was of no help in hastening Cartier's departure.

The old chief was no fool; he sensed that the French were not casual visitors; they had other objectives in mind. They could, therefore, be useful in the economic betterment of the Canadian people. Furthermore, Donnacona wanted his position as the master of the St. Lawrence recognised. Often the Hochelagans had impeded him and had become his rivals and enemies in the process. To have Cartier visit them and negotiate an alliance would be inimical to Donnacona's interests. So he used all his guile to force Cartier to stay among the Stadaconans. He gave Cartier a girl and two boys to show his good will; when that gesture failed, Donnacona tried to frighten the Frenchman by staging the visit of three evil spirits. They predicted that their principal god, Cudouagny, would imprison the French ships and their barges in thick ice, bury the sailors in deep snow, and send a freezing wind to inhibit their movements. Cartier laughed at it all and, to add insult to injury, refused to accept Donnacona's offer of his two sons as interpreters. Without taking leave of his host as courtesy demanded, Cartier left on September 19, arriving in Hochelaga on October 2.

More than a thousand people greeted him with great joy and amazement. Thinking him to be an emissary of the Great Spirit, they brought their children and even their chief for him to touch, bless—and to cure those who were ill or infirm. Cartier satisfied himself by reading to them the Gospel according to St. John and, to be on the safe side, he continued with the whole account of the Passion of Jesus Christ "mot à mot."

In his *Voyages en Nouvelle-France*, he didn't report whether or not the Gospel and the Passion relieved the pain of his hosts or cured their afflicted bodies. When they took him to their round city, he was impressed by the long houses in which they lived and the fortifications they had constructed. More compelling, though, was the high mountain at the foot of which the Hochelagans had built their town. He named it Mont-Royal.

Later, from the top of Mont-Royal, he saw the Laurentians reaching off to the northeast and northwest, and to the south he saw the Adirondacks and the Green Mountains of Vermont. Between all these ranges, he wrote, was a plain covered with rich soil and, in his judgement, easily tilled. In the southwest were "three beautiful round mountains": Saint-Bruno, Saint-Hilaire, and Rougemont. The Lachine Rapids worried him, for he was certain he could never navigate them. The Hochelagans pointed out the Ottawa River, flowing down from the northwest.

It was on the summit of Mont-Royal that the riddle of the Kingdom of the Saguenay became even more complex. Through the signs and pantomime of the three Hochelagans with him, Cartier was told that silver and gold came from the west, where the Ottawa River flowed, guarded by the fierce Algonquins, while the copper in his possession had come from the region of the Saguenay River. There was one Kingdom of the Saguenay, he was told, but two watery roads to get to it: the Ottawa River was one, the Saguenay River by Tadoussac the other. However, Cartier was not able at that time to situate the Kingdom nor even to determine whether it was just a fairy tale.

The day after his climb, he began his journey back to Stadacona, reaching it on October 11. Winter was just around the corner.

It was horrible . . . at least to the French, who had never experienced anything like it. They spent their time anticipating an attack from the Natives, and to add to the misery, scurvy practically destroyed them. Processions and prayers didn't help, but Domagaya did. He gave Cartier the cure: an infusion made from the leaves and the bark of the annedda, the tree of life, the white cedar. Before Domagaya's remedy, twenty-five Frenchmen had died.

When spring returned, the animosity between the two camps became more pronounced. Cartier determined to be rid of the meddlesome

Donnacona and his two sons. Unfortunately, Donnacona was the instrument of his own downfall. One of his chiefs, who went by the name of Agona, had become a rival. Donnacona asked for Cartier's support: "Take Agona to France," he pleaded. Instead, Cartier conceived a plot to be rid of the bothersome royal family by transporting Donnacona, his two sons, and two of his allies to France along with the four children he had received as manifestations of good will. The deed was carried out on May 3, the feast of the Holy Cross. After Cartier had erected a ten-metre "belle croix" with the words "Franciscus Primus, Dei Gratia Francorum Rex, Regnat," he seized his antagonists and kept them under "bonne garde." The Canadiens, as Cartier called the people of Stadacona, scattered weeping and cursing the French, but they returned in the night yelling and howling "as if they were wolves," insisting upon the return of their king. The next day, to pacify them, Cartier lied once more. He told Donnacona and the others that he was taking them to France and that they would all return "in ten or twelve moons." He had, of course, no intention of doing that. To maintain peace among his own people, Donnacona agreed and left with Cartier two days later, with three beaver pelts and a large, red copper knife that Cartier believed had come from the fabled Kingdom of the Saguenay. Before their departure, the Stadaconans, to show their respect to Cartier, made a sort of deal with him to ensure the safety of those kidnapped: they presented Cartier with a white shell necklace—white shells being the most precious possession they had. Thus, the wampum (beads as currency) came into our history.

⚜

Domagaya begins to row in the direction of the shore, finds a cove, and disembarks. He makes a fire and invites me to sit by him. The night is upon us, but I'm curious to know many things.

"When you first encountered him in this place, did you and your people take Cartier for a god?" I ask.

"Non," he replies emphatically. "For some time before your Monsieur Cartier arrived, some of our neighbours, like the Mi'kmaqs, had traded with the French fishermen and others whose languages I have heard spoken but do not know. At first the Mi'kmaqs were mystified by the wings of wind that made your ancestors glide over the water. They approached them with respect and awe as befits beings from another place—or even spirits returning from the dead." He looks at me and says with mockery: "We are not very different from your people in seeing ghosts. A man of your god told me when I lived in Saint-Malo that your god and his emissaries often visit those who live good lives. The same with us."

He takes his tobacco pouch from his neck, removes a small quantity and crushes it between his fingers. His pipe is like the one Cartier described in the account of his second voyage: it is shaped like a cone with the two ends opened. Filling one end with the tobacco, he lights it and sucks on the other end. It seems to me to last forever. Domagaya's body actually becomes larger as it fills with smoke. He then exhales slowly through his mouth and nose. With water running down his face, he sighs with great satisfaction and passes me the pipe. I hesitate, but think better of it. I too inhale, and I choke. As Cartier found when he first tried it, it's as hot as pepper. Domagaya laughs. "Just like your Monsieur Cartier," he says. "He did not like it." He takes back the pipe for another puff. Not offering it to me again, he replaces it in his pouch and suspends the sack around his neck.

"Most of the people," he continues, "in fact all of them whom we encountered in our fishing journeys, soon realised that your people were men like us. And so we traded with them. We ourselves had had commerce with fishermen who came from the same country as your capitaine and pilote. We were not afraid of them. And we certainly never thought that life could not pass out of them like it passes out of all of us, the children of the Great Spirit." He waits silently for the next question. Before I ask it, though, he tells me: "The sound of their guns and cannons frightened our people. That's all."

But I won't let go. "The people of Hochelaga," I say, "brought their sick and infirm to Cartier. Even their deformed king.

They must have thought that the capitaine had supernatural powers, that he could cure the sick."

He smiles. "The Hochelagans had had no contact with the likes of your Monsieur Cartier."

I stoke the fire as Mascou had taught me to do, and I ask: "What did you expect of the people who came to visit you?"

He turns the question in his head for a while. "Trade. Barter," he replies. "We are traders. The Mi'kmaqs, with whom we often waged war, had shown us some of the goods of your Monsieur Cartier: hatchets, knives, awls. We knew they performed better than our own tools. We wanted those." He smiles again and adds: "And yes, also his beads. We respect beads."

I mull over the matter of the glass beads that Cartier dispensed with relish. Somewhere I read that the First Peoples may have found similarities between his beads and the shells and the crystals they were familiar with. After all, their most precious possession, as Cartier noted, was the esnoguy, a small white shell ("blanc comme neige," wrote Cartier) that they used for money and other exchanges, in ornaments such as in collars and necklaces, as instruments for record-keeping and teaching, and as objects in ceremonies. The famous wampum originates in the esnoguy, which was the most precious gift the Natives could bestow.

Out of the blue, Domagaya interrupts my thoughts:

"The goods your capitaine and pilote exchanged with us," he says with anger in his voice, "were of inferior quality. They were worth nothing in his country. He found me difficult because I rebuked our people for being satisfied with so little in return for the food, the furs, and all the other things they supplied him with." He looks far away to the sea: "They took advantage of us." But he says that more with regret than in anger.

I wait for the tide of memory to subside, then I ask: "What did you do in France the second time around?"

He walks to his canoe, which he pushes into the water. Turning to me, he says: "We went to join our ancestors in the green and plentiful valleys that abound in the horizons of the stars." He gets into the canoe, and starts paddling out. Not far from the shore, he yells almost triumphantly, "I did not convert." And he disappears.

⚜

Five years after his second voyage, Cartier made a third and disastrous journey to Canada. His mission was to find the Kingdom of the Saguenay. However, a few months before he was to leave, the king issued new instructions. Even though Cartier was still ordered to search for the "Royaume du Saguenay," François I dedicated the enterprise to the colonisation of the new-found lands and entrusted the whole venture to his Protestant friend Jean-François de La Rocque de Roberval. Both expeditions were to leave together, but Roberval was delayed. He nevertheless allowed Cartier to sail on May 23, 1541. He had five ships at his disposal: the *Grande Hermine*, which was his property, the *Émérillon*, which had taken part in the previous voyage, the *Saint-Brieux*, the *Georges*, another ship the name of which is unknown, and 1,500 men.

There were no First Peoples aboard his ships. Nine of the ten whom Cartier had brought back with him to France in 1536, including Domagaya and Taignoagny, had died—no doubt of the Europeans' diseases. Only one of the little girls survived the ordeals of being transplanted into a new and strange life. Her name and whatever happened to her were never recorded.

On August 23, 1541, three months after his departure, Cartier arrived at Stadacona again, where he found Agona enthroned as the king of Canada. To Agona's persistent demands as to the whereabouts of Donnacona and the others, Cartier took refuge in a lie: Donnacona had died—which was believable—and the others lived as befits the grands seigneurs they had become. History does not tell whether anyone believed that.

Instead of anchoring in the Sainte-Croix River as previously, Cartier went up the St. Lawrence to the western point of Cap aux Diamants where the Rivière du Cap-Rouge flows into the St. Lawrence and where he founded

Charlesbourg-Royal. At the beginning of September, Cartier sent two ships back to France, but he stayed and built two forts, one at the foot of the cape and the other at the top of it. Satisfied with his defences, he left for Hochelaga, where he was well received. However, he wasn't able to conquer the rapids, which barred his way to the Kingdom of the Saguenay. He contented himself with seeing what he called "the fashion" of the rapids, and he returned to Stadacona to find that the Natives had made allies of practically every chief living along the St. Lawrence. Cartier, convinced that they were all plotting against him, took precautions. And there ends his story of his *Voyages en Nouvelle-France*.

The rest of his stay in Canada, it is said, was filled with trouble. Scurvy reappeared, but Domagaya's remedy kept it in check. The natives, annoyed at breaches of protocol, at the inferiority of French goods, and at the supercilious attitude of the French, who treated their hosts with disdain, laid siege to the settlement. Apparently, they killed more than thirty-five Frenchmen. Unable to fulfil his mission, Cartier left Stadacona at the beginning of May 1542 with eleven barrels of gold and one bushel of precious stones—so we've been told.

On June 8, he was at St. John's, Newfoundland, where he met Roberval, who ordered him to return to Stadacona and await the arrival of the colonists. Cartier wasn't prepared to do that. Scared of the Stadaconans and unwilling to share the glory of his gold and diamonds, he stole away in the middle of the night, reaching Saint-Malo at the beginning of September. In France, he was dismayed to discover that his gold and precious stones were an "illusion," giving rise to the French proverb: "as false as Canadian diamonds!"

In spite of his pomposity, his double-dealing, his cruelty, and his unwillingness to treat the peoples he encountered with dignity and respect, Jacques Cartier is still a name to be conjured with in the annals of the 16th century. In addition to his explorations, he left good descriptions of the life and manners of the First Peoples of Canada he encountered, particularly the Stadaconans and the Hochelagans—their long, wooden houses covered with strips of bark sewn together; their type of wheat called Ozisy; their vegetables: peas, beans, corn, and cucumbers; their pubescent girls entering a lodge, which Cartier called a "bordel," to receive the sexual advances of many males, one of whom they chose to be their husband; their living in common; the many wives of the braves; the loneliness of the widows; and the nakedness of the "savages."

Before Jacques Cartier, no European had known of the St. Lawrence, its approaches or its majesty. He charted our national river with reasonable accuracy all the way up to the Lachine Rapids. On his journeys on the St. Lawrence, he admired the whales and walruses at the mouth of the Saguenay River. He named many of the rivers, islands, and lakes, and a number of those names still endure. Thanks to him, the new explorers had some reliable information about the highway they were to use to make their fortunes, serve their God and King, or meet their destiny.

While Cartier was at the court of François I, Roberval was pursuing his mission to found a colony in the Canada of the Stadaconans. He failed miserably. At Charlesbourg-Royal, which he renamed France Roy, he rebuilt Cartier's outposts and prepared for winter with his two hundred men, women, soldiers, sailors, and "common people," many of whom he had recruited in the prisons of France, plus cows, bulls, sheep, and horses. The months from October 1542 to April 1543 brought a severe winter and scurvy (Cartier hadn't left Domagaya's remedy with Roberval, and the Natives weren't forthcoming); many of his men and women had to be flogged to keep them in line, and a couple were hanged; and the Stadaconans refused their co-operation. They didn't attack, however. Roberval had constructed an impregnable fortress and he had impressive military strength at his disposal. They came close enough, though, for it was noticed that the Natives had painted themselves red.

In the spring of 1543, Roberval decided to return the whole colony to France. Before that, however, he sailed to Hochelaga, but what he did there and whether he even tried to find the route to the Royaume du Saguenay is not known for certain. He left no record. In September, he and his surviving "colonists" were back in France. He made no peace with the Natives, he didn't find the treasures of the Royaume, he returned poorer than when he left, he couldn't stand the climate, and he left nothing about his passage up and down the Rivière du Canada. (He did rename it France-Prime or François-Premier, but the new appellation didn't last long.)

A love story. Marguerite de La Roque, a relative of Roberval's, came with him on the voyage, accompanied by a maid and a young man who was her lover. We don't know his name. As they sailed up the St. Lawrence, they were so public in their love-making that they upset the serenity aboard the ship. People talked incessantly; work stopped; the men were jealous and ornery, and the women cantankerous; the Calvinist Roberval was scandalised. Things got so out of hand that Roberval dumped his pregnant relative on Île des Démons (Devil's Island). Her lover wouldn't abandon her, nor did the maid. How long they were there, we don't know. What we do know is that her baby died, as did the young man and her servant. Marguerite stayed alone on the island and, with great ingenuity, strength of character, and her firearms, she survived until French fishermen found her and took her back to France.

Roberval, a devoted Protestant, was one of the first to die (1560) in the wars of religion that engulfed France.

After his futile attempts, it would take half a century before others attempted to establish a colony.

Castor canadensis: The beaver, often ridiculed by lesser mortals, has had a profound influence on our country. It also adorns our coat of arms. According to the Récollet missionary Chrestien Le Clerq, "The Beaver is of the bigness of a water-spaniel. Its fur is chestnut, black, and rarely white, but always very soft and suitable for the making of hats." Others found beavers with dark brown fur; for still others, it was closer to red, sometimes black, and even white. These variations usually depended on the location of the animal. The same can be said about the value of the pelts. The best were found north of the St. Lawrence, even though there were fewer of them than south of the river. When fully grown, the beaver weighs between fourteen and twenty-seven kilograms. The great geographer and explorer David Thompson—and many others—found the meat "agreeable . . . fat and oily," the tail being a delicacy.

A beaver lodge, usually consisting of up to nine creatures of various ages, is about six metres long, one and a half metres high, and, sometimes, thirty centimetres thick. The inside of the lodge is a round chamber about sixty centimetres high, almost two metres in diameter, and ten centimetres above the water. Made of sticks and branches held together by mud, it has two entrances with many burrows dug in the base of the pond or river and following the shoreline that leads to the lodge. To ensure an adequate water supply, beavers build dams.

Prior to the arrival of the Europeans, the population of the beaver was "more prolific than the sheep in France" in spite of its natural tendency to monogamy. They numbered between ten and fifty million, with densities of ten to fifty animals per two and a half square kilometres.

To the First Peoples and the Europeans, the beaver became a valuable source of food and, above all, its pelt the most important article of trade. At the beginning of the European experience, the Natives hunted the amphibious creatures with "a pointed stick shaped and hardened in the fire, stone Hatchet, Spear and Arrowheads of the same," methods that couldn't cause mass slaughter. But this situation changed dramatically with the supply of iron and steel weapons and tools provided by the Europeans—and the "fatal Gun." Hunted in all seasons, "their numbers soon became reduced," according to David Thompson.

In the first half of the 16th century, the fur trade, which included other animals beside the beaver, even though the latter was the most hunted, was incidental to the fisheries. In the second half of the century, however, its increased importance led to conflict between the Native tribes and the beaver's near extinction. Why? Everybody in Europe wanted a fur hat. And *Castor canadensis* was crucial to satisfying that urge. (The microscopic barbs in a beaver's fur are best suited for the making of felt hats.) A steady supply of beaver pelts was thus imperative. And with such a demand, more and more Aboriginals wanted to reap the benefits (iron tools) by having access to the beaver's habitat and by controlling the trade routes. In this context, rivalry and war were inevitable.

The first Natives to have access to European goods were those who encountered the European fishermen in their annual trips to North

America—particularly the Mi'kmaqs, the Malecites and others in the Abenaki Confederacy, who lived in what are now the Maritimes and parts of Maine, and the Montagnais-Naskapis, who controlled the vast territories that stretched from Tadoussac to Newfoundland and north to James Bay. Furthermore, not only did the latter have access to the rivers and lakes of the Canadian Shield, they also could reach the Iroquoian and agricultural St. Lawrence valley through the headwaters of the Saint-Maurice River (which "almost connects with the Saguenay River," according to a Native who informed the Jesuits) and the Ottawa. Of all those who participated directly or indirectly at the beginning of the fur trade, the Abenaki Confederacy had access to a limited supply of beavers, and the Montagnais and other Algonquin tribes who dominated the Canadian Shield had the most. For their part, the agricultural St. Lawrence Iroquoians (whom Cartier encountered) had very little.

For most of the 16th century, the trade became centred in Tadoussac, at the confluence of the Saguenay and St. Lawrence Rivers. Tadoussac is a Native word that means "breasts"—no doubt a reference to the hills that surround the place. Long before the arrival of the Europeans, it was an important trading centre for Natives from both shores of the St. Lawrence. By the middle of the 16th century, it became of the greatest importance to traffickers in a wide variety of goods. So important was it that between the Roberval adventure of 1542–43 and the founding of Québec in 1608, the French attempted, in 1600, to establish a colony there that would be open to both Huguenots (Protestants) and Catholics, thus helping to relieve some religious tension in France. It didn't work.

Three years later, in 1603, Samuel de Champlain, who was on his way up the St. Lawrence, concluded the first trade and protection treaty between Europeans and Canadian Aboriginals—the Montagnais and Naskapis. By this act, Champlain, in the name of the French king, recognised their importance as masters of the fur trade. The signing of the treaty was held after the tabagie (feast) that the Montagnais-Naskapis and their allies, the Algonquins, held to celebrate their victory over the Iroquois at the mouth of the Richelieu River (la Rivière des Iroquois). This historical river flows from Lake Champlain northward to the St. Lawrence, where it empties near Sorel. Champlain's new friends had killed one hundred Iroquois.

As the European demand for furs increased, more and more tribes became—or were determined to become—involved in the trade, most particularly the Hurons of Georgian Bay and the Iroquois of the five nations of the Iroquois Confederacy: Mohawks, Oneidas, Onondagas, Cayugas, and Senecas (who then mostly lived in upper New York). Throughout the existence of New France, the struggle to control the fur trade and supply the French, Dutch, and British traders was incessant. Bloody conflicts dominated the first part of the history of Québec—a brutal and violent war pursued by Aboriginals and Europeans with little respect for human life. The list of abominations on both sides is endless.

Unimpeded access to Europeans goods transformed irrevocably the Aboriginal societies of the 16th, 17th, and 18th centuries. Native self-sufficiency disappeared, replaced by dependence, as inter-tribal wars brought havoc to organised life. Almost as soon as the Mi'kmaqs encountered the Europeans, they determined to extend their hunting territories westward at the expense of their neighbours. Their struggle with Donnacona's people was only the first of a nearly endless sequence.

The fate of the Stadaconans and the Hochelagans—and other neighbouring tribes—is another example. Encountered by Cartier in 1534, particularly during his second stay, they had totally disappeared by the time of Champlain's arrival in Québec in 1608—no doubt conquered and dispersed by various Algonquin and Iroquoian warriors in search of control of the access routes to their European suppliers.

A final example was the coming together of the Iroquois and the emergence of two rivals: the Huron Confederacy and the Iroquois Confederacy, both created for self-defence, trade—and for control. It was probably the Hurons who destroyed the Stadaconans and the Hochelagans, and by 1570, the Mohawks and Oneidas were waging war on Montagnais and Algonquin bands living north of the St. Lawrence.

As Native relationships with Europeans intensified in the 17th century, disease was inadvertently added as an instrument of extermination. With no resistance to contagions such as smallpox, the Native peoples whom the French and other Europeans encountered lost their lives or liberty and way of life, and they became wards of the white man, particularly the missionaries. Emancipation from that dependency would take a long, long time. It is still an unfinished task.

Half a century after Roberval's departure, France returned to Canada with a new attitude. At the beginning of the 17th century, colonisation, or permanency, was the order of the day. For the merchants, access to the furs of North America was the compelling motive; it was they, rather than the Crown, who led the charge. In return for a monopoly, the trading companies were obliged to colonise. In 1603 the first attempt was made in Acadia, not in the St. Lawrence valley; that was because Île Sainte-Croix and then Port-Royal (which would become Annapolis Royal in Nova Scotia) were near the sea, the climate was temperate, the land fertile, and the Natives friendly. This first endeavour lasted until 1607, when the monopoly was revoked and the settlers returned to France. Then, under the impetus, skill, and determination of Samuel de Champlain, new commercial arrangements were made, and the town of Québec came to be on July 3, 1608.

Samuel de Champlain is one of the great heroes of Canadian history. His first Canadian biographer, Narcisse Eutrope Dionne (1848–1917), calls him the "founder of Québec and the father of New France." Dionne speaks of his "disinterested actions, his courage, his loyalty, his charity, and all those noble and magnificent qualities which are rarely found unified in one individual in so prominent a degree."

The great French-Canadian historian Marcel Trudel (*Dictionary of Canadian Biography*, vol. I) tells us that Champlain was a "draftsman, geographer, explorer, founder of Québec in 1608, lieutenant to Lieutenant-General Pierre Du Gua de Monts, 1608–12, to Lieutenant-General Bourbon de Soissons in 1612, to Viceroy Bourbon de Condé, 1612–20, to Viceroy de Montmorency 1620–25, to Viceroy de Ventadour 1625–27; commandant at Québec in 1627–28 . . . commander of New France . . . 1629–35; member of the Compagnie des Cents-Associés."

It is obvious from this litany that Champlain had many bosses and never knew how permanent his appointment was. This lack of a continuous authority to ensure the development of New France was its essential weakness prior to 1663, at which time Louis XIV proclaimed royal government in the colony. While the British colonies to the south thrived after 1608, New France languished.

Prior to his arrival in Québec in July 1608, Champlain was a soldier and a mariner, sailing as far as the West Indies. In 1603, he was in North America, travelling up the St. Lawrence to Hochelaga, where the rapids impeded his progress. A year later, he was establishing a colony on Île Sainte-Croix (now Dochet Island, in the Sainte-Croix River). The colony was short-lived due to the harsh winter and scurvy. When spring came, it was decided to move to Port-Royal. The choice proved successful and the winter of 1606–07 was a merry one, according to Trudel. But the trading monopoly was revoked, and the settlers returned home. A year later, Champlain was back, but at "the point of Québec." There, no one appeared to own the place. The Stadaconans (Cartier's Canadiens) had disappeared.

Champlain chose "the point of Québec" because of the advantages the site offered: easy access, the possibility of controlling the "highway" leading to the interior of the continent, the proximity to furs and friendly fur-trading Natives, a temperate climate, and its location on a promontory that provided certain security. Furthermore, much of the land appeared fertile, making it possible to feed a population, while the proximity of the riches of the Royaume du Saguenay fed everyone's dreams of wealth. Finally, the narrowing of the St. Lawrence at the "point of Québec" would not only permit the control of the fur trade; but also the desired "China" trade.

"From the island of Orléans to Québec is one league," he wrote in his *Voyages du Sieur de Champlain*, "and I arrived there on July the third. On arrival I looked for a place suitable for our settlement. . . ." He found it at the foot of Cap aux Diamants, in a place "covered with nut trees." There, he built his "habitation," lodgings for him and the thirty men accompanying him and their stores and munitions, on the site of the present church Notre Dame des Victoires. The habitation consisted of three main two-storey structures. "All the way around our buildings," he wrote, "I had a gallery made, outside the second storey, which was a very convenient thing." In addition, there was a moat over which was a drawbridge, one cannon, gardens "in which to sow grains and seed," and a large square "which abuts

upon the river's bank." It was, as Marcel Trudel has pointed out, "a repro-
duction in miniature of a European fortress."

His first winter started in mid-November with a heavy fall of snow. In
February "scurvy began . . . and lasted till the middle of April. Eighteen were
struck down with it and of these ten died: and five others died of dysentery."
By the spring of 1609, there were only eight men living in the habitation, one
of whom was a much afflicted and weak Champlain. Obviously, he didn't
know about the marvellous healing effects of l'arbre de la vie that Domagaya
had shown Cartier. The following June, Champlain declared war against the
Iroquois of the Five-Nation Confederacy.

Champlain was at Tadoussac at the time. The Montagnais, who were his
allies, wanted to take revenge against the Iroquois, and they sought
Champlain's help. Unwilling to insult them and curious as to the country of
the Iroquois, he, along with twenty Europeans stationed in Tadoussac, went
up the St. Lawrence with his friends. On his way, he came upon "some two
or three hundred Indians who were encamped near a small island. . . . We
approached to investigate and found that they were tribes of Indians called
Ochateguins and Algonquins, who were on their way to Québec to help us
explore the country of the Iroquois, with whom they are in mortal conflict,
and they spare nothing belonging to these enemies." Champlain met with
Chiefs Ochateguin (of the Hurons) and Iroquet (of the Algonquins). They
had another purpose in seeking out Champlain: they too wanted his help in
waging war against the Iroquois. After a long discussion, Champlain agreed,
and the entire party returned to Québec. A few days later, around June 28,
Champlain, with two French companions and sixty Native men, went out
again. A month later, on July 29, the encounter with the Iroquois took place.

Before it happened, however, Champlain had a dream. In his dream he
saw "in the lake near a mountain our enemies, the Iroquois, drowning before
our eyes." He wanted to help them, but his Native allies asked him to let
them all perish, "for they were bad men." When they awoke, as was their
custom on the voyage, he and his Native allies discussed his dream. The
scene he described gave them "such confidence" that they no longer had any
doubt as to the good fortune awaiting them. They spent the night preparing
for battle by singing, dancing, and yelling at mock enemies. Champlain put

four bullets into his arquebus. When daylight came, he and two companions hid from the main body of the Natives, who were arrayed in two camps facing each other. Champlain watched them and was impressed. Then, "our Indians began to call to me with loud cries and put me ahead some twenty yards, and I marched on until I was within thirty yards of the enemy, who as soon as they caught sight of me halted and gazed at me and I at them." When he saw them about to draw their bows, "I took aim with my arquebus and shot straight at one of the three chiefs, and with this shot two fell to the ground and one of their companions was wounded who died thereof a little later." Arrows flew all over the place and the Iroquois panicked and "took to flight." Fifty of them were killed and many were wounded. The "allies" had fifteen wounded and no dead.

This was the first skirmish in a war that was to last, on and off, for over 150 years. Thousands of men, women, and children on all sides would be terrorised and killed, Native tribes annihilated, and the survival of New France seriously endangered.

Why did Champlain do it? Some say he had no choice. In 1603, when he first went to Tadoussac, it was clear to him and his business associates that the Montagnais and the Algonquins were the masters of the Canadian Shield, and therefore the indispensable procurers of beaver pelts and other furs. Their allies were the Hurons, who were becoming the middlemen in the fur trade. These three Native tribes were therefore his only means of expanding his trading routes to the Great Lakes and beyond. An empire beckoned. He accepted the challenge. And to solidify his position, he stationed young and courageous men, like Étienne Brûlé, with the Natives, to learn their ways and their languages.

On the other hand, he may have merely continued the war with the Iroquois that Cartier had begun. It cost them both dearly.

Between 1608 and his death on Christmas Day, 1635, Champlain was the soul of Québec. For over a quarter of a century, he kept alive his dream of building a permanent French and Catholic colony in North America with its centre on the banks of the St. Lawrence. In pursuit of that objective, he spared little of himself. And he had no easy time of it.

To keep his French masters happy—king, courtiers, and merchants—he needed to make their investment worthwhile. That meant keeping the profits of the fur trade rolling in, hence the solidification of the alliance between the Hurons and the French. It was to that end that he undertook his famous journey to Huronia in 1615–16. The 1,100-kilometre journey there took him twenty-two paddling days—an average of fifty kilometres a day, by way of the Ottawa River and Lake Nipissing.

The purpose of his voyage, besides learning all he could about the lay of the land of the empire he wanted to build, was to plan a great campaign, and hopefully the last one, against the Iroquois who were ambushing the Hurons on their way to Québec. At the conclusion of the feasting and the arrangements for the strike against the Iroquois, Champlain left for Lake Ontario and the present State of New York. In early September, Natives under his command attacked the fortified town of the Onondaga Iroquois near what is now the city of Syracuse, N.Y. The town proved to be impregnable to both arrows and gunfire. (By this time, the Iroquois no longer feared the magical arquebus.) Champlain lost the battle, which some historians recognise as one of the decisive battles in North American history; the defeat almost cost him his alliance with the Hurons. However, he returned to Huronia that winter and spring, during which he was able to reaffirm his friendship with them and to cement the tripartite alliance among the Hurons and the Algonquins and the French. After all, their common enemy was not each other but the Iroquois. By the beginning of July 1616, he was back in Québec. A month later, he sailed for France and didn't return until the spring of 1620.

Besides strengthening the alliance with his Native fur-trading partners, he had to watch carefully the shifts of power in France, since they could easily threaten the survival of his colony at Québec.

Between 1608 and 1635, arrangements as to the governance of the colony and the pursuit of the fur trade changed nine times. The rivalry between the merchants, the positioning and repositioning of the courtiers, the fluctuations of the royal moods, and the imperatives of international politics made constancy of purpose and consistent management impossible. It was a miracle—due largely to Champlain's exertions—that the colony didn't perish in these formative years.

Between 1608 and 1635, Champlain made ten trips to France to clarify and maintain his position as de facto head and manager of French affairs in North America.

Between 1608 and 1635, the battle for Canada between the French and the British began with the capitulation of Québec to England's Kirke brothers in 1629. In July, six English ships were at Tadoussac and three off the Île d'Orléans. By the early afternoon of July 19, an emissary from Lewis and Thomas Kirke presented himself to Champlain with a note ordering him to "surrender the fort and the settlement to us." The Kirkes explained that they were doing this "in consequence of what our brother [David] told you last year that sooner or later he would have Québec." The time had arrived. Champlain had no defence, and the brothers knew "very well the extreme need of everything" that Champlain had. However, Champlain asked, "Why, then, do you come here to trouble us if our princes live in peace?" The question was never answered. Instead, Champlain was given three hours in which "to dictate the terms of capitulation," a courtesy offered him, no doubt, in lieu of an answer to his question. There was hardly any food and ammunition left in the colony; the Kirkes were determined; and there was no hope that ships from France would make it to Québec on time. And so he drafted his terms, which were more or less accepted, and, on July 20, Lewis Kirke slept in the fort as he had vowed. In September, Champlain left with two-thirds of the colony.

In the whole colony of New France, there were, at the time of the Kirkes' conquest of Québec, eighty-five French persons: twenty-three permanent residents (habitants), eleven interpreters (young men like Étienne Brûlé— who sold himself to the Kirkes, as did three others), fourteen clerks, ten missionaries (five Récollets and five Jesuits), seven domestics, and twenty French citizens living among the Natives at the time, most of whom remained. (By comparison, the English and Dutch population of North America was 2,610.) Of those living in New France in 1629, twenty-seven (twenty adults and seven children) stayed with the English, while many interpreters remained at their posts in the territories of various Aboriginal nations.

Dionne, Champlain's biographer, states that between 1608 and 1629, "there had been only seven births, three marriages, and forty deaths," including one man who was hanged, six murdered, four drowned, and sixteen dead from scurvy. After eleven years of perseverance, hard work, dedication, pleadings and humiliations, Champlain had twenty-seven people to continue his dream.

However, he wasn't without resolve. As soon as the Kirkes landed him in England, he began his efforts to have New France—"this part of America which extends to the Arctic pole northward"—restored to France. The Florentine Giovanni da Verrazzano, whom François I had dispatched to America, "discovered nearly all the coast" from the Tropic of Cancer to the fiftieth latitude, "and still more northerly, harbouring arms and flags of France." It was for that reason, Champlain insisted, "the said country is called New France." He laid no claims, though, to the lands around the Florida peninsula, including Virginia. After having submerged the English under an avalanche of words, he went to France to pursue his mission. And on March 29, 1632, the ambassadors of the French and English kings signed the Treaty of Saint-Germain-en-Laye, which restored New France, Canada, Québec, and Acadia to Champlain, whom Cardinal Richelieu named as the absolute ruler of the St. Lawrence. It was the first time in his long career in North America that Champlain wielded such authority, even though Richelieu had named him governor of New France, in 1627, in accordance with the Charter of the Compagnie des Cents-Associés, to which New France was transferred in that year.

Champlain arrived to take up his new duties in Québec on May 22, 1633, with two hundred men, one woman, two girls, and two Jesuits. But only a small fraction of them took up permanent residence in Québec or its neighbourhood.

There could be no permanent French settlement in North America without permanent settlers. Colonisation was, therefore, a fundamental instrument in Champlain's colonial policy, a policy that his masters and patrons pursued mostly unwillingly. In the twenty-seven years that he was, in one way or another, in charge of French affairs in North America, Québec was only a village; in Tadoussac, Trois-Rivières, and Montréal, there was no colonisation at all. Pierre-François-Xavier de Charlevoix, a Jesuit priest, once made the following inventory of New France: "The fort of Québec, surrounded by a few wretched houses and some sheds, two or three cabins on the island of Montréal, as many, perhaps, in Tadoussac, and at some other points on the river St. Lawrence . . . a settlement begun at Trois-Rivières and the ruins of Port Royal: this was all that constituted New France." Had the "many Frenchmen, who might have built up a great colony been well directed," he added, another story could be told.

However, upon his return to New France in 1633, Champlain pursued his colonisation policy with a vengeance. Aided by the publication *Relations des Jésuites* in 1632, the mystical appeal of the strange land that was Canada, inhabited by "savages," persuaded a great number of charitable and pious souls to donate money and goods and to encourage settlement. Slowly the population grew to about 150 settlers by the end of 1635. (Boston, no more than five years old, had 2,000 inhabitants.)

In Champlain's New France, no Protestants were allowed to settle. They could trade with the Natives and provide money and goods to the various companies that obtained trading monopolies over the years, but they couldn't live here permanently. Champlain agreed with this policy: to him, uniformity of religion was essential to the progress of New France.

The Jesuits, who had successfully lobbied to eliminate the Récollets (who had been the first missionaries in New France), looked after the spiritual life of the colonists and the conversion of the "Indians," particularly the Hurons in their own territory. The Jesuit Jean de Brébeuf moved to Ihonatiria (near Sault Ste. Marie) now St. Joseph Island, in September 1634.

Part of this mission of the Jesuits was to consolidate the Hurons' friendship with the French and to promote the supply of furs. According to historian Marcel Trudel, "the trade network was intact" upon Champlain's return after the English evacuation. This was because the French interpreters who had stayed in New France had lived in Native villages. However, many poachers often offered better terms—alcohol and guns—than the French. Furthermore, the Algonquins, masters of the Ottawa River and known to the Jesuits as the "Island People," had become the enemies of the Hurons, for they didn't relish "the Hurons . . . coming to the French, & the French . . . going to the Hurons." To fulfil their objective, the Algonquins, according to the *Relations des Jésuites* (1632), blocked "the road," thus replacing, temporarily, the Iroquois as the most important obstacle to the French for full enjoyment of the fur trade. To counter the Algonquins and others who endangered the network, the Jesuits were sent to live among the Hurons, and Jean Nicollet de Belleborne, a coureur de bois, undertook his famous journey of 1634–35.

Nicollet had come to Canada in 1618. Almost immediately upon his arrival, he was sent to Allumette Island in the upper Ottawa River where he stayed two years, learning the Alonguin and Huron languages and becoming one of their chiefs. In 1620, he went to live with the Nipissings on the shores of the lake that bears their name. He lived among them for nine years, becoming familiar with their lore, trading customs, and language. When the English arrived to occupy New France in 1629, he fled to the country of the Hurons and spent the years of the occupation there, using all his guile and charm to thwart all English attempts to make allies of the Hurons. He returned to New France in 1633, settling in Trois-Rivières as the clerk of the Compagnie des Cents-Associés (Company of the Hundred Associates), which Richelieu had established. It was from there that he began the mission Champlain entrusted to him: to make peace between the Hurons and the "Gens de Mer"—the "People of the Sea," or the Ounipigons, Winnebagoes, and Puants, as they are also known. They lived in a strategic location on the western shore of Lake Michigan, surrounded by Algonquins and courted by the Dutch. Champlain felt it imperative to bring them into the French camp by restoring peace between them and the Hurons—thus, Nicollet's mission.

Before he took to his canoe, he went shopping. The Natives had made the French believe that Lake Michigan (where the Puants lived) was near the Sea of China, the finding of which was still an obsession with many souls in North America. To be properly attired to meet the "Golden Tribe" somewhere in Cathay, he bought himself "a great robe of Chinese damask, with flowers over all & birds of various colours." How he knew what a mandarin robe looked like, let alone where he got it in Québec, is not known.

From Trois-Rivières, he followed the Ottawa River until he reached Allumette Island and thence to Lake Nipissing, down la Rivière des Français (the French River) to Georgian Bay, where he recruited an escort of seven Hurons. From there, he canoed and portaged to Lake Michigan and came upon the Puants in their main territory on Green Bay. They took him for a god, dressed as he was in his mandarin, damask splendour. He charmed them, spoke their language through one of his Huron interpreters, smoked their long-stemmed pipes, and made peace between them and the Hurons. The fur-trade network was safe.

Of course, the Puants were not the Chinese—or even near them. So he continued his journey down the Fox River to the Wisconsin River and, not finding the Sea of China, he set out again, southward this time, towards the Illinois River, but no Sea of China. He returned to Québec in the fall of 1635, bringing his robe back with him. Settling in Trois-Rivières, he married, had a son and a daughter, and lived an exemplary life (he fathered a child, a girl, by a Nipissing woman). He drowned in 1642 when the shallop he was in overturned.

Jean Nicollet de Belleborne (Belleborne being a fief on the Plains of Abraham) was a remarkable man, a great explorer, and an intrepid coureur de bois. His journey of 1634–35 introduced what is now known as the American Northwest to the French. He made easier the exploration of the Mississippi River, which René-Robert Cavelier de La Salle discovered some forty years later. He was a splendid negotiator and an effective peacemaker.

"In the autumn of the year 1635, Champlain suffered from a stroke of paralysis, which was considered very severe from the commencement," writes Dionne in his biography of Champlain, and he died at Fort St. Louis on the night of December 25, 1635. To this day, his remains have not been found.

Samuel de Champlain was a lonely man. His wife, Hélène Boulé, whom he married in 1610, spent only four years in New France with him (1620–24); he was thirty-one years older; and they had no children. His brother-in-law, Eustache Boulé, a Calvinist, came with him in 1618 and returned to France in 1629. Boulé had by then converted to Roman Catholicism. Some ten years later, he died in Italy, a member of the Minim Order.

In the interest of Québec, of New France, of Canada, Champlain was indefatigable. As Dionne reminds us: "He had to spend thirty years of the best years of his life in his endeavours to found a settlement on the shores of the St. Lawrence. Twenty times he crossed the Atlantic in the interests of the colony."

Charlevoix, who wrote the first history of Canada about a hundred years after Champlain's death, said of him that he was "beyond contradiction, a man of merit."

As I'm searching for more information about Champlain, Mascou enters to say, "The Reverend Mother has arrived."

I I

Building a Country
1639–1713

❧

*T*he nun's name is Marie de l'Incarnation. During the Christmas season of 1633, as a nun in a convent in Tours, France, she had had a dream, a dream that she described to her spiritual advisor two years later:

> . . . I found myself in close union with God. Thereupon, while I was asleep, it seemed to me that a companion and I were journeying hand in hand through a very difficult place. . . . From the place in which we were, there was a road to go down into these great vast spaces, but it was exceedingly dangerous because of having terrible rocks on one side and awful and unguarded precipices on the other. . . . At the beginning of this year, while I was at prayer, all this was restored to my mind and with it the thought that the afflicted place I had seen was New France. I felt a very great inward attraction in that direction and an order to go there to build a house for Jesus and Mary.

⚜

Three hundred and sixty-six years later, she is standing at the entrance to my study. Her eyes are cast down and she wears the habit of an Ursuline nun, the cloistered order to which she belonged. I find her different looking than the silly pictures we see of her oozing piety and stupidity. She is tall, handsome, graceful, and, no doubt the power she emanates made many take notice when she passed by or entered a room. Her silent command is for me to stand and offer her a chair. I do so. She sits, her back straight, her hands resting gently on her lap. After a while, she looks at me and says in a voice that I find pleasant, "God be with you."

Like an idiot, I can only stare. She smiles gently and says, "My son, in his biography of me, has described me well?"

"Yes, Madame."

Silence follows again. Eventually, she lifts her shoulders, deciding to take charge. "Mascou, whom I know well, has asked me to visit you. Since he seems to like you, I decided to take a chance. He tells me you ask many questions."

"Yes, Madame." She waits. I wait. "We'd better begin then," she says. To facilitate my task, she adds, "I was born Marie Guyart in the city of . . ."

"Tours," I say interrupting her. "The Capital City of old Touraine . . ." She looks at me somewhat perplexed. "In the rich valley of the Loire," I hasten to add with satisfaction.

She pays no attention to the geographic information I have given her. Instead, she tells me that she was one of seven children. Her father was a baker, well-off and devout. "I was happy growing up in my father's house. It was, though, a busy place."

"Not much time for prayers."

My words seem to surprise her. Why? She doesn't say. To fill the silence, I comment: "Your life is full of virtue, prayer, mortification, and penance. It amazes us in this century."

"I do not know about any of that. As for my piety and reverence for God, I let Him be my judge." She looks at me as if she were searching to see if she might entrust me with the confidences of her soul. Having made up her mind, she says, looking down at her hands, "When I was seven years old, Christ came to me in a dream. He asked me if I wished to be His!" She hesitates for a moment, then lifts her eyes towards me and adds gravely, "I said yes."

"This, then, was your mission. To be His?"

"Yes, Monsieur."

"But your father had a different mission for you!"

"Yes. I was led into marriage with Claude Martin. A master silkworker." Again she waits before going on: "My marriage was not a happy one. It lasted two years. My husband died after his business failed." Another pause. Then: "We had a child. Claude. Like his father."

I know, from my notes, that she was left destitute. She returned to her father's with the firm determination of becoming a nun. But that had to wait. Her son still had need of her. From her father's house, she moved to the home of her sisters- and brothers-in-law where her integrity, hard work, and intelligence led her to take charge of the household and her brother-in-law's business affairs. At the same time, she performed horrendous mortifications, wearing a hair shirt and punishing her body. She made a vow of chastity and denied herself the natural motherly demonstrations of affection towards her son. When I confront her with this litany, she simply replies, "I was preparing myself to be joined in a mystic union with my Lord, Jesus Christ."

"A marriage?"

"Oui, Monsieur."

"And it took place . . . this marriage?"

"When I was twenty-eight years old."

"In 1627."

She bows her head in acquiescence. "My martyrdom of love."

I don't understand what she's telling me and, if truth be known, I'm somewhat put out by what appears to me to be nonsense. I don't tell her, of course. Rather, I ask: "And your son?"

"He grew up . . . and . . . when he was twelve years old . . . I left him." It seems very difficult for her to admit that.

"You abandoned him?"

"As you wish. I prefer to think that I left him in the care of my sister and her husband." Her hands tremble and a cloud comes over her eyes. "I suffered a living death."

I won't be so easily put off. I feel no sympathy. "You abandoned your twelve-year-old son to pursue some fantasy?"

She chooses not to reply. Instead she looks at me as I read in her eyes: "You cannot or will not understand." She sighs and adds in a more cheerful voice, "I entered the Ursuline Convent in Tours." She seems happy, and she adds: "That was on January 25, 1633. From that day on, I became what I am: Marie de l'Incarnation."

The research scattered on my desk tells me that she advanced fast in her career. In 1634 she became assistant mistress of novices and three years later, the mistress of the boarding school.

"When did you find out about Canada?"

"Through the Jesuit Fathers who came to establish their convent in Tours a year or so before I entered the Ursuline Order. One of their priests became my confessor and spiritual director. He knew about Canada. Also the *Relations des Jésuites* were published in France in 1632, if my memory serves me. I became quite enthusiastic about their work in that far-away land. At my request, I was given permission to correspond with some of the missionaries who had served and were serving there." She looks out the window and remains pensive. She is obviously troubled. Some memory has touched her profoundly. Her eyes meet mine again and she says with tears in her voice: "The Jesuit martyr Charles Garnier used to reply to my importune letters with words of encouragement, written on a piece of white birchbark and polished as vellum." She looks at me, sensing that I have another question.

"Were the people of Tours as obsessed as you were by New France?"

"All over France." She leans forward in her chair. "It is perhaps difficult for you to capture what so many of us felt. Canada was a challenge. It was strange." She smiles. "We had no idea where it was. But the reality of it was powerful. In a faraway land, a land opened to us by our people, there lived creatures who knew not God. To convert them and lead them to civilisation became a cri de coeur." She leans back and adds: "God gave me the mission of my life in a dream."

"In December 1633. I have read your letter. But you weren't certain at the time of your dream that you were destined for Canada. How did you find out?"

"God revealed it to me as well, but a couple of years later."

"What did God say?"

"My Lord said: 'It was Canada that I showed you; you must go there.' I was to establish a seminary, a school, for the little Indian girls." She casts her eyes down and says humbly, "And I did."

⚜

That too I knew. She was thirty-five years old when she began her search for a way to get to Canada. However, she was a tough lady, determined, and cognizant of the ways she must use to get what she wanted. She would go to Canada. It was not easy and she had to spend close to five years before she had completed all arrangements necessary. Finally on May 4, 1639, she sailed for Québec, arriving there on August 1.

⚜

"You had a hard time. Yet you persevered," I say. "I admire you for that."

She doesn't acknowledge the compliment. "Yes, there were many trials and tribulations."

"Like what?"

"I was a cloistered nun. A cloistered nun in my day did not leave her convent for foreign missions. Permissions had to be obtained. Companions had to be found. And money. The Virgin Mary saw to it all. It was she who sent us Madame de la Peltrie."

⚜

Marie Madeleine de Chauvigny de la Peltrie was a rich Norman widow who became fascinated with Canada and, in the midst of a serious illness that threatened her life, she made a deal with St. Joseph. If the earthly father of Jesus restored her to health, she would go to Canada, found a house there under his patronage, and spend the rest of her life converting and teaching little Native girls. On the day following her vow, she became well again, determined to fulfil her promise.

⚜

"Madame de la Peltrie, who heard of your desire from a mutual Jesuit friend, came to see you in your convent at Tours."

"Yes. As soon as I laid eyes upon her, I recognised her to be the companion who had accompanied me in my dream. She agreed to help us, and she provided not only her encouragement, knowledge, contacts, and what have you, but also the means to realise our mission. We know her as the foundress of the Ursulines of Québec."

"A few more difficulties later, you left for Canada, New France, Québec?"

She bows her head. She must have communicated with Mascou, for he appears and they leave together. The door closes and I am left alone to ponder the country she embraced at the beginning of August 1639.

⚜

New France's existence was still precarious. The French population was only about two hundred. (There should have been three thousand according to the contracts between the Crown and the various companies that had obtained a trade monopoly.) And those few people were scattered along the vast St. Lawrence, while a few lived with the Natives in their territories. As for settlement, a few clerks worked in Trois-Rivières, some settlers occupied Beauport and the Côte de Beaupré, but the majority of the population lived in the town of Québec. An engineer had drawn up plans for the streets of Québec and built a new Fort Saint-Louis of stone and brick on top of the hill. Life was intensely calm and pious, with little possibility of escape. However, boys and young men did leave. They became coureurs de bois, living among the Natives, learning their languages and their customs while trading with them in the name of France. Their free ways were, for the moment, accepted and even encouraged. It was deemed a fair price to have interpreters for the complicated deals that the fur trade demanded.

Then there were the Iroquois, particularly the Mohawks. The Huron-French alliance excluded the Iroquois from the St. Lawrence fur trade. This didn't bother the Iroquois too much in the first quarter of the 17th century; they tended to concentrate on establishing a monopoly with the Dutch, and by 1626, after defeating, absorbing, and dispersing the Mohicans, they were successful in that objective. However, equipped with firearms for hunting beaver, they soon depleted their territory, obliging them to obtain furs elsewhere, namely in the areas north of the St. Lawrence. However, the Hurons controlled the supply of furs there, and they brought their cargoes down directly to the French by way of that river. To control that trade, the Iroquois had either to force the Hurons into an alliance or destroy them. The Richelieu River, the Iroquois' natural route and entry into Canada, was where they captured two coureurs de bois who were hunting near Trois-Rivières in February 1641. Negotiations to free them failed, shots were fired, the prisoners escaped, and the Mohawks sought revenge by attacking a Huron flotilla bearing furs to Trois-Rivières. This was the first skirmish in a war that would eventually see the destruction of several Aboriginal Nations allied to the French, the death of Jesuit missionaries, and the near destruction of New France.

Another momentous event was the arrival, in September 1641, of Paul de Chomedey de Maisonneuve, a gentleman, an officer, and a member of the Société Notre-Dame de Montréal. He came to Canada to found Ville-Marie and to become the first governor of the Island of Montréal. The island had become the property of the Société, which pious souls had established in France, five years earlier, to bring Christianity to the "Sauvages" in far-away Canada. The exact location, the Island of Montréal, had been revealed to one of the founders of the Société in a vision. This was indeed a holy undertaking. To those already established in Canada, however, extending the territory of New France almost to the door of the Iroquois, a situation that would tax the small defences of New France, was a "foolhardy under-taking." Everyone from the governor on down begged Maisonneuve not to go. But he was adamant. "Monsieur le gouverneur," he said, "having been instructed to go to Montréal by the Company that sends me, my honour is at stake, and you will agree that I must go up there to start a colony, even if all the trees on that island were to change into so many Iroquois."

Concurrently, the ships from France had been bringing the smallpox virus in their human cargo. Then, when Huron traders and Jesuit priests carried the infection with them to Huronia and to the territories of their allies, hundreds died. Survivors held the Jesuits responsible for the epidemics, which, by 1640, had cut the Huron population by half. The Natives residing within the town and neighbourhood of Québec were not immune either.

Marie de l'Incarnation was present at these events.

⚜

"What did you think of Canada?"

"It is where God wanted me to be. I surrendered myself to live or to die, whether on the sea or in the stronghold of barbarism, for all is alike to me in His adorable will."

I know that the three-month crossing had been no picnic. She and her companions were within a hair's breath of ship-wreck. Then, an iceberg as big as a city and towering over the ship threatened them. She's a woman of great courage and determination. However, in the appreciation of our First Peoples, she's not much better than Cartier was. I tell her so.

"Your choice of words to describe the humans, the creatures of God, you found here is somewhat offensive. You, and most of your people, refer to our First Peoples as barbarians, savages, and only your secret thoughts know what other names you gave them. You seem to despise them. It's unfortunate your God didn't instruct you. He could have told you that His Canadian children were different from His French children, not lesser beings."

She looks at me somewhat perplexed. I'm afraid she's going to leave. But no. Instead she says gently: "Since when is my God not your God?" But, not waiting for my answer, she continues, this time more severely: "Do not be harsh. And do not demand too much. I come from a different world, a different time than you. In my heart, the Indians were the children of God. And I loved them. God made me a gift of them. And through them, I found the strength to carry out His will."

I feel chastised. She smiles at me and proceeds to answer my first question.

"The Canadian landscape I saw upon my arrival was exactly as in my dream. There was a fort on a hill with a path leading down to a sort of square below, by the river. There was also a house halfway up the path and, in the square, warehouses and four or five houses, one of which became our home at the beginning of our stay in New France. We were received with much joy and dignity. Our most joyful moment was our visit to Sillery, downriver, where . . ." She hesitates, swallows, and says: "Indians lived . . . a few Montagnais families along with Algonquins and Hurons. We danced with them. Madame de la Peltrie was more proficient at dancing than I was. It was a pleasure to see her so happy, having been so ill during the crossing."

"I understand you lived in a house built on the quay from where you could see the ships in port. Where did you get the house?"

"Before we left France, Madame de la Peltrie rented it for us. That is where our work began: teaching and learning the languages of our Indian girls." She sighs and whispers: "I confess that there are many thorns in learning a speech so contrary to ours. Yet, no one else found it as difficult as I. Ah! But the desire to understand and be understood helped me in overcoming my difficulties." She looks away with mischief in her eyes and adds: "It was in that small house that I learned to make sagamite." She seems quite satisfied with that.

"I know what it is," I say. "It's a delicacy much appreciated by the people you found here. It consists of boiling cornmeal or other cereal, with plums. You were praised for it."

"Not as much as Sister Cecile de Sainte-Croix. God has forgiven me. I found sagamite quite sublime."

Quickly, to hide her embarrassment, she says: "Within a few days of our arrival we had six Indian girls and two French ones living with us, while other daughters of the settlers came to our school daily. It was a bark lodge in our yard."

"But your house was very small: two rooms, an attic, a cellar, and a small lean-to. Not much space for . . ."

For the first time, she laughs out loud and picks up from where I left off: "For a kitchen, refectory, retreat, classroom, parlour, and choir. It was such a poor house that we saw the stars shining through the ceiling at night, and we could scarcely keep a candle alight because of the wind. I had a little church built of wood. It was pleasing for its poverty."

"How did you ever manage?"

"Everyone wanted to know that. How do you hold so many people in so small a place?" She bends towards me as if to tell me a secret and whispers: "You see, we divided the ends of the rooms into alcoves made of pineboards. The beds were on top of each other and only accessible by ladder. It was luxury. After all, I expected to have, for all lodging, only a cabin made of bark."

"Eventually, though, you built yourself a monastery on two and a half hectares of land near the fort and which the Compagnie gave you."

She replies with some mockery: "Is that a question?"

It's my turn to blush. I nod my head.

"While Madame de la Peltrie was away on the Island of Montréal, we moved into a fine stone monastery. That was in 1642. We lived in it until it was destroyed by fire at the end of December 1650. Everything was lost except some papers God told me to throw out the window. By that time we had ten cloistered nuns, two lay sisters, a postulant, and many boarders. God in His mercy saved us all, but we were destitute. No clothes. No bedding. No linens. No food. Nothing at all. In the middle of the winter. But, in our poverty we continued our work and many, as poor as we, came to our help and, over the next two years, we were able to rebuild our monastery, occupying it for the first time on Whitsuntide in 1652. Madame de la Peltrie did not contribute, like everyone else, to the building; instead, she gave us a church. She was a woman of enthusiasms that prevented her from being able to mortify her own desires. I accepted her gift. You see, our first monastery was built against all reason. And so was the second."

Without giving her a moment to rest her mind, I say: "We need to talk about your 'Savages!'"

She looks at me in that forceful way she has, and her voice trembles with a mixture of anger and compassion: "Please, do not think that that word is meant to be disrespectful or that I used it—and will use it—to imply any superiority, or to insult or belittle them. That is not the case. I am sure you have read my letters. I had utter respect for your First Peoples, as you refer to them now. Unlike you, if you allow me, I lived among them. They enriched my life."

She stops and goes off in a world of her own. When she returns, she says simply but with much emphasis: "It was a pleasure to be

with so many Savage women and girls. Their candour and the sim-
plicity of their spirits were so delightful that I have no words
to describe them to you. Those of the men, no less so. I asked
everyone I knew to pray to Our Lord to give me the grace to love
them always. And He did."

Having said that as firmly as she could, she then asked me
what I wanted to know.

"Everything!"

"You are demanding! Let me see . . ."

Before she could continue, however, Mascou comes in with a
command to me of his own: "The Reverend Mother may want to
walk with you in the park."

"Oh yes, please! It is such a nice day."

So we did. In the park adjacent to my house, she and I walk
side by side while Mascou hovers discreetly behind. We can hear
the children playing at the far end; nearer to us, various
adults are attempting tennis. Marie de l'Incarnation pays no
attention to the tennis players but is obviously happy to hear
and see the children. As we walk, she talks for a long time. I
don't interrupt her. The past has become the present to her.

"It is hard to know where to begin." I hear her whisper a
prayer to the Holy Ghost. She makes the sign of the Cross and,
folding her hands on her heart, she continues: "This land of
Canada, which we have claimed for the honour of God and of our
king, is inhabited by various peoples with whom we trade. We
evangelize them to win their souls to Jesus Christ. We educate
their daughters and we share with them what we have." She stops
and looks at me, commanding me with her eyes to believe her as
she says: "We mean them no harm. After all, we live in a region
where Montagnais, Algonquins, Abenakis, and Saguenays come to
settle because they wish to believe and obey God."

Resuming our walk, she adds: "We are misunderstood, however,
by so many who are not Christians, especially in the Huron
Mission. These Savages hold the delusion that it is baptism,

instruction, and dwelling among the French that is the cause of the high mortality in their midst. Great assemblies are held with the purpose of exterminating the Reverend Fathers. But they are not afraid. Some are beaten, others wounded, and still others driven away."

She stops to look at the children running after a ball. Happiness returns to her eyes. She then resumes: "In addition, Monsieur, there are the Iroquois who constantly wage mortal war upon our faithful Savages around the colony and also upon those beyond as far as the land of the Hurons. If they dared, they would come down to Québec, but it would avail them nothing, and so they keep their distance. But the gentlemen of Montréal are not secure, because of the continual raids and warfare of the Iroquois."

⚜

What she's telling is well known. All through her life in Canada, Montréal was always in mortal danger. The Iroquois, particularly the Mohawks, were bent on controlling the Great Lakes fur trade where the Hurons dominated it. Until 1640, the Hurons were able to withstand the Iroquois attacks. After 1640, it was another matter. The Iroquois became more united in the pursuit of the fur trade, and they had firearms supplied by the Dutch; the Hurons, on the other hand, had none—the French refused to give them any. Every year, the Iroquois played havoc with the flotilla of canoes that brought furs to Montréal, Trois-Rivières, and Québec. By 1651, in spite of a "peace" that was arrived at in 1645, which lasted a couple of years, they had become the masters of the Great Lakes fur trade; they had destroyed the Hurons in 1649–50, and they dispersed all of the Neutral Nations a year later. They then acted as if they had decided to rid the settlements along the St. Lawrence of their inhabitants.

⚜

"We are all in danger. If the Iroquois continue their conquest, there will no longer be a place here for the French. Commerce will be impossible, and without commerce, no more ships will come; without the ships, we shall have none of the necessities of life. So the colony may have to be abandoned. Our foundress and I make plans in case we are forced to return to France." She waves her hands in the air to emphasize her thought: "We need military help desperately. But France does not seem to hear us." She looks again at the children playing not too far from us and adds: "In the meantime, like so many others, we await martyrdom." Then, she makes a remark that she knows addles me: "Oh, how sweet it is to die for Jesus Christ."

She knows what she's done. She walks briskly ahead of me. Then she waits for me to catch up, and she tells me at length about her holy Jesuit martyrs: Isaac Jogues, Antoine Daniel, Jean de Brébeuf, Jérôme Lalement, Charles Garnier, Noel Chabanel, and the deaf layman and surgeon, René Goupil, who was the first of the Jesuit martyrs. She follows that with the exploit of Dollard des Ormeaux and his sixteen companions, whom the Iroquois killed at the Battle of Long Sault in May 1660.

She's most enthusiastic about their courage. "Gallant men," she says, "filled with the wonder of God." Maybe she knows that there is much controversy about Dollard and his gang, for she adds, quickly abandoning the use of the present tense: "You see, at the time Le Sieur Dollard planned his worthwhile act, the Iroquois were arming a powerful army to come to carry off our new Christian Iroquois converts and as many of the French as they could." She doesn't tell me that the Iroquois were said to be massing troops on the Richelieu River and not up the Ottawa where Dollard went . . . to meet the Iroquois canoes laden with furs. "Le Sieur Dollard des Ormeaux saved the colony. We owe him much."

I don't dissuade her. We talk of the arrival of François de Laval, the first Catholic bishop of New France, in 1659.

"You didn't like him much."

"He is a man whose personal qualities are rare and extraordinary. He lives like a saint."

"Was he a saint?"

She laughs at that. "I do not say that he is a saint." She pauses and, with mischief in her eyes, says, "That would be to say too much."

"He wanted to change the constitution of your Order, and you weren't pleased at all."

Without hesitating, she says with conviction: "Change our constitution? Non, Monsieur LaPierre, he almost managed to ruin it. Of course, he left the substance, but he cut out everything that gave interpretation or could facilitate our living together and doing the work God had given us to do." She stops and turning towards me, she adds: "We considered his views with humility and, with the help of the Holy Spirit, we decided not to accept his version of our rules unless God ordered it and subjected us to His holy will. A zealous and worthy prelate. A holy priest. Unfortunately, he does not realize that experience—and I have a considerable amount of it—should prevail over all speculations. You know, Monsieur, as well as I, that when things go well, one should continue in these ways."

And with that, we return to the house to speak of her son. But, even before I could broach the subject, she refuses a chair and, with conviction and brooking no interruptions, she says: "I will now tell you about my son, Claude Martin. You may choose to believe me or not. It is as you wish." She bows her head. I bow mine.

She continues: "Yes, I abandoned him when he was twelve years old. I did it only with great convulsions, which were known solely to God. I had to obey His divine will. Besides, He promised me that He would take care of him. And He did! In 1641, Claude entered the Benedictine Order, an order of priests whom I infinitely honour and esteem. As you see, my abandonment of him was advantageous to him. He took his place among the principal members of his Order. I always carried him

in my heart. And I always will. Bonne après-midi, Monsieur
LaPierre. May God be with you."

She leaves me alone with my thoughts.

⚜

The story of Marie de l'Incarnation's passage among us in the 17th century is the story of the birth of Québec and, in some ways, of the Canada
we know. She was a remarkable person, knowledgeable, aware of what was
happening around her, and capable of sorting it all out. Feeling worthless
most of the time, she nevertheless pursued her mission and her mystical marriage to Christ with all the fervour and care she possessed. Difficult to get
along with, often opinionated, self-sufficient most of the time, she was also
judgemental and bitter "towards certain good and holy persons," as she
wrote in her spiritual biography in 1654. Reading her letters, particularly
those to her son, and other writings, we cannot but be amazed by her personality. She grew: one can see it. She matured: one can only be convinced of
that. Throughout all her self-doubts and travails, she arrived at a serenity
and tenderness that moves me to tears.

Marie Guyart, *dite* Marie de l'Incarnation, died quietly in her convent, in
the town of Québec, on April 30, 1672. She was seventy-two years old.

In 1663, nine years before Marie de l'Incarnation died, Louis XIV took
command of his most neglected colony. Aided by the genius of the useful
Jean-Baptiste Colbert (1619–83), the comptroller-general of finances and,
in fact, the king's chief minister, Louis XIV governed New France as a
province of France, thus ending the private monopolies of various companies that had succeeded each other without much benefit to the colony itself.
For the duration of the French regime (until 1763), Québec was headed by a
governor who had charge of defence and foreign affairs and who had some
supervisory responsibilities over the regular and secular clergy, and education. The intendant, the second most important civil personage, was left
with the entire civil administration. High justice was under the jurisdiction
of a Sovereign Council, the court of highest appeal. The bishop remained
the most important clerical personage. However, Louis XIV was not about

to allow the creation of a theocracy by permitting Laval and the Jesuits to wield too much influence and power. Economically, Québec was meant to be partly self-supporting through the fur trade and some agricultural products, and by developing its mineral and timber resources. The colony could even export to other parts of the French empire. As we shall see later, mercantilism and other weaknesses made that dream impossible. But in 1663, there was much hope that the new constitutional structure would herald an era of great expansion.

This general feeling was reinforced in the summer of 1665 with the arrival of Alexandre de Prouville de Tracy (1596–1670), lieutenant-general "throughout the length and breadth of the continental countries under our authority situated in South and North America . . ." and the commander-in-chief of the French troops in America. His mission was not so much to defend the towns and the forts of New France; rather, it was to exterminate the Iroquois completely by attacking them directly in their territories. (Colbert had made the royal mind-set quite explicit in his March 18, 1664, letter to Bishop Laval: the time had come, he wrote, "to destroy utterly these barbarians.") To accomplish this came the twenty companies of the Carignan-Salières Regiment, about one thousand men.

Two men completed the top echelons of the administrative and military structure of New France: the new governor, Daniel de Remy de Courcelle (1626–98) and the new intendant of justice, police, and finances in Canada, Acadia, the island of Newfoundland, and other possessions of France in North America—Jean Talon (1626–94). He followed Lieutenant-General Tracy to Canada in the fall of 1665.

At that time, about 2,500 people lived in all of New France, a thousand of whom inhabited the town of Québec, which had two separate sections. In the lower town, ordinary people, particularly those involved in commerce and service trades, occupied about seventy houses. The governor had his castle, the Château Saint-Louis, at the summit of the cape in the upper town. Nearby were various religious houses and, not too far away, on the Grande Allée, a few officials and rich merchants had fine residences.

With the implementation of Royal Government came settlers: 1,500 of them between 1665 and the death of Marie de l'Incarnation in 1672. In addition, the king sent one thousand young women (*les filles du roi*) from all walks of life, to become the wives of impatient young men who had been forbidden to hunt and fish if they weren't married within a fortnight of the girls' arrival. In 1667, when the Carignan-Salières Regiment was demobilized, the great majority of the young officers and men opted to remain in Canada. With this immigration and a most fertile birthrate (which became the envy of the world and caused much derision during great chunks of Canadian history), eleven years after the introduction of this new status for New France, the population numbered 7,800—a three-fold increase over 1663. Amen.

As the first responsibility of the new regime was to rid the colony of its Iroquois enemies, Tracy and de Courcelle built and garrisoned forts along the Richelieu River, which was still the Mohawks' main invasion route. Then they launched two expeditions against the Mohawks in their own territories (one other, against the Oneidas, who were as much enemies of New France as the Mohawks, wasn't carried out). When, in 1665, the Mohawks heard that a large number of well-equipped French troops had arrived at Québec, they sought peace. However, Tracy, Courcelle, and Talon rejected these advances and continued to make their plans for an invasion of the Mohawks' lands. By this time, everyone in the colony knew that the Iroquois Confederacy of Upper New York was vulnerable. The Iroquois had made innumerable enemies while attempting to control all the North American fur trade, and repeated epidemics of smallpox had considerably depleted their population and pool of warriors.

The first intended invasion of the Mohawks took place in the dead of winter, in January 1666. It was an utter disaster, even though the French regulars and Canadian militia were able to penetrate Iroquois territory for the first time. Fearful of a possible follow-up, the Iroquois sent twenty-four ambassadors to Québec to sue for peace in the summer of 1666. The pursuit of peace was short-lived, however. Mohawks attacked a French party of hunters on the Richelieu River, killed Tracy's nephew, and captured a number of prisoners, including one of Tracy's cousins. Enraged, Tracy imprisoned the ambassadors and sent a rescue party to the lands of the Mohawks. Fortunately for all, the prisoners were returned but the peace negotiations weren't resumed. Instead, Tracy hanged one the ambassadors to teach the Iroquois a lesson and launched his second expedition on September 14, 1666. It included French regulars, Canadian militiamen, Algonquins, and Hurons under Tracy's general command. Like everyone else in the colony, Marie de l'Incarnation was ecstatic: "1,300 picked men" she wrote, "who are all going off to a combat as if to a triumph." Reaching the Mohawks' villages, the invaders found them deserted. To the roll of drums, the French marched into them one by one and, one by one, burned them to the ground, along with their granaries and the growing corn. The army was back in Québec on November 5, having lost only eight men by drowning and not having fired a shot. It is said that four hundred Mohawks died of starvation during the winter. General peace followed in the summer of 1667 and it endured, more or less, until 1675.

While the defences of New France were being reorganized for the better, the civil administration wasn't forgotten. This was due to the intendant, Jean Talon, the most far-sighted administrator of the colony till then. From 1665 until his return to France in 1668, and during his second mandate, 1669–72, he transformed the colony. Knowing almost all the settlers by name, he used his charm, his influence, and the power of his office to encourage agricultural diversification, to build the small number of purebred cattle and sheep sent from France into useful herds, and to introduce the growing of hemp and flax, forcing the girls and women to learn spinning and weaving. With his own funds, he built a brewery to lessen the use of imported and expensive wines and brandy, and he underwrote the construction of a ship to transport dried fish, lumber, and other goods in a three-way trade: Canada–West Indies–France, with emphasis on the trade with the West Indies. He found the money to establish a tannery and a hat factory, to locate mines, to inspect the forests, to survey the land, to manufacture tar, and to develop the whale- and porpoise-fishing industry. Following Colbert's instruction, he was determined to make the colony self-sufficient, particularly as to food.

Nor did Talon forget his duties as the dispenser of justice and the maintainer of civil peace and order. He favoured out-of-court settlements, thus saving "valuable time for the parties that live in distant places which they can leave only by canoe." As for policing, most of his ordinances have been lost, but it does appear from other sources that here, again, he pursued an enlightened policy.

His determination in peopling New France can also be seen in his views on settlement. He created a land-holding pattern that had been unknown here. The plots of land given or sold to the settlers were triangular, with direct access to the water. The houses were built at the apex of the triangle and grouped around a square where the church or the chapel was. He also invigorated the seigneurial system, which was hardly developed upon his arrival. He granted new fiefs, but only to persons who were determined to live on the land, to clear it, and to develop its resources.

There remained the fur trade. This became the primary focus of his second term. It consisted mainly in sending ambassadors and discoverers to all parts of America that could be reached. "This country is laid out in such a way" he wrote to Colbert in 1670, "that by means of the St. Lawrence one can go everywhere inland, thanks to the lakes which lead to its source in the West and to the rivers that flow into it along the South." He thus set in motion what the historian André Vachon called "a veritable exploration programme" ("Talon," *Dictionary of Canadian Biography*, vol. I), the purpose of which was to confine the English by the seashore, to secure the fur trade for French interests, to reach the Sea of China, and to search for mines. In his relentless pursuit of this policy of expansion, Talon acted contrary to his instructions, for Colbert preferred to first solidify the colony along the St. Lawrence rather than scattering its resources all over the map. However, Talon acted as if he hadn't heard.

One of the central figures in this program was the Jesuit Claude Allouez. His journey to Lake Superior in 1665 led to the establishment of mission posts at Sault Ste. Marie, Green Bay, and Michilimackinac. Above all, it opened the way to the discovery of the Mississippi—that most mystical of all rivers and the obsession of so many adventurers, explorers, missionaries, and administrators who, in their dreams of grandeur, saw it as "the way to the Southern Sea and thereby the route to China." One so possessed was René-Robert Cavelier de La Salle (born in Rouen, Normandy, in 1643, assassinated on March 19, 1687, in Texas).

There is serious doubt that La Salle discovered the Mississippi, but he was the first to travel the last 1,100 kilometres of it, assuring the world that indeed the Mississippi emptied into the Gulf of Mexico. On April 9, 1682, he took possession of the valley of the Mississippi in the name of the French king and celebrated the birth of Louisiana. The honour of the discovery of the Mississippi River belongs to a French Jesuit, Jacques Marquette, and a Canadian explorer, Louis Joliett, who reached it in 1673. Meanwhile, at an imposing ceremony at Sault Ste. Marie in early June 1671, France claimed all the territory west of the Great Lakes, as far as the Rockies. Furthermore, on the same day on which Marie de l'Incarnation died in Québec, another Jesuit, Charles Albanel, was on his way to attempt the first overland trip to Hudson Bay, which he reached in June 1672. Unfortunately for him, he was too late to claim it for France—Médard Chouart des Groseilliers had already done so for England in 1668.

To conclude the age of Marie de l'Incarnation, Courcelle and Talon returned to France a few months after her death. (Tracy had left in 1667.) With her death and the departures of the governor and the intendant, New France's period of transformation ended. There was now no money to pour into the colony. The king's and Colbert's attention (and money) were needed in France's war against Holland. It was then decreed that New France existed only for the enrichment of the mother country, to supply her with raw materials and provide her a market for her products. Mercantilism was the policy.

Three fundamental issues dominated the last forty-one years of this period, during which a French colony, as Gustave Lanctot reminds us, became "firmly rooted in the soil of Canada": the struggle with the Iroquois, the English threat, and the peopling and expansion of New France, Canada, Québec.

Between the end of the 1670s and the beginning of the 18th century, the Hurons and the Ottawas were allies of the French and of the Canadiens, as the fur trade moved west. Members of these two nations acted as the middle-men between the authorities in Montréal and Québec and the Native hunters (the Sioux, the Miamis, the Illinois, etc.) on Lake Superior and Lake Michigan and in the Illinois and Ohio country. The Iroquois, on the other hand, wanted to capture that western trade for themselves and their partners, the English traders of New York and Albany.

From roughly 1675 to 1695 (and on and off thereafter), they pursued that policy relentlessly by attacking French forts in the west, capturing fur cargoes on their way to Montréal, and pillaging the western missions. However, it was mostly in the St. Lawrence settlements that they carried on an endless and destructive guerrilla war in which raiding parties of Iroquois destroyed the crops, killed the settlers, and made peaceful life impossible. One has only to recall the so-called Massacre of Lachine in 1689 when, in the middle of the night, they killed twenty-four settlers, took more than seventy prisoners, and burned some sixty houses, or the attack upon the fort at Verchères, where the fourteen-year-old daughter of the seigneur, Madeleine, with her ten- and twelve-year-old brothers, two soldiers, one servant, and a few women kept the Iroquois at bay for three days. Incidents of these kinds happened constantly, forcing the settlers to be constantly on their guard. It was an untenable situation.

Unfortunately for the well-being and the security of the Canadiens, Louis XIV was busy in Europe with various wars, which he was waging to make himself the supreme monarch of Europe. This left New France to the fate of the governors. The pedantic Louis Buade de Frontenac et de Palluau served two terms in Canada: 1672–82 and from 1689 to his death in Québec. During his first term, he was too interested in what he could get out of the fur trade. However, during his second term, he proved himself to be determined and capable of great leadership. As for Joseph-Antoine Le Febvre de la Barre, 1682–85, he was too incompetent to be of any value. Jacques-René de Brisay de Denonville, 1685–89, was decisive, but he found his experience in the wilderness of North America oppressive. These three governors and commanders-in-chief spent an enormous amount of time procrastinating or trying to buy off the Iroquois, and, in the case of Frontenac and La Barre, pursuing their personal interests at the expense of the colonists' well-being.

The only "success" was Frontenac's expedition of 1696. He was, by then, seventy-four. At the head of an army of 2,150 men—French regulars, Canadiens, and Native allies—he invaded the main village of the Onondagas and that of the Oneidas. Finding them practically empty of people, his soldiers plundered, destroyed, and burned all they could find. Although Frontenac didn't put an end to the guerrilla war nor weaken the Iroquois' military might, he did, nevertheless, humiliate them by penetrating so deeply into their territory and leaving many of them destitute. In the process, he kept the loyalty of the western Native nations and ensured French domination of the fur trade.

When war between England and France ended in Europe in 1697, the Iroquois of the Five Nations sent ambassadors to Frontenac to negotiate a peace treaty. His death at the end of November 1698 temporarily stopped the pourparlers, and it took the following three years to achieve an acceptable treaty. In return for some involvement in the fur trade, the Iroquois promised to stop harassing the traders and the settlers, and to remain neutral should a conflict develop between the French and the English. On August 4, 1701, the treaty was signed in Montréal between France and thirty-one chiefs. A few days later, the Mohawks, who hadn't participated in the peace process for reasons of their own, came to Montréal to signify their assent to the peace that their brothers—the Onondagas, the Oneidas, the Cayugas, and the Senecas—had entered upon. New France was finally at peace with all the First Nations within its North American sphere of influence.

This sorry chapter of the rivalry between the Iroquois and the French (Canadiens) cannot be closed without mentioning several other factors. French alliances with such western tribes as the Hurons and the Ottawas had, as their goal, the shutting-out of the Iroquois from the most lucrative part of the fur trade. In retaliation, the Iroquois Confederacy waged only one war, a war that began with Champlain at the beginning of the 17th century and, except for short intervals of peace, that ended a century later. In the pursuit of the objectives of that war, they gave as much as they received; they betrayed as much as they were betrayed; they suffered and died just as their enemies did; and their villages and farms were as much devastated as those of the Canadiens. As for cruelty and the treatment of prisoners, they weren't any worse or any better than those who massacred them or starved them in the name of their vital interests, including delusions of religious superiority. As for courage, the Iroquois had an ample supply of it and they often demonstrated—more often than historians have granted—a capacity for compassion and care. This could have amazed those who sought the glory of martyrdom had they been willing to see with their hearts rather than through their prejudice.

But the Canadiens faced a second threat during the last quarter of the 17th century.

When Denonville arrived in Québec as governor in 1685, he perceived that the real menace to New France didn't come from the Iroquois. It was the English who threatened the security, even the survival of the colony itself, from two directions: from New York and Albany in the south and from Hudson Bay in the north. (The New England colonies concentrated on Acadia, which was a distinct colony from New France.) New France couldn't be secured until this situation was reversed. A year after his arrival, Denonville sent an expedition to James Bay, composed of thirty French soldiers and seventy Canadiens, with two of the Le Moyne brothers: Jacques Le Moyne de Sainte-Hélène (1659–90) and Pierre Le Moyne d'Iberville (1661–1706). Within a year, the French were in command of the lower part of Hudson Bay.

In 1688, William of Orange became king in England, and war with France ensued, making New France a more than probable target. This is why Frontenac returned, in 1689, for a second term. He was to attack New York and rid North America of the English. For a variety of reasons, that idea was eventually abandoned. The Canadiens, who blamed the Albany traders for inciting the Iroquois, wanted him to destroy Albany. Frontenac refused on the grounds that he didn't have enough troops to be successful. Instead, in the winter of 1690, he allowed a military force, made up mostly of Canadiens and Indians, to raid three small settlements in New York and New England. At Schenectady, near Albany, they burned all the houses (except for the home of Mrs. Alexander Glen, who, it was reported, had often been kind to French and Canadian prisoners) and killed many male inhabitants, but not the elderly, the women, or the children. At Salmon Falls, north of Boston, they achieved the same results. And at the fort at Casco Bay in Maine, they burned everything to the ground and turned over its inhabitants to the Abenakis.

In retaliation for these raids, a guerrilla party of English militia from New England, with some Indians, attacked La Prairie (near Hochelaga) where they killed or captured about twenty settlers and soldiers. This was to be the prelude to an Anglo-Iroquois, full-scale military attack by land and one by way of the St. Lawrence. Although smallpox forced the abandonment of the land invasion, the water-route offensive was another story. Its commander, Sir William Phips, was successful in bringing thirty-two small ships and two thousand militiamen before the town of Québec on October 16, 1690. That same day, Frontenac uttered those glorious words: "I have no reply to make to your general other than from the mouths of my cannon and muskets." And he sent back the officer whom Phips had dispatched to demand the capitulation of the colony. Three days later, harassed by Canadian guerrillas, the English navy sailed away. The colony was safe . . . at least for the moment.

In the last year of the war between France and England, 1697, Louis XIV was determined to re-establish his most Christian suzerainty over Hudson Bay. To that end, Pierre Le Moyne d'Iberville, with five ships, sailed north. Only Iberville's ship (fog and other mishaps delayed the others) made it to Fort Nelson at the beginning of September when three English ships arrived, one armed with fifty cannons, the others with thirty-two each. Against this vast force, Iberville had a total of only forty-four guns. In spite of the odds, his audacity and superb skill won the day, and on September 13, 1697, Hudson Bay became part of France again. Seventeen days later, France and England signed a peace treaty in the Dutch town of Ryswick.

To contain the English on the narrow band of land between the Atlantic Ocean and the Allegheny Mountains, Iberville was then entrusted to found a colony in Louisiana. In March of 1698, he planted a cross in the Mississippi delta, claiming all the lands north and west of that mighty river in the name of French king, confirming what La Salle had done seventeen years earlier. In 1700, the Canadien, Pierre Le Moyne d'Iberville, became the first governor of Louisiana. The empire of the French in North America, an empire maintained and defended by the Canadiens, stretched from Hudson Bay to the Gulf of Mexico.

There was yet another war between France and England at this time: the War of the Spanish Succession (or Queen Anne's War), which began in 1702. For New France, this meant that New England might invade Acadia in retaliation for not being permitted to fish the waters around Cape Breton and that New York might launch an expedition against Québec for having been excluded from the western fur trade. Hopefully, the Indian allies of the French—the Abenakis and the Iroquois—would assist the French where possible, or at worst, remain neutral. The Abenakis participated in the raids against settlements in New England, particularly the village of Deerfield, Massachusetts, where settlers were killed, houses burned, and many prisoners taken. In spite of the New Yorkers plying them with brandy, gunpowder, clothing, and weapons of all sorts, the Five Nations remained largely neutral. The situation was more complicated, however, in the west. There, hostilities could break out at any moment, endangering the precarious French/Canadian fur trade. However, due to the intelligence and considerable diplomatic skills of the new governor, Philippe de Rigaud de Vaudreuil (1643–1725), who was married to a Canadienne, no damaging incident occurred on that front.

Vaudreuil's success with the Native tribes angered the English-Americans and made them more determined than ever to rid themselves of the French. Accordingly, they sent a naval and military force against Port Royal, in Acadia. The fort capitulated to the English on October 13, 1710. The English also determined to attack Québec by land, through Lake Champlain and by way of the St. Lawrence. Nothing came of that effort: the English fleet floundered in the fog and, discouraged upon hearing the news, the land army went back the way it had come. However, the Canadiens were ready. The English had a force of about 12,000 men; Vaudreuil had only 2,300, to which was added 600 militia from Montréal and a large number from Trois-Rivières, along with 700 Natives. In the defence of their country, the Canadiens did all they could. Then, peace came in 1713 with the Treaty of Utrecht, which ceded Hudson Bay, Newfoundland, and Acadia to England, but left intact the rest of the French possessions in North America. That satisfied the Canadiens. The people of New France were then ready to enjoy the fruits of their sufferings and labours.

One of the most important results of the 1639–1713 period was the considerable growth of the population. In 1663, when the colony's Royal

Government was established, the population numbered between 2,000 and 2,500. By 1713, in the space of fifty years, it had increased seven-fold, to 18,179. The vast majority of the people living here by then were Canadiens, the descendants of the 4,000 who had immigrated between 1663 and 1673. Since there was hardly any immigration after 1673, the birthrate must have been phenomenal and the infant mortality low—and all that in spite of the destructive war among the Iroquois and the Canadiens and the French, which had lasted over twenty years. And all that, too, in spite of the epidemics of 1685, 1701, and 1703, which killed over three thousand.

Most of the people lived on farms, under the seigneurial system, along both sides of the St. Lawrence, while 1,819 lived in the capital of New France, Québec (its population had been 547 at the birth of Royal Government), 1,200 occupied Montréal, and 299 lived in Trois-Rivières. The young men of New France lived on their farms or in the towns, but they spent much time away—too much, according to the authorities—trapping, fur trading, and exploring. The phenomenon of the coureurs de bois grew in spite of all attempts to curtail it. Once the war with the Iroquois ended in 1701, and the English menace became somewhat controlled, New France was a good place to live.

In the face of the great hardships that had to be met in tilling the land, or exploring it, or defending it, it was said that you had to be a Canadien to endure it all. And *Canadiens* they were. They knew who they were and what they wanted, and they strove to achieve it. The Jesuit historian and traveller Pierre-François-Xavier de Charlevoix (1682–1761), among so many others, noticed the difference between the people of France and the people of Canada. The Canadiens, he wrote, "breathe from birth an air of liberty which makes them very pleasant to associate with, and nowhere else is a purer French spoken." Even though we were not very rich, we were vain; we lived well; and, above all, we dressed much above our means. "Everyone here," he added, "is well built . . . You couldn't find better types of either sex anywhere. Even the people in the most rural districts have alert minds and gentle, polite manners."

All that remains to be said is that in the space of barely half a century, a people took root in the land of Canada—a people who spoke French; a people attached to their ways and traditions; a people determined enough to build and to hold an empire that stretched from the Atlantic to the foot of the Rockies, and from Hudson Bay to the Gulf of Mexico. Whenever part of their land was lost, my people were not at fault: forces in France or elsewhere in Europe controlled their destiny. Canadiens were determined, however, to remain in Canada, come what may. This constitutes the lesson of the days of Champlain, of Marie de l'Incarnation, of Frontenac, of Vaudreuil, and of all the Canadiens who valiantly built themselves a country to have and to hold.

⚜

"I see that you've taken us to 1713," a voice says out of nowhere. "It's the beginning of a new era. But, of course, I won't be there."

I'm in Toronto, Ontario, Canada, in the house of a friend. In the breakfast room, in fact—a breakfast room that is attached to a rather attractive kitchen. I have turned around and there, in the middle of the room, is a not-so-tall man of a certain weight. I would say he's about my age, seventy, and he's dressed in a pair of grey flannel trousers; a white shirt trimmed with lace, over which he has a sort of red vest; a beat-up beaver hat on his head; and a pair of leather boots that have seen better days. He holds a book in his left hand.

"You haven't mentioned my name at all," he reproaches me.

"Who are you and why do you deserve to be included?"

"My name is Charles Aubert de La Chesnaye. I was . . . I am! . . . the most important businessman of the century you've just finished writing about, and probably the largest landowner of my time. And, unless you've forgotten, the king ennobled me in 1693." He bows his head and says: "He said flattering things about me. Vive le Roi!" He bows again and adds: "As you can see, I'm somewhat important. So why not include me along with Champlain, the Holy Ursuline Mother, and the others?"

"You didn't seem to fit," I reply with some sarcasm. "But, since you're here, come and sit down and we'll talk." He approaches the table and lays down his book. As he sits, I take a peek at what he's reading. It's the works of François de Sales, a religious leader of the early 17th century in France. I offer my visitor some tea, which he accepts, and I say: "I know who you are! You were born in Amiens, France, in 1632. You came to Québec in 1655 as the agent of some merchants, I think from Rouen. You amassed a fortune but practically lost it all before you died in the town of Québec in 1702. When in Québec, you lived on Sault-au-Matelot Street where you built a commodious stone house that served as your residence. Attached to your house was a large store where you charged exorbitant prices for the various goods you sold. You also had a magnificent summer house, known as La Maison Blanche, on what is now St. Vallier Street in the City of Québec."

I look at my research notes. "Oh! Yes. Your marriages! . . . Your three Canadian wives gave you eighteen children, eleven of whom lived beyond adulthood. One of your sons, Pierre, was le Sieur de Gaspé and the great-grandfather of Philippe Aubert de Gaspé (1786–1871) who is the author of a fine book about us all, called *Les Anciens Canadiens,* published in 1863. I must add that you're mentioned in every book about New France that I've read; that one of our best historians, Professor Yves F. Zoltvany, presents a long article about you in the *Dictionary of Canadian Biography;* and that one of your descendants, L.C. Audette, has written about your life in a manuscript that awaits publication. There! You haven't been forgotten."

"Except by you."

"Well, I don't like you very much."

"Why is that?"

"It's hard to say." I think about it as he finishes his tea. "You were all over the map."

He looks at me pensively, assessing me. "You're not a businessman," he says. "It's obvious. A businessman always needs to diversify . . . at least in my time. However, there was a core to my economic or entrepreneurial activities. That core consisted of the fur trade in the west and in the north, merchandising at my store in Québec, and agriculture throughout my landholdings and seigneuries. The rest—lumbering, fishing, exporting, shipping, and the lending of money to whoever wanted to accept my terms—all that was ancillary to the core." He ponders what he's just said and adds: "It was no easy matter to do business in the France of my time, especially in this colony. Until 1690, we had no currency. We had to sell on credit. Mon ami, it was most difficult to collect. The inhabitants here may have been Canadiens, but they had kept that infuriating Norman characteristic of litigating everything. It took a long time for me to get paid. Much of my capital was trapped in what merchants, explorers, the government, and the inhabitants owed me."

"You didn't get along with many. You fought with Talon, Frontenac, and only Zoltvany knows who else. Oh! Yes: that fraud La Barre, you didn't fight with him. In fact, you helped him." La Chesnaye doesn't look guilty at all. "So, what do you have to say for yourself?" I ask with some annoyance.

He asks for more tea and when I've served him, he replies: "I didn't always fight or argue or whatever you want to call it. Take the intendant Talon. In his first term, Monsieur l'Intendant was all exercised about free trade in furs. It was a silly idea. You need a lot of capital to trade in furs. None of us had it. We needed a monopoly to ensure access to the furs, to bring them to Europe to be sold there, to procure the supplies the trade expeditions needed, to pay the taxes the Crown and everybody else in power charged and . . . Oh! I could go on and on. I won't, except to tell you that the fur trade was an intricate and far-reaching economic activity." He shrugs his shoulders as he adds: "Free trade was a silly idea."

"You lost, though. In spite of you and your memoranda to Louis XIV's court, it was decided to accept Talon's policy."

"In business, you lose some, win some. I liked Talon. And I helped him. That you must grant me."

"Yes, that is so. Without you, his plans for a lumber and fishing industry, not to mention exporting all that to Europe and to the West Indies, wouldn't have materialised to the degree that they did."

"Governor Frontenac and his cohort, the explorer La Salle, were out to ruin me economically by their manipulations of the western fur trade. I had to put an end to it. As for La Barre." He hesitates. "He was a weak man," he finally says. "A good man, no doubt about that. But quite weak and, above all, indecisive. I helped him because he looked to me for advice. He trusted me."

"He allowed you to smuggle furs to the enemies of France, the enemies of your king: the English. It was illegal, probably treasonous."

"Please, don't get carried away. The English paid more for the furs than did the French. I made a lot of money. The king made a lot of money through me. So did Governor La Barre. Everyone was satisfied . . ." He smiles and adds: "Especially when I pursued . . . things for which they had no funds." He doesn't elaborate. But I think he refers to the Compagnie du Nord, which he founded in 1682 to take advantage of the fur trade around Hudson Bay. Instead, he repeats, "I made them all a lot of money. That helped me."

"What do you mean?"

Again he considers what he's about to say. Finally, he taps me on the shoulder and says: "In my whole life, I had two basic principles outside, of course, the religious ones that I inherited and upon which I built what I consider to be a good spiritual life. As for business and the political aspects of my passage on this planet, I gave myself two maxims. The first one was: 'Seize whatever opportunity there is and go for it. If you have reverses, forget them, for the future is where life is.' " He sips his tea.

"And your second principle?"

He puts down his cup. For the first time, I notice that he shakes. Old age, I tell myself. The cup safely in the saucer, he continues: "In the narrow mercantilism of our day and the precarious situation of those to whom the king granted his favours, exercising power—in whatever limited way—meant survival. To have power, you have to have access. And to have access, you had to make yourself noticed." He smiles again. "I'm certain it's not that different in your day!"

"I can't argue with that!" We're both silent. "Tell me," I ask him, "you who traded with the English, did you find much difference between the French or Canadiens and the English and the English-Americans in their dealings with the Natives?"

"Yes. I can fairly say that we were respectful of the partnership we had with your Indians. We dealt with them as equals, and we didn't want their lands. We wanted to trade rather than to colonize. The English saw their mission differently. Take, for instance, the New Englanders! They were merciless in forcing the Indians off their lands and, more often than not, they killed them. We didn't do much of that." Again he thinks over what he has said, as the nodding of his head indicates. Looking at his hands, he finally says: "Our rhetoric and our paternalism, though, were the same."

"From that lofty pinnacle where you placed yourself, is this why you objected strongly to the sale of liquor to the Natives—the so-called Brandy trade?"

"The sale of alcohol to the Indians! Horrible. I opposed it. Frontenac knew my views, and when he held his Brandy Parliament, he didn't invite me to participate."

"But you had everything to gain by getting the Indians drunk."

He looks at me as if I were drunk myself. With some anger, he lectures me: "Don't be so flippant. The Brandy trade was immoral. And I wanted no part of it." He looks out at the patches of snow in the yard and, using the present tense as if he were still in the New France of the 17th century, he adds: "I don't know what hell is all about, really. But I'm certain that there is no greater hell on this earth than the sight of these savages, men and women, drunk and capable of every kind of brutality, violence, and murder: father and son, husband and wife, etc. All these disorders take place very often because there is no will to punish the authors of the evil. Bishop Laval did the right thing by threatening to excommunicate those involved in the sale of liquor to the Indians. You see, there is nothing to gain by being lenient towards those who practise this horrible and immoral trade."

"The king, though, forced a compromise, forbidding the sale outside of the towns of New France."

"I disapprove of His Majesty's decision as well."

We are both silent, then I ask him if he wants to hear what Professor Zoltvany concludes about him.

"That would be nice," he says with enthusiasm.

I search DCB's vol. I and find the conclusion to that biography. I tell my visitor that Zoltvany pays homage to his sense of duty, his piety and austerity, his devotion to New France, his charity particularly after the disastrous Québec fire of 1682 when you "made generous loans to help your fellow-Canadians rebuild their homes." I read on to the effect that none of these fine qualities and acts "should obscure the fact that the driving force in his career had been the spirit of gain . . . With money, in other words, came power, the quest for which cannot be discounted as a factor in La Chesnaye's career."

I close the book but when I look up, his chair is empty.

⚜

III

The Making of les Canadiens 1713–1763

✣

*E*arly in the morning of September 13, 1759, two messengers arrived at the headquarters of Governor General Vaudreuil, which was situated not too far from the main French camp at Beauport, a few kilometres east of the town of Québec. They reported that the English army, under the command of Major-General James Wolfe, had probably landed at L'Anse-au-Foulon, above Québec. Once disembarked, the troops were said to have walked up a narrow path that led to the heights above the St. Lawrence River. Confused by the word "probably," the Marquis de Montcalm, commander of the French troops in New France, along with several troops, went to investigate.

If Vaudreuil was confused, Wolfe wasn't. He knew what he was doing. He would fight the French army on his chosen territory. The rain came and went, but by eight o'clock most of his troops had climbed the ravine and were on what we call the Plains of Abraham (which is now a national park that commemorates the central battle between France and England for our country, Canada). He had an army of over four thousand men: some he used to protect his rear, others to give himself a reserve, and with the rest he formed two thin lines on the ridge of a shallow ravine about one and a half kilometres from the walls of Québec. He didn't have enough men for the usual three lines. In the midst of the Canadien guerrilla fire coming from the bushes and shrubs that dotted the entire landscape, Wolfe waited for Montcalm's soldiers to arrive.

While Wolfe was drawing up his troops on the Plains of Abraham, Montcalm, on his black horse, was riding to his rendezvous with destiny, followed by his aides, his valet, his coachman and the horses, and a few soldiers. He entered the town of Québec through the Porte du Palais and exited on to the Plains through the Porte Saint-Jean. When he saw the English army six hundred metres in front of him, he whispered to himself: "Ils sont là où ils ne devraient pas être!" (There they are where they ought not to be!)

The French army numbered well over 11,000 men, made up of regulars, colonials, Canadian militia, and Indians. However, Montcalm had at his disposal only 4,500 soldiers on the Plains of Abraham. About 1,500 regulars remained in their camp at Beauport; about 2,000 colonial troops and militia guarded the town; three thousand soldiers, with the entire cavalry, and well over 900 Grenadiers were encamped at Cap-Rouge above Québec. His second-in-command, le Chevalier de Lévis, was also absent, having been sent to protect the French fort at Niagara.

Shortly after nine o'clock, what was left of the French troops had arrived on the Plains, and their officers were lining them up in battle formation— one long line. Some of the colonial troops—with an unknown number of militia from Montréal and Québec—were on the far right of the line; next came the five regiments of regular troops, with a large number of Canadian militia mixed in with them; and closing the line, on the far left, was the rest of the Montréal militia, along with the men from Trois-Rivières. Indian and Canadian sharpshooters continued to harass the English from every vantage point they could.

At 10 a.m., Montcalm raised his sword, pointing it at the English; the flag-bearers unfurled their flags; and the drummers, beating away, led the charge. The rain stopped and the sun bathed the Plains in light. Montcalm's soldiers and militia advanced. Wolfe, with a bloody handkerchief tied around his wrist, smiled as he saw them coming. He ordered his soldiers, who had been lying down, to their feet and his front line to drop to one knee. Montcalm's line continued its erratic advance with great speed, causing many soldiers to stumble over the uneven ground. As they advanced, much too fast, Montcalm thought, the Canadian and Indian sharpshooters joined the ranks. Without waiting for the order, a shot rang out from the French line, followed by a general volley. Their guns empty, the Canadiens and the Indians fell to the ground to reload, as was their custom. This, however, caused the regular troops to become confused and disoriented as they tripped over the Canadiens. Nevertheless, Montcalm and his officers were able to restore some semblance of order, and the French line pursued its course.

When the French and Canadiens were forty metres away from the English, Wolfe yelled: "Fire!" The right and the left of his front line shot at intervals while the middle did so simultaneously. When they had fired one of the two balls that Wolfe had ordered them to place in their muskets, Wolfe's army took three steps forward and the front line dropped to one knee. They waited for the smoke to clear. It took seven minutes. Then came Wolfe's second command: "Fire!" Apparently, the sound of the English muskets was like a single, gigantic cannon shot. Two minutes later, a Canadien sharpshooter, hiding in the bushes above the ridge, aimed and fired, hitting Wolfe in the chest and fatally wounding him. He died half an hour later, happy to have won the day. He was thirty-two years old.

The first English volley froze the French and Canadien soldiers in their tracks. Soon, too many corpses littered the battlefield. Montcalm managed to hold the centre, but only for a while. The second volley, however, found him without an army. Some of the regulars ran to the town or across the St. Charles River for cover, while many of the Canadiens took cover in the bushes from where they fired on the pursuing redcoats, permitting many French soldiers to escape. Vaudreuil, who had witnessed the two English volleys in his calèche (open carriage) from the north end of the Plains, attempted to rally the French fugitives, but to avail. As for Montcalm, his retreating army swept him to Québec by the Porte Saint-Louis.

The battle of the Plains of Abraham was over. It had lasted less than half an hour.

As he was about to pass through the Porte into the town, Montcalm was severely wounded. At five o'clock the next morning, he died. He was buried in a bomb crater in the chapel of the Ursulines.

At about the same time, Montcalm's demoralised army, led by Governor General Vaudreuil, was fleeing to a refuge of sorts at Jacques-Cartier, where the city of Longueuil now is, abandoning thousands of Canadiens in the district of Québec, living on both sides of the St. Lawrence—in one town, and in fifty-nine villages, parishes, and seigneuries. On September 18, 1759, they became the subjects of the English king.

To understand the people who were suddenly subject to an entirely new authority, we need to see their world with a couple of perspectives in mind.

Geography: somebody once said that geography is everything. Perhaps. It certainly dictates a large portion of the metamorphosis that makes one people become another. In this case, it was the transformation of French men and women into Canadiens and Canadiennes, a process that, as we have seen, didn't take much time.

Geography gave the French and the Canadiens a splendid river to work their destiny. The St. Lawrence and many of its tributaries provided agricultural lands, more plentiful on its south shore than on the north. "Consequently," as Professor W.J. Eccles concludes, "throughout the French regime, land settlement was concentrated in the St. Lawrence Valley from a point a few kilometres west of Montréal to a little below Québec, with pockets of settlement on both sides lower down the river."

The St. Lawrence made transportation and communication possible between the settlements, especially among the three towns of Québec, Trois-Rivières, and Montréal, and the settlers around them—by means of canoes and barges in summer, and sleds on the ice in winter. Furthermore, it was the St. Lawrence, as we noticed earlier, that dictated the land-holding pattern: a narrow strip of property from the water to the end of the concession, with the houses and the barns a little way up from the river bank. The "neighbour" was but a few metres away. Now and then, there was a manor house for the seigneur, a mill, and, more often than not, a stone church. Roads, when they began to appear, followed the same configuration. When certain

French officials attempted to herd settlers into villages, to protect them from the Iroquois raids, the Canadiens vehemently refused to limit their liberty: they preferred to live in danger rather than to abandon their way of life: living on their land, apart from their neighbours, and being easily able to reach the world beyond by means of their river.

Why was that world beyond so important to the Canadiens, particularly to the young men of the colony? Because the search for and the capture and enjoyment of freedom was the essence of who they were and the fulfilment of their existence. The St. Lawrence and its tributaries opened for them a whole continent, stretching from Hudson Bay to the Rocky Mountains to the Gulf of Mexico. They could leave their farm or their little house somewhere within the confines of the colony and canoe to Montréal. From there, and paddling to their hearts' content, they could travel west on the Ottawa, Mattawa, and French Rivers to Georgian Bay and thence to the most important fort and fur depot for the northern trade of the Old West, Fort Michilimackinac, situated between Lake Michigan and Lake Huron, where Mackinac City now is. The St. Lawrence also permitted access to the southern fur trade, by leading to Detroit and the country of the Mississippi and Ohio Rivers. Then, after the Treaty of Utrecht in 1713, they paddled even farther west of Lake Michigan, into Lake Superior and beyond.

"The West" was what it was all about. The colony was, of course, where home was. But the West was the source of the Canadiens' livelihood and where their social and economic standing in their communities came from. As Professor Dale Miquelon has remarked: "For the Canadian psyche, the West was a counterpoise to all that was traditional and that had behind it the full weight of rural life and of the imperial connection."

That continent, which the St. Lawrence opened up for the Canadiens, was theirs for the taking. And they did take it.

The river also made sailors out of them, permitting them to crew on fishing boats in the Gulf of the St. Lawrence and on whale-hunting expeditions up the Labrador coast. The St. Lawrence, as well, allowed them to serve their country in time of war, by serving as privateers along the New England coast, where they were much admired for their toughness, endurance, and aggressiveness—and all of this when their counterparts in France hardly travelled more than a few kilometres from their villages.

Most important, the St. Lawrence provided the Canadiens with the epitome of the freedom they sought. And the Natives were everywhere. In the West. In the lands adjacent to the colony. Up the coasts. (In Hudson Bay and Labrador, they encountered those whom they called Eskimos.) Around the towns and settlements (in Lorette and Saint-François near the town of Québec, and at Oka and Caugnawaga near Montréal). The Canadiens had no difficulty joining the Natives on their travels everywhere, trading and exploring, to make war, peace, and love, and to learn how to live in this land.

Slowly and gradually, but faster than many anticipated, Frenchmen were transformed into Canadiens. No sooner had Governor Denonville arrived in New France in 1685 than he deplored the attraction "that this Indian way of life has for all these youths," who were "very self-willed and inclined to dissoluteness." The bishop, the Jesuits, the clergy, and the officials shared this view and tried every which way to put an end to it. But they couldn't, for as Charlevoix reported in the 1740s: "They love to breathe a free air, they are early accustomed to a wandering life; it has charms for them, which make them forget past dangers and fatigues, and they place their glory in encountering them often. . . . It is alleged they make bad servants, which is owing to their great haughtiness of spirit, and to their loving liberty too much to subject themselves willingly to servitude."

Professor Eccles states that even those who didn't participate in these escapades, "could feel that the opportunity was there, and this must have given them a sense of freedom. They could not help but hear the tales of those who had voyaged far afield, of the strange peoples with stranger customs in the distant lands. They, too, shared the experience vicariously."

To the vast majority of the Canadiens, the Natives were their equals, and they dealt with each other on the basis of that equality, in spite of the fact that often they had to defend themselves against each other. Without the First Peoples, the first French settlers would not have survived to become Canadiens. Domagaya gave them a cure for scurvy; others introduced them to tobacco, a custom that, in time, made the Canadiens of all ages confirmed pipe-smokers. From the Indians, the settlers also learned to eat corn, squash, and pumpkins; to travel by means of snowshoes, toboggans, and canoes; and to dress à l'indienne, which soon became to dress à la canadienne. It may even be possible that the Canadien aptitude for storytelling and myth-making came from the Natives, as did the Canadien cupidity and spendthrift attitudes.

"They are not thrifty and take no care for the future," wrote a French observer a couple of years before the battle of the Plains of Abraham. Pursuing his thought, Bougainville added: "They endure hunger and thirst patiently, many of them having been trained from infancy to imitate the Indians, whom, with reason, they hold in high regard." As for war, their masters were the people they called fondly "les sauvages," who taught them to make war "only by swift attacks," using guerrilla techniques and, through forest warfare, the adroit use of firearms. Did they also teach the young men of New France to be harsh, cruel, to give no mercy, to forgo chastity for the necessary pleasures of the flesh, to father "bastard" children, to take more than one wife, and the rest of it? Who knows? All of that probably came naturally to them!

The English and the Anglo-Americans admired and, at the same time, resented the relationship between the Natives and the Canadiens. It was well known that the First Peoples preferred to trade with the Canadiens rather than with the English—the price of the goods being the only obstacle. The Canadiens were able to conciliate "the affections of the savages," as someone once put it. No one did it better than they.

Did the Canadiens have a beneficial impact upon the Native Peoples? We certainly know much—and can imagine what we don't know—about the harm that was done. However, there is ample evidence to suggest that the record is not totally bleak, in spite of the paternalism and the arrogance that too often characterised the dealings between Natives and visages pâles. Even though there is, at the present time, a national prise de conscience—which is all to the good—about the impact of Christianity, the work of the missionaries and nuns, and other religious-minded people on the First Nations, it is fair to say that the Christians of New France had enough respect for the Indian people to attempt to save their souls and to "civilise" them through education and contact. These objectives now appear misguided, but they weren't in the 17th and 18th centuries—they were fundamental to the exercise of the faith that animated those who came here.

However, there appears to be a difference in attitude when one talks about the relationship between the Indians and the Canadiens as opposed to the relationship between the French and the Natives. Canadiens learned Indian languages and respected Native ceremonials. Both shared the land and associated freely and equally in trade. Both also undertook wars against common enemies, to satisfy different but mutually accepted objectives. The Canadiens found refuge on Native land, and the Natives were given it, as well, in the settlements and towns. Both showed real affection towards each other. And both were victims—a word much used these days to account for what fate ordains—of the yoke their cultures had imposed upon them. All and all, it seems that both benefited by their being together and attempting to co-exist.

War: between 1608 and 1753—nearly a century and a half—the Canadiens enjoyed only forty-two years of peace; the other hundred-plus years brought war.

The major conflict of that period in New France was with the Iroquois nations for the control of the North American fur trade. That violent struggle lasted about a century and, as we've seen, almost destroyed both groups.

The British-American settlers along the coast of the Atlantic didn't threaten the Canadiens, even though their population grew much faster than their northern neighbours. (In 1763, there were a half million British colonials and only seventy thousand Canadiens.) Natural barriers (the Green Mountains in Vermont, the White Mountains in New Hampshire and Maine, the Adirondacks in New York, and the Appalachians in the Carolinas, Virginia, Maryland, and Pennsylvania) helped considerably to keep both sides apart. The colonials to the south lacked cohesiveness, and argued relentlessly with each other, but both sides participated in illegal fur-trading—it was very lucrative. Besides, I have no doubt that the Canadiens were better fighters, more experienced, and certainly more aggressive than their southern neighbours. In the era of New France, they proved that. They managed to keep the "Americans" prisoners on the Atlantic seaboard.

No, the threat to the Canadiens didn't lie in America; it lay in Europe.

After the escapade of the Kirke brothers in 1629, the first major European war that had colonial repercussions in North America was the War of the League of Augsburg (1688–97), which pitted France against England and Holland. The Iroquois, still smarting over Denonville's invasion of Seneca lands in 1687, got revenge by attacking the settlement of Lachine near Montréal in the summer of 1689. At the same time, the Abenakis, aided by their Franco-Canadien allies, intensified their battles against the New Englanders, by invading settlements in the region in 1689 and, especially, in 1690. These attacks provoked the Sir William Phips expedition in the summer and autumn of that same year. Phips captured Port Royal, Acadia, in May; but when, later, he demanded the surrender of Québec, Frontenac, relying mostly on the Canadien militia, sent him on his way with his two thousand militiamen and thirty-two small ships. When the European war ended with the Peace of Ryswick in September 1696, everything was as before: neither the French nor the English gained anything, except that the English lost the support of the Iroquois, who complained that the English hadn't helped them against the Canadiens. They sued for peace. It was signed in Montréal in 1701.

The peace, however, lasted only a year, for in 1702 Louis XIV went to war against Spain and England. The War of the Spanish Succession lasted eleven years.

The new European madness was slower to catch on here, but in 1703 the Canadiens and their Indian allies struck the first blow by raiding various New England settlements that summer, and totally destroying Deerfield, Massachusetts, in February 1704. In reply, American colonials attempted to mount a land and sea expedition against Canada. But for a variety of reasons, that failed. However, in 1710, with the decisive assistance of an English five-vessel squadron and four hundred marines, Port Royal was finally captured and renamed Annapolis Royal. A year later, the English government sent over six thousand of their most seasoned regular troops and a forty-five–vessel armada to conquer Québec. However, that attempt came to naught because of fog and the stupidity of the admiral in command. For the second time in the memory of many, the English offensive to take Canada failed. So the war was all but over.

Even though the Canadiens had fought valiantly to protect their homes and lands, and had survived against the most gigantic odds, the French lost at the peace table in 1713—as they would later in the century—weakening the people at Québec in the process. A few days after the news of the European peace reached the colony at the end of June 1713, the Canadien nun who kept the logs of the Hôtel Dieu of Québec wrote: "The state of French affairs permitted the court no thought of us." Yet she, like everyone else in New France, was of the opinion that the peace "cannot but give us hope for better days and hope that by peace all our past losses will be made good."

Thirty-three years of peace followed the War of the Spanish Succession, a peace marked by intense competition in the colonies for imperial power and prestige. Furthermore, by opening the West to all comers, the Treaty of Utrecht forced a long and protracted struggle between France and England for land and trade.

During that uneasy truce, one of the most remarkable Canadien families stepped in to bridge the gap—the family of Pierre Gaultier de Varennes et de La Vérendrye. With his sons, Jean-Baptiste, Pierre, François, and Louis-Joseph—and his nephew, a fine and bright young man by the name of Christophe Dufrost de la Jemerais—La Vérendrye was the first of my people to walk the Canadian prairie. From there, he found the route that became "the great highway to the northwest" and which every explorer and fur trader used for decades afterwards. From there, as well, he pushed the western frontier of New France to at least within sight of the Rockies. But he never found the western sea.

Because of his accomplishments and selfless contribution, La Vérendrye is known as "The Explorer." His story, and that of his sons and nephew, is one of valour and sacrifice, pain and anguish, endurance and courage, with little return.

Pierre, the father, was born in Trois-Rivières, in 1685, the son of the governor of that little town. His education was most rudimentary, and he chose to become a soldier, enrolling as a cadet in the colonial regular troops when he was eleven. At nineteen, he helped to burn Deerfield, Massachusetts, to the ground. A year later, he was fighting in Newfoundland, becoming an ensign shortly thereafter. When he was twenty-three, five years before the end of the War of the Spanish Succession, he opted to fight in Europe, hoping to find glory and advancement. Upon his arrival, he was made a second lieutenant in the Régiment de Bretagne. On September 11, 1709, he was left for dead on the battlefield at Malplaquet. His valour on that day caused him to be mentioned in the Order of the Day. For over a year, he was a prisoner of war, during which he was promoted to rank of lieutenant. Upon his release, he returned to Canada with the reduced rank of ensign, and when the war ended in 1713, he was without employment. However, a year before, he had married the daughter of a rich landowner. For the next fifteen years, he lived on his wife's property on Île aux Vaches on Lac Saint-Pierre, near Trois-Rivières, siring six children—four sons and two daughters—clearing the land, struggling to make ends meet. At thirty-five, he felt he hadn't done very much with his life. So change was imperative.

For several years he had traded with the Natives who came to sell him furs at his small post, La Gabelle, on the Saint-Maurice River. In these encounters, he made an important discovery about himself: the Indians trusted him and confided in him. He had learned their languages easily, and he was fair, courteous, diplomatic, and non-judgemental when dealing with them.

In 1726, his brother had received le poste du nord, as a trading fief; this was a vast fur-trading area north of Lake Superior. Its main post was at Kaministiquia (Thunder Bay) with two smaller ones, at Nipigon and Michipicoton, north of Sault Ste. Marie. La Vérendrye became his brother's partner and two years later he succeeded him as commander-in-chief, and he moved to Thunder Bay. That's when his "new" life really began.

His stay there coincided with the renewal of the search for la mer de l'ouest or la mer du couchant. That sea filled the imagination of most of those who set out from Québec and Montréal to explore the vast hinterland that is North America. It also fed their dreams with visions of wealth, recognition, and *gloire*, for it led directly to the jewels of the fabled East. During the first years of Canada, the western sea always lay somewhere west of known territory. Somewhere in that immense space lay a body of water—a gulf—that led directly to the Pacific Ocean. That gulf was the western sea. But where was it?

For Canadian explorers and fur traders, the western sea—if it existed at all—was somewhere in the Lake Ouinipigon (Lake Winnipeg)–Lake of the Woods complex. On the other hand, to Charlevoix, that indefatigable Jesuit, it was somewhere else. In 1720, the French authorities asked him to locate it. In January 1723, after a perilous journey that took him from Montréal to the Great Lakes and thence to New Orleans, England, and back to France, he reported that la mer de l'ouest could, in all probability, be found between forty and fifty degrees latitude, relatively close to the lands of the Mandan Indians, who lived along the banks of the Missouri River. For Charlevoix, the source of the Missouri River "is certainly not far from the sea."

La Vérendrye was certain that the western sea couldn't be found in the upper regions of the Mississippi River. Rather, after talking to many Indians who came trading at Thunder Bay, especially an old Cree by the name of Auchagah, he became convinced that the western sea was the Pacific Ocean and, therefore, farther west than was being advocated. As for the route to it, it was to be found from Lake Ouinipigon and through the river system that surrounded it. To get there, he would use the Pigeon River, some sixty-four kilometres southwest of Thunder Bay. That route, a perilous one, with as many as forty portages over difficult terrain, would take him to Lac La Pluie (or Tekamamiouen, or Rainy Lake) situated on the present Ontario-Minnesota border, 240 kilometres west of Lake Superior. Lac La Pluie was important because its waters flowed westward.

In spite of all that route's difficulties, La Vérendrye chose it. He knew the Indians used it regularly, and he had great faith in Auchagah, whom he considered "the man most capable of guiding a party and with whom there would be no fear of our being abandoned on the way."

After much deliberation between the many levels of the French autocracy—and with various partners who, at vast cost, would supply him the money he needed—he was given permission to search for the western sea. He set out on his quest from Montréal on June 8, 1731, accompanied by three of his sons: Jean-Baptiste, Pierre, and François, his nephew, and fifty *engagés*. Almost three months later, he was at Grand Portage, at the western end of Lake Superior. But he wasn't able at that time to proceed to the mouth of the Pigeon River: most of the engagés were in no mood to go farther. It was the only mutiny La Vérendrye had to put up with in his twelve years of exploration. All was not lost, however. Jean-Baptiste and Christophe volunteered, with some others, to proceed to Lac La Pluie, where they built a fort (Fort Saint-Pierre) and began trading. In the following summer (1732), La Vérendrye joined them and, hardly stopping, he canoed down the Rainy River to the west end of the Lake of the Woods (Lac des Bois) where he built a fort thirty metres square, with a palisade about three and a half metres high. Fort Saint-Charles, as it was called, contained a small church, a house for him, one for the missionary accompanying him, barracks for the men, and a magazine. It was to serve as La Vérendrye's headquarters for the next several years. Out of the Lake of the Woods flowed a small creek that grew into a river, which is known to us as the Winnipeg River. To La Vérendrye, it was the river that would lead him, he hoped, to the western sea.

The year that followed was particularly harsh. But the meagre food supply and the intense cold didn't prevent La Vérendrye from making plans for his third fort, Fort Maurepas. He built it in 1734 on the lower Red River, but before it was finished, he had to return to Montréal to replenish his funds and obtain new concessions. He was gone a year; it wasn't a pleasant one. The governor general wrote that "The Explorer" had "failed to secure any associate who like himself, prefers the glory of success to gain in money." However, La Vérendrye's will prevailed and he returned to Fort Saint-Charles with his fourth and most versatile son, the eighteen-year-old Louis-Joseph, also known as Le Chevalier.

Until 1743, when he resigned his commission, La Vérendrye had no easy time of it. He was constantly in debt, besieged by his creditors, abandoned by his partners, and rejected by the authorities in France. Yet, he accomplished much.

⚜

The books, the documents, the maps are scattered all over my desk, and I'm having difficulty making sense of them all. Then, there is the complication of what territories, rivers, mountains, lakes, etc., lay in what is now Canada and in the present United States of America. I'm beginning to despair when a hand appears, the rough right hand of a young man, with the index finger jabbing at a point on the map in front of me, and I hear a voice say: "I'm buried here."

The figure bends his head and reads the name of the place he is pointing at: "Létellier! Ah! I know this Létellier as the Fourche des Roseaux. That's where they laid me to rest, as they say." The same finger circles the whole area around Létellier, stopping under the word Manitoba. "What is this Manitoba?" he asks impatiently.

"A province of Canada."

"You still call this country Canada?"

"Of course," I say with some irritation.

"Well, all isn't lost!" He withdraws his hand and sits on the edge of the desk. "Do you have a drink? Some . . ." But he interrupts himself and says: "My name is Christophe Dufrost de la Jemerais."

"You're the nephew." Without thinking, I add: "You had a short life."

"But a full one." He gets up and walks around my scriptorium (I always wanted to be a monk). He's in his late twenties, tall, compact, long legs, a pleasant face, blue eyes, small forehead, and he appears full of an endless energy that must have been contagious in his time. He wears short baggy pants that were green in an earlier era and that are padded with leather at the knees and on the seat, a reddish shirt with a sleeveless jacket that may have been leather, moccasins that nearly come up to his knees, and he has no hat.

"You had a famous sister. I think she's a saint of the Church—or on her way there."

"That must be Marguerite. She was so pious. What did she do to deserve sainthood?"

"She founded an order of nuns, known as the Grey Nuns. She began it unofficially around 1737, a year after your death. In 1755 she was issued letters-patent. She was a widow by then."

"Yes. I found that out when I came back to Montréal in 1734, I think. By that time, her widowhood had made her even more dedicated to religion and service to the poor than she was before her marriage. What happened to her two surviving children? They were boys, I think."

"They became priests as did your own two brothers, Charles and Joseph. As for your sisters . . ."

"They married well," he says, interrupting me. He turns away from the window. "I'm glad Marguerite did what she wanted to do. Good for her! Maybe I'll go and see her up there!" He laughs and starts walking around the room. Without stopping his hike, he says: "I'm a Canadien. That was a good thing to be in my day." He stares at me as if to find out if it still is. He seems satisfied and goes on: "I was the youngest in my family and, as such, entitled to a good education. But it was far from easy. My father died even before I was born. We may have had a noble name, but there wasn't much money to go with it. We struggled. We were fortunate though—we had influential relatives." He smiles and says under his breath: "I knew how to measure an elevation. So I was a good cartographer."

"You left us the first map of the West. Experts consider it to be the best available. I've a copy of it here somewhere."

"Find it," he orders.

"How did you get out of your native village, Varennes?"

"I had a good home, but there were many of us. A small fief. Life was hard. The army was the only way out. I was fifteen when I was sent to the West, before my uncle. It was exciting, but not pleasant."

"Why?"

He thinks about that for a moment, ordering his thoughts, as it were. "Have you found the map?" he asks.

"I haven't had time."

"Well, keep looking, as I tell you more for your book. You've read about the Peace of Utrecht? . . . Of course, you have. Well, the peace solved nothing for us. In fact, it made things worse. The Anglais, those people who lived by the Atlantic to the south of us: they wanted what we had in the West. Land and trade." He comes closer to my table. "Prior to Utrecht, we had it," he almost yells, spreading his hand all over the western part of my map. "And at Utrecht, the fools in Versailles made the West a no-man's land. Imagine that! Such a stupid policy almost destroyed our trade alliances with the Indians." He begins marching again. "I need a drink. What do you have?"

"A Scotch. Single malt!"

"What's that?"

"It's very good. Trust me." And Mascou appears with a tumbler full of my best single malt. Of course, they know each other! They talk away in a tongue I don't understand. After a few minutes of conversation, Mascou leaves the room and Christophe gulps down the Scotch. "Jesus! . . . Bonne Sainte-Vierge! . . . Saint-Joseph! Aidez-moi!" he yells. "What did you put in this? Fire?" he asks, croaking away. But not waiting for my answer, he adds: "Never mind. It does what it's supposed to do." He sits on the sofa and continues his tale. "We had so many Indian allies. Keeping them all loyal was a great problem. That's the history of my time: keeping the Natives friendly. We build our forts on the land of some tribe. By that simple act, the allies of that tribe become ours. Unfortunately, so do their enemies."

"Why unfortunately?" I ask, trying to gain time to find his map.

"We needed all the Indians we could get. . . . Take my uncle. When he arrived in the West, he built his forts on the lands of the Assiniboines and the Crees who were—and had been for a long time—at war with the Sioux whose lands were . . . Have you found my map?"

"Yes, here it is."

He joins me at my desk. Pointing to Lake Superior, he says: "Here is where we traded with the Ojibwas and their allies; the

Sioux occupied many villages . . . here in the upper Mississippi, while the Assiniboines lived by what you call now . . . Lake of the Woods and the . . . Red River. Their lands also extended far to the north, we were told. As for the Crees, they had a lot of land south of Hudson Bay and in your northern Manitoba. By the way the Foxes, with whom I had some dealings, were the middlemen at the Baie des Puants . . . I see it's your Green Bay. They controlled the passage of furs from north and west to the Mississippi trade route. Important people. But, nasty to us. They wanted to ally themselves to the English. We had a hell of a time with them. And they had enemies everywhere. All these nations were almost constantly at war with one another. Then, there were the English, who, from their colonies in the East and from Hudson Bay, breathed down our necks with cheaper goods, better prices, and a lot of lousy liquor. So we had to thread our way very carefully. And all that because of that damn treaty!" He finds a drop of Scotch in his glass, swallows it without choking, and adds: "That's why we built these forts and caused wars to be fought among our allies. Oh well. We simple colonials don't know much. We just know how to do the best out of the stupid interests of the mighty. Left to ourselves, I could tell you another story."

As he's about to go back to the sofa, I stop him to tell him what was good about his map and how useful it has been. "You see, you dated this map October 1, 1733, and we know that you had not yet descended the Red River to Lake Winnipeg. Yet, you tell us much about the lake, the river, and the system around them. Here is the Red River, the Assiniboine, and the Souris. There is Lake Manitoba. The Pembina escarpment is up there, and here in the south is the upper Missouri, which was known to you as the River of the Mandans and which became your uncle's River of the West. How did you figure all this out?"

"I had good informants. Mascou was one of them. You see the Indians travelled a lot. They told me and I wrote it down." He goes back to his seat. There he takes out his pipe and the foul air of his tobacco fills my room. I open the window. He smiles but continues puffing as he asks me: "You know what this map tells you?"

"I think it says that your uncle changed his mind about how to get to the western sea. He seems to have decided to prove the accuracy of Charlevoix's opinion."

"And what was that?"

"Charlevoix believed that the route to the sea didn't lie north and west as had been believed. Rather, it lay south and west, through the land and the river of the Mandans. We must talk about them. But before we do, I must tell you that one year or so after your death, your uncle changed his mind again. Or at least he returned to the earlier possibility, that . . ."

"The Lake Ouinipigon water system?" he asks, interrupting me.

"Yes. And he also came to the conclusion that the western sea was to be reached by means of the Saskatchewan River. Now . . ." I anticipate what he's going to ask. "Our Saskatchewan River," I inform him, "is your Rivière Blanche. Now, tell me about the Mandans."

"The Crees were supposed to know about them. They talked a lot about a race of Natives, the Mandans, who were more like us than the Sioux or any other tribe we had encountered. They were blond men; they spoke a language that wasn't unlike ours; and they lived in well-constructed villages that also resembled ours. We came to believe that the Mandans were the key to the route to la mer de l'ouest. I never visited them. I was supposed to but, instead, I was given the command of Fort Maurepas. In the winter of 1736, I became quite ill and, as my two cousins were bringing me back to my uncle, I . . . I never saw my uncle again."

The silence that follows is rather long. After a while, I break it. "Your uncle went to them in November 1740. He was disappointed." I find one of la Vérendrye's letters on my desk and I read to Christophe what his uncle wrote about the Mandans:

"'They are just like the Assiniboines; they are naked, a buffalo robe perhaps thrown carelessly about them, but they have not even a breech cloth.' But your Crees were right: the Mandans were paler than the Natives your uncle had encountered, and many of the women had pale hair. They also lived in well laid out villages."

"Did he find the sea?" he asked, almost yelling out the word "sea."

"No. It wasn't beyond the villages of the Mandans. So Charlevoix was wrong."

"And so was my uncle. Oh well! We lacked information that could be trusted." He lights his pipe again and asks me to tell him about his cousins.

I decide to start with the eldest. "Jean-Baptiste," I reply, "died about a month after you." He looks at me, eager to know what happened. "A group of Sioux massacred him and twenty other companions as they were on their way to get supplies. And all that because his father had, two years before, shown some favouritism to the Crees in their never-ending war against the Sioux. Jean-Baptiste was twenty-three years old."

Christophe hasn't moved. He keeps puffing and looking out the window at the snow falling in the park. Finally, he says: "I suppose they chopped their heads off and laid them on beaver robes. They did that, you know. Well, I guess he was given a decent Catholic burial. He deserved it. He and I were very close." He adds, "We had known each other all our lives. I was a year older. We worked together. We froze together, and only God knows how many portages we made in that wild and never peaceful country." He looks back at me and asks about Pierre, his uncle's second son.

"He was forty-one when he died in 1755 in Québec," I reply.

As I'm about to tell him more, he interrupts me and says: "I knew Pierre very well. He was a most cheerful man. Nothing seemed to harm him or trouble him."

85

"Like all of you, Pierre built and manned forts and went on many expeditions. During one of the many wars with the English, he found himself in Montréal and, instead of returning to his western post, he was ordered to fight in the war. He eventually went back and stayed until the death of his father and yet another war. He died in Québec in September 1755."

"Then there was François, the third son. He was always a little slow. What happened to him?"

"Well, he was barely sixteen when he went west, and he didn't return to Montréal for nineteen years. He did what you all did. He also died in Montréal in 1794. With his death, your uncle's family came to an end. You see, only Louis-Joseph married, but he had no children."

"Louis-Joseph, the fourth son. I hardly knew him. He was a good man?"

"Historians have judged him so. He was honest, fearless, and was gifted with much initiative. To him goes the honour of discovering that the Saskatchewan River has two branches. He journeyed up there with only one companion in April 1739."

"Did he find out anything about what you call the western sea?"

"The Crees told him that the river came from the land of the high mountains and that on the other side of those mountains was a large lake, the water of which was undrinkable. What they were saying, in essence, was that the western sea lay beyond tall mountains. We didn't find that out, though, until fifty years later."

"What happened to him?"

"He fought the English when they invaded Canada in 1759. Two years later, on his way to France, he was shipwrecked."

"He had a good life?"

"Yes, including that breathtaking adventure with François."

"What adventure?"

"In 1742 and the next year, they made one of the great marches in the annals of our history. But first, I must tell you that after the murder of his son, Jean-Baptiste, your uncle refused the offer of the Crees and Assiniboines to take revenge upon the Sioux."

"Revenge wasn't part of his nature," Christophe says. "He was a man of honour who accepted the fate God gave him. Tell me more."

"In 1737, burdened by debts and with his supply line endangered, he went to Montréal to straighten things out. He had a hard time, but his perseverance won out. A year later, he was the first white man to reach where the city of Winnipeg stands today, and the first to walk into the Canadian prairies. And he also began the construction of a fort, Fort la Reine, on the present site of the city of Portage la Prairie." I bring him my map and point out where his uncle went. I sit beside him and continue the tale. "In that year, 1738, he went to the country of the Mandans on the upper Missouri. They were the same as other Indians; however, their villages were well laid out. But there was no western sea in the vicinity of where the Mandans lived. He was ill by then and returned to Fort la Reine. Upon his recovery, he went back to Montréal another time to straighten out his affairs. Again, after many difficulties, he returned west, and in May 1742, he sent Louis-Joseph and François back to the lands of the Mandans. This is when they went south to find the famous sea. But of course it wasn't there. They and two others walked and walked for days, weeks, and months. We don't know how many kilometres they covered, but we are pretty certain that they sighted the Rocky Mountains. And, to everyone's astonishment, when they returned to Fort la Reine in July 1743, they were riding horses."

"Horses? Damn, I should have lived longer." He thinks for a while and then says: "We had a good family. We did what we wanted to do. And, as you say, we did it honourably."

I don't reply. Instead I think of the slave trade La Vérendrye had set up. It bothers me. In my eyes, it tarnishes the great explorer's reputation. Finally, I say: "Your uncle sold slaves. Was that honourable?"

"In my time, yes. It wasn't immoral, and the Church didn't forbid it. It was the way things were done." Staring at his feet, he asked: "Do you have slaves?"

"No, we stopped doing that a long time ago. However, by the last quarter of the 18th century, there were 3,604 slaves in Canada. Most of them were Indians, but 1,132 were black. It's not to our honour."

Suddenly he gets up and says, "To ease your mind—if you care at all about my reputation—I didn't have any slaves either." He examines Sir Wilfrid Laurier's portrait above the armoire. He doesn't ask who he is and what it's doing there. Instead, he says: "I'd better go. Before I do, though, what happened to my uncle?"

"In 1743, your uncle resigned his position, being besieged by creditors and detractors. He lived in relative obscurity until 1746, when he was reappointed to his western posts. But he wasn't able to fulfil his mission of trying to find the western sea by way of the Saskatchewan River, for he died in 1749. He was sixty-four. A man with large dreams . . ."

"It went with the territory. But I must say goodbye."

"He was a great man," I say before he reaches the door. He nods in agreement, and as he is opening the door, I ask, "Of the five of you who journeyed with your uncle and were of his family, only Louis-Joseph married. Why didn't you?"

"There was no time . . . at least for marriage. But for what goes with it . . ." He laughs merrily and adds before walking out, "That's for your next book."

I hear him say goodbye to Mascou, and I return to the curse of wars.

⚜

As we've seen, the peace after 1714 was precarious at best. However, it hadn't weakened the general prosperity of New France; nor did it implicate whole armies and bring massive destruction. The sacking of Cartagena (now in Colombia) and the War of Jenkins's Ear (1739–41) came and went without unduly disturbing the tranquility at Québec. However, the War of the Austrian Succession (King George's War), 1740–48, did. The hostilities, here, began in Acadia with the capture of the fishing station at Canso, Nova Scotia, by the French forces at Louisbourg on Île Royale (Cape Breton) in May 1744. This led to British retaliation, with Louisbourg being forced to capitulate to an army of four thousand New Englanders in June 1745, after a forty-eight-day siege. While they were at it, the English-Americans took possession of Île Saint-Jean (Prince Edward Island) a month later. However, a planned excursion against Québec didn't materialise. The Americans and the British had no appetite for it. The main war activities, then, were the Canadian raids against the British and American settlers and settlements. The Treaty of Aix-la-Chapelle in 1748 changed nothing, except that the fortress at Louisbourg was restored to the French, along with all hostages and prisoners. But there was no settlement of the boundary questions on the frontiers of Acadia or on the Ohio. This led to the usual: rivalries and raids, the construction of forts, and the expansion of military and trade alliances with the Natives.

During this time, as well, the British expelled the Acadians from their lands in 1755. Originally there were two branches of Canadiens: those living in Québec and those living in Acadia. Four years before he built his habitation in Québec, Champlain, in 1604, had founded Acadia, a piece of heaven known as Port-Royal (now Annapolis Royal) on the south side of the Bay of Fundy, in Nova Scotia. The French behaved towards the Acadians in the same way they did to their Québec counterparts: they neglected Acadia, they did little to defend it, they allowed the Jesuits and other priests to quarrel with everybody in sight, and they passed it along to the English whenever it suited them. And, after the War of the Spanish Succession, Acadia belonged to England and was never to be a French possession again.

In spite of all this, the Acadians survived. By the middle of the 18th century, they numbered thirteen thousand. In their isolation from France and also from the Canadiens, they constructed a different identity and *sense d'apartenance* from the French and from the Canadiens. In the whirl-wind of the violence that surrounded them for over a century, they kept to themselves and maintained a strict neutrality, hoping to be allowed to live their lives, farm their farms, and watch their children grow. It was not to be.

In 1755, the British-Americans, aided by the English, scattered the Acadians to the four corners of the earth in an act of brutality and racism as evil as any we have experienced in the 20th century. The fact that some of the names of the men who perpetrated this crime are celebrated in statues and in names of towns in Nova Scotia, New Brunswick, and Prince Edward Island compounds the evil. Between 1755 and 1763, over ten thousand Acadians had their families broken up, husbands taken from their wives and young children, from their brothers and their sisters, from their friends and their loved ones.

However, in spite of that ethnic cleansing, Acadia survived. Some Acadians hid in the woods, others seized the ships they were on and escaped, and, eventually, thousands found their way home. By 1800, they had grown to eight thousand; 140,000 by 1900; and by the last census, 1991, they numbered over half a million—a glorious, courageous, and determined people. Canada owes them much. They enrich our culture and add to our identity. More than the Canadiens of Québec, they may emerge intact in a break-up of Canada, should that tragedy ever happen.

Between 1749 and 1756, just before the Seven Years War, the Franco-Canadiens' main success was in restraining the advance of the British-Americans in the Ohio valley. But the awakening of the Virginians, who became for the first time the direct foes of the French and Canadien interests in that territory, meant the entry of a population four times larger than that of the whole of New France. The contest had become unequal.

Then came the Seven Years War in 1756. At first, the French and Canadien forces were successful in defeating the British: at Fort Ontario (at Oswego, on Lake Ontario) in 1756, only to fall to British in 1758; at Fort William Henry on Lake George (1757); and at Fort Carillon at Crown Point, Lake Champlain (1758), which became Fort Ticonderoga when the British reconquered it in 1759. A proposed British attack on the fortress of Louisbourg on Cape Breton Island couldn't materialise in 1757 since the

French fleet in the North Atlantic was the most powerful in the world. In July 1758, however, the mighty fortress fell after a long siege and a display of rare courage on both sides.

The success of the British after 1757 was due to William Pitt the Elder, who became head of government in that year. He reformed England's army, limited her commitments in continental Europe, and built the mightiest navy in the world. He also made the conquest of Canada the centrepiece of his military and political policy.

At the time of Pitt's coming to power, France was the supreme military power in Europe. In America, she had established her preeminence in the West and was developing a plan for the security of Québec and her colonies in New France. In the spring of 1756, a new commander-in-chief of the French forces in America arrived in the person of Louis-Joseph de Montcalm, along with two regiments of troops to be added to the three that were already in place.

In North America, the progress of the Seven Years War may be divided into three periods: first, the French successes of 1756–58 (the only Franco-Canadien defeat of this period being the British victory at Louisbourg); second, the fall of Québec and Montréal in 1759–60; and third, the Military Regime, which lasted from 1760 to 1763. It was in the second period (1759–60) that Pitt's strategy prevailed. For the conquest of the French empire in America, he committed one-quarter of the Royal Navy and three fully equipped and well-supplied armies. The army, commanded by Major-General Wolfe, was to conquer the town of Québec (by way of the St. Lawrence) and from there it was to proceed to Montréal. Another army was to march to Fort Niagara and thence to Montréal. The third army, led by Jeffrey Amherst, was to proceed to Montréal by way of Lake Champlain. And so, on June 26, 1759, the English arrived at the door of Québec.

Geography and war made Canadiens and Canadiennes out of French men and women. But the greatest influence was Canada. Canada gave them—us—birth.

It wasn't only the vast land—the St. Lawrence and its tributaries, the Great Lakes, the First Peoples, and the presence of Anglo-Americans to the south. It was more than that. Far away from France, isolated a good part of the year, subject to low levels of immigration, unsure of assistance from the mother country, and lacking confidence in the paternalistic autocracy that ruled them, they forged a liberty to adapt, experiment, and become.

Fewer than eight thousand immigrants came from France to the land of Québec—by 1713, for instance, that population had scarcely increased. This, after a hundred years of potential immigration, was very low indeed. And it meant, according to several governors general of the time, that the small size of Canada's population endangered every undertaking for the colony's development. Various schemes—turning Canada into a penal colony, importing slaves to do the dirty work, using *engagés* (settlers who would have to repay the cost of their transport), and sending the unproductive sons of aristocratic families—were advanced and even tried in some cases. But the results were poor indeed. Between 1713 and 1758, Canada received only 3,880 new inhabitants: 1,500 engagés, 80 so-called black sheep, 700 salt smugglers, and 1,600 soldiers, who decided to stay after their tour of duty. If we count the wives and children with the men, a couple of hundred English and Irish families, and those few that weren't registered, the total might reach five thousand over a period of thirty-three years—France had a population of twenty million. Obviously, the colonies didn't interest the French.

What saved the colony—at least for a while—was the high fertility rate. "Astonishing!" "Miraculous!" and several other adjectives were used to describe the phenomenon of the population doubling every twenty years after 1713. A total of 76,172 settlers (the figure of the English general, Jeffrey Amherst) were transferred to the authority of the British king between 1760 and 1763.

There were also those who were called "domiciled" Natives, who lived in villages under the protection of the clergy. Perhaps three thousand can be added from this source. They retained their languages and customs, and attempts to francise them failed miserably. Intermarriages between coureurs de bois and Native women happened from time to time, even though they were considered "dishonourable"; the children remained "little savages" as it was said. However, the records don't show any figures. There were, as well, about three thousand slaves at the time of the "Conquest."

The non-Indian population lived mostly in rural areas along the St. Lawrence. However, eight thousand lived in the town of Québec, four thousand in Montréal, and six hundred in Trois-Rivières. The population comprised three orders, or estates: the clergy, the nobility, and the common people.

The Church: There were two kinds of clergy—the secular, those who were diocesan priests; and the regulars, those who followed a *regula* (rule). In all, there were 163 priests at the time of the Conquest. The 84 who belonged to the secular clergy lived mostly in the 124 parishes that existed in New France. The 79 regular priests comprised 30 Sulpicians (the order of priests who were the proprietors of most of the Island of Montréal and who had come from France in 1657), 25 Jesuits (who arrived in 1625), and 24 Récollets (who were the first clergy to come to Québec, in 1615). Most of the regular clergy were born in France, but over half of the secular clergy came from good Canadien, habitant stock. The bishop was French. An attempt was made in 1737 to have a Canadien nominated, but the king refused his consent because these Canadiens were said to possess a proud and hasty temper and to have the tendency to independence and insubordination.

In addition, there were lay brothers, mostly attached to the regular clergy, who performed various tasks. A rich merchant in Québec gave a small fortune to a group of men to establish a hospital in Québec for the poor, the orphans, the cripples, and other unfortunate people. These men were known as the Hospitaliers de Saint-Joseph-de-la-Croix, and, even though their numbers were relatively small, they were known for their devotion and energy.

By the time the English took over Canada, there were 204 nuns in our country. The Ursulines who taught in Québec were the most famous because of Marie de l'Incarnation—"the Saint Teresa of Canada," as theologian Jacques-Bénigne Bossuet called her. Her cloistered nuns also founded a convent in Trois-Rivières in the late 1690s. In the town of Québec, the Ursulines occupied a large and beautiful convent with extensive gardens.

In addition, the Augustines' Hospitalières de l'Hôtel-Dieu, who had come from Dieppe at the same time as Marie de l'Incarnation in 1639, had a hospital in the lower town, the Hôtel-Dieu. At the end of the 17th century and due to the influence of the bishop of the time, some hospitalières broke away from their original community to found a new congregation known as the Hospitalières de l'Hôpital Général de Québec. Their hospital was outside the walls of Québec and at the other end of the Plains of Abraham.

In Montréal, Jeanne Mance (1606–73), who came with de Maisonneuve, founded a hospital, the Hôtel-Dieu of Montréal, in the fall of 1642. In 1659, the Réligieuses hospitalières de Saint-Joseph took over her work. In 1694, the painter Pierre Le Ber (1661–1707), the son of a wealthy family, established a lay congregation of men, the Frères Hospitaliers, to serve the sick and the poor in a hospice known as the Hôpital Général de Montréal. However, by 1737 the arrangement was dissolved, and ten years later Marie-Marguerite d'Youville (Marie-Marguerite Dufrost de Lajemmerais [1701–71] and a group of women took over the Hôpital Général. In 1722, she had married François-Madeleine d'Youville and they had six children, four of whom died in infancy. Her husband died in 1730, and her two surviving sons became secular priests.) Five years before the capitulation of Montréal (1760), her order of nuns, commonly known as the Grey Nuns, received letters patent from the French court. In addition, Marguerite Bourgeoys (1620–1700), who arrived there in 1653, founded the Congrégation de Notre-Dame de Montréal in 1658 and dedicated herself and her community to the teaching of girls. She is now a saint of the Roman Catholic Church.

The nuns didn't have an easy time of it. They worked hard, had difficulties making ends meet, and were forever fighting with the various bishops to curtail episcopal interference in their affairs. They were also more subject to the civil authorities than were the orders of priests. With the exception of the Ursulines, the kings of France didn't relish their citizens relinquishing their personal liberty by making binding solemn vows. Their royal majesties were also concerned with the multiplication of convents, which seemed to them to be the civil instruments of theocratic power. Louis XIV and XV were not about to allow the usurpation of their rights as the guardians of religion. They contributed money for the upkeep of the religious, but were determined to control their power, their numbers, and their wealth.

The people were attached to the Church: it was their main institution, ever-present but not domineering. (The phenomenon that led to my people being called "priest-ridden" is a post-Conquest one. Real clerical control of

Québec, aided by the support of the so-called bourgeoisie, began only after 1840.) The Canadiens tended to accept the dictates of the clergy in religious and spiritual matters, but not in civil spheres. They rebelled against high tithes, and found the clergy to be an economic burden; they argued with their parish priest over such matters as the control of parish finances; they disobeyed the bishop; they sided with the governor in many matters dealing with episcopal privilege and clerical power; and they had definite ideas as to where the spiritual ended and the temporal began. Canadiens also used magic potions and other practices, which the priests declared to be superstitious and, therefore, forbidden. In church, they were often boisterous and, on solemn occasions and holy days, they "played" too much. And they sinned privately and publicly.

Because of the absence of priests in the rural areas to witness marriages or to make legitimate what wasn't, there developed a marriage ceremony that was particular and, to many, irregular. The most famous instance of that kind of marriage didn't take place in rural New France, however. It was performed in Montréal when Marie-Isabelle-Élisabeth Bégon de la Cour married. She was the eldest of the family of the king's shopkeeper in Montréal, a post that was not considered of high prestige. When she was between sixteen and eighteen, she fell in love with a French officer quartered in her father's house, the sub-lieutenant Claude-Michel Bégon de la Cour, who was the intendant's brother. They wanted to marry, but the authorities wouldn't give them permission; she was of lower rank than her husband-to-be. It was felt he could do better. But love prevailed. Using a practice known as *"mariage à la gaumine"* and condemned by the Church, they married, probably in November 1718. During a Sunday Mass, they found themselves in the same pew. At the moment of the elevation of the Host for the veneration of the people, they joined hands and pronounced their vows "loudly" in the presence of two witnesses in consort with the two love birds. Later, they would argue with the authorities that they did marry in the presence of a priest and two witnesses as the law demanded. After a period of frustration, the authorities agreed to regularise their marriage, which lasted thirty years. It is interesting to note that, after the death of her husband, Mme Bégon had a platonic-love relationship with her son-in-law. She left us a series of fine and useful letters, known as *Lettres au cher fils*.

The clergy and the nuns provided basic social services: hospitals and homes for the sick and the aged, schools for the education of boys, and convents for educating girls—not only in the three towns, but often in rural areas. The Jesuits founded the Collège de Québec in 1635; Bishop Laval established the Grand Séminaire de Québec to train priests, in 1663, and a Petit Séminaire for the general education of boys five years later. There was a trade school that also served as one for artists at Saint-Joachim, near Cap Tourmente, and Latin was taught practically everywhere. The Royal School of Hydrography trained sailors in mathematics and navigation, and lawyers gave lectures to those desiring to enter this blessed profession.

What we call social welfare, however, was dispensed by the intendant. That public assistance came out of the royal treasury and was deemed to be generous. No one in misfortune appeared to have been excluded: illegitimate or abandoned children, or victims of accidents, poverty, or famine.

Of the Roman Catholic bishops of the French regime, the first to arrive was Monseigneur François de Laval (1623–1708) who came here as vicar general in June 1659. He was a man with a forceful personality, stubborn will, and of an uncompromising attitude on all issues. His single goal was to maintain the primacy of the Catholic religion and the power and prestige of the Catholic Church in the territory of New France. He didn't consider himself or the Church subject to the will of kings. At the same time, he was wise enough to placate Louis XIV, who supported him financially and politically. However, many didn't welcome the theocracy that Laval, aided by the Jesuits, favoured.

In 1674 Laval was made bishop of Québec. He created new parishes, trained a secular clergy, and interfered in everybody's business. Eleven years after his nomination, he resigned because of ill health. However, he resumed his duties when his successor was detained in France at the beginning of the 18th century. He died in Québec on May 6, 1708. Laval was a holy man, difficult as he might have been to get along with. He made the Catholic Church the national church of the Canadiens, and he created it as an Ultramontane Church, tied closely to the authority of Rome and determined to control the State. His 16th-century presence had much to do with the clerical-lay troubles of the 19th century and parts of the 20th.

Laval's successor, Jean-Baptiste de la Croix Saint-Valier, was a man of the same cloth, but without the political acumen of the first bishop. He was more stubborn than Laval, if that was possible, tactless, and spent money without a thought for tomorrow. This led him into a series of conflicts with governors, intendants, the laity, and officials at the court. However, he was kind to the poor, notably by founding the Hôpital Général.

Three bishops followed Saint-Vallier: Bishop Mornay, who never set foot in Canada; Bishop Dosquet, who was here only two years; and Bishop Lauberivière, who died upon disembarking at Québec. The sixth bishop of Québec was Henri-Marie Dubreil de Pontbriand (1708–60). He served for about twenty years and died in Montréal. Energetic, he had to deal with matters that had been left in abeyance during the fourteen years of episcopal absenteeism. During his years in office, he did well, rebuilding the institutions that Laval had put in place and establishing new ones. He was kind and generous; he was, however, very weak. He hadn't the mettle of a Laval, nor, for that matter, of a Saint-Vallier, when it came time to confront the authorities at home and abroad. He never condemned the civil abuses that marked the last years of the French regime, which inflicted much harm upon the population. After the Battle of the Plains of Abraham, he maintained a conciliatory attitude towards the British and ordered his priests to do the same. He may well have saved the Church at a critical time.

The nobility: This was the second order of New France's social construct. Two hundred heads of families, said to be of the nobility, stood between the clergy and the members of the third estate. They were granted seigneuries, but unlike their counterparts in France, they were allowed to engage in trade. The only particular "right" they had was to wear a sword.

The third estate was everybody else. Its leaders were the officers of justice and the merchants. In fact, the "syndic" of the merchants spoke as the representative of the people and was accepted as such. In the rural areas and on the seigneuries, the captain of the militia, elected in most cases, was the link between the central administrative structure of New France and the habitants. In the fulfilment of his military duties (making sure the male habitants had guns and had manufactured their own ammunition, that they were ready and available to go to fight at any moment), he fell under the authority of the governor general. But the intendant supervised the captain's administrative duties, such as the building of roads, fortifications, and bridges, and the provision of other public services. The captain also saw to it that the ordinances and edicts were obeyed. Should the people in his jurisdiction object to any order emanating from the centre of power, only that rural officer was empowered to present the feelings and the opinions of his electors to either the governor general or the intendant.

The system of land distribution in New France, known as the seigneurial system, was established in 1627. (It was abolished in 1854.) Even though it came from the feudal system of France, it worked differently here. The people living on seigneuries weren't tenants but habitants who owed the seigneur some well-defined and much-supervised compensation and obligations in return for the land they obtained. Two hundred such seigneuries were granted during the French regime—to the nobility, religious institutions, military officers, and civil administrators.

There were, of course, no political rights as we understand them today. New France's government was autocratic and paternalistic. The king of France, his court, and his administration assumed a large responsibility for the spiritual and temporal development of Canada, much more so, in fact, than did the British Crown. Furthermore, the king of France was an absolute monarch, which was not so of the British king. And, Canada, as a colony, was subordinate to the power residing at Versailles. Therefore, it's not surprising that Louis XIV and XV exercised their royal authority over the minutest details of the civil and military administration of New France. Since most of the people lived mostly in what is now Québec, that authority extended to every aspect of the people's lives. The role of a centralised and paternalistic State is firmly embedded in the consciousness of those who are today called Québécois.

But New France wasn't France. This was a new land, far away from the centre of power, and Canadiens discovered—and exercised—a freedom of action not possible in France. They refused to be overtaken by absolutist power, regardless of whether it came from the State or from the Church.

Added to this was the fact that many of those sent here to administer my people were essentially mediocre. So, there was much adaptation and innovation. Lastly, the ministers at the court protected, in some ways, the people in Canada. Often Canadiens criticised their officials for being unjust in their autocratic exercise of power. For instance, acting upon a comment by Vaudreuil that Montcalm "mène durement les Canadiens" (was too harsh on the militia), the minister of marine affairs ordered him to change his ways and those of his officers and soldiers, who often brutalised and pillaged the population. Had there been a French victory on the Plains of Abraham and no capitulation of Montréal, I have little doubt that the next generation or so would have thrown off the French yoke and discarded the incompetent military establishment. The young aide-de-camp to Montcalm, Louis-Antoine de Bougainville (1729–1811), sensed this when he wrote: "Il semble que nous soyons d'une nation différente, ennemie même." (It seems we are different nations, enemies even).

From the beginnings of the colony, the administration was quite simple, and it remained so for the duration of the French regime. The king held all the power and authority that precedent and tradition dictated, and he exercised that might through ministers and officials. From 1627 to 1674, the immediate administration of the colony, its colonisation, and the evangelisation of the Indians was entrusted to companies, such as the Compagnie des Cents-Associés, in return for a monopoly in trade. After that, royal government was firmly established.

The governor general was the supreme authority in New France. As representative of the king, he had a large power source, prestige, and a preeminent status. All matters of civil government were his domain, but he had to share much of it with the intendant. In addition he was also commander-in-chief of the armed forces; however, at the beginning of the colony and during the Seven Years War, that power was shared with a general, like Montcalm, named for the purpose of conducting military affairs. This state of affairs led to constant recriminations, jealousies, and conflicts of authority.

This is well illustrated by the example of Vaudreuil and Montcalm. Vaudreuil was a Canadien of recent lineage; Montcalm was a Frenchman, belonging to an old and noble ancestry. They disliked each other from the moment they met. Vaudreuil found Montcalm vain, tactless, opinionated, and a potential usurper of his military power; Montcalm found Vaudreuil irresolute, mean, and a civilian playing at war. They both, however, lived in mortal fear of being repudiated by the court.

The command structure was also not conducive to a close relationship. Vaudreuil was commander-in-chief of all forces in New France, the direct commander of the colonial troops (known as the troupes franches de la marine), of the Canadian militia, and of the Indians fighting on the side of the French. He was the strategist, the planner, and he was to be obeyed. Montcalm was the commander of the French regular troops (the troupes de terre) and of the overall forces in the field. However, in the spring of 1759, secret directives made Montcalm de facto commander-in-chief of all forces and responsible for the conduct of the war. Vaudreuil was ordered, at that time, not to interfere in Montcalm's conduct of the war.

Both men argued continuously about the way to fight the English. Both were terrified of making the wrong decision and, therefore, considerable delays resulted. Both tripped over each other in their demonstration of loyalty to the king and in courting ministers and officials in France, while reproaching each other for every possible slight and humiliation. This rivalry, exacerbated by the confused directives emanating from France and, above all, by quarrels over status, weakened the war effort considerably. That they were from opposite sides of the ocean had much to do with it as well.

But there was more. Montcalm didn't think Canada could be saved. "The colony is lost unless peace comes," he wrote to his second-in-command, in February 1759, and he added: "I can see nothing that can save it." Because of that opinion, which he had formed after his famous victory over the English at Carillon in 1758, he made a plan that Bougainville, his aide-de-camp, took to France in November of that year: the army should take refuge in Louisiana, by way of the Ottawa River, the Great Lakes, and the Mississippi. In Louisiana, the army would regroup and invade the Carolinas. Consequently, the French government shouldn't do too much for the defence of Canada.

The king, however, rejected Montcalm's plan. He was to stand or fall in Canada.

But the country mattered to Vaudreuil. It was his. And the habitants were his people, his children. He was therefore a torn man. He had a duty to his king and a duty to his people. (After the Seven Years War, he was imprisoned for a while in the Bastille but was later rehabilitated.) He had no easy time of it.

After the governor, the next most powerful person was the intendant, who was the administrative head and the chief dispenser of justice. Here again, conflicts, jealousies, and silly battles over precedence between him and the governor occupied much of his time. Yet, the authority of the intendant was substantial, and since it dealt with the day-to-day activities of the people's lives, he tended to be as powerful—if not more so—than the governor. Montcalm recognised this when he wrote that the authority resided in "two, you might almost say one" person, and he meant the intendant. As an example of that person's power, it was Intendant François Bigot who drafted the articles of the capitulation of Montréal in 1760, not the governor general.

The most famous of the intendants were Jean Talon (at the beginning of royal government) and François Bigot (at the end of it). The former is remembered for his administrative skills, the latter for being a most intelligent crook. As the controller of finance, of trade, and of services, Bigot was able to determine the prices at which he bought supplies and the prices at which he sold them to the state. Using his authority and with the help of his cronies, among whom were the butcher Joseph Cadet and Michel-Jean-Hugues Péan, the husband of his mistress, Bigot erected a system known as the "Grande Société." The purpose of this was to enrich them, all the while defrauding the royal treasury, thus adding immensely to the cost of doing business and to the price of goods, not to mention scarcity of all sorts, particularly in food. The activities of "the rogues" cost the treasury in France a large amount, so large that the minister responsible threatened to "abandon" the colony. Public opinion was also seriously influenced: more than a few wondered if New France was worth the cost.

Bigot's mistress was Angélique-Geneviève Renaud d'Avène des Méloizes, known as Lélie (1722–92). Recognised as "La Pompadour," she was "remarkable for her beauty, her charms, and her wit," according to the recordkeeper of the Ursuline convent where Angélique went to school. In 1746, she married Michel-Jean-Hugues Péan, who became one of Bigot's cronies shortly after the intendant's arrival in 1748. That relationship made Péan one of the richest men in the colony—and his wife had much to do with his success. Gossip said that all his talents "lay in his wife's charms." The Péans entertained lavishly at their château in the upper town. "All the elegant people" met at their house, where life was "carried on after the fashion of Paris." She was young, witty, charming, alluring, a superb gambler, and prepared to do much to ensure her position, that of her husband, and that of her family. When she met Bigot, she was twenty-five; he was forty-five and quite ugly. But love conquered all and she soon became his "Pompadour," as people remarked. Péan accepted his wife's indiscretion as it made him richer. When they went to France after the fall of Montréal, her husband was arrested and imprisoned. She was, though, allowed to visit him, which she did fifty-eight times between March and June 1764. After he was released, they went to live on their property near Blois in Touraine. She spent the last twenty years of her life a widow and devoted herself to helping the Canadien families who had settled not too far from her residence.

Bigot was also arrested after his return to France in 1760. He was tried, convicted of fraud, and banished. But in 1771, he was allowed to visit the Péans (La belle Lélie was, by then, in her late forties) at Blois. No documents tell us what happened.

"Mon pays ce n'est pas un pays, c'est l'hiver" sings Gilles Vigneault. Voltaire, on the other hand, sang another song, even though he never visited Canada: "Le plus détestable pays du Nord! Pays couvert de neiges et de glaces huit mois de l'année, habité par des barbares, des ours et des castors" (Canada the most detestable country, covered with snow and ice eight months of the year, inhabited by barbarians, bears, and beavers). Winters were tough. Periods of intense cold and frightful snow storms isolated neighbours for long stretches of time and caused much suffering and death. On the other hand, winter played a key role in the transformation of French men and women into Canadiens and Canadiennes. It taught us to adapt and to find ways of doing things and surviving. We learned how to dress warmly, to discover the foods that would keep us comfortable, to build our houses able to withstand the cold, to find games and songs and dances that filled the leisure time available, and to come closer together as one people. Winter may have been harsh, but it was also a good and friendly companion.

With due respect to Francis Parkman and Mason Wade, the arts weren't absent from New France. Artists were everywhere, as were the people who built and embellished churches, created sacred ornaments and statues, and constructed homes and châteaux, institutional houses, convents, seminaries, and hospitals. The settlers adapted the songs, the dances, and the music of the old country to their new temperament. They had plays and concerts. The bishop was upset and banned the work of Corneille and Racine, and Molière's dancing—and the "immodesty" that went with such an art form. However, the people did as they wished, realising that their bishop was holy but, at the same time, a little silly. And they told stories. Stories that embodied their sense of humour, their concerns, their joys, and their pains—stories that continue to be told.

Pehr (Petter) Kalm (1716–79), from Sweden and Finland, was a natural historian, botanist, environmentalist and keeper of notes. In 1747 he was sent to North America to study plants and determine if any could be imported to Scandinavia. After a couple of years in the American colonies, he came to New France. Then after a return visit to British colonial America, he sailed for Europe in February 1751. Later, he published the diary of his travels. Here, in part, is what he had to say about us.

July 24, 1749

This morning I went from *Prairie* in a bateau to *Montreal*, upon the river St. Lawrence . . .

The difference between the manners and customs of the *French* in *Montreal* and *Canada,* and those of the *English* in the American colonies, is as great as that between the manners of those two nations in *Europe*. The women in general are handsome here; they are well bred, and virtuous, with an innocent and becoming freedom. They dress out very fine on Sundays; and though on the other days they do not take much pains with other parts of their dress, yet they are very fond of adorning their heads, the hair of which is always curled and powdered, and ornamented with glittering bodkins and aigrettes. Every day but Sunday, they wear a little neat jacket, and a short petticoat which hardly reaches half the leg, and in this particular they seem to imitate the *Indian* women. The heels of their shoes are high, and very narrow, and it is surprising how they walk on them. In their knowledge of economy, they greatly surpass the *English* women in the plantations, who indeed have taken the liberty of throwing all the burthen of house-keeping upon their husbands, and sit in their chairs all day with folded arms. The women in *Canada* on the contrary do not spare themselves, especially among the common people, where they are always in the fields, meadows, stables, & c. and do not dislike any work whatsoever. However, they seem rather remiss in regard to the cleaning of the utensils, and apartments; for sometimes the floors, both in the town and country, were hardly cleaned once in six months, which is a disagreeable sight to one who comes from amongst the *Dutch* and *English*, where the constant scouring and scrubbing of the floors, is reckoned as important as the exercise of religion itself . . .

The men are extremely civil, and take their hats off to every person indifferently of whom they meet in the streets. It is customary to return a visit the day after you have received one . . .

Mechanics, such as architecture, cabinetwork, turning, and the like, were not yet so forward here as they ought to be; and the *English*, in that particular, out-do the *French*. The chief cause of this is, that scarce any other people than dismissed soldiers come to settle here, who have not had any opportunity of learning a mechanical trade, but have sometimes accidentally, and through necessity, been obliged to it . . .

The Making of les Canadiens (1713-1763)

July 27, 1749

The common houseflies have but been observed in this country about one hundred and fifty years ago, as I have been assured by several persons in this town, and in Québec. All the *Indians* assert the same thing, and are of opinion that the common flies first came over here with the *Europeans* and their ships, which were stranded on this coast . . .

The peace, which was concluded between *France* and *England* was proclaimed this day. The soldiers were under arms; the artillery on the walls was fired off, and some salutes were given by the small fire arms. All night some fire-works were exhibited, and the whole town was illuminated. All the streets were crowded with people till late at night. The governor invited me to supper, and to partake of the joy of the inhabitants. Present were a number of officers, and persons of distinction; and the festival concluded with the greatest joy . . .

July 28, 1749

The scarcity of labouring peoples occasions the wages to be high; for almost every body finds it so easy to set up as a farmer in this uncultivated country, where he can live well, and at a small expense, that he does not care to serve and work for others.

Montreal is the second town in Canada, in regard to size and wealth; but it is the first on account of its fine situation, and mild climate. . . . The town has a quadrangular form, or rather it is a rectangular parallelogram, the long and eastern side of which extends along the great branch of the river. On the other side it is surrounded with excellent corn-fields, charming meadows, and delightful woods. It has got the name of *Montreal* from a great mountain, about half a mile [.8 kilometres] westwards of the town, and lifting its head far above the woods . . . The priests who, according to the Roman Catholic way, would call every place in this country after some saint or other, calling *Montreal, Ville Marie,* but they have not been able to make this name general, for it has always kept its first name. It is pretty, well fortified, and surrounded with a high and thick wall . . . However, it cannot long stand a regular siege, because it requires a great garrison, on account of its extent; and because it consists chiefly of wooden houses. Here are several churches . . . Some of the houses in the town are built of stone, but most of them are of timber, though very neatly built . . . The long streets are broad and strait, and divided at right angles by the short ones: some are paved, but most of them very uneven . . .

Every Friday is market-day, when the country people come to the town with provisions . . .

August 3, 1749

Trois-Rivières is a little market town, which had the appearance of a large village; it is however reckoned among the three great towns of *Canada,* which are *Québec, Montreal* and *Trois-Rivières.* It is said to lie in the middle between the first, and thirty French miles distant from each. The town is built on the north side of the river *St. Lawrence,* on a flat, elevated sand, and its situation is very pleasant . . . In the town are the two churches of stone, a nunnery, and a house for the friars of the order of *St. Francis.* This town is likewise the seat of the third governor in Canada, whose house is likewise of stone. Most of the other houses are of timber, a single story high, tolerably well built, and stand very much asunder; and the streets are crooked . . . Its present inhabitants live chiefly by agriculture, though the neighbouring iron-works may serve in some measure to support them. About an *English* mile below the town, a great river falls into the river *St. Lawrence,* but first divides into three branches, so that it appears as if three rivers disembogued themselves there. This has given occasion to call the river and this town, *Trois-Rivières (the Three Rivers)* . . .

August 4, 1749

At the dawn of day we left this place and went on towards *Québec*. We found the land on the north side of the river some-what elevated, sandy and closely inhabited along the water side. The south-east shore, we were told, is equally well inhabited; but the woods along that shore prevented our seeing the houses, which are built further up in the country, the land close to the river being so low as to be subject to annual inundations . . .

August 5, 1749

The shores of the river grow more sloping as you come nearer to *Québec*. To the northward appears a high ridge of mountains. About two *French* miles and a half from *Québec* the river becomes very narrow, the shores being within the reach of a musket-shot from each other. The country on both sides was sloping, hilly, cov-ered with trees, and had many small rocks; the shore was stony. About four o'clock in the afternoon we happily arrived at *Québec*. The city does not appear till one is close to it . . . As soon as the sol-diers, who were with us, saw *Québec*, they called out, that all those who had never been there before should be ducked, if they did not pay something to release themselves. This custom even the gover-nor general of *Canada* is obliged to submit to, on his first journey to *Montreal*. We did not care when we came in sight of this town to be exempted from this old custom, which is very advantageous to the rowers, as it enables them to spend a merry evening on their arrival at *Québec*, after their troublesome labour.

August 6, 1749

Québec, the chief city in *Canada*, lies on the western shore of the river *St. Lawrence*, close to the water's edge, on a neck of land, bounded by that river on the east side, and by the river *St. Charles* on the north side; the mountain, on which the town is built, rises still higher on the south side, and behind it begin great pastures; and the same mountain likewise extends a good way westward. The city is distinguished into the lower and the upper . . . The upper city lies above the other, on a high hill, and takes up five or six times the space of the lower, though it is not quite so populous. The mountain, on which the upper city is situated, reaches above the houses of the lower city. Notwithstanding the latter are three or four stories high, and the view, from the palace, of the lower city (part of which is immediately under it) is enough to cause a swimming of the head. There is only one easy way of getting to the upper city, and there, part of the mountain has been blown up. This road is very steep, notwithstanding it is made winding and serpentine. However, they go up and down in carriages, and with wagons. All the other roads up the mountain are so steep, that it is very difficult to climb to the top of them. Most of the merchants live in the lower city, where the houses are built very close together. The streets in it are narrow, very rugged, and almost always wet. There is likewise a church, and a small marketplace. The upper city is inhabited by people of quality, by several persons belonging to the different offices, by tradesmen, and others . . .

August 22, 1749

There is no printing press in *Canada*, tho' there formerly was one; but all books are brought from *France*, and all the orders made in the country are written, which extends even to the paper-currency. They pretend that the press is not yet introduced here, lest it should be the means of propagating libels against the government, and religion. But the true reason seems to lie in the poorness of the country, as no printer could put off a sufficient number of books for his subsistence; and another reason may be, that *France* may have the profit arising from the exportation of books hither . . .

The meals here are in many respects different from those in the
English provinces . . . They eat three meals a day, *viz*. breakfast,
dinner, and supper. They breakfast commonly between seven and
eight. For the *French* here rise very early . . . Some of the men dip
a piece of bread in brandy, and eat it; others take a dram of
brandy, and eat a piece of bread after it. Chocolate is likewise
very common for breakfast, and many of the ladies drink coffee.
Some eat no breakfast at all. I have never seen tea made use of . . .
Dinner is pretty exactly at noon. People of quality have a great
variety of dishes, and the rest follow their example, when they
invite strangers. The loaves are oval, and baked of wheat flour.
For each person they put a plate, napkin, spoon, and fork.
Sometimes they likewise give knives; but they are generally omitted, all the ladies and gentlemen being provided with their own
knives. The spoons and forks are of silver, and the plates of
Delftware. The meal begins with a soup, with a good deal of
bread in it. Then follow fresh meats of various kinds, boiled, and
roasted, poultry, or game, fricassees, ragouts, &c. of several sorts;
together with different kinds of salads. They commonly drink red
claret at dinner, mixed with water; and spruce beer is likewise in
use. The ladies drink water, and sometimes wine. After dinner the
fruit and sweetmeats are served up . . . Cheese is likewise a part of
desert, and so is milk, which they eat last of all with sugar. Friday
and Saturday they eat no flesh, according to the Roman Catholic
rites; but they well know how to guard against hunger. On those
days they boil all sorts of kitchen-herbs, and fruit; fishes, eggs,
and milk, prepared in various ways. They cut cucumbers into
slices, and eat them with cream, which is a very good dish.
Sometimes they put whole cucumbers on the table, and every
body that likes them takes one, peels, and slices it, and dips the
slices into salt, eating them like raddishes . . . They say no grace
before, or after their meals, but only cross themselves, which is
likewise omitted by some. Immediately after dinner, they drink a
dish of coffee, without cream. Supper is commonly at seven

o'clock, or between seven and eight at night, and the dishes are the same as at dinner. Pudding and punch is not to be met with here, though the latter is well known . . .

August 23, 1749

In many places hereabouts they use their dogs to fetch water out of the river. I saw two great dogs to-day put before a little cart, one before the other. They had neat harness, like horses, and bits in their mouths. In the cart was a barrel. The dogs are directed by a boy, who runs behind the cart, and as soon as they come to the river, they jump in, of their own accord. When the barrel is filled, the dogs draw their burthen up the hill again, to the house they belong to . . .

September 12, 1749

Near each farm there is a kitchen garden, in which onions are most abundant; because the *French* farmers eat their dinners of them with bread, on Fridays and Saturdays, or fasting days. However, I cannot say, the *French* are strict observers of fasting; for several of my rowers ate flesh to-day, though it was Friday. The common people in Canada may be smelled when one passes by them, on account of their frequent use of onions . . .

Every farmer plants a quantity of tobacco near his house, in proportion to the size of his family. It is likewise very necessary that they should plant tobacco, because it is so universally smoaked by the common people. Boys of ten or twelve years of age run about with the pipe in their mouths, as well as the old people. Persons above the vulgar do not refuse to smoak a pipe now and then . . . People of both sexes, and of all ranks, use snuff very much . . .

Though many nations imitate the *French* customs; yet I observed, on the contrary, that the *French* in *Canada*, in many respects follow the customs of the *Indians*, with whom they converse every day. They make use of the tobacco-pipes, shoes, garters, and girdles, of the *Indians*. They follow the *Indian* way of making war with exactness; they mix the same things with tobacco; they make use of the Indian bark-boats, and row them in the Indian way; they wrap square pieces of cloth round their feet instead of stockings, and have adopted many other *Indian* fashions. When one comes into the house of a *Canada* peasant, or farmer, he gets up, takes his hat off to the stranger, desires him to sit down, puts his hat on, and sits down again. The gentlemen and ladies, as well as the poorest peasants and their wives, are called *Monsieur* and *Madame*. The peasants, and especially their wives, wear shoes, which consist of a piece of wood hollowed out, and are made almost as slippers. Their boys, and the old peasants themselves, wear their hair behind in a cue; and most of them wear red woollen caps at home, and sometimes on their journies . . .

The farmers prepare most of their dishes of milk. Butter is but seldom seen, and what they have is made of sour cream, and therefore not so good as *English* butter. Many of the *French* are very fond of milk, which they eat chiefly on fasting days . . . The French here eat near as much flesh as the English, on those days when their religion allows it. For excepting the soup, the sallads, and the dessert, all their other dishes consist of flesh variously prepared . . .

The houses in this neighbourhood are all made of wood. The rooms are pretty large. The inner roof rests on two, three, or four, large thick spars, according to the size of the room. The chinks are filled with clay, instead of moss. The windows are made entirely of paper. The chimney is erected in the middle of the room; that part of the room which is opposite the fire, is the kitchen; that which is behind the chimney, serves the people to sleep, and receive strangers in. Sometimes there is an iron stove behind the chimney . . .

September 13, 1749

It is inconceivable what hardships the people in *Canada* must undergo on their journies. Sometimes they must carry their goods a great way by land; frequently they are abused by the *Indians,* and sometimes they are killed by them. They often suffer hunger, thirst, heat, and cold, are hit by gnats, and exposed to the bites of poisonous snakes, and other dangerous animals and insects. These destroy a great part of the youth in *Canada,* and prevent the people from growing old. By this means, however, they become such brave soldiers, and so inured to fatigue, that none of them fear danger or hardships. Many of them settle among the *Indians* far from *Canada,* marry *Indian* women, and never come back again . . .

Louis-Antoine de Bougainville, Montcalm's aide-de-camp, also had some opinions about the people. In letters home, he stated that we were "vainglorious, mendacious, obliging kindly, honest; tireless for hunting, racing, and journeys to the pays-d'en-haut; lazy at cultivation of the land." We drank too much brandy and we weren't concerned enough about "the education of youth, since one early devoted oneself to hunting and warfare." However, he agreed that "despite this lack of education, the Canadians have natural wit, speak with ease, although they do not know how to write; their accent is as good as at Paris; their diction is full of vicious phrases borrowed from the Indian tongues or natural terms used in ordinary style." We robbed the king too easily and without guilt and paid too much attention to commerce rather than to military glory. Finally, he sent us to hell: "Woe to this land! It will perish the victim of its prejudices, of its blind confidence, of the stupidity or crookedness of its chiefs."

And so, on June 26, 1759, les Anglais arrived. They were to stay forever.

Vice-Admiral Charles Saunders, commander of the English fleet, was now the fourth Englishman to sail up the St. Lawrence to Québec. But he was the first to attempt to do so with large ships. He had two hundred sails under his command. Forty-nine of them were ships of the Royal Navy; the rest served as transports, hospitals, sounding ships, or as tender, provision, and ordinance vessels. It is said that Saunders's "armada formed a line fifty miles [eighty kilometres] long."

Along with Saunders, 13,500 sailors and 8,500 soldiers crowded on his vessels. In addition there was a scattering of camp followers, mostly women who, among other services, provided sexual favours—for a price.

The siege of Québec lasted eighty-five days, seventy-nine until the Battle of the Plains of Abraham, and the five days afterwards were used to organise the surrender of the town of Québec.

On the fifth day of the siege, following a failed attempt to destroy the English fleet, the British, under Brigadier-General Robert Monckton, the second-in-command in Wolfe's army, landed on the south shore facing Québec. On the fourteenth day, Wolfe, after a bout of indecision caused largely by his morbid insecurity, moved most of his army to Beaupré, almost directly across from the French lines at Beauport.

Prior to May 1759, there had been no fortifications at Beauport. By the time the English were already in the St. Lawrence, over ten thousand men, mostly Canadiens under the command of Bougainville, spent five weeks digging kilometres of trenches, building dozens of redoubts and other fortifications, and erecting numerous campsites. It rained almost constantly, and often the men were almost buried in mud. The few times the sun shone, its heat broiled them and made the earth as hard as rock. For transport, only a few carts were available and the timber was a long distance away. Their shelter was inadequate, the food inadequate, and the flies and mosquitoes relentless. But the Canadiens achieved what they had set out to do: build a line of defence winding nearly twenty-five kilometres, from the St. Charles River in the west to Montmorency Falls in the east.

Food: prior to the summer of 1759, there had been several major crop failures, and the war activity of those years had drained the intendant's available resources. Bread rations were cut drastically and the people ordered to eat horsemeat. The Canadiens refused, arguing that the horse was their friend. Those living outside of Québec had food but they refused to sell it to Bigot at low prices and in return for paper money of little value. To meet the emergency, more food had to be imported from France. However, with the

British where they were, on the north and south shores, famine was more than a probability.

On the fourteenth day, as well, English soldiers on a reconnaissance mission, on the south shore, captured an old man and his grandchildren. And the soldiers killed the two children because they were crying too loudly.

The bombardment of Québec began on the seventeenth day. It lasted until practically the end of the drama. During that time, ten thousand cannon balls and nine thousand bombs fell on the town, destroying three-quarters of it. The most dramatic fire occurred on July 28 as incendiary bombs fell on the cathedral. The principal church of the Canadiens had stood for a hundred years, a symbol of their faith and survival. Its tall belfries could be seen for kilometres around. Now they lay on the ground, and their three bells had melted in the intense heat.

On day forty-five, 160 houses fell to the flames, as did Notre-Dame-des Victoires, another symbol of life and victory.

From mid-July to the end of August 1759, the English were mired in mud. But between the siege's twenty-first and twenty-fifth day, many of Saunders's ships passed successfully above Québec. A day later, twelve ladies dined with Wolfe on the *Sutherland*. By all accounts, it was a pleasant evening with soft music, impeccable service, and excellent food and wine. Wolfe was in fine form.

The French attempted, again, to destroy the English fleet on day thirty-three. They failed.

Three days later, on July 31, Wolfe attacked the French positions at Beauport. The Battle of Montmorency was an utter disaster for him. He lost more than four hundred men, including one colonel, two captains, twenty-one lieutenants, and three ensigns. He had to retreat. The French casualties were twenty-six dead or wounded.

But Montcalm didn't pursue the English. In fact, he allowed them to cross the Montmorency River in safety. At the time, it was argued that he had run out of ammunition and that the rain had soaked the gunpowder. However, there is a more compelling reason: Montcalm was in his trenches and he was there to stay, and Wolfe wasn't about to lure him out. On the other hand, Montcalm had no precise information as to the number of English troops that had not participated in the battle and who were stationed on the Île d'Orléans and on the south shore. Then there was the fleet.

As for Wolfe, he wrote: "It is unfortunate that a man sees his error often too late to remedy it." But, he wasn't discouraged. The defeat was, in his words, "inconsiderable" and could be "easily repaired when a favourable opportunity" came his way.

On day forty-five, Captain Joseph Goreham, of the "American" Rangers, by all accounts a vicious man, was on the north shore, burning every house, every barn, every building except churches, according to Wolfe's order—and plundering. The terror had begun.

Meanwhile, the supreme English commander, Jeffrey Amherst, was doing his bit far away from the town of Québec. Wolfe didn't often hear from this most overrated man (who had a penchant for incompetence and lived in a chronic state of insecurity), but he did on the seventy-first day, September 4. On that afternoon, two officers and four privates arrived at Wolfe's headquarters with a letter from Amherst, who was near Lake Champlain. The message informed Wolfe of the surrender of the French fort at Niagara and included the admonition, "I want to hear from you. . . . You may depend upon my doing all I can for effectively reducing Canada. Now is the time."

What is more interesting about that event is the journey the officers and the men had made. They had travelled 965 kilometres in just over twenty-seven days. Unable to use the Canadian route, they had first gone from Crown Point (on Lake Champlain) to Boston, then through the wilderness of Massachusetts to the Kennebec River in Maine. Following that 264-kilometre river, they arrived at a large lake, now known as Lac Mégantic, and then canoed down the Chaudière River to within 24 kilometres of Québec, on the south shore. It was roughly the same journey that Benedict Arnold took when he was sent to capture Québec in 1775, during the American Revolution.

On day seventy-three, September 6, Wolfe boarded the *Sutherland* to search for a suitable landing place for his attack on Québec. It appears that from that day on, his mind was made up: he wanted to surprise Montcalm. To do that, he had to choose a place that Montcalm wouldn't possibly think of. On the seventy-seventh day, Wolfe wrote to an officer at Pointe-Lévy, across from Québec: "Tomorrow [September 11] the troops re-embark, the fleet sails up the river a little higher, as if intending to land above upon the north shore, keeping a convenient distance from the boats and armed vessels to fall down to the *FOULON* and we count (if no accident of weather or other prevents) to make a powerful effort at that spot about *FOUR* in the morning of the 13th."

Anse-au-Foulon was about four kilometres above Québec. Its steep and wooded escarpment rose fifty-three metres above the St. Lawrence, and the ravine of the Saint-Denis brook was covered with trees and rocks. But 180 metres to the right of it, there was a slope that Wolfe, alone, might have noticed. That declivity, Wolfe thought, might "answer the purpose" and make it easier for those who were ordered to climb to the plateau above.

During his inspection, he also took notice that only a few soldiers guarded the Foulon, and he knew that Bougainville, with an army as large as his own, was stationed at Cap-Rouge, eleven kilometres west.

It appears that he didn't tell his three brigadiers—Monckton, George Townshend, and James Murray—about the Foulon. No doubt infuriated at Wolfe's pretensions, they had the audacity to meet in private to draft a note to Wolfe, which stated in part, "We must beg leave to request from you as distinct orders as the nature of the thing will admit of, particularly to the place or places we are to attack." When he received it, Wolfe became enraged and sent a nasty note to Monckton, the officer on whom would fall all responsibility should Wolfe be incapacitated. "It is not a usual thing," he wrote, "to point out in the publick orders the direct spot of an attack, nor for any inferior Officer not charg'd with a particular duty to ask instructions upon that point." Monckton's reaction is not recorded, but he was probably satisfied that Wolfe had told him that the landing would take place at the Foulon.

There was hardly any food left in Québec, and at Beauport the troops had food for only two more days, unless the supply ships made it to Québec.

On the night of September 12, Wolfe, dressed in his grey coat, sat in his long boat, waited for his destiny, and read the poetry of Thomas Gray:

The boast of heraldry, the pomp of power,
And all that beauty, all that wealth e'er gave,
Await alike the inevitable hour,
The paths of glory lead but to the grave.

✥

Day eighty: September 13, 1759

1 a.m.—The moon is in its twentieth day. It is high and casts a shadow on the advance party waiting in the boats.

3 a.m.—More troops embark in the boats to proceed to the Foulon.

4 a.m.—The first boat approaching the Foulon is halted by a sentry: "Qui vive? Qui vive?" A French-speaking officer replies immediately: "La France et vive le Roi!" The sentry is fooled. "Ce sont nos gens," he yells to his comrades, "laissez-les passer." And with that the English advanced guard of twenty-four volunteers land and start to climb the ravine to the top, with their guns tied to their back. By this time, it is beginning to be light enough to see what one is doing.

4:45 a.m.—At Sillery, there's a battery of four guns, the Samos battery. Hearing the sound of guns at the Foulon, the soldiers peer out to the St. Lawrence and see many English boats and ships. They open fire and cause much damage. At Beauport, Montcalm is on the beach. He also hears the rumbling. He doesn't investigate.

4:50 a.m.—Montcalm, who had ordered the troops to stand at the ready in case of an attack, allows them to return to their tents. He spends the rest of the night drinking tea, worrying, and talking to one of his aides.

5 a.m.—Wolfe is on the beach.

5:15 a.m.—Bougainville, who is in bed—some evil tongues say with the wife of his cousin—is awakened in his headquarters at Cap-Rouge and told of the commotion east of him. He does nothing, militarily speaking.

5:20 a.m.—Wolfe begins his ascent.

5:30 a.m.—The red flag, signifying that the English have landed above Québec, is flying over the Citadel. An officer informs Montcalm, who finishes his tea, changes into a clean uniform, has his horse saddled, and leaves to go to meet the governor general at the latter's camp, which is at La Canardière, named because the priests of the seminary kept ducks there.

An hour or so later, Bougainville can no longer tarry now that Vaudreuil has sent a messenger to tell him about the English. Bougainville is eleven kilometres away from the Plains of Abraham. He figures that it will take him two hours to get there, but his departure is delayed; he wastes an hour attempting to dislodge the English who have captured the Samos battery, loosing eighteen men in the process. He gets to the Plains when the battle is over.

7:20 a.m.—After Montcalm has already left for the Plains, Vaudreuil writes to him: "The success, which the English have already gained in forcing our posts, should be the ultimate source of their defeat; but it is to our interest not to be overly hasty. It is my view that we should attack the English only when all of our troops are assembled. You should therefore bring together on the Plains to join our army, 1,500 men from the garrison in Québec and all of Bougainville's corps. In this way, the enemy will be completely surrounded, and will have no other resources than to retreat towards their left, where their defeat would again be inevitable." Montcalm never receives the letter.

⚜

To conclude the story of this most important battle in which many Canadiens (and many others) who would become Canadians participated, here is some of what I wrote ten years ago, in *The Battle for Canada:*

> It is an historical axiom, challenged by few historians, that Wolfe made no errors on the Plains, that Montcalm committed more

than his share, and that what defeated the French was the superior calibre of the English army. I disagree with this assessment in the following way:

I believe that the way Wolfe planned his landing at Foulon and assembled his army on the Plains proves that he was incompetent, if not insane. What destroyed Montcalm was his pessimism, his paranoia, and his incapacity to act resolutely. As for the English army, it was no better and no worse than the French one—and both were not worth much. That leaves the Canadians.

It is often stated that Montcalm's fatal mistake was to incorporate Canadians into the regular troops. Perhaps this is true, since the two were accustomed to different forms of warfare. However, only the Canadians behaved well and with any semblance of honour on the Plains of Abraham. Left to themselves, it was their courage, their fine marksmanship, and their initiative that made it possible for many of their French comrades to find safety in the trenches of Beauport and behind the walls of Québec. The Canadians—at great cost in human lives—salvaged at least part of the day.

In the Battle of the Plains of Abraham, the English lost 658 men from all ranks; there were 644 casualties on the French side; however, many Canadien and Indian losses were not recorded.

Between September 14 and 18, the inevitable happened. The town of Québec capitulated and was turned over to the English, who entered it at 4 p.m., on the eighty-fifth day of the siege.

However, it still wasn't over.

François-Gaston de Lévis (1719–87), Montcalm's second-in-command, and, therefore, his successor, was absent at the Battle of the Plains of Abraham. He had gone to Lake Ontario following the loss of Fort Niagara (near Youngstown, N.Y.) to prevent the English from reaching Montréal, should they have had the intention to do so. After the battle of September 13 (which, by the way, might have been won had Lévis been in command—or so Vaudreuil thought), Lévis rushed to Jacques-Cartier (now Longueil) arriving where the French army had taken refuge on September 17. He was furious at the rout of his army and at the capitulation of Québec. He was able to send a message to France for more troops and more supplies which, hopefully, would come the following spring. And he decided to retake Québec.

And so, seven months later, in April 1760, he and his army of seven thousand men, three thousand being militia, beat Murray and the English on the Plains of Abraham, and the siege of the town began again, the French being outside the walls this time. There, they waited for the first ship to sail up the St. Lawrence. It was an English one; the ships sent from France never arrived. Lévis had no alternative but to return to Montréal to await the convergence of three English armies, with seventeen thousand men, to descend upon him. They arrived at the beginning of September.

At the same time, the Canadiens—abandoned, betrayed, and alienated—refused to bear arms any longer. Lévis was left with an army of two thousand soldiers. Vaudreuil sued for peace and forbade Lévis to pursue the war.

On September 8, 1760, Montréal and the northern and western territory of the French empire in North America were handed over to the English.

As the war continued in Europe, the English settled in Montréal, in Trois-Rivières, and in Québec. Life returned to some form of normalcy. The clergy were accommodating; so were the girls; and the merchants made money. Most of the militia returned to their farms, while others went to rebuild the town of Québec.

French nobility, officers, and many soldiers returned home, some accompanied by their wives. Merchants went as well. There, a few were thrown in prison and, after fifteen months or so, some were banished, others were fined, still others were pardoned, while the king dispensed Crosses of Saint-Louis everywhere. There were people, however, who pleaded for Canada and the maintenance of French presence there.

François-Charles de Bourlamaque, a gallant, competent, and quiet officer who had served in New France from 1756 until 1760, had been third-in-command, after Montcalm and Lévis. In 1762, he sent the Duc de Choiseul, the minister of war, a *Mémoire sur le Canada* in which he argued that

Canada should be retained, for it would be beneficial to France should improvements in its administration and development be made. Canada was governed on false principles, he argued. The dual administration of the governor and the intendant was nefarious; the refusal to allow Protestants and foreigners to immigrate was a mistake; and too much attention was paid to the fur trade at the expense of the development of the St. Lawrence valley, of fisheries, and manufactures.

No one listened to him, and on February 10, 1763, we were ceded to England's rule.

I V

Here We Are and Here We Stay
1763–1867

❧

*I*n the hundred years following France's betrayal, the Canadiens living in Québec devoted much of their energies to the quest for survival. That survival was to be achieved through political means, including a revolution—or "rebellions," as Canadians and Canadiens like to call the insurrections of 1837 and 1838 in both Upper and Lower Canada—and, at the same time, through a cultural transformation. The most far-reaching of these two processes is to be found in the political realm. When the dust had cleared, political adaptation was inevitable. It brought us Responsible Government which, along with Representative Government, is the cornerstone of our political democracy; and, also, the British North America Act, which made us a new country on an ancient land and brought all our people together—with the cruel exception of the First Peoples—under one constitution. No doubt, many will argue that such developments would have taken place without the so-called Rebellions of the 1830s. Perhaps, but it would have taken a hell of a lot longer and with great disruptions to the tranquility that must exist between peoples of different languages, cultures, ways of doing things, and religions who occupy the same country.

In the pursuit of this political/constitutional/cultural scenario, the Canadiens, no doubt, were quite difficult, if not impossible, to deal with. The search for "ambiguity" however, has not been one our traits. On the other hand, les Anglais—as we called the English who came to live among us after the conquest—weren't easy to get along with either. Sure of themselves, determined to have their way, and racist in too many instances, they rushed to keep the purity of the British stock—which meant excluding, as much as possible, the new subjects of His Imperial Majesty in the whole economic and political process. That they didn't succeed wasn't for lack of trying.

As for the cultural transformation that occurred roughly between 1815 and 1850, it considerably delayed the social and economic modernisation of Québec. It tended to favour a new oligarchy made up of the bourgeoisie canadienne (individuals trained in the Collèges classiques to be doctors, lawyers, notaries, and members of other such professions). Another group in this oligarchy was the clergy, often educated in the same colleges. Both groups conspired to keep the Canadiens (habitants) obedient to what the oligarchy considered to be in the best interest of this Catholic and largely illiterate people. That this "best interest" often coincided with the class interest of the bourgeoisie and of the clergy will come as no surprise. The nefarious Ultramontanism that prevailed in clerical quarters was meant to bend the State to the will of the Church and its allies. This is what the oligarchy wanted—and the clergy were happy to oblige. The effects of this were felt throughout the 19th century and the first sixty years of the 20th. Vestiges can still be found in the xenophobic nationalism of the Parti Québécois and the Bloc Québécois. The most tragic consequence of it all was to keep the French-speaking people of Québec ignorant, in the name of God, as there would be no comprehensive public secondary school system until the Révolution tranquille of the 1960s.

The most important contribution to the cause of survival came from some of our leaders, who articulated clearly what made us different from the English who came to occupy our ceded or conquered lands. That articulation brought about Responsible Government and Confederation.

On the other hand, it wasn't entirely the fault of the French-speaking and Catholic people of Québec that some of their efforts for survival became extreme and disoriented. A good part of the blame must be laid on many of those who came to occupy the land of Canada with us. More often than I care to state or remember, their refusal to accept us as we were—as we are—endangered our survival. Our identity and future have always been—and still are—irrevocably linked to the French language, to the country that gave us birth—namely Canada—and to the full participation of the Province of Québec in the affairs of the larger Canada.

What Canadians and Canadiens must understand is that infections like modern-day Serbian xenophobia, which leads to many forms of ethnic cleansing, exclusion, victimisation complexes, and to apartheid—which has been far too present in our past on both sides of the great divide—must be avoided. Or else we perish. That lesson was made quite clear between 1763 and 1867.

Politically speaking, three events, during the 104 years under review, are of supreme importance in understanding the life of the Province of Québec: the Rebellions of 1837 and 1838, the arrival of Responsible Government in the 1840s, and the British North America Act of 1867.

On the cultural side of the equation, we have four significant moments: the Québec Act, the French Revolution, Lord Durham's report, and Confederation.

The heroes and villains shall be revealed.

On February 15, 1839, at the new Prison of Montréal, François Marie Thomas Chevalier de Lorimier was hanged. He had participated in the Rebellion of 1837–38, and in his cell, at seven that morning, he wrote to his wife.

> Ma chère et bien-aimée,
>
> À la veille de partir de mon lugubre cachôt pour monter sur l'échafaud politique, déjà ensanglantée de plusieurs victimes qui m'y ont devancé, je dois à mon devoir conjugal, ainsi qu'à ma propre inclination, de t'écrire un mot avant que de paraître devant mon Dieu . . .

Sois donc heureuse, ma chère et malheureuse épouse, ainsi que
mes chers petits enfants; c'est le voeu le plus ardent de mon âme.
Adieu, ma tendre épouse, encore une fois, adieu. Vis et sois
heureuse.

Ton malheureux époux

Chevalier de Lorimier

Who were Chevalier de Lorimier and the four others who were hanged
with him—Charles Hindenlang, Amable Daunais, François Nicola, and
Pierre-Rémi Narbonne—and why were they hanged in 1839? To answer
that, we all have to return to 1760.

Immediately after the surrender of Montréal in September 1760, the British government installed a military regime until the fate of Canada and its inhabitants
had been decided. In the four years that followed—between the capitulation of
Montréal (1760) and King George's Proclamation (1763)—martial law was
imposed. The town of Québec lay in ruins; the farms on the North Shore and
the rest of the lower countryside were virtually destroyed; and the farmers and
the merchants who stayed in New France were ruined. Murray, who inherited
the government of the new colony, wrote to Amherst about the "miserable condition of His Majesty's Canadian subjects . . . to describe it is really beyond my
powers and to think of it is shocking to Humanity." He and others helped my
people rebuild, but that took many years.

The four-year military regime wasn't as cruel as some historians have
suggested. Most Canadiens would now agree with Murray when he wrote to
a business partner in 1764: "No Military government was ever conducted
with more disinterestedness and more moderation than this has been." There
has been much exaggeration, as well, as to the number of seigneurs and merchants who left for France, thus impeding the development of Québec after
the Seven Years War. It now appears that only 3,000 persons left Canada for
France, mainly government officials, military personnel, and those closely
tied to the French regime. We know that "130 seigneurs, 100 gentlemen and
bourgeois, 125 notable merchants, 25 legal authorities and lawyers, 25 to 30
doctors and surgeons, and nearly as many notaries . . ." remained to help

rebuild, in addition to most of the clergy. Consequently, the people had potential leaders to make their aspirations and problems known.

The Royal Proclamation of 1763 considerably reduced the territory (of the old French empire) administered from the town of Québec. The new boundaries of Québec were Lake Nipissing in the west; the St. John River (Labrador) in the east; the 45th parallel in the south to the shore of the Baie des Chaleurs, and then up to the western end of the Île d'Anticosti. However that island, along with Labrador, the Gulf of St. Lawrence, and the Îles de la Madeleine, was given to Newfoundland. The land to the west of the Canadiens, beginning approximately at the Ottawa River, became, more or less, an Indian reserve that the First Peoples occupied. It isn't any wonder that they consider the Proclamation of 1763 as their Magna Carta.

The civil government of the Province of Québec now rested in the hands of an all-powerful governor general, with a council of some twelve members to assist him and to act as the legislative body. Justice in both criminal and civil matters was to be carried out in accordance with the laws of Great Britain. Since Canadiens couldn't take the anti-Catholic oaths demanded of British officials, they couldn't serve on the council or in the courts. It's fair to say that the essential purpose of this arrangement was to assimilate the Canadiens and turn them into English men and women. As well, it was meant to create compatible conditions for a British immigration. Although the new subjects were protected in the exercise of their faith, the Protestant religious way of life and influence was to be paramount: "To the end that the Church of England may be established both in Principle and Practice, and that the said Inhabitants may by Degrees be induced to embrace the Protestant Religion and their Children be brought up in the Principles of it." Lastly, an elected and representative Assembly could be empowered, but, there again, no Canadiens could serve in it. The future wasn't bright.

Another factor threatened the Canadiens: the influx of merchants, mostly from the American colonies. In 1760, there were about fifty of them; by 1766, close to six hundred. Their agenda was vastly different from that of the habitants: what the newcomers wanted was to fully inherit the benefits of the "conquest"—in which they had little participated. In the pursuit of their goals, they became to Murray and a couple of other governors: "the

Licentious Fanaticks Trading here." Filled with contempt for the Canadiens; animated by the anti-popery syndrome that affected most American colonists, especially New Englanders; and obsessed by the conviction that a Frenchman lurked in everyone who spoke French, the "Fanaticks" plotted to have Murray recalled, because they judged him too friendly with the Canadiens. They succeeded two years after Murray had assumed his duties.

His successor, Guy Carleton, 1st Baron of Dorchester (1724–1808), arrived in 1766 but took up his office two years later. (He had served with Wolfe on the Plains of Abraham.) He remained here for ten years, and through it all he, too, had to battle the English-speaking merchants and settlers, for he also had a policy of conciliation towards the "New Subjects," as Carleton referred to us. This long-lasting opposition of the vast majority of les Anglais to anything that appeared a concession to the "French" (as they came to call us—an appellation that has carried on to this day, unfortunately) would eventually lead to the troubles of the 1830s—and beyond.

At the start of his term, Carleton tended to pacify the "old subjects," meaning the Anglais made up of "disbanded Officers, Soldiers, or Followers of the Army . . . Adventurers in Trade, or such as could not remain at home." But, he soon realised that his pacification might well precipitate a crisis with his "new subjects," whose numbers were increasing almost daily. Since he believed Québec's high birthrate would continue unabated, he considered that "barring a Catastrophe shocking to think of, this Country must, to the end of Time, be peopled by the Canadian Race." He had, so he felt, to govern in such a way as to not alienate the vast majority of His Majesty's subjects in the former French territories. He hoped that such treatment would mean that the Canadiens would become "inspired with a cordial Attachment, and zeal for the King's Government."

The growing dissatisfaction in the American colonies also played an important role in his pursuit of this policy. Like many others, Carleton was aware that, to the south, there could be all sorts of troubles: civil disobedience, uprisings, rebellions, revolution, and a possible French invasion of Canada, at worst, or assistance to the British Americans, at best. Canada might even face an American invasion. Since he had only 1,627 British

troops, 500 British immigrants, 76,675 habitants, and 7,400 Natives techni-
cally under his command, it was imperative, then, that he buy the loyalty
of the Canadiens.

Consequently, he went about governing the "new subjects" through those
he considered to be their natural leaders: the seigneurs and the clergy. He
favoured a Canadian economy by promoting increased production in grain,
hemp, flax, iron, and manufacturing, at the expense of importing British
goods. He also made possible the participation of Canadiens in the fur trade;
he supported the habitants' claims to the winter seal fishery on the north shore
of the St. Lawrence; and he argued that the people he governed had the right
to be indemnified for the worthless paper money handed out during the last
days of the French empire in Canada. He repaired highways, built bridges,
and initiated many social reforms. Helping him out, the British government,
in 1771, allowed that seigneurial tenure govern the allocation of all lands.

His greatest contribution, however, to the pacification of the Canadiens
was the Quebec Act, one of the five intolerable Acts that are said to have
precipitated the American Revolution.

The Quebec Act, officially known as *An Act for making more effective
Provision for the Government of the Province of Quebec in North America*,
received royal assent on June 22, 1774, and was proclaimed on May 1, 1775.
It was Carleton's handiwork. Through the Act, the boundaries of Québec
reverted to those that had existed prior to the Royal Proclamation, thus
stretching into western Indian territory south of the Great Lakes, between
the Mississippi and the Ohio Rivers. The government of the province rested
in a governor and seventeen to twenty-three appointed councillors, but there
was no provision for an elected assembly, let alone for Responsible
Government. However, religious freedom was guaranteed, and the Test
Oath was reworded to enable Catholics to assume public office. French civil
law was made mandatory, as was British criminal law. Land tenure remained
within the seigneurial system.

As is customary in human affairs, the Act didn't please everyone. The
Anglais, though they welcomed the extension of the frontier of the fur trade,
were annoyed that an elected assembly wasn't granted. The main reason for
that may well be found in an argument put forward in 1766: "Bigoted as they

are to the Popish religion, unacquainted with, and hitherto prejudiced against, the laws and customs of England," the Canadiens wouldn't be willing to promote any policies that might assimilate them to the English way of things. Moreover, since the habitants spoke no English, the business of the Legislative Assembly would have to be "carried . . . in the French language, which would tend to perpetuate that language and postpone to a very distant time, perhaps for ever, that coalition of the two nations, or the melting down the French nation into the English in point of language, affections, religion, and laws, which is so much to be wished for, and which otherwise a generation or two may perhaps effect, if proper measures are taken for that purpose."

As for the Americans who considered the Mississippi-Ohio territory as morally theirs, the Quebec Act was the "worst of laws" because it recognised as almost official a "religion that has deluged our island in blood, and dispersed impiety, bigotry, persecution, murder, and rebellion throughout every part of the world."

The habitants were grateful for some of the provisions of their Magna Carta, as the Act was called, but they abhorred the reimposition of seigneurial dues and clerical tithes. Some considered it as intolerable as the Americans did. On the other hand, and in the view of many historians, "by bolstering French Laws and Canadian customs and institutions," Carleton enabled them (the Canadiens) not just to survive, but to flourish. The argument goes further to state: "And although it might be argued that the 'charter view' of the Quebec Act has been overstated, it does seem that a groundwork was laid for the special status that many French Canadians have claimed to the present day. In so far as he can be held accountable for this groundwork, Carleton maybe praised, or blamed accordingly."

Moreover, many historians have also pointed out that "the real importance" of the Quebec Act lay more in the future than in 1774. This is so, they argue, because it created a precedent for the British empire that was to evolve in the 19th century: that a British subject didn't have to be English. Multiculturalism was born.

If Carleton expected that a grateful people would embrace the British cause during the American Revolution, he must have been sorely mistaken and greatly displeased.

❧

In a place that is not here and at a time that is not now, there are chat rooms on an Internet site known as explor'.ca where Canadians and Canadiens, interested people from other societies, angels and saints, living in the past or present, can come together to tell stories about this country and their passage through it. In the chat room reserved for the stories of Canada between the passage of the Quebec Act and Confederation, I log in and take a colour (grey) that labels me as a non-participant. The rules ask me to identify myself, which I do, and I inform the facilitator that I came to find out what some of the people who lived in Québec or Lower Canada or Canada East (all the same thing) around 1774 have to say about themselves and that era's events.

The facilitator, in red, tells me, "We have just begun."

Carleton is already at it: "Why don't the Canadiens help us beat the Americans?" Then, an American, identified by the colour blue, wants to know why my people don't want to partake in the benefits of the American Revolution. "Your destiny is with us!"

"That's what your first Congress writes to us in an address dated October 26, 1774," replies a seigneur and, no doubt, a beneficiary of the Quebec Act. "Your Congress is hypocritical. On the one hand, you bombard us with slogans against our religion, and on the other, you beg us to stand with you. Reconciled to Great Britain, we aren't willing to enter into your adventure."

"But the American adventure is appealing!" This comes from a Montréal lawyer. "Monsieur Carleton, your Quebec Act guarantees us some rights; but the people have serious doubts about the application of these rights. They certainly object to your reliance on pacifying the seigneurs and the clergy, who will then become your allies in keeping us quiet and docile. Well, it doesn't work. Why? you ask. Because the English merchants, who are supposed to be on your side, plot with the Americans as do too many seigneurs—don't bother denying it. It's a fact. In regard to the priests, let me just say that joining the American Revolution or not, and helping you to defend the British empire: these are NOT spiritual matters. They are temporal ones. The bishop's role is to make priests, not soldiers. In other words, it's none of his business."

A habitant from the Richelieu valley insists: "We've nothing to lose by not making a choice. On the other hand, we can lose everything if we back the wrong side. So neutral we'll remain."

"You see," says a Canadien, a tavern-keeper in Montréal, "you, the British, are unable to defend us. Why, then, should we antagonise the Americans, especially when many of your countrymen are siding with them. They talk of nothing else in my tavern."

"But there's more," the lawyer writes. "Monsieur Carleton, you're indecisive. You don't know when to pursue or when to act decisively. In a fit of what can be nothing else but insanity, you send the bulk of your army to the American colonies, leaving us stranded and vulnerable to attack."

"I follow my orders," replies Carleton. "Is that a valid reason for so many of you to withdraw from the ranks of the militia, as you do?"

"Yes, it is. But I prefer to see our dilemma in another way," an unidentified participant adds. "We've been on this land for a long time, and keeping it ours has meant almost a constant state of war." In capital letters, he writes: "WE'RE TIRED OF WAR!" There is a pause, after which this person says: "Barely ten years have passed since the English took over our land. We're still rebuilding. War isn't an option, Monsieur Carleton. It's as simple as that."

Carleton: "Even when American rebels invade your land and threaten your homes?"

⚜

While the participants juggle for position, readers may need to know that in November 1775, a "genteel appearing man, tall and slender of make," and "of an agreeable temper and a virtuous General" invaded Montréal. He was Richard Montgomery from New York. Carleton was nowhere to be seen. During the various "invasions" of the land he was sworn to defend, the governor's entire behaviour was strange indeed. Two months before Montgomery's entry into Montréal, the Americans had set up camp, in Canada, in the Richelieu valley. Carleton did nothing to dislodge them, but spent all his time trying to raise the militia. Unfortunately, he entrusted that task to the seigneurs instead of the captains of the militia, who had performed that duty since the establishment of New France. It's not surprising that, at first, Carleton had little success. But when, in the middle of September, a combined force of British regular soldiers, Canadian militia, and Indians defeated a group of Americans and Canadiens near Montréal, close to 1,200 habitants enlisted. Soon, their numbers climbed to two thousand. However, Carleton, not trusting them, made no use of them, and he spent three important weeks dilly-dallying instead of pursuing the enemy. Bored, and probably insulted, the militiamen decided to return to their farms, leaving him with barely 150 British soldiers. On November 11, Carleton decided to abandon the city, leaving a committee of leading citizens to negotiate the fate of the town with Montgomery.

Carleton and his Regulars commandeered various schooners to take them to Québec City. Unfavourable winds, however, forced them to take refuge at Sorel, where, on the 16th, American batteries attacked them. Still determined to reach his capital as quickly as possible, Carleton disguised himself as a peasant and entrusted his fate to Joseph Bouchette, a mariner of great experience. Bouchette was "not a handsome lad," while his wife, it was reported, was "beautiful, buxom, and well-built." According to the gossip of the time, Bouchette and his wife "knew" each other for a long time before their marriage. But he was good at his trade, and he brought Carleton safely to his destination on the 19th. For his skill and bravery, Bouchette was well rewarded. In Québec, Carleton had 1,800 men (Regulars, Canadiens, seamen, and Indians) to defend the honour of Great Britain and the 3,200 inhabitants of the city. He had also ample food and supplies for eight months.

Meanwhile, another American, Benedict Arnold (1741–1801), was advancing towards Québec. Arnold had left Cambridge, Massachusetts, in early September with 1,100 men. He marched them through the wilderness of the Kennebec River (Maine), losing 500 men in the process. Starving and practically naked, he reached Pointe-Lévy, across from Québec, on December 9, where he waited for Montgomery to arrive. When he did, the third battle on the Plains of Abraham took place in the middle of a fierce snow storm on the night of December 30–31. The Americans were routed and Montgomery was killed. The remnant of his army, decimated by smallpox and other illnesses, remained in the vicinity of Québec. Carleton, again, didn't act, leaving the Americans to do pretty much as they pleased. In the following spring, British reinforcements arrived, putting an end, for the moment, to attempts to make Americans out of us.

In Québec, there was much criticism of Carleton's generalship and, after the usual quarrels with his advisors, he left in July 1778, still bearing a grudge against the habitants. They were influenced, he said, "only by hopes of gain, or fear of punishment." But the essential reason he gave for their lackadaisical attitude was that "these people had been governed with too loose a Rein for many years, and had imbibed too much of the American Spirit of Licentiousness and Independence administered by a numerous and turbulent Faction here, to be suddenly restored to a proper and desirable Subordination." He never noticed that, for a multitude of reasons, the Canadiens were becoming more and more anti-American all through the American invasion and occupation of their homeland.

The Canadiens, if they weren't prone to spontaneous loyalty, were adept at seizing the opportunity to make money. Carleton had dismissed them with a wave of the hand: "I think there is nothing to fear from them while we are in a state of prosperity, and nothing to hope for while in distress." Neither did Montgomery believe the eloquent declaration of support and brotherhood some of the Montréal élite, known as the "Congressites," made to him. He had no doubt that they and the habitants "will be our friends as long as we are able to maintain our ground." He was right: as soon as his money ran out, they withdrew their support.

If Carleton couldn't count on the gratitude of the Canadiens, he had no problem with the vast majority of the clergy, who were loyalist to the core and quite anti-American. Québec's bishop issued several *mandements* (episcopal letters), ordering the people to be loyal and serve the British cause, to enlist in the militia under the seigneurs, and to obey their priests—who knew best. If they didn't abide by these edicts, or if they, in any way, supported the American invaders, his clergy was to refuse the sacraments. Like the other Frenchmen who served in the high echelons of the Church hierarchy, the bishop didn't relish the American appeals to liberty, to direct election, and to any notion that authority comes from the people and not from God. He saw grave dangers for the Church in the politicisation of the habitants towards democracy and liberty. He considered feudalism and absolutism to be the natural condition of his people. His priests, a majority of whom were French and better educated than their native colleagues, followed him. With the Quebec Act, Carleton had bought the loyalty of the bishops and his clergy, as he had with the bulk of the seigneurs.

The notion that the French-speaking people of Québec, at the time, could think for themselves might seem questionable to some. However, there is much evidence that the American views on liberty and democracy were known and discussed widely, particularly in the towns.

Although perhaps only five thousand people in the province could read (out of a population of 140,000), they were attuned to contemporary ideas. Voltaire was known and discussed, as were Montesquieu, Rousseau, the encyclopedists, and many other "radical" thinkers. Their books, after all, were banned in Québec only in the middle of the 19th century, when the dreadful Jansenism and Ultramontanism took over the Catholic clergy of Québec.

However, if only a few could read the American summons to liberty and democracy—or the Voltarian pamphlets—those who could read could talk! News of the Americans and of the French "radicals" was read where groups gathered, on occasion even on the steps of the parish church after High Mass on Sundays. In that way, ideas were spread during the dangerous period of transition that existed before the troubles of 1837. It's also fair to remember that people were busy surviving, and protecting their religion, their laws, their customs, their language—and attempting to reconcile themselves to the grow-ing domination of a culture they had not wished for.

Gustave Lanctot, an eminent historian, has suggested that "perhaps no event has exercised so much influence upon Québec, directly or indirectly, as the American Revolution." For his part, another historian, Mason Wade, writes: "The Revolution settled the fate of French feudalism and absolutism; it caused a split between the largely pro-British élite and the largely pro-American masses, which had important and lasting results."

Besides influencing the habitants of Québec, the American Revolution had four other spectacular effects. The Treaty of Versailles (1783), which ended the struggle between Great Britain and her American colonies, stripped Québec (or Canada) of the hinterland south and west of the Great Lakes. By doing so, it laid the geographical foundation for the Canada of Confederation. Second, it made Canada British *and* French/English, for it brought among us about forty thousand Loyalists. The bulk of them settled in New Brunswick, Nova Scotia, and Ontario, but a substantial number built their homes in the Gaspé Peninsula and in the Eastern Townships. Third, it contributed to that laid-back and non-affirmative attitude that so characterises us, Canadians and Canadiens, and that also tends to enrage many of us. And it gave us a neighbour—a neighbour to compare ourselves with, to envy, to want to emulate, and to use as the cause of whatever fail-ures we may have. In the heart of every Canadian and Canadien would there lurk an American?

The American Revolution came and went without resolving the issue of Canadiens' "loyalty" to their British overlords, but it soon became obvious that the changing political landscape had made the Quebec Act of 1774 out-dated. By the end of the 1780s, Great Britain had six colonies in North America: Newfoundland, Nova Scotia, Cape Breton (created in 1784 but united with Nova Scotia in 1820), New Brunswick (also carved out of Nova Scotia in 1784), the Island of Saint John (Prince Edward Island), and Québec (which included land that would become Upper Canada/Canada West/Ontario). There was, as well, Rupert's Land, that vast territory in the north and in the west granted to the Hudson's Bay Company in 1670 and transferred to Canada in 1870. Close to half a million people lived in that

Canada, two hundred thousand of them were First Peoples and roughly the same number were Canadiens.

The Loyalists, who had lost everything in their former colonies, were not to be denied the rights of British subjects here; they wanted British parliamentary institutions—and the Constitutional Act of 1791 granted them those. This time, Québec was divided along ethnic lines: an English majority in Upper Canada, a French-speaking one in Lower Canada. The Constitutional Act also guaranteed to all subjects, the same rights and privileges that British subjects were said to enjoy everywhere, and provided the Canadas with colonial assemblies with the authority to raise taxes in order to pay for the cost of government. The Act bolstered the power, prestige, and status of the governor general and limited the powers and rights of the newly created assemblies through an appointed Legislative Council, which was to act as a sort of House of Lords and defend the interests of the Crown. It maintained seigneurial tenure in Lower Canada, instituted the Clergy Reserves in Upper Canada, and held Crown lands in freehold tenure.

The privileged position of the Roman Catholic Church and the status of the laws in Lower Canada were also maintained, so the Quebec Act was not repealed. On the other hand, the Constitutional Act made sure that British North America wasn't "abandoned to democracy." To have done that would have meant instituting Responsible Government (the system we enjoy today, whereby the executive is subject to the will of a duly elected parliament). And there lay the fundamental weakness of the Constitutional Act of 1791, which inexorably led to the debacle of 1837.

Dividing Québec into two distinct provinces or colonies satisfied the Loyalists in Upper Canada, but they were about the only ones who were satisfied. They were now free from the "French domination" they had endured since coming to the old Province of Québec.

In Lower Canada, however, it was another story. The seigneurs were happy with the maintenance of their land-holding system, but not pleased at all by the removal of Crown lands (from their grasping hands) or by the creation of an elected Legislative Assembly, which would inevitably rob them of their status. The "English merchants," particularly in Montréal, and the Loyalist immigrants to Québec (Lower Canada), were infuriated. The former were fearful that their potential economic empire might be lost to them, because of the conservatism and lack of "entrepreneurship" of the habitants, whose representatives controlled the Assembly. As for the new settlers, they found themselves in a minority position, subordinate to a majority they despised, a majority obsessed with itself, a papist majority, and a republican one—or so they thought.

Neither the merchants nor the Loyalists would accept that destiny. They would refuse the Canadiens the self-government implicit in the Act of 1791. In the meantime, they would feather their nests at the expense of their co-citizens. Racists, they didn't foresee that their attitudes would provoke the events of 1837.

As for the clergy and the habitants, they were largely indifferent. Such representative institutions were foreign to them. They only hoped that they wouldn't be subject to more taxation.

By not imposing the full force of English laws and customs on the French-speaking majority of Lower Canada, the Constitutional Act preserved the notion of the multicultural empire that the Quebec Act had enunciated. On the other hand, it was the fervent hope of the British government that its "French subjects" would come to admire English law and custom and adopt them of their own free will. "It will be experience which will teach them that English laws are the best," said the colonial secretary at the time, William Pitt the Younger, during the debate. In the meantime, though, "they ought to be governed to their satisfaction."

Whatever the appreciation of the Constitutional Act, it assured the survival of my people for all time, to paraphrase a statement from Mason Wade. It "armed" us for the half-century of constitutional struggle that lay ahead.

For the first elections of the new regime in 1792, the province was divided into twenty-one counties or electoral circumscriptions—most of which had been given English names! (The French-speaking population of Québec, at the time, was 156,000, the English-speaking one barely 10,000.) At that election, thirty-four Canadiens and sixteen Anglais were elected. (Many of the latter were bilingual, but the vast majority of the Canadien representatives were unilingual.) The most important debate was over bilingualism—shades of things to come. A unilingual French-speaking deputé was elected speaker, after a debate marked by the stupidity of many members. It didn't bode well.

This was followed by a protracted and intense discussion of the Assembly's official language—French or English, English or French, or both! After a three-day debate, the members agreed to introduce and debate bills in their "language of choice," to instruct the clerk to read the bills to be voted on in both "official" languages, and to consider English the "legal" language for those bills that pertained to criminal law, and French for those that had French civil law at their source.

James McGill was a merchant, office holder, politician, landowner, militia officer, and philanthropist. Born October 6, 1744, in Glasgow, Scotland, he was the second child and eldest son of James McGill and Margaret Gibson. He died on December 18, 1813, in Montréal. McGill was twenty-two when he arrived in Montréal in 1766. At first, he was a fur trader, and he travelled extensively pursuing that trade. When Montgomery invaded Montréal, he helped negotiate the terms of the surrender. After the American Revolution, he had to reorganise his mercantile interest, all the while keeping many of his old partners who then resided in the new United States of America. Bilingual, he was elected to the new Legislative Assembly in 1792 for the riding of Montréal-West, and he was also appointed to the Legislative Council. At the time of his death, he was very wealthy, and he willed ten thousand pounds and forty-six acres (nineteen hectares) of land to establish a college, which became McGill University.

McGill, a rich and influential merchant, had all the attendant characteristics of that position. He viewed the Canadiens as too conservative, not entrepreneurial enough, and too dedicated to their own way of life. Like the other members of his class, he thought that, as a patriotic necessity, the Assembly should be free of "party" politics. However, this wasn't to be. "Unhappily the Session commenced with a determined spirit of Party amongst the French members," wrote a disgruntled merchant to a colleague in Great Britain, "for they had a private meeting, at which it was decided that an Englishmen should on no account be elected speaker." McGill, like the other Anglais, feared that the "Out of Door Meeting," as they called caucus meetings, would disrupt the proceedings of the Assembly. This, however, didn't prevent them from caucusing themselves, especially when they felt that the Canadiens were using the Assembly to foster and entrench their agenda.

A colleague of McGill's wrote to one of his partners: "I fear that there are Two Parties amongst the French—one obnoxious to the New Constitution, as they opposed our procuring it—the other more dangerous as being infested with the detestable principles now prevalent in France." However, there was light at the end of the tunnel: "These being my fears, my hopes of course are slender—still as questions will arise on which they will split, it will give the English (who have no wish but the happiness of this country as a British Colony) a preponderance."

Professor John Irwin Cooper describes McGill (in the *Dictionary of Canadian Biography*, vol. V) as "an 18th century man," whose economics "were those of the pre–Adam Smith world." And what is to McGill's credit: "He shared the Enlightenment's tolerance of confessional divergences; born into the Church of Scotland, he died an Anglican, and half-way through life married a Roman Catholic." He was so much attached to Montréal that he not only very seldom left it, he also "with characteristic practicality . . . gave land and the nucleus of a university."

No sooner were the effects of the American Revolution beginning to be felt than it was followed by another, no less spectacular—the French Revolution. In Québec, it seems to have all come from Vermont.

Why Vermont? I return to the chat room to find out.

⚜

There are only two participants: Ira Allen (1751–1814) and Edmond-Charles-Edouard Genêt (1763–1834), better known as Citoyen Genêt.

Ira Allen, the brother of Ethan Allen, is a Vermonter, a businessman, a francophile, and not much like his unpredictable brother. Ethan spent his life trying to make his state independent of New York and of the British. His journey to independence took him to Canada in the early years of the American Revolution. There he was most influential in spreading propaganda about the blessings of the Revolution. With his militia, the Green Mountain Boys, which he founded, he invaded Canada at the beginning of the war and was captured by the English when he impulsively attacked Montréal prior to the arrival of Montgomery's army. So angry was he about the "Yorkers," as he called the people of New York, that he had discussions with the British about making Vermont a Canadian province. However, his discomfort with the British quickly put an end to that possibility. In 1779, he was sent back to Vermont, where he developed trade with Québec and sought to expand the territory of Vermont at the expense of Canada.

Ethan's brother, Ira, whom I find in the chat room, wasn't much involved in these activities; but he did favour trade with the English merchants in Montréal and the settlers in the Eastern Townships, of which Vermont is a natural extension.

Citoyen Genêt, a French revolutionary, belonged to the Girondins. He arrived in the United States in 1793 and served as Minister representing revolutionary France. Due to his meddling in the internal affairs of the United States, Washington asked that he be recalled. However, when it was realised that his return to France would mean certain death (the Girondins had now fallen from grace), Washington allowed Genêt to remain. He married an American and kept alive the flame of revolutionary France for the rest of his life.

I sign myself in, pick a colour, and am greeted warmly. I ask my companions if we can talk about their influence on Canadian affairs during the French Revolution. They agree, and I direct my first question to Ira Allen: "Why did the American and the French Revolutions come to Québec through Vermont?"

"Vermont is hemmed in. We need room to expand. So your Eastern Townships are natural to us." He stops, and I suspect he is smiling. "We seize every opportunity we can. Also we trade extensively with your people: timber, potash, grain, and the rest of it. In that way, the principles of our Revolution and of the French Revolution, including those principles identified with what Citoyen Genêt calls the Enlightenment and the Age of

Reason, are passed on to your masses as we push along the St. Lawrence. And that's where the Citoyen comes in."

Gênet picks up the tale. "It was I who drafted an appeal to your people in June 1793. I must say that a young and kindred spirit from Montréal helped me out."

I interrupt him: "That's the document known in English as *The Free French to their Brothers in Canada,* in which you write: 'Imitate the examples of the peoples of America and of France. Break with a government which degenerates from day to day and which has become the cruelest enemy of the liberty of peoples.' "

"Good prose!" Genêt replies. "Je leur ai demandé aussi: 'Canadians arm yourselves; call the Indians to your aid. Count on the support of your neighbours and on that of the French.' Nous sommes vos amis!"

"But you caused enormous trouble."

"Voyons! C'est la vie! La liberté ça se prend! Nobody gives you liberty. You have to seize it."

I reproach him: "Citoyen, between 1793 and 1797, we feared an American invasion from Vermont—and many French ones from Hispaniola or Saint-Domingue. The militia was called out; some of the people refused to bear arms, stating that they were disobeying 'in the name of the people, which is above the law.'"

"Ah! Some learn."

"A Vermont vessel was seized with 20,000 muskets for my people to use should the French Revolution come to our shore. And in 1797, a man was hanged for treason."

"Oh! Yes," intervenes Allen. "David McLane, a Scottish merchant. He was about thirty years old when the hateful English hanged him. He helped us a lot. In fact, he's around. I'll fetch him."

Both Genêt and I wait. I gather that Citoyen hasn't met McLane. No doubt, though, he has heard of him. Suddenly, a green colour appears on the screen with the name "David McLane."

Without hesitation, he tells me: "Let me instruct you, young man. I was born in Scotland, but I live in Providence, R.I. By trade, I'm a merchant and I have many contacts in your country as well as in Vermont. I'm also an enlightened man: I believe in equality, liberty, and fraternity. I have to spread these ideals to oppressed masses. Yours, for instance."

He waits as I digest all this information, then continues. "When I visit your country, particularly Montréal, to sell my lumber, I encounter people hungry to be liberated from the heinous English, whom we have cast away from our land. Many of your people, whether they be French or English, are aware of our Revolution—and of the noble one in France. Many are converts to our ideals. And they want them actualised. Your oppressors, aligned with your priests and seigneurs, oppose them. This is why they create a reign of terror, accusing people of treason, searching for spies under every woman's bed, and conscripting you into their army, so that they can send you to far-away places. You do well to resist them."

"So, Mr. McLane, you came to our country," I find myself saying pompously, "to foment insurrection. In May 1797, a ship's carpenter and member of the Legislative Assembly by the name of John Black reported you to the authorities, who arrested you in his house. When he had met you in the forest as pre-arranged, you told him that you were a 'French general' sent to overthrow the legitimate government of Québec. That subversive act caused you your life."

"That bloody blackguard. A horrible little man. No vision. He lies through it all. He perjures himself at my trial and you use his name and mine in the same sentence? You insult me, sir."

"There were also five other witnesses. Were they liars too?"

"What do you think? Or have your oppressors succeeded in impairing your mind?" After a string of exclamation marks, he goes on: "Of course they lie! No doubt, they will be well rewarded."

I can't resist the riposte: "They were—with land!"

"I am a foreign citizen," David writes. "As such, I can't be charged with treason. But the jury, made up of twelve English oppressors and accomplices, finds me guilty, after only half an hour of deliberation. I die. And here I am. I hope you and your countrymen are free now." The green colour disappears. I'm left alone—Allen and Genët have vanished, too.

⚜

On July 21, 1797, David McLane was taken outside the city walls of Québec and publicly executed. He was first hanged, then his head was cut off and he was disembowelled. His body, however, was not dismembered as the sentence had ordained. The population was horrified, but the government made the most of McLane's "treason," widely distributing a transcript of the trial, and they were determined to uproot other spies. The Anglais helped the States by yelling into the wilderness that the "French" living among them weren't to be trusted. In all this commotion, the priests didn't find it in their interest to be left out. They exhorted their parishioners not to fall to the temptation of sedition, reminding them that "the bonds which attached them to France had been entirely broken, and that all the loyalty and obedience which they formerly owed to the king of France, they now owed to His Britannic Majesty." The people's duty was clear, the bishop thundered, as only bishops can, "to drive the French [revolutionaries] from this Province."

A would-be bishop, Abbé Joseph Octave Plessis (1763–1825), even went so far as to recapitulate what we had become. A newspaper reported:

> Our conquerors, regarded with a suspicious and jealous eye, inspired only horror and a foreboding chill. We could not persuade ourselves that men strange to our land, to our language, to our laws, to our usages, and to our belief would ever be able to give to Canada that which she had just lost in changing masters. Generous nation, which has proved with so much evidence how false were these prejudices; industrious nation, which has brought to bud the riches which this land enclosed within its bosom; charitable nation,

which has just rescued with such humanity the most faithful and most maltreated subjects to the kingdom to which we formerly belonged; kind nation, which gives each day new proofs to Canada of your liberality; no, no, you are not our enemies, nor those of our Holy Religion, which you respect. Pardon this early distrust in a people who still had not the happiness to know you; and if, after having learned of the overturn of the state and of the destruction of the true Faith in France, and after having tasted during thirty-five years the mildness of your rule, some amongst us are still found so blind or so evil-intentioned as to entertain the same suspicions and to inspire in the people criminal desires to return to their ancient masters, blame not on the whole what is only the vice of a small number.

The records do not show if the parishioners left the church in disgust. However, many such examples of episcopal and clerical foolishness abound in the annals of the history of Québec, even to the Révolution tranquille of the 1960s. The Abbé Plessis, of course, became a bishop.

As for the Assembly, filled as it was with clerics disguised as laymen, fearful of losing their position and perks, the members took money from the taxpayers to help Great Britain defeat France.

The French Revolution broke the ties that bound us to France. Furthermore, just as we inherited the negativity of the American Revolution, we inherited the Jansenism and the Ultramontanism that afflicted those who rejected the French Revolution, particularly in the ranks of the clergy. Émigré-priests arrived here in great numbers and drew us back into the confines of the ancien régime. We remained there for over a century and a half, during which time untold damage was done to the development and survival of the Québec people. We became fearful of change, servile in our acceptance of authority, xenophobic in the defence of our rights, and distrustful of modernity.

Yet it wasn't all negative. The émigrés, clerical and lay, brought culture and intellectual power. Dedicated to education, they spent their lives among us fostering it, a benefit we too often rejected. In the space of thirty years—between 1802 and 1832—they help found and staff many classical colleges, and they furthered the cause of local/parochial education.

In the final analysis, though, we were "much tinged with Yankee politics" and much influenced by republican France. Populism reared its head, and it couldn't be chopped off. However, it would have to be suppressed—and that is the story of the following two hundred years.

Around the beginning of the 19th century, the mission of anglicizing the "ignorant" French-speaking people began in earnest. The Château Clique—made up of English merchants, Loyalist hangers-on, and the not-so-Christian Anglican bishop of Montréal—was born. (A word about the Reverend Jacob Mountain [1749–1825]: he was the first Anglican bishop of Québec, taking up his task in 1793. He was a superb preacher and indefatigable in the pursuit of the interests of his Church, which he considered to be the "Established Church" of Canada. However, he wasn't able to convince anyone of the value of that exercise, and his attempts to limit the power and freedom of the Roman Catholic Church failed.)

The Château Clique wasn't alone in trying to marginalise the Canadiens. It found collaborators in "les vendus," habitants who had been bought by perks, positions, and benefits of patronage.

To the English-speaking authorities, anglicization was necessary because Québec "is much too French for a British colony. To unfrenchify it as much as possible . . . should be our primary purpose." So proclaimed an English newspaper from Québec. Unfrenchify the Canadiens also meant, as Thomas Chapais has remarked in his *Cours d'histoire du Canada*, "garrotter l'Église catholique et pousser à l'apostasie les Canadiens" (muzzling the Catholic Church in order to force the habitants to deny their faith).

There was another reason as well, and it lay in the Constitutional Act of 1791. Pitt's central principle in that Act was that the French-speaking and Catholic-British subjects living in Québec would have some opportunity to govern themselves. To that end, a Legislative Assembly was created, and since those new British subjects formed the majority of the population in the province, they would form the majority in the Assembly and act accordingly. For the principle to work without repudiating the rights and privileges of the

Executive Council and of the Legislative Council, it was necessary to make the three institutions work together "without losing sight," to quote Chapais again, "that the central fact was the Imperial Parliament had wanted to institute in Canada the principle of the governance of the majority." The Anglais didn't fancy the application of that principle. Their agenda demanded an emphasis on the industrial and commercial development of Lower Canada. To that end, it was necessary to curtail the power of the Assembly, filled as it was with a majority of lawyers and notaries belonging to a culture and a way of life, a religion and a language, that they considered inimical to their mercantile interests, to their attachment to British institutions, to their loyalty to the British Crown, and to their power as conquerors. That fear of the Assembly was, of course, irrational and a camouflage for racism. After all, this Tory Party controlled the Executive Council and the Legislative Council. It could achieve practically all that it wanted.

Naturally, the governor and other officials sent to Québec to administer the affairs of the province were the political allies of the Tory Party, especially between 1807 and the Troubles of 1837. For the most part, these personages, by their actions, decisions, and pronouncements, intensified the state of dissatisfaction and disharmony between the various segments of the population.

In those thirty years, only two or three of the eight governors proved to be decent, trying to hold back the tide through conciliation. The others were martinets, political thugs, and the chief architects of the violence and the loss of property and life in 1837 and 1838. Sir James Henry Craig initiated a reign of terror during his term of office (1807–11). Sir George Prevost spoke French, had colonial administrative experience, and spent the two years he served in Canada embroiled in the War of 1812, leaving him little time for conciliation. Sir John Coape Sherbrooke devoted his term (1816–18) to making peace, a process that gained him the loyalty and affection of the king's subjects in Canada and that caused the deterioration of his health, forcing him to resign. Charles Lennox, 4th Duke of Richmond, was a silly man who came here in 1818, after an undistinguished career in the British Army and parliament, not to mention his year here, during which he managed to insult all those he had come to pacify; he died of rabies in 1819, after his pet fox (who probably understood his personality better than most) bit him. George

Ramsay, 9th Earl of Dalhousie, was the most authoritarian governor we had, exercising his functions from 1820 until his recall in 1828, after innumerable clashes with the Assembly and especially its speaker, Louis-Joseph Papineau. Sir James Kempt wasn't really a governor but the administrator of the Government of Canada between 1828 and 1830; in that capacity he wasn't very dangerous—in fact, he was able to bring some harmony between the various branches of the government. Matthew Whitworth-Aylmer came to our shores in 1830 and, even though he wasn't well served by the Assembly, which became more and more difficult to deal with as his term progressed, his dismissal in 1835 was justified, for he consistently failed to reconcile the warring factions. Finally, Archibald Acheson, 2nd Earl of Gosford, tried hard between 1835 and 1837, but he was too late to achieve the necessary peace.

To defend themselves from cultural and national alienation, the Canadiens resorted to shoring up their nationalism—or sense of collective appartenance.

That some form of *Canadienisme* existed prior to the "Conquest" of 1760 cannot be denied. It expressed itself as a community of persons who shared a common heritage, lived in a specific geographic area, spoke a common language, had a recognisable temperament and spirit—along with a distinct culture, traditions, laws, and ways of doing things—and possessed a *vouloir vivre collectif* (a will to live as a distinct people). Nor can anyone successfully question that what is called the "Conquest" resulted in a particular way of looking at ourselves—a sense of being an unfinished people or one prone to being victimised by the "conquerors," whoever they may be at any given time. At the beginning of the 19th century, social and economic circumstances led to a political crisis that hasn't been entirely resolved to this very day—and to the acceptance of a nationalism that became combative, self-centred, exclusive, and conservative, as the years and crises passed between 1800 and 1960.

For the years following the "Conquest," the Church was the only institution of the people that remained familiar. In time, it became a refuge around which the people grew, awakening to their sense of identity. The Church was conservative, authoritarian, and hierarchical. It controlled, as well, the temporal via the spiritual. It had been all that in the days of New France, but after 1759, seeing its duty as the protector of the faith (and, in some way, the language and way of life) of the people, it became even more involved in the daily activities of the Canadiens. Compassionate, it knew how to temper the rod with the velvet glove. Finally, to protect the people, it saw its political role as rooting obedience—to the "legitimate" authority of the British—deep in the people's psyche. That it brought about its own survival, numerous perks, and much power was the natural outcome of the episcopal and clerical strategy of those days.

Between 1763 and 1837, a variety of circumstances brought about the violence of 1837–38.

As we've seen, the Royal Proclamation of 1763 created a province that was much smaller than the original territory of New France, centred as it was along the St. Lawrence River. Eleven years later, the Quebec Act re-extended the territory to almost its original size and shape. But, by the Treaty of Paris (1783), which ended the War of the American Revolution, the boundary of my province was altered again, being pushed farther north. However, for the next thirteen years, until the Jay Treaty of 1796, Great Britain (therefore Montréal) had access to the fur-trading posts south of the Great Lakes. Then, in 1791, Québec lost its western territory with the creation of Upper and Lower Canada.

Those changes in the boundaries disrupted the livelihood of the Canadiens, which was primarily based on the fur trade, even though other exports, especially wheat products, contributed to the overall economy of the province. However, the fur trade was what they knew. They had portaged, hunted, and been wounded, killed, flourished, and reduced to destitution by it. In time, they considered themselves the owners of "the West" —what was called the North-West, the entire territory between Lake Superior and the Rockies, which was in fact the territory of Québec, explored and linked to the colony along the St. Lawrence by the voyageurs and the fur traders.

After the events of 1760, the habitants' capacity to exploit that fur trade was considerably reduced, mainly because of the non-availability of capital and credit from a friendly metropolis, not to mention the sorry state of public and private finances in Québec. Furthermore, the authorities in Québec had become more receptive to the economic aspirations of the *Anglais*. And so, between 1760 and 1790, the English merchants of Montréal acquired practically all of the fur trade of North America, although the *Canadiens* continued to be involved in it to a certain degree. A few participated with their capital, and some as clerks, but it was as *voyageurs* that the *Canadiens* made their mark.

The *voyageurs*—those characters who have entered the romantic mythology of our country—were young men paddling canoes in the fur caravans of the 19th century. They traversed almost an entire continent, living lives filled with perilous and glorious adventures, incredibly hard labour, and a camaraderie that wasn't only boisterous but caring. They are the early heroes of Canada—as the *coureurs de bois* were the heroes of New France—and the prototype of what a *Canadien* was and is.

To conquer the West and the fur trade, the Montréal merchants gave themselves the North West Company, which dominated the mercantile life of Canada from the 1780s to 1821. One name stands out when referring to that company: Alexander Mackenzie (1764–1820). He set out to find the sea beyond the mountains in 1789, but the river that was supposed to lead to the Pacific Ocean actually led to the Arctic. In his honour, it is known to us as the Mackenzie River. At over four thousand kilometres, it is the second longest river in North America.

Still determined to find the Pacific, though, he headed westward again in 1793. He crossed the Great Divide, discovered the Fraser River, and pioneered the first overland route to the Pacific. It is said that no harm came to his crews and that he never fired a shot in anger at the many Natives he met along the way. In 1795, he returned to Montréal, and four years later he was in England, where he published his *Voyages* and was knighted for all his efforts. But he didn't live to witness his dream of bringing the North West Company and the Hudson's Bay Company together. He died on his estate near Dunkeld, Scotland, in 1820.

The rivalry between the two companies was intense, leading to violence, seizures of goods, and the Seven Oaks Incident, on June 19, 1816—a massacre in which twenty men of the Hudson's Bay Company were killed by Métis who were working for, or were allies of, the North West Company. Peace had to come, especially after the rivalry caused profits to plummet. The Colonial Office stepped in, and Parliament gave exclusive trade to the Hudson's Bay Company and devised a coalition of sorts between the partners of both companies. All this occurred a year after Mackenzie's death.

Between 1760 and the beginning of the 19th century, the economy had two tracks: one, dominated by the English, took it towards commerce with the mother country; the other, followed by the habitants and the seigneurs, was agricultural, artisanal, and oriented towards the local market. That domestic market was not insignificant. The increase in Québec's population did the trick—161,000 by 1790—the vast majority of whom were pure laine. That had a considerable impact on the growth of the domestic market; immigration into Québec had little to do with it.

However, in the first thirty years of the 19th century, several factors contributed to the weakening of the active participation of Canadiens in the overall economy of Lower Canada. First, they had only a secondary role in the fur trade. Second, they didn't participate as investors or developers in the timber trade, which became so important after 1806, but they did supply most of the labour force. Third, they lost their international agricultural markets, which had developed steadily since the 1730s—particularly with the West Indies and, then, after the events of 1760, with Europe and Great Britain. During the first decades of the 19th century, agricultural production fell sharply because of droughts and the emphasis, in Lower Canada, on subsistence farming. This deficit had to be remedied through imports from Upper Canada, causing a serious decrease in the standard of living.

What can be described as overpopulation didn't help either. The French-Canadian birthrate was about fifty per thousand; the mortality rate was half that, which meant a doubling of the population about every twenty-five years. This massive increase and the seigneurs' determination to benefit from the boom in forest products naturally led to a decreasing availability of good lands. And this resulted in a third of the rural population becoming indigent. To find refuge, many moved to the towns of Lower Canada and to the United States.

In the late 18th century, and moreso in the years that followed, the British government, in order to swamp the Canadiens, vigorously pursued a policy of immigration of English-speaking people to Lower Canada. After all, it was preferable to have subjects "of English stock, professing the same religion, speaking the same language," and "who would therefore be more easily assimilated and would become better subjects than those which we now possess." This policy was also encouraged because British speculators (and their allies in Lower and Upper Canada) made fortunes in land speculation. In the Eastern Townships, especially, the land was fertile, well watered, and accessible; by 1805, five thousand had settled there. After 1816, a great number of British immigrants also arrived, looking for jobs and lands.

By 1831, Québec was 45 percent English-speaking, Montréal 61 percent. The new immigrants (Anglais) took 50 percent of the available menial (day labour) jobs in Québec, 63 percent in Montréal.

Canadiens weren't pleased with this government-encouraged immigration. They had looked towards the Eastern Townships to relieve the problem of land for those unable to obtain it on the seigneuries, and they had wanted the day-labouring jobs in the cities to alleviate employment problems. And, as if events weren't unfolding badly enough, epidemics of cholera reached their shores with the immigrants. The first occurred in 1832, another followed two years later, and more would devastate the country between 1849 and 1854. All in all about twenty thousand people would perish. Suffering and courage, fear and anxiety, anger and revenge, and the inevitable death toll became an increasing part of daily life.

It was easy and self-serving to blame the immigrants: "When I see my country in mourning and my native land nothing but a vast cemetery, I ask what has been the cause of all these disasters? And the voice of my father, my brother and my beloved mother, the voices of thousands of my fellow citizens respond from their tombs: It is émigration." The following remarks of a nationaliste were published in the Montréal *Gazette* of August 21, 1832: "It was not enough to send among us avaricious egotics without any spirit of liberty . . . they must rid themselves of their beggars and cast them by thousands on our shores; they must send miserable beings, who after [having] partaken of the bread of our children, will subject them to the horrors following upon hunger and misery; they must do still more, they must send us in their trains of pestilence and death."

The article found fertile ground. The loss of economic power and independence, the demands of the new economy for large investments in road and canal constructions, tariffs, the growing Canadien proletariat, the unavailability of lands, particularly in the Eastern Townships, the ever-increasing foreign immigration with its epidemics, and the antics of the Château Clique all caused the Canadiens to conclude that the Anglais had a plot to destroy them once and for all.

But before those epidemics and many other events, they helped fight a war in the early 19th century.

On June 18, 1812, the United States declared war on Great Britain. Canada couldn't escape being involved, as the Americans were determined to capture it. "A mere matter of marching," reasoned Thomas Jefferson.

The battles of the war were fought mostly in what is now Ontario. However, the Americans twice launched attacks against Montréal. One of these led to the Battle of Châteauguay, on October 26, 1813—Châteauguay being a river some fifty kilometres south of Montréal. Under the command of Charles-Michel d'Irumberry de Salaberry, the Voltigeurs Canadiens, a light-infantry corps formed shortly before the beginning of the hostilities, drove an American army of four thousand men across the river. To confuse the Americans, they blew horns and made loud noises in the woods, pretending they were far more numerous than they actually were. Two weeks later, the same unit participated in the decisive Battle of Chrysler's Farm, near Morrisburg, in Upper Canada.

The Canadiens, a group of voyageurs this time, also helped to rid "western Canada" of the Americans: they seized a fort on the upper Mississippi and repelled an attack on Fort Michilimackinac by capturing two warships on Lake Huron.

But 1812 was not 1775. All the elements of the society of Lower Canada coalesced to defend the country: the clergy, because legally constituted authority must be supported; the merchants, because the benefits of the British Empire were far superior to the Americans' "manifest destiny"; the bourgeoisie, because they valued the British parliamentary system—even if it wasn't as yet complete—as superior to the American model; and the general French-speaking population, because of the nationalism growing in their hearts and their need to defend their interests, along with protecting their cultural heritage. For all of the above reasons, neutrality wasn't possible in 1812.

Although the war was mostly fought in Upper Canada, repercussions were felt in Lower Canada and among the Canadiens. The historian Fernand Ouellet enumerates the following consequences: greater commercial exchanges between Lower Canada and Upper Canada became the order of the day; a possible St. Lawrence Seaway entered the national agenda; and banking institutions were found to be a necessity. Furthermore, it confirmed once and for all the failure of the Anglican Church to become the established church, making the Catholic bishops and clergy victorious in that long conflict. Above all, the war stimulated what Ouellet calls le nationalisme canadien-français. Although Thomas Chapais might have been exaggerating, he wrote the following about *la victoire canadienne-française*—the Battle of Châteauguay: "It was our vengeance. Châteauguay was the affirmation of our undeniable loyalty and of our ardent patriotism. Châteauguay was the heroic manifestation of our national will."

Finally, the war may have fostered in the hearts and minds of many the idea or the possibility that the diverse peoples of Lower Canada—different in religion, values, and language as they were—need not be enemies. If that is the case, then it made possible the collaborations of LaFontaine and Baldwin and of Macdonald and Cartier, collaborations that illuminated the second half of the 19th century.

After the War of 1812, the Canadiens began to challenge more rigorously those whom they came to identify clearly as their enemies. To that end, they gave themselves a party, a newspaper, and a leader.

The Parti Canadien was the first political party that combined the aspirations of the Canadiens. Its founding catalyst was Pierre-Stanislas Bédard (1762–1829), lawyer, politician, journalist, judge, and perhaps the most well-read person in Québec. He was also quite ugly, awkward, socially inept, and timid, particularly with his wife. In 1792, he became a member of the Legislative Assembly for Northumberland, which was situated on the north shore of the St. Lawrence, down from Québec and the Côte de Beaupré—a constituency that had an entirely French-speaking population, to whom the British authorities, as in many other instances, denied the pleasure of a French name. Bédard remained as their representative until 1808, when he sought and won the Lower Town of Québec, retiring from politics to become a judge in 1812.

He was convinced that British institutions were the best to govern what he called the "nascent people" to whom he belonged. In the newspaper *Le Canadien*, which, with a group of colleagues, he founded in 1806, he wrote that the British Constitution was "perhaps the only one under which the interests and rights of the various classes composing society are so carefully arranged, so wisely set off against one another and linked to one another as a whole, that they illuminate and sustain one another through the very conflict which results from the simultaneous exercise of the powers that are entrusted" to the members of the various classes.

It goes without saying that the French Revolution had no message for him.

That appreciation of the British political way of life was one of the three fundamental principles of the Parti Canadien and of the Parti Patriote, which succeeded the former.

The second principle, which also came from Bédard, was that the Assembly, in concert with the Crown, was dominant. What he was talking about was ministerial responsibility—or Responsible Government. In that sense, he predated Baldwin and LaFontaine, who brought it about in the late 1840s. As Professor Fernand Ouellet has written: "Pierre-Stanislas Bédard, whose name is closely linked with the birth of political parties in Lower Canada and of Québec nationalism, was the first person in the British empire to formulate in a coherent manner the theory of ministerial responsibility."

During the debate as to the language to be used in the Assembly in the early 1790s, Bédard, in a way, gave the Parti Canadien its third principle, by asking a simple question: "Is it not ridiculous to wish to make language the test of a people's loyalty?" Out of that question, which is the source of many of our conflicts about national unity, arose the notion of the existence of the nation canadienne (or the French-Canadian nation), which some, to the detriment of many, have, in our day, transformed into the nation québécoise.

What were the identifiable characteristics of this "nation"? To Bédard, they were as follows: Catholic, French-speaking, agricultural in economic endeavour within the seigneurial system, and adherent to the *coutumes de Paris* or French civil law. The natural leaders of that nation were the members of the bourgeoisie; that is, the seigneurs, affluent and influential entrepreneurs, and, above all, the professional middle class. Aligned with the clergy, whose responsibility it was to keep the "masses" in line, this bourgeoisie would safeguard the rights of the people and the survival of the nation, while maintaining a democratic paternalism in accordance with the British parliamentary system. British power would also be used to provide the necessary protection from the Americans.

To a very large degree, these characteristics endure to this day.

Founded on an ad hoc basis at the beginning of the 19th century to regroup the French-Canadian middle class or bourgeoisie—that coterie of "six petty shopkeepers, a Blacksmith, a Miller, and fifteen ignorant peasants . . . a doctor or Apothecary, twelve Canadian Avocats and Notaries," as someone described it at the time—the Parti Canadien did attract some Anglais, who were reformers, and some Irish patriots. Its platform was simple: to defend the rights and the security of the people and the social and political prerogatives of the bourgeoisie through ministerial responsibility (Responsible Government) and the control of patronage. Bédard was its first leader; but, after the War of 1812, Louis-Joseph Papineau succeeded him.

Bédard was a torn man. His marriage was essentially on the rocks, his financial resources practically non-existent, and his views resulted in his being sent to jail for almost a year, in 1810–11. Then, this man, "possessed by the passion of politics," fell victim to the lure of patronage, accepting a judgeship in 1812. From the bench, he watched the Parti Canadien, which he had founded, transform itself into a nationalist movement, as the demographic, economic, and social conditions of the Canadiens disintegrated.

However, it was under the aegis of the Parti Canadien that Papineau and all the others—including Bédard—battled governors, the Château Clique, and the British authorities, to prevent the union of the two

155

Canadas, as proposed in 1822. It wasn't a new idea: it had been suggested in 1805, in 1807, and again in 1810. This time, though, it was more serious and dangerous.

The British authorities, along with others in "Canada," welcomed the union proposal, in order to rein in the Legislative Assemblies of both Upper and Lower Canada. Both colonies were quarrelling with their respective governors and Legislative Councils over the control of the public purse, the power of the Château Clique in Lower Canada and that of the Family Compact in Upper Canada, and the division of import duties. In the view of the British, one governing authority would remedy that situation. Furthermore, the union of both colonies would also permit the full exercise of the "British way of life" over the recalcitrant Canadiens, who would be turned into a minority.

When, in September 1822, the news arrived in Québec that the British government had introduced such a bill, all hell broke loose. Canadiens and some "Britishers" joined forces to oppose the bill and the "unionists" who desired it. Resolutions of protest were passed, and 60,000 people signed a petition, which Papineau and the politician/journalist John Neilson took to Great Britain in January 1823. As Mason Wade has remarked, this was the "first major collaboration of Canadians of different ethnic backgrounds in the common interest."

Born in Scotland, John Neilson immigrated to Canada in his fourteenth year. Seven years later, he succeeded his brother as publisher-editor of the bilingual *Québec Gazette*, which he ran for fifty years. A supporter of Responsible Government, he formed an alliance with Papineau, which endured until after 1831, when Papineau became more despondent and discouraged—in the face of the growing difficulties with the British authorities both in Canada and in Great Britain—and turned to encouraging violence. Moreover, the temperament of both men differed substantially: "You are disposed," Papineau wrote to Neilson in 1831, "to believe that the government can be pushed into the right path and will follow it passably well; I am disposed to believe that it goes from bad to worse." History doesn't hesitate to suggest that Neilson was right.

Meanwhile, though, in July 1828, the British authorities, for reasons that had nothing to do with Lower Canada, declined to give life to the union of the two Canadas. Papineau proclaimed that he had won and, through him, the Canadiens. However, this was not the case. The Château Clique continued to dominate the political, social, and economic agenda, and the French-speaking majority became more determined than ever to win its case.

As the movement towards a more defined French-Canadian nationalism progressed—due to the defence of the homeland in the War of 1812 and over the Union Bill—the Parti Canadien changed its name to Parti Patriote after 1826. Its members continued to control the Assembly and push for ministerial responsibility. The majority of the membership certainly weren't radical. To keep their following, conservatism was embraced as a virtue: the maintenance of the seigneurial system, support for agriculture rather than commerce, respect for the Church and the clergy, no cosying up to the Americans and republicanism, and, above all, no violent tactics.

The party's centre of power, however, moved from Québec to Montréal, and this move had serious consequences. It became a Montréal party ruled by a political mafia associated closely with its leader, Papineau. It exercised a ruthless control over the members of the party, which grouped together many of the diverse elements of the society of Lower Canada: the French-speaking bourgeoisie, the English liberals, the Irish, many of the American farmers who had settled in the Eastern Townships, and the "peasants."

In 1827, a year after the birth of the Parti Patriote, Ludger Duvernay, a follower of Papineau and a member of the party, purchased the Montréal newspaper *La Minerve*, which another Patriote member had founded a year or so before. Duvernay transformed it into "the national newspaper" of French Canada, and the principal organ of the party.

The party, with a charismatic leader, a platform, an effective party discipline, and a great following, was ready.

Until the 1830s, there was not much to show for the struggle. Britain appeared deaf to the demands of the politicians of Lower Canada—as it did to those of Upper Canada. So a new strategy had to be developed. It was simple and natural: the Assembly systematically obstructed government proposals—refusing to vote and thus paralysing the administration and grinding public works to a halt. But here again, Great Britain wouldn't make the necessary reforms to the system and, to make matters worse, it encouraged, through its officials, the development of an ethnic struggle between the majority represented by the Parti Patriote and the British minority with its British Party. Violence was just around the corner.

Meanwhile, the economic situation disintegrated considerably, with many Canadiens finding themselves on the verge of starvation.

The result of this deterioration was twofold: something drastic had to be attempted, and the leadership of the Parti Patriote began to lose its faith and confidence in British institutions and to look elsewhere for the realisation of its political and national goals.

On February 17, 1834, the Parti Patriote issued its ultimatum. On that day, it introduced, in the Legislative Assembly, its Ninety-Two Resolutions, most of them drafted by Papineau. The Resolutions are a mishmash of varied objectives and a catalogue of grievances and affirmations of nationalism. Essentially, Papineau and his allies asked that Responsible Government be introduced in to Lower Canada and that legislative councillors be elected. In opposition to the Resolutions and their proponents, the "Tories" organised themselves in order not to submit any longer to the "domination of a party adverse to emigration, to commerce, to internal improvements, and to all those interests which maybe regarded as British."

The Resolutions were sent to Great Britain, commissioners were appointed to review the situation yet again, and, on March 2, 1837, the British government, through Russell's Ten Resolutions, handed down its answer: NO. To make matters worse, it allowed the governor to seize the revenues of Lower Canada without the consent of the Assembly.

The die was cast. All that remained was "agitate! Agitate!! AGITATE!!!" The agitation was to become a rebellion—perhaps, a revolution.

In 1806, to defend their people against the Tories' derisive and racist attacks, a group of Canadiens, again led by Pierre-Stanislas Bédard, founded a newspaper called *Le Canadien*. The newspaper abhorred the often-repeated allegations that the "Conquered" had no rights but only privileges that could only be exercised in the English language. It rejected the utility of the Legislative Council, packed as it was with "vendus," selected appointees, and merchants, and it opposed the dissolution of the Legislative Assembly at the governor's whim. It stood for Responsible Government, control of the civil list (government expenses), and the rights and privileges of the bourgeoisie. This version of *Le Canadien* endured until 1810. However, it had a second existence from 1817 to 1825, and a third one after 1831. The dominant figure of the last two incarnations of the paper was Étienne Parent (1802–74).

Étienne Parent, journalist, lawyer, member of the Legislative Assembly, public servant, and essayist, was a most remarkable man who, as of yet, has not been accorded the tribute of a full-scale biography.

He became known as *"le Père Parent,"* for, as Professor Jean-Charles Falardeau states in his fine entry on Parent in the *DCB*, vol. II, he appeared so much as the "prototype" and "example" of what we ought to be. To Falardeau and many others, Parent "incarnated," as did no one else of his time, "the ambitions of a new social type, that of the intellectual and political élite, which at the turn of the 19th century was replacing the gentleman class of land-owning seigneurs, and, along with the ecclesiastical leaders, resolutely taking hold of the destiny of the French-Canadian people." It was Parent more than anyone else in the first half of the 19th century who gave his people their national objectives.

His physique was as strong and powerful as his intellect. His hands and brow were those of a farmer, marked by sweat and effort. The spoken word didn't come to him easily; his eyes were permanently focused on some inner thought or conclusion; and he carried himself with aplomb and authority. He is said to have been endowed "with a Herculean constitution," working eighteen hours most days.

In 1819, while still a student at the Petit Séminaire de Québec, Parent began to write for *Le Canadien*. Three years later, at the advanced age of twenty, he became its editor. During those crucial days and months when the debate of the Union Act raged all about him, he was influential in bringing about the collapse of the effort to unite both Lower and Upper Canada into one legislature. His messages, strongly and effectively stated in *Le Canadien*, argued without respite that the Constitution of 1791 had to be respected, and that the flouted rights of the people had to be restored and safeguarded. Unfortunately, he lost his job in 1825, when the owners of the paper closed it down.

For the next seven years, he wandered about, occupying his time with a large number of tasks: he served as editor of the French section of the *Gazette de Québec*, which had become the organ of the Parti Canadien in 1825; at the same time, he served as the French translator and law officer of the Legislative Assembly, studied law (becoming a lawyer in 1829), married, and, in time, became the father of five daughters and one son. (One of his daughters, Marie-Augustine, married the historian Benjamin Sulte three years before her father died in Ottawa in 1874.)

On May 7, 1831, with borrowed capital, he revived *Le Canadien* as a bi-weekly. Devoting it to "notre langue, nos institutions, nos lois." He wrote: "It is the lot of the Canadiens to have not only to preserve civil liberty, but also to struggle for existence as a people. . . . No middle course: if we do not govern ourselves we shall be governed. . . . Our politics, our aims, our senti-ments, our wishes and desires are to maintain all that constitutes our exis-tence as a people, and, as a means to that end, to maintain all the civil and political rights that are the prerogative of an English country." To make cer-tain that this path was followed, he wrote many articles explaining the British parliamentary system, discussing ministerial responsibility, emphasising dan-gers that lurked in the shadows of the Château Clique, and advocating con-stitutional means as the best way to pursue the desired political and constitutional goals. These articles and editorials made him the intellectual leader of the Parti Patriote. He was accepted then, for the vast majority of the members of the party were "constitutionalists."

However, after 1833, matters deteriorated, making life most unpredictable. When, in 1835, the leadership of the Parti Patriote began to preach the possi-bility of violence against the constitutional authority, Parent was one of the few dissenters, and he spent the next two years insisting on non-violent means. His message was clear: changes to the constitution were urgently necessary, and the peaceful struggle against the nefarious government of the Château Clique had to be carried on, for it was vital. At the same time, he continued what he had begun so long before: defining the constitutional and political reforms that Great Britain had to sanction. But he wasn't listened to, and the rhetoric became more and more bellicose on the both sides of the great divide. He condemned them all. This won him the enmity of the leadership of the

Parti Patriote. In 1835, he broke with them and they, in turn, condemned him as a traitor.

Yet, many of his ideas found their way into the Ninety-Two Resolutions of 1834, and he placed his hope in them. But, as we've seen, the British government rejected them in the spring of 1837, making inevitable numerous public protests, which took place in the summer and autumn of that year, followed by bloody clashes in November and December. A month before the fatal mistake of the British government, he wrote: "We are ready for independence; let us have patience, let us prove ourselves, the law will resume its course . . . let us work for improvements [in the constitution]; let us educate the people in its affairs; let us open the schools that have been closed as the result of political upheaval." A month later, he was at it again: "We impute to them [those advocating violence] the blame for all the blood that will be shed . . . the wailing of widows, mothers, and orphans, and the lamentations of a whole people brought to social abasement."

And the day before the hostilities broke out at Saint-Denis, in the valley of the Richelieu River, he could hardly contain his rage and contempt for those who were leading the people down a gully full of suppression: "After the sword of the soldier has cut off the thousand heads of anarchy, then will come the law, which will arm the government with repressive measures that will necessarily retard the progress of the liberal cause. Thus we shall perhaps soon see the government vested with extraordinary powers which its creatures will certainly abuse. What will have caused that? The fatal agitation which has been imprudently aroused in this country, and which the leaders are no longer able to control. Once again, let this be at least a lesson for future, if Providence reserves for us a future, which we must still hope."

Then, shattered by the bloodshed, he was silent for two months.

Louis-Joseph Papineau (1786–1871), seigneur, lawyer, politician, orator, rebel, exile, pontificator, nationalist, deist, and coward—a man of contradictions and of eternal discontent. This was the leader whom the Canadiens gave themselves to from 1814 to 1837.

Papineau was born in Montréal in the family of a seigneur (the Seigneurie de la Petite-Nation, now Montebello). His father was a notary, a member of the Legislative Assembly, a merchant, and a man of moderate liberalism. His mother was pious and devout to a fault, cold and authoritarian, and obsessed with the pettiness of daily life.

Given a good education with the Sulpician Fathers of Montréal and then with the priests of the Petit Séminaire de Québec, Louis-Joseph became what they taught him: traditional in his social thinking, authoritarian and hierarchical in his political thought, and non-entrepreneurial in his economic pursuits. His destiny was marked: unwilling to enter the priesthood, he was made ready to join the ranks of the liberal professions.

It was in the Québec seminary that Papineau said he lost his faith, becoming a deist—that is, a believer in a God-Creator, since nature and reason demanded it, but not in supernatural revelation. On his deathbed, he would say, "I believe in the existence of God and in the moral obligations of man; but, I cannot make myself believe in revelation." Even when he was refused a resting place in the consecrated ground of his funeral chapel, a historical monument on the Montebello estate, next to his parents, his wife, and his children, he would not relent. Although he was unable to have a religious ceremony, he did receive a civil one and was interred where he wanted to be.

Why this denial of his ancestral Christian faith? It's hard to say. He read an enormous amount: Voltaire, the Encyclopaedists, and many others of the Enlightenment. Perhaps it is there that can be found the basis for his decision. Maybe the pretensions of organised religion bored him, even though he never denied the place of it in the make-up of his people, nor the place of the episcopacy and clergy in the reality of everyday life and of the national structure. Or perhaps his rejection of Catholicism satisfied his deeply embedded anti-clericalism. For he was, in fact, "violently anticlerical," as Fernand Ouellet puts it. Papineau never hesitated to criticise the clerical autocrats for putting every aspect of human life on the turntable of religion. He also railed against the privileges of the Church and, above all, against the union of Church and State. For him, the clerical certainly was not a state within a state and it had no right to "dictate how a part of the fruits of the labour of citizens should be employed." However, he never attempted to uproot or even modify the status of the Catholic Church in the mind and in the reality of the Canadiens. That would be too dangerous—and perhaps even play into the hands of his enemies.

On the other hand, his deism was—just maybe—an element of his eternal discontent. Perhaps.

Among the books to be found on the table beside his deathbed (in addition to the works of Seneca and of Marcus Aurelius, the poetry of Horace, the history of the Goths, and the life of George Washington) was *The Imitation of Jesus Christ*!

After much procrastination and indecision, Papineau was admitted to the bar of Lower Canada in 1810, at the age of twenty-four. A year before, he had been elected to the Legislative Assembly, where he was to remain until his flight to the United States and his exile in France after the Rebellion of 1837. During that time, he became leader of the Parti Canadien (around 1814) and, later, of the Parti Patriote. For twenty years, from 1815 to 1835, he was also speaker of the Assembly. During the first five years of his speakership, he didn't take an active part in the deliberations of the Assembly beyond those demanded by his duties. His spent his spare time studying history, reading all he could, and assimilating knowledge from a considerable number of sources. He became an expert in constitutional law and, now and then, worked at being a lawyer.

Julie Bruneau, the daughter of a Québec fur merchant, married Papineau on April 29, 1818. Between 1819 and 1834, they had nine children, one of whom, the youngest, Marie-Julie Azélie, married the artist Napoléon Bourassa, and their son Henri Bourassa (1868–1952) became an eminent politician.

Julie Bruneau Papineau was strong, opinionated, and overly religious. Often ill, she also suffered from melancholia, which frequently made her impossible to live with. On the other hand, she was devoted to her husband and to her children. During Papineau's exile, she joined him in France from 1839 until 1843. In 1843, she returned to Montréal and Montebello, while Papineau continued to live in France until 1845. Their living in France was painful for both of them, away from their families, friends, and former colleagues. They were also poor. He could have returned to Canada in 1842, but he chose instead to remain in exile. In 1844, he was given a full amnesty, and, a year later, upon his wife's insistence, he came back to Canada.

Professor Ouellet writes that Papineau's choice of a wife "who projected an image rather like his mother's may be considered significant" in understanding Papineau's character.

In 1817, his father sold him the seigneurie, Petite Nation, in Montebello, a property of some 7,200 hectares. He liked being a seigneur. It provided him with prestige, power, and a good living. He looked after his affairs with care, especially after his return to Canada from France, and he didn't hesitate to prosecute his farmers who didn't meet their obligations or who frustrated his ambition. He was, in more ways than one, a lumber baron, exploiting the rich timber of his fief without a thought to tomorrow. After he built himself a fine *manoir*, he nevertheless had great difficulty convincing his wife and most of his children to live with him. They preferred the city. There is no need to add that, all through his public life, he opposed every attempt to abolish the seigneurial system. For a supposed democrat, liberal, and social reformer, this attitude is most revealing.

During the first fifteen years of his political career, he was a constitutionalist, deeply in favour of British institutions. He was, as well, a nationalist, dedicated to linguistic survival and the maintenance of traditional institutions, none of which were liberal or democratic in any sense of those words. To succeed in these nationalist goals, however, he was prepared to use the inherent powers of the Assembly—particularly those of obstruction—to achieve his ends, while convincing the British authorities to expand upon these powers through the election of legislative councillors and of ministerial responsibility.

But after 1830, he changed. He became convinced that it was the republicanism of the United States, and not the monarchical-representative institutions of Great Britain, that would ensure the survival of the *petite nation* on the shores of the St. Lawrence.

Why this about-face? We have, in the midst of his political and social thoughts and actions, some indications. When he went to Great Britain in 1823 to battle the Union Bill of 1822, the pomp, wealth, and circumstance of the aristocracy scandalised him, and the poverty of the urban masses shocked him. Perhaps he never forgot that. Maybe he also saw the same pattern in his homeland: a rich and privileged élite and a poor citizenry, made poorer by the rapid deterioration of the economy. Maybe the over-crowding in the liberal professions disturbed him, and he sought other out-lets. Maybe the Paris Revolution of July 1830 took its toll, with its emphasis on liberty and democracy. Maybe, like so many others, he became convinced that there was indeed a plot to destroy his people and their way of life—through the British imposition on Canada of a narrow, aristocratic and privileged élite who would dominate and manipulate the political process. Maybe he saw new possibilities for him and his people in the American way of life. Maybe it was the only way for him to become the president of the small nation he strove to save. Maybe. But with Papineau, nothing was ever constant or final.

In any case, by 1835 he was the leader of a national majority that demanded redress as the condition of its loyalty. Unable to obtain it, he found other means.

That the struggle ended in the loss of life and property was the natural outcome of his rhetoric. He might not have imagined, though, that it would go so far. But more of that later.

When he returned to Canada, he re-entered politics as the member for Deux-Montagnes, from 1848 until 1851, and then from 1852 until 1854. That part of his life was a great disappointment. Times had changed. He couldn't exercise the influence he had previously. He was out of touch and incapable of serving under anyone but himself. As an annexationist and an implacable enemy of British institutions ("Aristocratic England"), he rejected the Union of the Canadas. Unable to have his way, he retired from politics and took up permanent residence in his *manoir*. He died on September 25, 1871.

"We will not withdraw the requests [that is, the Ninety-Two Resolutions] we have made for the full measure of our political powers and rights. . . . We hope, but with some unease, that the British government will give us justice. In this hope we will do nothing to hasten our separation from the mother country except to prepare the people and make them ready for an age that will be neither monarchical nor aristocratic." Thus spoke Papineau in 1835, two years before the British government declared his position untenable and rejected his Resolutions.

The spring and summer of 1837 were followed by a period of reflection, in which the two wings of the Parti Patriote—those favouring a revolution and those who cautioned prudence—argued it out. It appears that they reached a consensus: there were to be two stages to the struggle. The first would be dominated by speeches and public assemblies, along with smuggling and the boycott of British goods and all other products that were taxed, in order to deprive the government of needed revenues. But constitutionalité (peaceful means) through civil disobedience would be maintained. However, if the British government didn't give in, then the second stage would begin, but only in December, after the freeze-up, and it would include the use of force.

Two meetings of some importance were held on the way to armed combat. The first one was the assembly the Patriotes held at Saint-Ours-sur-Richelieu (the district of Richelieu was perhaps the most affected by the disastrous economic situation that prevailed). There, in early May, 1,500 persons adopted a manifesto that declared the government of Lower Canada to be "an oppressive power and a government of force." In light of that, the people then had the right not to submit to such tyranny. Consequently, the "sad experience" of the people "forces us to recognise that our true friends and natural allies were on the other side of the 45th parallel." The declaration went on to deny the British Parliament the power to "legislate on the internal affairs of this colony without our consent, our participation," and it affirmed that it was the duty of the citizens "to resist by all means now in our possession a tyrannical power, in order to diminish as much as we can these means of oppression."

The appeal to a show of force was just around the corner.

The government saw this and other assemblies as dangerous enough to declare them seditious. And the Church stepped in at the end of July to agree with the governor. "It is never permissible to revolt against legitimate authority or to violate the laws of the land." Priests were ordered to refuse absolution and the sacraments to those who held the opposite view.

On June 23, Russell's Ten Resolutions were suspended upon the accession of Queen Victoria, and the British government assumed the responsibility of paying for the civil lists in Lower Canada.

This gesture, however, didn't temper the animosity and the political rhetoric, with the result that a direct appeal for the use of force was issued at the end of October 1837 in Saint-Charles-sur-Richelieu. At a large assembly there, organised by the Confederation of the Six Counties, the people enthusiastically endorsed the summons—in spite of Papineau's protest. He continued to favour the course of constitutionalité and civil disobedience. But the people would have none of it. The "time has come to melt our spoons into bullets" since the "time for speeches has passed; we must now direct a lead against our enemies." To that end, Papineau, as the undisputed leader of the Patriotes, was enjoined to call a Popular Convention to replace the Assembly, which had been indefinitely prorogued in August. He was to create a state within a state—maybe even a sovereign and independent one.

After that, nothing—either from the Church or the government—could stop the storm that had been unleashed. The bishops cajoled and threatened the people, but to no avail. For his part, the governor, who had up to then sought conciliation and had tempered his anxiety with moderation, prohibited all public meetings and processions, ordered reinforcements from the Maritimes and Upper Canada, allowed volunteer regiments of Loyalists to be raised and even to do mischief, and issued warrants for the arrest for treason of twenty-six Patriotes, Papineau being chief among them. That was on November 16.

Seven days later, an uprising took place at Saint-Denis-sur-Richelieu. It was the only victory the Patriotes had during all of this sorry affair. Two days later, they were roundly defeated in Saint-Charles and also at Saint-Eustache, northwest of Montréal.

The first Rebellion was over. It was a fiasco (as in Upper Canada).

What followed was a period of intense destruction and abuse by the victors. Whole villages were burned and hundreds of farms destroyed. All liberties were suspended in favour of the brutal force of martial law. Rewards were offered for the capture of Papineau and other leaders of the Rebellion. Life became more miserable than before. Étienne Parent and the bishops had been proven right.

"Emporté par le vent": the people, overwhelmed by the injustices and indignities they had suffered at the hands of their governors—and by the terrible economic conditions that prevailed—tried to find salvation in the words of those they respected as their defenders.

But where was Papineau?

After the battle of Saint-Denis, Papineau went to Saint-Charles and then proceeded to Saint-Hyacinthe, where his sister lived. Soldiers searched diligently for him, but his sister had hidden him well. When, at the beginning of December, the governor offered a thousand pounds for his head, he decided that he couldn't risk arrest nor the harm that could befall his family. From Saint-Hyacinthe, he proceeded to Saint-Césaire and Saint-Georges-d'Henriville. A day or so later, he was in a boat, crossing the Bay of Missisquoi. Then, by January 1, 1838, he had arrived in New York, where his eldest son, also a fugitive, met him. After a year and a month in which he tried in vain to obtain aid and support from the United States, he left for France. He was to remain there until 1845.

Meanwhile, on February 28, 1838, the second phase of the Rebellion was launched. Robert Nelson, a major participant in the 1837 uprising, crossed the border into Québec at Alburg, Vermont, and proclaimed Lower Canada an independent and sovereign state, with himself as president of the Provisional Government. In this undertaking, some American sympathisers with a thousand muskets—no doubt stolen from a military arsenal—accompanied him. After this show of power, Nelson returned to the United States, where he was promptly arrested.

What to do next? This was the quandary of the Patriotes-in-exile, who were much divided as to the course of action to be taken. Papineau and many others felt that without the support of the United States, no progress could be made nor success ensured. In fact, President Martin Van Buren had declared that neutrality was the order of the day on January 5, 1838. Until circumstances changed, Papineau reckoned that it was futile to pursue the matter.

Others, though, had a different idea. A secret society known as the Frères Chasseurs—whose goal was to invade Lower Canada and declare the independence of Québec—fomented discontent in many counties around Montréal and threatened unwilling souls with death or other dire consequences if they didn't cooperate.

The 1838 uprising began on November 3 and was over a week later. Its centres were Châteauguay, Laprairie, Napierville, and Odelltown. In revenge, the British forces destroyed many villages, including Saint-Eustache and Saint-Benoît, where there had been no fighting at all. They desecrated churches, burned farms, and took 850 prisoners, charging over a hundred of them with high treason. At their courts martial, between November 1838 and May 1839, ninety-nine were condemned to death (only twelve were executed); fifty-eight were deported to Australia; two were banished; and twenty-seven were released conditionally.

One of those hanged was Chevalier de Lorimier, whose letter to his wife appears early in this chapter.

⚜

Through mysterious ways that only Mascou knows, he brings me to de Lorimier's cell early in the morning of the day of his execution, February 15, 1839. On our way there, Mascou tells me that, on the previous night, the warden gave de Lorimier and his four companions permission to have a dinner: le banquet des Girondins. There were speeches. No regrets.

François-Marie-Thomas Chevalier de Lorimier, a notary and a Patriote, is a handsome man of medium height with a dark—quite dark—complexion, black hair and black eyes. He has a high forehead, and those who know him tell me that he is gentle and intelligent, good-hearted, imaginative, and possessing a fine intellect.

It is about seven o'clock in the morning. He has had his breakfast, the soldiers inform me, and a priest will come to be with him from about 8:00 until his execution. De Lorimier has written all his letters and finished his political testament. He is ready.

He finds me sitting in front of him. I explain who I am and what I am doing. He will not grant an interview. Instead, he will dictate what he wants my readers to know. I can't refuse. And so, he begins. He speaks in a monotonous voice. No emotion, no

169

inflection to express his passion, his anger, or his sadness . . . except when he speaks of his wife and children. The rest is only a steady stream of words.

"I became active in the political life of my country and people around 1821. I was about eighteen years old. I was—am—a nationaliste. I will bring that conviction with me to the beyond God has reserved for me.

"At twenty-nine, I married my dear Henriette. She is my constant companion and of great assistance to me. She understands who I am and what I need to do. She has never reproached me for my political activities, nor did I ever do anything to harm her—at least, until now.

"We have five children. God has taken three of them, including my only son. I have always provided for them. My notarial practise was quite successful and we live in a house that her father left to her."

He stares at his hands—long hands, not made for hard labour. Tears begin to flow down his cheeks. He wipes them away and continues whispering in despair: "I do not know what will happen to Henriette and the two little ones."

While he eases himself through his pain, I recall that his wife, unable to meet the mountain of debts he had accumulated, renounced his estate and, with her daughters, lived in abject poverty in L'Assomption. In 1883, a public subscription was organised to help them. I hear a cough and de Lorimier appears ready to proceed.

"I admire Louis-Joseph Papineau, at least I did for a long time. During that period, I was close to him and other Patriote leaders. I followed orders and accepted the policies, especially the Ninety-Two Resolutions, which the people supported. I am a democrat!

"My career—if I can call it that—as a resistance fighter began in April 1837, after Lord Russell had rejected our demands and, thus, annihilated all our constitutional rights.

"I attended most of the assemblies that were organised and, with my friend George-Étienne Cartier I was co-secretary of the Comité Central et Permanent du District de Montréal, which oversaw the activities of the resistance in the Montréal district.

"In October, I was present at the Assemblée des Six Comtés at Saint-Charles-sur-Richelieu. An amazing moment! We resolved to plan to take our freedom, and to be responsible for it. Amazing! A month later, in fighting for that liberty, I was wounded in the thigh during the confrontation between our Fils de la Liberté and the English Doric Club. That incident was the beginning of my sixteen-month pilgrimage as a resistance fighter for my country.

"Fearing arrest due to my patriotic activities, I left my wife and children in Montréal and sought refuge in the county of Deux-Montagnes, where I served at the battle of Saint-Eustache on December 14. When I realised the futility of continuing the battle, I advised my commanding officer to lay down our arms. He refused, and so I left. In secret, I made my way to the Eastern Townships and, thence, to the United States."

(De Lorimier doesn't tell me that his commander, Jean-Olivier Chenier, died during the battle as he was trying to escape the burning church in which he and some of his men had taken refuge. At least, Chenier was consistent. He died bravely.)

"After my escape, I lived in the United States until I returned to Canada as a resistance fighter yet again in November 1838. During that time, there were meetings to determine the best course of action. But the Patriotes were drifting apart. I noticed great divisions among our leaders—divisions I had not fully grasped between April 1837 and the uprising of November of that year. But now it all came to the surface and was—at least to me—devastating.

"Take, for instance, the meeting that I attended in the town of Middlebury. As I said, I was always a supporter of Papineau.

But, in Middlebury, I became most disappointed with his attitude. He turned his back on the struggle. First, he refused to
accept the declaration of independence that we had prepared,
because it demanded the abolition of the seigneurial system, the
coutumes de Paris, and, for God's sake, tithes to the clergy . . .
Unbelievable! He considered these outdated practices and systems to be at the core of our nationalité. Unbelievable! From a
man so learned and so liberal.

Second, Papineau didn't want us to pursue the resistance,
since the United States would not assist us. I am telling you, he
disappointed me. Here was the greatest leader our people ever had
not prepared d'aller jusqu'au bout (to go all-out). A word from
him would have inflamed our souls and those of our people. He
was extraordinarily popular with the people—but he didn't act.
He wanted us to resort to la constitutionalité, to civil disobedience—as if we could get rid of the Anglais with that.

"Thank God some of us were not prepared to wait. Instead, we
got ready for the action that was necessary.

"And so, when Robert Nelson crossed the border to proclaim
the independence of my country, I was there. It was a providen-
tial moment.

"When the Frères Chasseurs began their activities, I was one
of them." (He seems rather pleased with himself. But he doesn't
tell me whether he agreed with one of the policies of the Frères
Chasseurs—the one about strangling the Jews after robbing
them of their property.)

"While I waited for the moment to strike, I lived in
Plattsburgh, where my wife came to join me in January and
stayed until August—an important time for both of us, a pleasant time as well, marred only by what was going on in my country and by the condition of our family. I was torn between my
duty as a Patriote and my duty to my wife and children. With my
wife's consent and participation, I reconciled both of these
duties. I told her that I was ever ready to spill my blood on the

soil that had given me birth, in order to dislodge the infamous British government—top, branches, roots, and all. I was going to make sacrifices for the liberation of my country. She was prepared to do the same as well. A remarkable woman."

He looks at his hands again, and the tears come. Eventually, he moves impatiently and continues his monologue.

"Then, the war started again in November 1838. I was by then a brigadier-general in our small but patriotic army. I fought at Beauharnois, and then at Sainte-Martine, where I encouraged the people in their resolve. Liberty was at hand, I told them. By that time, though, Nelson had been defeated at Odelltown, and the American army he had promised us never materialised. It was hopeless.

"On the morning of November 12, as I was trying to escape to the United States, I lost my way and the Anglais captured me."

One more time, his hands become the focus of his attention. He seems angry with himself. Staring at the dirt under his fingernails, he says between deep, deep breaths: "Like Papineau, I ran away . . . Escaped . . . leaving others to meet their fate . . . I shouldn't have done that . . . yet, I needed to do so. I wanted to live to fight another day. I wanted to live to provide for my family. I wanted to live to prepare the day of deliverance for my people. And so I fled . . .

"He takes a deep breath before he resumes: "I was court-martialled on January 11, 1839. Les Anglais would not grant my request for a civil trial. But I knew they wouldn't. So I made it as difficult as possible for the officials to condemn me. I defended myself, cross-examining witnesses, many of whom contradicted themselves over and over again. Fiercely, I denied all the accusations against me, but it was to no avail. Even the court martial: just a pretense that justice was being done. The English officials at the trial wanted me dead. That is all there is to it. Even the witnesses against me, and many were my comrades, were bought with promises of leniency. And so the trial ended with a guilty verdict, with no recommendation for any form of amnesty."

For the first time since the beginning of his tale, he really looks at me and says: "And here I am."

As the priest comes in, de Lorimier adds with great dignity: "I am a Patriote."

As he leaves his cell, I see him out of the corner of my eye holding the priest's hands and hear him, in a tearful voice, say: "Ma pauvre Henriette . . . Mes pauvres enfants."

I wait at the entrance of the prison. At about 8:40, the guards lead de Lorimier out. He looks at me and . . . smiles. A little, sad smile.

At 9:00 a.m. I see him mount the scaffold with four of his comrades. There are too many people around who have come to see, jeer, and witness this sordid execution. I'm not one of them. I walk away.

Suddenly a jubilant roar coming from the place of execution stops me. The deed is done! De Lorimier was the last to be executed. What is left of this horrible affair?

De Lorimier is an honest man—a pathetic one no less—who lived in accordance with his emotions, passions, and enthusiasms. He paid the price. It's better to let others judge him.

Mascou materialises beside me and returns me to the present.

⚜

On February 11, 1839, a report was lodged in the British Parliament that served as a catalyst in changing the face of Canada. It was the work of John George Lambton, Ist Earl of Durham (1792–1840), who was a Liberal associated with the Whig party and was known as "Radical Jack" for his part in the drafting of the important Reform Bill of 1832. He had served as the British ambassador to Russia and in 1838, was appointed governor general of British North America with the special mandate to report on the Rebellions of 1837 in Lower and Upper Canada. He arrived on our shores in May 1838 and left us in November of that year, having resigned when the

British government censured him for deporting prisoners to Bermuda without due process.

Less than two years after the publication of his report, Durham died of tuberculosis.

Durham's *Report on the Affairs of British North America* is an important Canadian historical document. It certainly is one of the most talked about documents we've ever had. He was convinced that in Upper Canada, the essential reason for the disenchantment and uprising was "a petty, corrupt, insolent Tory clique"; in Lower Canada, however, it was another matter. There, he didn't find a petty, corrupt, insolent Tory clique—although he was critical of the uses of power that he was certain the Château Clique abused more frequently than not. What he did find were "two nations warring in the bosom of a single state." What he had expected to find was "a contest between a government and a people." And so, as opposed to the struggle in Upper Canada, the struggle in Lower Canada was not one of "principles, but of races." In that situation, he perceived that "it would be idle to attempt any amelioration of laws or institutions, until we could first succeed in terminating the deadly animosity that now separates the inhabitants of Lower Canada into the hostile divisions of French and English."

Durham found us "habituated to the incessant labour of a rude and unskilled agriculture," too "fond of social enjoyments," and a people who were "unstructured, inactive, unprogressive" and exhibited "the characteristics of the peasantry of Europe." In our static state, we "clung to ancient customs and ancient laws," too "uneducated and unprogressive" to be able to do what was needed to get out of that pattern.

To resolve the political dilemma of the six colonies of British North America, he recommended government that was responsible for its internal affairs, leaving to the British authorities "the regulation of foreign relations, and of trade with the mother country, the other British Colonies, and foreign nations . . . and the disposal of the public lands." After all, "the British people of the North American Colonies are a people on whom we may safely rely, and to whom we must not grudge power."

For the French-Canadian problem, Durham recommended that we be assimilated. That assimilation was long overdue, in his view. It should have been done in 1759–60. It had been an error then; for, instead of the policy of assimilation, the authorities pursued the "vain endeavour to preserve a French-Canadian nationality in the midst of an Anglo-American colonies and States." To be the recipients of the blessings of being British, we had, therefore, to be integrated into the promise of the Empire. In other words, we had to become like the Anglais; or, to put it in his words: "I entertain no doubt of the national character which must be given to Lower Canada; it must be that of the British Empire; that of the majority of British America; that of the great race which must, in the lapse of no long period of time, be predominant over the whole North American Continent. . . . It must henceforth be the first and steady purpose of the British Government to establish an English population, with English laws and language, in this Province, and to trust its government to none but a decidedly English Legislature."

To achieve his goal of assimilating us, he recommended that Upper and Lower Canada be united in one legislative union with, of course, Responsible Government. "Such a union," he wrote, "would at once decisively settle the question of races; it would enable all the Provinces to co-operate for all common purposes; and, above all, it would form a great and powerful people, possessing the means of securing good and responsible government for itself, and which, under the protection of the British Empire, might in some measure counterbalance the preponderant and increasing influence of the United States on the American continent."

Radical Jack was a racist! Or was he just an English Liberal caught up in the glory of race and the potentials of the Empire? Who knows? He certainly didn't think that by assimilating us he was doing us a disservice. Quite the contrary. After all, we were a people "destitute of all that can invigorate and elevate a people," since we were determined to retain our "peculiar language and manners," and one "with no history and no literature."

John George Lambton, 1st Earl of Durham, was a man susceptible to the charms and the illusions of being part of an empire—along with the great, powerful, and intrepid Englishmen who built that empire (he was one of them). He found no contradiction in his refusal to accept the genuine national characteristics of colonials of non-English stock and in his dismissal of the validity of diversity. He was a racist because of that. He was unliberal because he couldn't accept that equality implied diversity.

Moreover, he undid the promise of the Quebec Act—the promise that the nationality of my people could be preserved with the tolerance and the help of Great Britain. Durham betrayed us.

In spite of all of that, we, Canadians and Canadiens, owe him a debt of gratitude. He made imperative the building of our nation on principles that had little to do with his report. In some way, he made us see the follies of our ways. He directed us to the fundamental ingredient of our nationality: diversity.

And so, the first nation builders of the new Canada were Robert Baldwin and Louis-Hippolyte LaFontaine—and the history of Québec became the history of Canada.

That, of course, couldn't have been done without Québec.

Étienne Parent translated Durham's report and published it in *Le Canadien*. With his confidence in British justice and process, Parent had welcomed Durham's mission; however, he had a falling-out with Durham's successor, Sir John Colborne (1778–1863). Colborne's savage persecution of everyone he thought had participated in the uprisings attracted Parent's anger. On December 24, 1838, he wrote in *Le Canadien*: "We should like to spare England the unenviable honour of seeing its name associated with that of Russia, the 'executioner of Poland.' There is all our crime. It is a great crime, we admit, in the eyes of all those who are plotting the annihilation of the Canadian people." Two days later he was arrested on the accusation of "seditious scheming." He was to remain in prison, without trial, until April 1839. However, he continued to direct, write, and publish his newspaper by smuggling his articles out of prison. It was while in prison that he became almost totally deaf, and he lost his position as a law officer of the government.

Parent's views on Durham's report were essentially the same as those of every other Canadien editor. He had hoped for better from Durham. Now, it was apparent to all that the "English cannot pronounce an impartial judgement between us, poor French Canadians, and our adversaries, who have the good fortune not to be stricken like us with original sin." The proposed union meant assimilation, and he condemned it, then and later, as another proof of the contempt of the British for the Canadiens and the British determination to shower favouritism on their minority "regardless of acts and guarantees that were equivalent to a sworn social contract."

But he wouldn't capitulate. Instead he would fight on and try with all his might to make the union—should it come—work, and to derive benefits from it. The articles that he wrote on the issue of union and the actions he took to reinforce the presence of the Canadiens in the whole sorry process became the inspiration of all those who hoped for a better tomorrow.

However, in spite of Parent's best efforts and the many petitions against union—one of which contained 39,928 signatures—the British Parliament approved the Act of Union creating the Province of Canada in July 1840. On February 10, 1841, it was proclaimed in Canada.

All things considered, it was an unjust act, not befitting the British people and their institutions. There was to be no Responsible Government, as it was judged to be incompatible with imperial responsibility. Furthermore, although the population of Lower Canada was larger than that of Upper Canada—650,000 to 450,000—representation in the Legislative Assembly was to be equal, the use of the French language was proscribed, and the Québec people were forced to pay part of the public debt of the Upper Canadians—the debt of Lower Canada being hardly more than one hundred thousand pounds, while that of Upper Canada was well over a million. (Oh, if only we could remember the lessons of those days when the have-nots, as the Anglais would call the Québec people, would subsidise the haves.)

And Lower Canada became Canada East, and Upper Canada became Canada West.

To make matters worse, as if that were possible, Kingston (*cet enfer*—that hell—that little, little town that had been Cataraqui when the Natives lived there and Fort Frontenac when the French lived here) became the capital of the new colony.

But all was not lost, as Parent reminded his readers and the whole population of Québec. His people could still win the day, he was certain of that. The goals, though, had to be clear. To him they were equality of the two communities—the one that spoke French and the one that spoke

People and places I met along the way . . .

Coureur de bois
From *Dent Illustrations*, vol. 2, no. 418
Artist: Arthur Heming, 1870–1940
(Arthur Heming / National Archives of Canada / C-005746)

Le combat de Dollard des Ormeaux, 1660 (1926)
Artist: Marc Aurèle de Foy Suzor-Côté, 1869–1937
(Marc Aurèle de Foy Suzor-Côté / National Archives of Canada / C-003018)

Blue Hyacinth with Scroll: "Ven. Mère M. de l'Incarnation"
From *Lady Belleau's Album*, folio 15, recto
(National Archives of Canada / C-119375)

French Canadian Habitants Playing at Cards, Quebec, 1848
From *Life in Lower Canada* (Montreal: R.& C. Chalmers, 1848)
Artist: Cornelius Krieghoff, 1815–1872
(Cornelius Krieghoff / National Archives of Canada / C-000057)

Louis Joseph Papineau, ca. 1852
Photographer: T.C. Doane
(T.C. Doane / National Archives of
Canada / C-079114)

Sir Louis Hippolyte LaFontaine,
prime minister of the United Canadas
(National Archives of Canada /
C006068)

Molson family brewery, Montreal, after the fire in 1858
Photographer: T.C. Doane
(The Molson Archives Collection /
National Archives of Canada / C-089689)

Joseph Brant, Thayendanege (ca. 1875)
Artists: Ezra Ames, 1768–?; George Catlin, 1794–1836
(Ezra Ames and George Catlin / National Archives of Canada / C-007095)

La moisson (1879)
From *l'Opinion publique*, Sept. 25, 1879, p. 466
Artist: William de la Montagne Cary, 1840–1922
(William de la Montagne Cary / National Archives of Canada / C-003614)

Through the French Country, Quebec, 1882
From G.M. Grant, ed., *Picturesque Canada* (Toronto: 1882), vol. II, p. 730
(National Archives of Canada / C-085488)

E.C. Genêt (1896)
(National Archives of Canada / C-006843)

The Liberal Cabinet of Canada, 1896 (ca. 1896)
(National Archives of Canada / C-001869)

Relief Projects, No. 7—The Citadel in Québec, Québec (April 1936)
(Department of National Defence Collection /
National Archives of Canada / PA-034657)

Monseignor Joseph Charbonneau,
archbishop of Montreal, 1940–1950,
Ottawa, Ontario (August 7, 1940)
Photographer: Jules Alexandre Castonguay
(Jules Alexandre Castonguay / National
Archives of Canada / PA-804435)

Major Paul Triquet, V.C., Royal 22ᵉ
Regiment, Québec City, Québec
(April 12, 1944)
(Photographer unknown / National
Archives of Canada / PA-157376)

Signing of the Constitution, Ottawa, Ontario. R to L:
Mr. Gerald Regan, minister of Labour; Rt. Hon. Pierre Elliot Trudeau,
prime minister; H.M. the Queen; Mr. Michael Pitfield, clerk of
the Privy Council; Mr. Michael Kirby (April 17, 1982)
Photographer: Robert Cooper
(Robert Cooper / National Archives of Canada / PA-140705)

René Lévesque, U.L.
Artist: Nickolay Sabolotny
(National Archives of Canada / C-045062)

English—and Responsible Government. To those ends, alliances could be formed, especially with the Reformers of Canada West, who were aghast that Responsible Government had been denied. As well, the Canadiens, who had become masters of the British parliamentary process in their previous battles, could use that knowledge to their advantage to obtain their rights.

And this is exactly what happened. It took ten years—ten years of advances and retreats—but it was done.

Unfortunately, Étienne Parent wasn't in the Assembly to be a part of it, although he served for a while, during which time he introduced a bill to recognise French as an official language. However, his deafness prevented him from meeting his responsibilities, and when he was offered the post of clerk of the Executive Council, he resigned.

At the same time, he ceased his activities with *Le Canadien*. He had been its soul for fifteen years.

Parent spent the rest of his life working as a public servant, writer, and lecturer. He retired in 1872. By then he was totally deaf and partially blind. And he died in Ottawa on December 22, 1874, still unable to understand, as he once stated, "that God would have imposed work upon man as a punishment."

⚜

As agreed, Sir Louis-Hippolyte LaFontaine arrives at 4:00 a.m. He's a portly man, a little above average in height, with black eyes, and exuding confidence, or is it self-assurance? He stands in my living room looking like Napoleon—he bears a striking resemblance to the emperor; he combs his hair the same way, and the fingers of his right hand are inserted in his jacket. His biographer, Jacques Monet, says that LaFontaine wasn't a thinker; he was cold and dour and uncommunicative; he had few friends, and he was more or less a recluse; but he was most able, capable of distinguishing the important from the secondary, and was dedicated to his work. He was also quite anticlerical. But I have made up my mind—I will not talk about Church politics with him.

We sit facing each other. He will have no tea, no coffee. I have the feeling he wants to get on with it and return to his world. So, I begin.

"Do you still play tennis?" I ask, thinking I shall put him at ease. I fail. He stares at me and replies: "There is no possibility for that entertainment where I am." He gives me the impression that if that's going to be the level of my questioning, he really wants to leave.

"You began your political life in 1830 as the member for Terrebonne. You were re-elected in 1834. And you supported Papineau. Why?"

"There is no one else to support," he replies in a monotonous voice as if totally uninterested in our proceedings. He would answer me like that practically all throughout the hour we spent together. And, like Marie de l'Incarnation, everything's in the present tense. "Monsieur Papineau's struggle is *our* struggle. We are fighting for our rights."

"But you didn't follow him into insurrection? You abandoned him."

"As you wish. The appeal to violence and insurrection is not a practical alternative. Sound and effective political manoeuvring is. But it demands compromises. Monsieur Papineau does not understand that simple truth. Unlike him, I do not consider compromise as a betrayal. Nor does he—or those who join him in this suicidal adventure—understand that we can only survive as a people within the context of British institutions. Without the help of the British, we shall be the creatures of the Americans. There is no hope for us there. And we are too fragile to occupy this vast land on our own."

"Where were you during the 'troubles'?"

"As Lord Gosford, the governor, will not understand the sensible course of action for him to take—recall the Assembly—I need to go to England. My wife understands well what my mission there is and promises me to visit our people in prison and to help their families. In England, I struggle, with some British allies, to arrive at a constitutional solution, even if it means swallowing our pride and compromising. I work at that until March, and when my efforts are futile, I travel to France, returning to Montréal in June."

Thinking that I may conclude that he betrayed Papineau, he adds, looking at me: "I do stop in Saratoga, New York, to meet with Monsieur Papineau." But he doesn't add that in 1840, he had credit extended to Papineau. LaFontaine takes a sip of water from the glass I have left on a table near his chair, then tells me that when the uprising began again in November, he was arrested and detained until the middle of December. "All of these experiences are not negative for me. They help shape my political views and determine my life's work."

He continues, still as if it were nothing of great importance. "You see, sir, Canadiens have become British subjects by treaty. They must be treated as such. We must have an Assembly, for without it we will certainly become just like the Acadians, incapable of reforming our institutions and shaping our destiny. The Assembly I am talking about is not a constitutionally useless thing. There, we are to have the majority. It is our right to influence the government as a majority. This is not being allowed. It is easy to understand why men lose their patience."

"Lord Durham, though, insisted that a political and constitutional compromise or solution wasn't possible, for the conflict was essentially racial."

"He was wrong. It is a great mistake to suppose that there is no means of rapprochement between the two parties. It is even easy to re-establish harmony among the majority in the two political parties, for their interests are the same. If we put an end to discrimination, favouritism, and "la dictature," there will be peace. Before the "troubles," as you call them, we had a bastard, unnatural government that refused to apply all the principles of the British Constitution insofar as some form of ministerial responsibility is concerned. Furthermore, that bastard administration of ours saw fit to act as if valid political differences were based on origins rather than on distinctions. Had it recognised distinctions, your friend de Lorimier would still be alive and his family taken care of." He sighs, rubs his eyes, and adds: "Ministerial responsibility or Responsible Government: that is my political philosophy. I will not derogate from it."

"Why then did you accept Union Government? It was, after all, a rebuke of your philosophy."

"Ah! Ye of little faith." He smiles and makes the only attempt at humour during our entire interview. "For a violent anticleri-cal, I have, after all, a Catholic education." That taken care of, he explains: "Lord Durham's Union, with Responsible Government, makes sense to me. I see that this measure contains the means by which the people can exercise the control over government to which they have a just claim. With it, I can place my countrymen in a better position than they have occupied before."

He takes a breath and I say, not allowing him to continue on his own: "But the British government gave you Union without Responsible Government!"

He doesn't like being interrupted. He actually glares at me and puts his right hand more deeply between the buttons of his jacket. "Even without Responsible Government, Union still has possibilities for us." And in a voice one would use to explain something to a child, he says: "Union will give us a party, made of Reformers from both Canada East and Canada West. We shall have the majority, an immense majority. We already have. And our principles, our policies, will be based on Reform principles and not on origin. We cannot escape our destiny. We, the Canadiens and Canadians who are party to this arranged marriage of convenience, as Étienne Parent would say, share a common cause and, therefore, we have a common interest in meeting at the legislative level in a spirit of peace, union, friendship, and fraternity.

United action is more necessary than ever. I am in favour of the English principle of Responsible Government. I see in its operation the only possible guarantee of a good, constitutional, and effective government. It is also indispensable to our survival as a distinct people, co-inhabitants of this great and vast territory. We will form a majority that will make our tyrants succumb. That I promise you, Monsieur. So Union is the price we have to pay for Responsible Government. On ne peut en sortir! The rest will follow. I shall be there to see that it does."

I look at this man. He is mysterious. Condescending. Abrupt. But ever in command. He was thirty-two when he embarked on his mission, with most of the senior politicians of Lower Canada fervently opposed to Union. He manoeuvred magnificently. He lent his support where it could best be profitable; he travelled to Toronto to court Reform politicians; he became friendly with many of them and received them in his house; he organised meetings and coalesced with Parent. But, when the elections were held in March 1841, he withdrew his candidacy in Terrebonne to prevent violence between the Canadiens and the supporters of the English candidate. When Robert Baldwin, who had been elected in two constituencies, learned of LaFontaine's withdrawal, he offered him York, where LaFontaine was easily elected on September 23, 1841, with a majority of 210 votes. In 1843, LaFontaine paid back his debt to Baldwin by having him elected in Rimouski. Then, there was Parent!

As if LaFontaine is reading my thoughts, he says: "In my three-week campaign in York, Étienne Parent accompanied me. A fine man. A great philosopher. You should meet him. He is quite deaf, but, I swear to you, he will hear you. He is like that." Again, he refuses to use our conversation to bask in his glory. So he doesn't admit that he had Parent appointed clerk of the Executive Council. Nor will he brag about his maiden speech in the Assembly. As the member for the fourth district of York, he spoke in French, and when he was told to speak the

Queen's language, he replied: "Even if I were as familiar with the English as with the French language, I should nonetheless make my first speech in the language of my French-Canadian compatriots, were it only to enter my solemn protest against the cruel injustice of that part of the Act of Union which seeks to proscribe the mother tongue of half the population of Canada." After that date, it was accepted that anyone who wanted to speak French could. Seven years later, French would become one of the official languages of the Assembly.

"In the summer of 1842, you became attorney general for Canada East, resigning that position in November 1843." I state a fact; I don't ask a question.

He shakes his head: "I have a program, the elements of which are to reconcile my people to the new constitutional arrangement. So I will have a polling station in every parish; I will have a new electoral map of Canada East adopted so that my people are better represented and will have more influence; Montréal will become the capital city [the first session held there took place on July 1, 1844, in the Marché Sainte-Anne on McGill Street. Montréal had by then a population of 45,000]; and I will manage to authorise the use of French in the records of the legislature and in the courts. And, as a good politician, I will favour the exercise of patronage." He laughs and adds: "Ironically, it is my use of patronage as an instrument of power that brings me into conflict with the governor general. The governor Lord Metcalfe, unlike another governor Sir Charles Bagot, has no understanding of ministerial responsibility. He is quite determined to govern. He will have to do it without me and my friends. So in opposition I will go, and there shall I remain until my way becomes the way of all."

He was to stay in opposition until 1848. I do not need to ask how difficult that time was. His health and that of his wife deteriorated, and the death of his adopted daughter left an immense emptiness in his heart and life. "You have children," he wrote to Baldwin, "we have not. Corine was our adopted daughter. Her death

will, I am afraid, greatly influence my plans and calculations."
In spite of his pain and ill health, he kept alive the flame of
Responsible Government as the best guarantee for survival. He
never lost the opportunity to raise the question of French as an
official language of the government. The great majority of the
people of Canada East accepted him as their best defence and
offence. To cement that feeling, he had to have political unity
among the French Canadians. Voting en bloc! As his colleague
Jacques Monet has remarked: "This theme, that la survivance could
be achieved only by the united effort of all French Canadians
voting together, has, of course, remained almost a cardinal tenet
of Québec nationalist ideology ever since."

My guest is getting impatient. I tell him, "Your exile from
office ended with the elections of 1847–48, which you won
resoundingly. The country had a new governor general in the
person of Lord Elgin. You became attorney general. You were, in
effect, the first Canadian to become prime minister and the
first French Canadian to be elected by his own people to direct
their national aspirations. You preceded Sir Wilfrid Laurier.
Moreover . . ."

LaFontaine interrupts me: "Monsieur, before you go on ad
infinitum, did you know that James Bruce, 8th Earl of Elgin and
12th Earl of Kincardine, married, en deuxième noce, Lord
Durham's daughter? Ironic." A big smile spreads across his face.
"His moral mission is to undo Durham. And he does." LaFontaine
settles more deeply into his seat and, for a time, looks comfortable. "On January 18, 1849, British troops line the streets of
old Montréal. The streets and sidewalks are covered with snow.
The women in their best attire—too many low décolletées for
the bishop—fill the galleries of our Parliament, and we, the
men, also in our best clothes, wait for the governor to arrive.
He leaves his residence, Monklands, at the west end of the city,
in a large sleigh escorted by his guards. When he arrives,
Robert Baldwin and I greet him at the bottom of the stairs and

escort him to the Red Chamber, where, under a bright red canopy with gold tassels, he reads in his highly refined English the Speech from the Throne, which we, his ministers, have prepared. When he is finished, instead of handing the speech to the clerk, so that it can be read in French, His Excellency looks around the room, and, with a flickering smile on his face, he reads it again, in French. It was done. Elgin has indeed undone Durham. Canada is bilingual!" He appears moved by a great emotion. Hardly audibly, he adds: "It is a glorious moment."

A few sips of water later, he says: "We take office in uneasy times. The economic recession is hard on our people, a recession caused by the British repeal of the Corn Laws, which loses us the guarantee of British markets for our goods, and also by the collapse of the railway boom in Queen Victoria's kingdom. Our commerce is disrupted, bankruptcies are on the increase, and the people are restless. In addition, there is the terrible Irish tragedy—70,000 immigrants from Ireland came to our shores last year, 1847. Many of them have died of cholera, leaving us with orphans to look after, or widows. Then, we have the school question: many in the rural areas are opposed to a centralised school system. They take their fury out in arson and riots. And as you know, Monsieur Papineau has returned. More people than I care to admit are turning to him in their time of misery. Dissension is rampant, as is the desire for annexation to the United States. But that is more of a problem for my friend Robert Baldwin, even though many merchants here appear to be in favour, as is Monsieur Papineau." He loses himself in his thoughts. "I suppose we can isolate Monsieur Papineau, but we are still left with the Rebellion Losses Bill. I have to act upon that. I will be accused of paying the rebels. But it shall be done. Otherwise, Monsieur Papineau will win the day. That I cannot allow." Again he is lost in some memory bank of his own.

I wait patiently for him to tell me about the Rebellion Losses Bill, which established forever the principle of Responsible

Government; that is, that the Executive governs only with the consent of the elected people as represented in the Assembly. LaFontaine and Baldwin had a large majority. The purpose of the bill was to indemnify those in the then Lower Canada whose property had been lost or damaged by the government of the day and its soldiers and officials, during the Rebellion of 1837, as had been done in Upper Canada. Even though it passed by good majorities from both Canada East and Canada West. . . . Now, it's my turn to have my thoughts interrupted. Monsieur LaFontaine is ready again.

"Lord Elgin is steadfast and exhibits a courage rarely seen. It is April 25, 1849, and he comes down to Parliament to give royal assent to our Rebellion Losses Bill, which will finally bring justice to this country and closure to these sad times. The Anglais who have lost their position of favouritism rebel. As His Excellency drives away, his duty done, the mob pelts his carriage with stones and rotten eggs. His guards protect him, but many are hurt. I am told Lord Elgin wrote to his Minister that the Queen's representative was in grave danger."

I wonder what he remembers about that very night. The mob, which is said to have included many respected citizens, invaded the Parliament, which was still in session. They tore down draperies, smashed windows and lights, broke furniture, and slashed paintings. Not satisfied, they set fire to the building. But the speaker was adamant: he would not adjourn the Assembly until a proper resolution to that effect had been passed. That being done, he took his place behind the mace and led the procession of the members out of the Assembly, while the flames roared and curses and jeers, shouted in the English tongue, engulfed them. Montréal fell prey to an organised and violent Tory and Orange mob. On the next day, not satisfied, they went to LaFontaine's house, where they broke in and did much damage. They also set fire to the stables and burned a few coaches. The riots continued, off and on, until the end of August.

Out of the blue, he chuckles and says: "We have to give up Montréal as the capital, in favour of Toronto alternating with Québec." He chuckles again.

A word about the capital: between 1841 and 1866, it moved from Kingston to Montréal, to Toronto, to Québec, and then to Ottawa (Queen Victoria had declared it the capital in 1857), when the Parliament buildings there, begun in 1859, were completed.

Suddenly, he stands up and declares: "My time is up. I did what I had determined I would do." And he disappears.

⚜

In 1851 LaFontaine retired from politics. He was, by then, weary of public life, especially after the retirement of his friend Robert Baldwin, who had encouraged him to tie his fate and that of his people to the liberal-minded people of Canada West. LaFontaine also suffered from severe insomnia and rheumatism, as did his wife. He returned to his law practice and was appointed chief justice of the Court of Queen's Bench in 1853. A few months later, he became a papal knight and a baronet, "the first French Canadian on whom this dignity has been conferred"; thus confirming his long-held belief, as he wrote to Lord Elgin, that his compatriots needed no longer to feel that "political and social inferiority" was their lot. All doors were open to them. He was proof of that.

On the night of February 25, 1864, he died.

It is sad that Canadians hardly know this man, who, more than anyone else, saw to it that Canada was a parliamentary democracy, in the fullest sense. It is also sad that the few Canadiens who know about him generally dismiss LaFontaine as inconsequential to the Québec brand of nationalism.

More than Papineau, LaFontaine assured the survival of my people. He paid dearly for it. I thank his memory.

LaFontaine's passage through the affairs of our country was done in the midst of severe economic downturn. On July 4, 1849, hundreds of houses in Montréal flew the American flag, and on October 11, a manifesto appeared in the Montréal *Gazette*, signed by 325 of the most important ("solid") personalities of the city. These business leaders, politicians, journalists, agitators, etc. (mostly English-speaking and Conservative and a few French-speaking Rouges) declared:

> The number and magnitude of the evils that afflict our country, and the universal and increasing depression of its material interests call upon all persons animated by a sincere desire for its welfare to combine for the purposes of enquiry and preparation with a view to the adoption of such remedies as mature and dispassionate investigation may suggest.
>
> *This remedy consists in a friendly and peaceful separation from the British connection and a Union upon equitable terms with the great North American Confederacy of Sovereign States.* [This last paragraph was published in full capital letters.]

There were different reasons why such a disparate group signed this self-serving document. The Rouges signed it because they wanted to free themselves from the British connection and, following Papineau, they admired American democracy and institutions. The same may be said of certain English-speaking Liberal politicians and journalists. The vast majority of the signers, however, were English-speaking, business oriented, and Conservative. They led the movement because their ambitious "vision of a great commercial empire, based on the St. Lawrence waterway system, and stretching into the rich lands of the West, was now just a mirage," as Professors Ramsay Cook and Kenneth McNaught remind us in *Canada and the United States, a Modern Study*.

In their opinion, the mother country had betrayed them at least twice. The first betrayal was in allowing Responsible Government—according to them, it placed the destiny of the country in the hands of the "disloyal" French Canadians; the second betrayal was Great Britain's termination of the old colonial system between 1846 and 1849, by adopting free trade and abolishing the Navigation Acts. Through free trade, the Montréal businessmen and their allies lost their preferential treatment in the imperial markets—a great advantage over the Americans—while, with the repeal of the Navigation Acts, their favoured access to British and imperial markets was abrogated. It's no wonder that they were "disillusioned, fearful and angry" and that they came to the conclusion that "if they could not defeat their competitors in the United States, they had better join them."

Even though the collective action was a severe indictment of the British connection—and the people suffered from the serious economic problems of the times—the population of the Canadas rejected such a solution. The political consequences were too great. And, in time, the fury passed. Lord Elgin negotiated a Reciprocity Treaty with the United States in 1854, which was a boost to the Canadian economy. The treaty was in effect between 1854 and 1864, when the Americans put an end to it, furious as they were about Great Britain's involvement in the American Civil War in favour of the South. And when the British government opened the St. Lawrence to international navigation, prosperity ensued.

So British North America remained intact to become, in 1867, our country, Canada. In time, we became the largest country on the planet. (Some evil tongues rate us second. Maybe that is part of our national obsession with humility.)

⚜

On July 9, 1852, I find myself on Saint-Laurent Street in Montréal. It is as hot as a furnace. I'm sweating and my blood pressure is shaky.

Not far from where I stand, looking up and down the street, a fire breaks out in one of the houses. Soon, it is engulfed in flames, the families living there rushing out to save themselves and whatever belongings they can. Volunteer firemen arrive with portable fire equipment that turns out to be useless. Near me a man is swearing to every saint in the calendar: "Christ! De Christ! Le maire et les échevins . . . partis! Les Tabernacles!" And he stands there, yelling all the swear words he has learned in the half century he has lived.

A woman runs by screaming: "Les pompiers ont pas d'eau."

"Ben non!" yells a man. "The reservoir is being cleaned. Hostie! I hope this doesn't spread."

No sooner has he uttered these words than a gust of wind carries the flames to the houses on each side, which, in turn, spread it up and down the street. Before I know what is happening, the entire square bordered by Saint-Denis, Craig, Saint-Laurent, and Mignone is ravaged. People run every which way, not knowing what to do. Some try to go back into their houses to retrieve a few things, but the flames, the smoke, the heat turn them back. The thermometer, I'm told, is at one hundred degrees Fahrenheit.

"The hospital!" someone screams. With a few people whose houses have already been destroyed, I rush to the Protestant Hospital on Dorchester Street to see what state it's in. The building is made of stone. "Don't abandon us! Save us!" cry old men and old women in their hospital clothes; children with canes and crutches try to escape along with other patients hardly able to walk. The doctors and the nurses rush about draping wet blankets around their charges. We help the best way we can. It seems so hopeless. The flames are coming closer and closer. We make haste, carrying those who can't walk. But, miracle of miracles, the wind changes direction and the hospital is spared. At sundown, the fire has spent its fury. Of the buildings in the square, only those in stone have survived in one form or another.

By the time I return to Saint-Laurent Street, the police are ushering the people out of the neighbourhood. They encourage the victims to take refuge at la ferme Logan (which, in the century I live in, is the Parc Lafontaine). Others make their way to the slopes of Mount Royal. Most damn the mayor and the city administration for emptying the reservoir on that day of all days. A few attribute the disaster to the sinful state in which too many find themselves. "C'est le Bon Dieu qui nous punit!" says a nun in a torn habit, rushing and shepherding a couple of children and a few elderly.

Those in the city who are not affected arrive with food and blankets, while the army and municipal officials, with volunteers, erect tents on the Champ-de-Mars. I help. Tired, red eyed, I'm having some soup, when suddenly Mascou appears before me. "Come quick," he whispers. "The fire has broken out again, in a stable this time." The news spreads quickly, and Mascou and I, with a large crowd, soon find ourselves near a square of streets bordered by Saint-Laurent and Lagauchetière. A river of fire flows everywhere. Before our eyes and without anyone being able to help, the residence of Bishop Ignace Bourget, the bishop of Montréal, who is out of town, is burned to the ground, and soon his cathedral suffers the same fate. I feel sorry for the bishop—whom I don't like and whom I consider to be pompous, arrogant, and interested only in his prestige, which he confuses with that of the Church; but who, just the same, is dedicated to his pastoral duties and indefatigable in the pursuit of his goals. He always has to watch his back, for the Sulpician Fathers, an arrogant and uncooperative gang of speculators if there ever was one, are constantly trying to stab him through the Vatican authorities. Two of them are walking by, admiring the handiwork of God. Their cassocks are spotless, their faces clean, their eyes bright, and their hair combed, while the rest of us are filthy with black soot running down our faces, and our eyes red with smoke. "Where the hell have they been?" I ask myself. Many must share my opinion, for they stare at the Vatican authorities. The clerics stop near me and Mascou, and I hear them say to each other: "It is the hand of God. His Excellency shouldn't have made our life so difficult, trying to destroy our parish and our properties as he has done. It is the hand of God." And they walk on. I look at Mascou and say as loud as I can: "The smug bastards!"

He laughs. "No one but me can hear you. I suppose you won't write about them."

"I'm forgetting they exist."

Early the next morning, before he returns me to my time, Mascou informs me that over a thousand homes have been destroyed; in all, the fire has created ten thousand victims.

Two days after the most disastrous fire in the history of the city, Bishop Bourget tells his flock: "It is the breath of God's anger that has fed the flames. It is He who has chosen to light the fire on the very day our reservoirs of water were empty. He has plotted the course of the fire to punish those who deserved His wrath and to reward those who do His will. In all of this, He is adorable!"

Bourget would have been a star on Christian television. But then I wonder: if God chose fire as the means to punish sinners, did He destroy Bourget's home and cathedral because of the bishop's sins? Mascou smiles and orders me to eat my lunch.

⚜

After LaFontaine's departure, but not because of it, there followed some thirteen years during which the Province of Canada, over which he and his friends had presided, came to fall apart for all sorts of reasons that I need not go into.

However, the years gave rise to a new breed of politicians and leaders who would lead us to the fulfilment of our destiny, the making of our country, through Confederation—men like John A. Macdonald, George-Étienne Cartier, George Brown, and Antoine-Aimé Dorion.

As far as Canada East was concerned, Cartier dominated the political scene there for a generation. He took part in the "troubles" of 1837 and escaped to Vermont, where he lived until 1838, when he was granted leave to return to Montréal and practise law. A close ally of LaFontaine's, Cartier was associated with the struggle for Responsible Government and the use of the Union to expand the rights of the Canadiens. He entered the Legislative Assembly in 1848 as a Liberal Reformer. In 1861, he became the leader of Liberal-Conservative Party of Canada East, known in popular parlance as Bleu, and served with Macdonald in the administrations of 1857–58 and 1858–62 and in the ministry that brought about Confederation. Cartier was known as the lawyer of the railroads, particularly the Grand Trunk Railway, for which he was the solicitor. (The Grand Trunk Railway of Canada was a company empowered to provide a railway "throughout the entire length of the Province of Canada, and from the eastern frontier thereof . . . to the city and port of Halifax." It was formally incorporated in 1852, and its goal was to construct the line from Toronto to Montréal. The greatest achievement of the company was the construction of the tubular Victoria Bridge over the St. Lawrence River at Montréal. Costing seven million dollars, it was opened to traffic in 1859. The Prince of Wales inaugurated it in August 1860.)

Cartier was a tireless defender of Confederation. It was, for him, an absolute necessity. Left to themselves, the British North American colonies, especially Québec, would become the toys of the Americans: "We must either have a Confederation of British North America or else be absorbed by the American Confederation." He worked hard to bring it about as, I think, it would realise the dream that he and LaFontaine shared: a dream that made it inevitable that one day there would be a way found to bring us all together. "We are of different races," Cartier would say, "not for the purpose of warring against each other, but in order to compete and emulate for the general welfare."

During these years, Cartier's main opposition came from the Parti Rouge, led by Antoine-Aimé Dorion. He and a few young radicals founded it in 1848 to promote their views and political goals: repeal of Union, free trade, annexation to the United States, election of all officials, abolition of the seigneurial tenure and tithing, universal suffrage, representation by population, and limits on the influence of the Church in political, economic, and social affairs. They read books that Rome forbade.

Dorion and his friends were fierce opponents of Confederation. As soon as the Québec Conference of 1864 had taken place, they denounced it furiously as nothing else but Union government in disguise. French Canadians would be swamped, their power base destroyed, and their capacity to govern themselves limited because of the powers to be given to the central authority. What was needed to replace the defunct Union, the Rouges argued, wasn't confederation of all the British colonies; rather, it was the federation of Canada East and Canada West, leaving the larger union to later.

One who fought Confederation with Dorion, his brother, and their allies was Wilfrid Laurier, of whom much will be said later. Laurier, who was then in his mid-twenties, considered Cartier's proposed scheme false in its conception and iniquitous, immoral, and cruel "dans ses détails."

Cartier won the day.

Mason Wade, in his monumental study of the French Canadians, wrote:

> It had taken only ten years for the French Canadians to rally from the death sentence pronounced upon their nationality by Lord Durham's Report and the Act of Union. Under the sage leadership of LaFontaine, their constitutional resistance had been so successful that they had gained undisputed political power. . . .
>
> Both ethnic groups had now resorted to rebellion when dominated wholly by the other; the great achievement of the next two decades was to be the working out of a partnership of English and French which guaranteed the rights of both. . . . Thanks largely to George-Étienne Cartier, the French Canadians were led to support the project of the Confederation of British North America into a Canada that was both French and English. . . . Thanks largely to him, an English-French Canadian solidarity was achieved, as a result of which it was definitely settled that the continent was to be divided between two powers, rather than to be a political entity; and that one power was to be bicultural.

In these years as well, Canada East won some, lost some. Such is life.

When we, the Canadiens, were forced to change our allegiances in 1759, we were an intrepid people, open to the future and determined to achieve great things—which we often did. Although often on the move, we had, nevertheless, established a permanent presence along the shores of the St. Lawrence, where we built our homes, worked the soil, and harnessed, other resources, and laid the foundation of a civilisation that was imaginative—and on the move. We had lived on the edge constantly. It was good for us.

After 1759, due to factors such as having to share the land with a people and a way of life we didn't know, we turned inwards and became sedentary, closed, and *replié sur nous-mêmes*. I suppose we were afraid what would happen to us in a world that became more and more hostile, as too many powerful beings wanted to transform us into English men and women and thus destroy us. They wanted to take what we had and, too often, they excluded us from being able to participate in the promise of the land.

Also we were badly led. The priest became our jailer, and the Church our jail. The episcopacy and clergy, of course, had our welfare at heart, but not as much as their own. For their own purposes, they manipulated our allegiance to God into our acquiescence to their power and prestige, influence, and control. Having little respect for us, they forced us to accept that they were the most important bulwark against those who endangered us. We were different! Such was our identity. What made us different was primarily our adherence to the Catholic Church, which was the way of God, Who had chosen the priest as the interpreter of His will. We could not be French Canadians unless we were Catholics, and we couldn't be Catholics unless we defined ourselves in terms of the clerical apparatus.

It was their allies, the professional classes, that added another dimension to our identity. We belonged to a *petite nation* . . . we who had built an empire that stretched from Hudson Bay to the Gulf of Mexico, and from the Atlantic to the base of the Rockies, traversing an entire continent in the process. Few of these professional men had our welfare at heart. They made speeches about how useful they were to us and how much they would bring us to the light of day. But they ghettoised us to serve their own purposes. We became a small agricultural people, parked on too many small farms incapable of producing a living.

We also became afraid of learning and fought to keep our young illiterate—literacy might endanger their faith. We refused social change, as if there was virtue in the status quo. The seigneurial system and tithing became the symbols of the differences that had to be preserved, while, in fact, they were instruments to control the poor and to deprive us of our liberty.

The language we spoke was also a guarantee of our survival, not because it lived through knowledge and literature, but because it was another element of la différence—and in la différence resided survival. And there certainly wasn't much opportunity to learn the language well.

Then there was entrepreneurship and commerce and development. We couldn't participate in those because we would be contaminated, losing our Faith and our language. We could work in the factories and tanneries; we could be lumberjacks in the forest; we could perform petty urban jobs: that was all right.

To save their skins, the middle class, the professionals, and the clergy betrayed us. They made us the hewers of wood and the drawers of water for the Anglo-Saxon economic empire.

There were many exceptions: the LaFontaines, the Cartiers, the Lauriers, and many others were cut from a different cloth. However, their attempts to lead us to a more participatory and modern society got them branded as vendus and anticlerical.

This manipulation of the people in the name of God, and la survivance through isolation and the pursuit of ignorance, lasted for close to a hundred years. It may still be going on—some in the province are still caught in the petard of a narrow, xenophobic, separatist nationalism.

A very tragic consequence, and one of the great tragedies of this state of affairs, this lack of opportunity for our people, this ghettoisation, was the birth of the Franco-American. It began approximately in the 1830s, when a few crossed the American border to work in the fields of Vermont or in the lumber industry of Maine, then a largely seasonal/temporary emigration. But as the industrialisation of the United States progressed prior to Confederation, and the economic situation deteriorated in Québec, the flow became an hémorragie: whole families left and didn't return. By 1850, one hundred thousand Canadiens lived in the United States.

During inquiries made in 1857 and 1861, many reasons were given for this vast exodus, among them lack of roads, land speculation, inability to find part-time or full-time jobs, overpopulation of the rural areas (in 1861, 85 percent of the people of Québec lived in rural areas), positive propaganda by Canadien exiles, bad harvests, no efficacious government policy, lumber barons' opposition to making more land available for agriculture, and poor agricultural technology and inefficient farming methods.

The inquirers could have added one more reason: the clergy's constant preaching about the value of our agricultural vocation and our spiritual need to suffer while trying to make a living in unproductive rural areas. After all, the temporal reality of their silly sermons only drove people to a mediocre way of life, propelling an exodus to the cities, to Upper Canada (in 1861, 33,287 Canadiens lived there), and to the United States.

In the last three decades of the 19th century, Québec lost 10 percent of its population to emigration. Most of the emigrants came from rural Québec and went to find jobs and economic security in the textile and shoe factories of New England, which employed men, women, and children. In all probability, there is not a single Canadien family today who doesn't have a relative in the United States. The descendants of these emigrants now number close to five million, but few of them still speak French.

Les Anglais: At the time of Confederation, over a million people lived in Québec, 75 percent of whom were French-speaking. In the two largest towns or cities, over 58,000 lived in Québec City, of whom about 23,000 were English-speaking; the population of Montréal was over 90,000, but more than half of them were English-speaking. Furthermore, many Anglais lived in the semi-rural suburbs of Montréal, in the Eastern Townships, in the Outaouais (the Ottawa Valley was known as "Little Ireland" in 1851), and here and there across the province.

The quarter of the population that was English-speaking wasn't all bad. The Anglais built educational facilities (McGill University, primary and secondary schools), economic associations (Boards of Trade), along with cultural and social institutions of their own (the Art Association of Montreal, the Protestant General Hospital of Montreal, the YMCA—the first one in North America, Orange Lodges, etc.). They had newspapers (the *Gazette*, the Protestant *Herald*, the very Catholic *True Witness*, etc.) that mirrored their lives and defended their causes, often as vociferously as their French-speaking counterparts. Most were journeymen having a hard time making ends meet. They drank beer in taverns made for them. (When French and English drank together, these sessions often ended in brawls.)

A few, only a few, built large, transnational economic empires. But most

Anglais—at least those who didn't go to the United States or Ontario—had a sense that Québec was also their land, and on it they would make their stand. They didn't have an easy time of it, boarding themselves up in areas that were their territories, just like their French-speaking neighbours did. The two groups seldom fraternised—Anglais and Canadiens. The two lived apart: the two solitudes of the Montréal writer Hugh MacLennan.

How many Anglais were francophobes? Probably the same proportion as those across the great divide who were anglophobes. In reality, both groups were scared of each other.

However, from time to time, bright lights shone. Carolus Laurier of Saint-Lin, Québec, sent his ten-year-old son, Wilfrid, to an English-speaking Protestant school in New Glascow, eleven kilometres away. That was in 1851. Wilfrid spent two years in New Glascow, being educated by Protestants, but living with an Irish Roman Catholic family. It was a most formative experience for him and he never forgot it.

There is no doubt that, at the time of Confederation—and long there-after—the Anglais controlled the economic life of the province. In Montréal, it was their entrepreneurship, their money, and their contacts that built the industries (sugar refining, flour milling, iron making, wood processing, and shoemaking) that made the city into a Canadian metropolis. They controlled the Bank of Montreal; they opened the Sun Life Insurance Company; they developed the port and transportation; they financed the ship construction and the grain elevators and public transport; they built the railroads and the canals.

The language of commerce, like the language of industry and money matters, was English, particularly in Montréal. The Canadiens appeared to have no objections, extolling too the virtues of their businesses in English—no sign laws in those days and no language police.

However, the French Canadians weren't totally absent from the economic life that swirled around them. They owned the Banque Jacques-Cartier; they had large and profitable stores of all kinds, and the wholesale food business was in their hands; they controlled the ship-building industry of Québec City, and in Montréal they owned tanneries, shoe and cigar factories; they were involved in land speculation and development; and a couple of millionaires built international businesses. They (along with the Irish) also supplied the labour force to staff these industries. They were also wise enough to give themselves a labour union: the Union des Cigariers de Montréal—cigars being very popular.

However, the economic activity of Canadiens, when compared with that of les Anglais, was negligible.

Being annoyed at the economic power of les Anglais, and seeing it as an instrument of domination, is a useless exercise. They did what they had to do, and many thrived. We should have done the same. We chose not to. Instead, we built religious institutions, seminaries, churches, convents, and classical colleges. There wasn't even a French-speaking university in the largest French-speaking city in North America. Why? Certainly not because of the English. Rather it was due to the folly of Rome and the eternal battle between bishops for prestige, and between ecclesiastics for material goods and control.

Professor Arthur Lower once wrote that, in those days, "French Canada's imagination was for the past, rather than for the future." According to him, we "sighed after stability, the perpetual Eden . . . without any English-speaking snakes to whisper in Eve's ears." We also possessed a Latin-Catholic mind, which was focused on the family, religion, and intellectual concepts, especially that of nationalism. Never did revolution cross our mind.

Maybe so. In those days, we weren't too sure of ourselves. Time, though, brought changes in attitude.

When Durham imposed the death penalty on my people, he didn't shed a tear. For him and others, we were a people without a history, and our future lay in having one through belonging to the British Empire and becoming Anglais. That understanding of who we were caused a revolution to take place, a revolution in attitudes and one that didn't mean that we had to sacrifice the best parts of ourselves to be ourselves. In the world of politics, we saw this revolution in attitudes through LaFontaine and Cartier. But we were also to see it in the area of literature and other aspects of the intellectual world.

In effect, Durham called us to arms, literary ones, and the name that dominates here is that of the notary, poet, and historian François-Xavier Garneau (1809–66). In the late 1830s he began collecting documents and information for his *Histoire du Canada*, published in three volumes (between 1845 and 1848, with a supplement in 1852), which covered our history from its beginnings to 1840. It was a clear and solemn statement of our struggle to survive with quality—and our determination to do so. For over a century, his work dominated the Canadiens' understanding of themselves. (The first translation, in English, of Garneau's *Histoire* was done by Andrew Bell and published in 1860.)

"The destiny of Canada," Garneau affirmed, "is dependent on the cause which we vindicate in this work; namely, the conservation of our religion, our language, and our laws." His view of what happened from the time of Champlain until the Act of Union was his "stand upon the old ways." Even though no one, he urged, should believe that "our nationality is secured against all further risks," Canadiens should take solace in the fact that "the existence of the Canadians as a distinct people is not more doubtful than it was a century ago." At that time, he went on to argue, "we were a population of 60,000; we now exceed a million souls."

Garneau's history brought courage to a rather traumatised people, and gave them hope for the future. He also inspired an astonishing number of writers, great and not-so-great. Among them we find the names Philippe-Joseph François Aubert de Gaspé, who wrote what is recognised as the first classic of French-Canadian literature, *Les Anciens Canadiens*, published in 1863; Antoine Gérin-Lajoie, who saw the much-hoped-for survival in the clearing of the land as he demonstrated in his *Jean Rivard, le défricheur* and *Jean Rivard, économiste*; and Octave Crémazie, who was determined that the Canadiens should achieve their destiny through economic and cultural development. That approach made him different from many of his contemporaries, even though his poetry was evocative of the grandeur of the past, as in his *Le Vieux Soldat Canadien* and *Le Drapeau de Carillon*.

And of course, there was the Institut Canadien. A group of young intellectuals founded the institute in 1844 as a place where intellectual pursuits and political debate could be carried out with the greatest possible freedom. It had a large library (8,000 books), a reading room, and it organised debates and discussions on a whole range of subjects, particularly political ones. The members (seven hundred in 1857, in sixty branches across the province) were mostly Rouges, if not in affiliation, at least in the openness of thought that the institute considered to be a fundamental condition of human life. They read American authors and debated the virtues of the American way of life. They didn't, however, attach much importance to British thought, which they considered to be most illiberal in its treatment of Canada, particularly Canada East. And they delved, with great enthusiasm, into the books that Rome, in a fit of dictatorial pretensions, condemned in its infamous Index.

It wasn't possible, as you can well imagine, for the institute not to attract the ire of the bishop, Ignace Bourget, who was the second Roman Catholic bishop of Montréal (1840–76). His view of the French-Canadian Catholics was that they should be obedient servants to the will of God—as expressed by Bourget. The lay order had to be subordinated to his will: the Church was supreme over the State. There could be no division of Church and State in Bourget's world. The institute, and the Rouges affiliated with it, were evil—they didn't share his view. When the institute refused to remove the condemned books from its library, Bourget put it under interdict and excommunicated all those who didn't obey him.

The Institut Canadien suffered a severe blow; but it maintained its course. The spirit of free inquiry lived on.

In 1760, New France was finished for the Canadiens. A new regime began, and an abyss opened under our feet, separating our past from our future. We were alone! "What will happen to us?" we asked nervously? "Will we survive?" In 1760, the only certainty was that the present was bleak and the future sinister. Then a century passed, bringing us to July 1, 1867. We were still here. We had endured the conquerors. We still had our country. In 1867, the only certainty was that the present was good, the future promising. We had triumphed.

Part Two

A People of Canada

V

Adjusting
1867–1920

⚜

On July 1, 1867, Nova Scotia, New Brunswick, Canada East (Québec), and Canada West (Ontario), were "united in Holy Matrimony" as Sir John A. Macdonald, the first prime minister of the new Canada, wrote to a friend in New Brunswick. It was an uneasy union, even though, in most places, the occasion was celebrated with gun salutes and pealing bells, high masses and special church services, Te Deums, parades and speeches. Yet, in the Maritimes, which was largely anti-Confederation, flags flew at half-mast, and many of the inhabitants hung black crepe on their doors.

In Québec there was general resignation, since a large number of people, both lay and clerical, acknowledged that Confederation was necessary. A still larger number, particularly of French Canadians, weren't too certain about the impact of the new constitutional arrangement.

This mixed reaction was to be expected. Confederation began as little more than an act of faith in a still-undefined common destiny. The Union government (1841–67) had proved a disappointment and had failed to establish a workable order between the Canadiens of Canada East and the Anglais of Canada West. Granted that the new constitutional structure was founded on the principle of bilingualism and the duality of the Canadian heritage; yet, only Québec, where the French Canadians were the majority, and Ottawa, where they were a minority, gave formal recognition to this fact. Should English Canada ever unite against them, it was obvious that the French Canadians would have no alternative but to turn to Québec for the protection they needed.

But, like the other provinces, Québec's capacity to act was severely limited by the highly centralised structure created in 1867. The federal government was almost absolute in its authority. It had the power to disallow provincial legislation, and it received the most profitable sources of revenue. Furthermore, it was given the responsibility for appointing and dismissing the lieutenant governors (who were not meant to be figureheads), plus all residuary powers, and full control of the most important legislative fields. Obviously, there was no guarantee that the conflicts that had troubled the country since the days of 1760 would not visit us again.

The Fathers of Confederation sincerely believed—and if they didn't, they certainly hoped—that the unification of the British North American colonies would solve the country's economic ills. Canada would regain the markets lost with the abrogation of the Reciprocity Treaty with the United States in 1864. Canada would attract the foreign capital necessary for the construction and maintenance of railways and the development of our natural resources, particularly in the West. And Canada would be better equipped to compete with the Americans for immigrants. It was a large dream. And the pursuit of that dream would go a long way in minimising the "racial" tensions of the past.

However, there were still the immediate effects of the terms of Confederation, which attempted to unite, in the bosom of one country, peoples of different cultures and languages, backgrounds and religions. Yet, the new state was based on the principles of "representation by population." What would happen if the Protestant English-speaking majority tired of minority rights and began to assert its influence? As for Québec, the Catholic French-speaking majority started to argue that it was not "une province comme les autres." Nor had Confederation successfully disposed of regional and sectional interests.

In light of that situation, federal politicians quickly realised that, in the final analysis, their power-base was provincial—federal parties being federations of provincial parties—and found a great source of success in exploiting sectional rivalries to their own ends. At the same time, provincial leaders of all shapes and forms recognised the value of making the federal government the scapegoat in any issue, and increasingly attacked the federal authority as the chief obstacle to provincial progress. Not much different from today.

In the first thirty years of Confederation, the dream wasn't fully realised, in spite of all the efforts that were poured into it. What caused the dream to falter? The principal cause was the economic challenges of those years. Between 1873 and 1879, there was an economic depression of international dimensions: it disrupted the banking system; many companies went bankrupt; industrial output was suspended for a period of time; unemployment was high; wages were cut drastically; and strikes turned into riots more often than not. It took a long, long time for the economy to recover in spite of the gains made just prior to that period. That turn-around was made possible by Macdonald's national policy of the late 1870s, which advocated protection of Canadian industries, the building of a transcontinental railway, and the settlement of the West. Textile industries grew in Québec; construction of the Canadian Pacific Railway was resumed; and immigrants came to Manitoba.

After that, though, falling prices continued to play havoc with the Canadian economy. All in all, the economic circumstances of these first thirty years hindered the flow of capital, the development of industry, and the settling of the West. It also caused the emigration to the United States of more than a million Canadians.

The record wasn't totally bleak. Three new provinces were added: Manitoba in 1870, British Columbia in 1871, and Prince Edward Island in 1873—*A Mari usque ad Mare* became a reality. By 1876, the Intercolonial Railway, begun as a condition of Confederation, was completed between Québec and the Maritimes—1,100 kilometres long. As well, in 1885, one could take the Canadian Pacific Railway in Montréal and travel to Vancouver.

A great feat; for, in spite of continuous financial difficulties, bitter political feuds, a national scandal, and almost insurmountable natural obstacles, it was a permanent monument to what vision and determination could accomplish within and through Confederation. Moreover, industrialisation did grow in the '70s, '80s, and '90s; so did agriculture as it underwent revolutionary changes for the better. And immigrants began to arrive—and they stayed.

However, the benefits of Confederation didn't materialise fast enough.

Québec, as we shall see, was not left out of the miseries or the blessings of the new reality. Yet, Québec had a particular problem, a particular concern: la survivance nationale. What that expression meant—from 1867 until our era—is important to understand.

We are talking here of the survival of the French-Canadian people—or the Canadiens français, or as I prefer to call them: the Canadiens—and the term has nothing to do with living in Québec, even though it was recognised that the province was the "foyer" of the peoples of America who spoke French. (The Acadians were recognised as a distinct people, but because of their speaking French and having the same roots as we did, for all intents and purposes, they were also Canadiens français. Their struggle was our struggle—or so it was said.)

For the Canadiens to survive, the following assurances were needed: that the French language would survive as well as the institutions inherited from 1608 onwards; that guarantees would be honoured to maintain the importance of the Canadien presence within Confederation; that the majority would not use its power to crush the Canadiens' legitimate rights and goals; and that the Province of Québec would be accepted as a province that wasn't like the others, because it had a special responsibility and because it was the berçeau and foyer of those Canadiens who were born of France. Of course, it wasn't articulated that way, but in searching for the words used to describe la survivance nationale, these were the fundamental elements.

In the beginning, Québec's French-speaking people trusted the constitutional provisions of language and culture that the British North America Act had established to guarantee their survival. However, these were dependent on their maintaining a powerful presence and influence at the federal level.

But they soon found themselves vulnerable to the power of a large English-speaking population, larger than in the days of Union, which had been so perilous for them. More and more, the Canadiens asked themselves, Can we maintain the influence we need? Can we play a dynamic role in this Confederation? Can we make our will known and our objectives realised? Or will we need to retreat within the only province where we have the majority? Will that province, then, become our only homeland?

We can find this anxiety in speeches, editorials, sermons, episcopal letters, documents in public and private archives, memoirs, biographies —practically everywhere one turns. So much material is there on this matter that it forms an integral part of the history of the Province of Québec.

What to do about it, though, was a question that wasn't so easily answered.

⚜

I hear Chazy bark and a noise coming from my dining room. I rush downstairs. Four gentlemen are sitting around the table, and Mascou is busy passing cups of coffee around and pouring glasses of cognac for those who indulge; but there are no cigars, to some of my guests' dismay. Without welcoming them, I rush to my scriptorium to get my tape recorder, remembering that Mascou had offered to organise round tables, to make my passage through time easier.

By the time I return, Chazy has made peace with the guests and lies peacefully next to my chair, and Champa has curled up on the lap of one of the gentlemen. I take my seat at the table, welcome them, thank them for coming, and ask permission to introduce them to you.

Monsignor François-Xavier-Antoine Labelle (1833–91), known affectionately as "le curé Labelle," is a colossal man and quite merry-looking. His cassock is spotless, and he drinks his cognac with flair, but I know he's annoyed that Mascou didn't offer him a cigar. In his time among us, Labelle became known as the Apôtre de la Colonization. As the curé of the prosperous parish of Saint-Jérôme in the Laurentians for over twenty years—and the friend of practically everybody—he was a tireless promoter of settlement in the Ottawa Valley and in the Laurentians. In politics, he tended to be a Bleu, being a great friend and supporter of Cartier's successor, Sir Joseph-Adolphe Chapleau. Yet, he could work with anyone, as long as his dream advanced. For instance, in 1888, he became a sort of deputy minister of agriculture in the national government of that time, remaining in his post until Rome sent him back to his parish a year before he died. Labelle was no idle dreamer; he was determined that his schemes would make sense economically. He belonged to the messianic-religious nationalist school, but he wasn't an Ultramontanist. To him, the Catholic religion was at the core of our nationalism and the only guarantee of our survival. We were chosen, he once said, "to play the role of the Jewish people in the midst of the heathen nations" that surrounded us. He had also no doubt that it was through colonisation that we would undo the Conquest of 1759: "The revenge of Montcalm . . . the greatest victory ever achieved by a nation: to conquer our conquerors."

To the curé's right is a nervous and excitable little man by the name of Joseph-Israel Tarte (1848–1907), a notary (he practiced law only a few years in his youth), an editor (among the most important newspapers he edited and owned were *Le Canadien, L'évènement, La Patrie*), a political organiser sans pareil, a clever politician, a master at patronage, and a minister in Laurier's government. In spite of his slight size, he's an impressive figure, with a shaggy beard and grey hair. He's dapperly dressed in a redingote and a grey topper. In his mortal existence, he was always in frail health. Tarte never smoked or drank hard liquor and urged others to refrain as well. (The smell of either tended to make him ill, which is why the curé is not able to enjoy a cigar.)

Tarte was a devout Catholic and travelled extensively on this continent and in Europe. He is said to have been the best political organiser between 1874 and his retirement in 1902. It's also to his credit that he never was interested in personal wealth—and not once was he accused of mishandling the thousands of dollars that passed through his hands as the financial manager of both political parties, in a career that spanned thirty years. (In an era when many politicians used dubious means to amass fortunes, Tarte's is an unusual record.) He was also known to change his mind frequently, not to mention his political affiliations. But he was always true to a few basic principles: strong leadership to maintain the influence of the Canadiens, protection of Canadian industries, and effective political organisation. Someone once referred to him as a "stormy petrel." He certainly was never afraid to venture into unknown seas, and a storm rarely forced him to take shelter. Instead it would embolden him to fly more deeply into its centre.

Beside Tarte, and with Champa, the cat, on his lap, is Clément-Arthur Dansereau (1844–1918), known as "Le Boss Dansereau"—a journalist of great skill and with an infinite number of contacts in all parts of the Québec population. A conservative of the school of Cartier, he supported Chapleau, and when Wilfrid Laurier's star began to shine, he helped transfer all moderate Liberal-Conservatives to the Liberal Party. He looks like Honoré de Balzac. During his life, he was a bon vivant, erudite, fond of theological arguments, and quite knowledgeable about the history of Canada and of many other places in the world. I think I would have liked to have been Dansereau's contemporary.

To Dansereau's left is Christopher Dunkin (1812–81) professor, lawyer, public administrator, politician, judge, and farmer. Before coming to Canada in 1837, he had been a Greek and Latin scholar who taught at Harvard University. He entered politics in 1857 as a representative of the Eastern Townships of Québec, and in 1864, by refusing to support the government of the day, he precipitated with his vote the political crisis that led to

Confederation. He went on to oppose the Macdonald-Cartier scheme in a brilliant speech in the legislature. At Confederation, though, he accepted the inevitable and was appointed provincial treasurer, ushering in a tradition that lasted over a hundred years: Québec's provincial treasurer was always English-speaking, no doubt to give security to the lords of national and international high finance. In 1869, he entered the federal cabinet as minister of agriculture, a post he retained until 1871, when ill health forced him to leave politics. He then became a judge. He was known to be brilliant, well organised, officious, bad-tempered, cold, and quite conceited. Chazy is asleep at his feet.

Now I'm ready to begin the session. (In the transcript that follows, "LP" stands for me.)

LP: Mascou has given you my comments on Québec and Confederation. Am I on the right path?

Labelle: Yes. We were all concerned. The bishop of Montréal may have had many faults, but lack of patriotism wasn't one of them. He was afraid that, in time, what he cherished most would disappear.

LP: Mr. Dunkin, I suspect it was different for you.

Dunkin: I'm a Protestant and an Anglais. It had to be different. (He stops for a moment before quoting the Old Testament.) "If the prophet had bid thee do some great thing, wouldst thou not have done it?" He looks at me and asks: Wouldn't you?

Dansereau: What the hell does that mean? Never mind! Confederation was a good thing, but it wasn't foolproof for us. A majority could be fashioned to threaten, even harm us.

Dunkin: That's nonsense. In a system of Responsible Government, you don't easily fashion majorities. I understand the anxiety and share it. But too many of you journalists made that up to give you comfort. You thought that when you didn't have your way, the whole country was against you. Concessions had to be made and compromises worked out.

Dansereau is so annoyed that Champa has sought refuge with the curé. Mascou replenishes the cognac for Labelle and Dansereau but offers water to Dunkin and Tarte.

And it's Tarte who breaks the silence with the slight stutter that was his trademark: As long as Cartier was there, there was little to fear. His influence in Québec and in Ottawa—he took over from Sir John A. often, when the old man was either sick or drunk—offered us some assurance that our rights would be recognised and maintained.

LP: Why did you say "some" assurance?

Tarte: Well, there were problems with Cartier's leadership.

Dunkin: He interfered too much in the politics of Québec. It was either his way or no way at all. That's a weakness in a leader.

Dansereau: The reason Tarte has used the right word—"some"—is that you refuse to recognise that the majority worked against us. (Dunkin doesn't move or say a word. But my friend Dansereau is all worked up again.) Not long after 1867, it became apparent to us that Cartier's strength and powers were limited. You can't deny, Christopher, that in spite of his presence and his hard work in keeping us all going in the same direction, we, the Canadiens français, began to feel your power, the power of the majority. No one can deny that!

Dunkin doesn't reply to that either.

Instead I ask: You mean that after 1867 racial and religious antagonism returned to haunt the Canadian nation?

Tarte: Yes. I'm sorry to say. (He stands up, obviously becoming excited.) Louis Riel! Manitoba! And 1869! That was our first hint that things weren't as we had hoped.

Dunkin: Monsieur Tarte, please sit down. You were hardly out of school. If memory serves me right, you left the classical college that you, Arthur, Chapleau, Laurier, Jetté—and only God knows how many others—attended, at the end of the school year of 1867. When Riel caused all this mess, you were learning to be a notary in the office of my friend Louis Archambault. So, please spare us the editorials you would have written had you been old enough.

Labelle comes the rescue. In a gentle voice, he says: Monsieur LaPierre, you will recall that when Canada purchased the lands of the Hudson's Bay Company in 1869, no guarantees were given to protect the collective rights of the Métis of those territories. They were largely Catholic and French-speaking. Under the leadership of our friend Riel, they prevented the peaceful takeover of the territory of Manitoba until their demands for legal guarantees that their schools and language would be protected were granted.

Dunkin: Monsieur le curé, this "incident" greatly embarrassed the federal government. It was necessary to show the Americans—who were just waiting for an opportunity to do mischief—that we could protect our territory. So an expeditionary force was sent to put them in their place and exhibit Canadian sovereignty over the lands we had just acquired. At the same time, the Catholic archbishop of those parts was summoned from the Vatican Council to use his influence with Riel and the other Métis. Canada did what she had to do. You would have done the same.

Tarte: That's not the issue. Macdonald and Cartier promised Archbishop Taché an amnesty for all those who participated in the conflict. It wasn't respected. That's the issue.

Dunkin: But, Monsieur Tarte, no one knew when this so-called promise was made that Riel would have been foolish enough to execute Thomas Scott. We didn't know that! Scott's execution—or murder—changed the whole situation.

Dansereau: Thomas Scott. That Ontario bandit. A good-for-nothing tramp.

Dunkin: Let's not debate Scott's character, please. After his death, there was a powerful riot in Ontario, demanding Riel's blood. If you ask me, Riel brought about his own demise. And while I'm at it, Macdonald did the only possible political thing he could do: delay. Meanwhile, Cartier negotiated the terms under which Manitoba became a province of Canada in 1870. The rights of the Métis were protected. And, oddly enough, Riel, I'm told by Mascou, is now considered a Father of Confederation and is recognised as the Father of Manitoba. You'll pardon me for saying so, but I think it's utter rubbish!

Tarte has become all excited again: Was it rubbish (he practically screams at Dunkin) that Macdonald continued to avoid any decision? It was left to Alexander Mackenzie, a Liberal, to deal with it when he became prime minister after the Pacific Scandal. We wanted an amnesty for everybody. But non! We were denied again. There was no "total" amnesty for Riel. He was banished for five years. That's where the rubbish is, Monsieur Dunkin.

LP (soothingly): I think there's much that's valid in Monsieur Tarte's statement. French Canadians could only view with alarm both the Ontario riot and the government's delay in granting the amnesty.

Dunkin: I agree. But they don't have to argue that Confederation is already a failure or that we, the nasty Anglais, are constantly conspiring against them.

LP: Mr. Dunkin, you're using the present tense. Why?

Dunkin: Did I? It just seems as if it were yesterday. (He scratches Chazy's ears and adds mockingly) If you ask me, they were more concerned about their prestige than about the rights of the Métis and their vital interests.

Before war breaks out again, Mascou comes in to announce that lunch is served in the garden. While they're having lunch, I consider another issue of importance that did much to add to the Canadiens' worries.

⚜

At Confederation, education became the exclusive responsibility of the provinces, with the provision that the separate schools (Catholic schools in

215

Ontario, Protestant schools in Québec) existing by law at the time of Confederation should be maintained. On the other hand, should the minority ever feel deprived of its rights in this matter, it could appeal to the federal government for redress. However, all efforts to have this provision extended to those separate schools that existed by custom—but not in law—had failed.

In 1869, in accordance with the provision of the British North America Act, the then premier of Québec, the novelist Pierre-Joseph-Olivier Chauveau (1820–90), introduced legislation that, in effect, created a Protestant (English-speaking) school system. He did so by splitting the Conseil de l'Instruction Publique into two committees: one Catholic and one Protestant. The funds earmarked for education, $275,000 in Dunkin's first provincial budget in 1868, were divided according to the Catholic and Protestant populations in the province.

In 1870, the New Brunswick government ended subsidies to the Roman Catholic schools in the province. One fanatical superintendent applied the law, brutally closing schools and leaving the Acadian and Irish populations—most of whom were poor fishermen, farmers, and urban workers—unable, in most instances, to have their children educated in their faith. The Catholic population of Canada led the charge to have the decision reversed, but to no avail. The federal government argued that it couldn't consider any appeal and, in time, the Privy Council decided that New Brunswick was empowered to do what it wanted in matters of education.

For the first time, the Canadiens of Québec were confronted with the fate of their French-speaking co-religionists in other parts of Canada—the Acadians in this case. (Later it would be the Canadiens living in Manitoba, in the North-West Territories, and in Ontario.) The French-speaking people of Québec followed the debate—a debate begun under the Conservatives and that continued when the Liberals formed the government in 1878—with interest and growing anxiety. During it, many in the province argued, for the first time, that it was the duty of Québec's French Canadians to defend the rights of "their people," wherever they lived in Canada. Few had doubts that if the French-speaking majority of Québec had acted in the same way toward the Protestants of that province, there would have been hell to pay.

Interestingly enough, the bishops of Québec sided with the federal government. They feared that federal intervention would endanger provincial autonomy. It was more prudent, then, to tolerate an unjust law than to risk weakening the emerging provincial powers.

The questions of the "amnesty" for Riel and the New Brunswick school "policy" weren't conducive to affirming the security of the French Canadians within Confederation. What measures, then, should be taken to ensure that security, to decrease the apparent French-Canadian impotence, and to force the federal government to redress what they, the Canadiens, considered infringements of their rights?

It's the question that I ask my panel after lunch.

⚜

Dansereau: To answer your question, we obviously had only one option: find ourselves a leader that was indispensable, as Cartier was.

Dunkin: Come, come, Arthur. By 1872 Cartier's power was all spent, sad to say. But it's a fact. As I said before, he was too authoritarian. His handling of patronage, his constant interference, and his fixation on Montréal divided the party and sapped his authority and control. We know that. And you, you're too intelligent not to have realised that Cartier had become set in his ways and was unwilling to adjust to people like you—young, able, ambitious as you are. I'm no fool. I realised that the young in our party resented him. God knows how that hurt when he lost his own election in 1872 and had to be elected in Provencher, in Manitoba. Of course, he was quite ill by then. He died in the midst of the Pacific Scandal, on May 20, 1873 . . . He was never able to clear his name.

Tarte: Unfortunately, there wasn't much to clear. Money did change hands between the Conservative Party and the consortium the government was negotiating with to build the CPR from Montréal to Vancouver. Over $300,000 changed hands. There is no doubt about that.

Dansereau: It was all the fault of that old geezer Hugh Allan. He wanted to be president of the company. He hunted down Cartier, promising him that the terminal would be in Cartier's riding in Montréal. The money flowed into the Party's coffers, and we used it all over the country to fight the elections of 1872. Macdonald got some, Cartier too, and others too numerous to name. I can assert, though, that not a single person appropriated one cent for his own personal purposes. Allan knew that Cartier was vulnerable. Well? That's that. (He looks around the room, then continues.) Four thousand people lined the streets of Montréal at my friend's funeral.

Labelle: There's more than that. You see, Cartier wasn't certain if Allan was the best man for the job or if the terminal should be in Montréal or elsewhere. But Allan was insistent. He worked up the electorate in favour of his scheme. Unfortunately, Cartier's agreement came too late. He was defeated largely because his ability to protect our interests was openly questioned.

There follows a lengthy silence as each is caught in his own thoughts about Cartier's fate.

Eventually, Tarte brings us back to the question: Le bas Canada, as we called ourselves then, didn't have as powerful a leader until your friend Wilfrid Laurier came our way in the '80s.

Labelle: My great friend Chapleau could have been such a leader. But for all kinds of reasons, he wasn't accepted as Cartier's successor.

There follows another period of silence as Mascou brings refreshments. It gives me time to think of Chapleau.

Sir Joseph-Adolphe Chapleau (1840–98), lawyer, teacher, politician, premier of Québec (1879–82), member of Macdonald's cabinet (1882–92), and lieutenant governor of Québec (1892–98), never had Cartier's following either inside or outside Québec—or his prestige and power. Chapleau was a tormented soul, often unsure of himself, and not much appreciated by Macdonald. It must also be admitted that after Cartier's death, the inherent contradictions and divisions in the Liberal-Conservative Party, which Cartier had built from the coalition created by LaFontaine in the days of Union, became more pronounced. Chapleau wasn't able to overcome that.

LP: The Liberal-Conservative Party to which all of you belonged in different ways and at different times (I point out to my guests) was torn apart by the increasing influence of the Ultramontanists.

Monsieur Tarte: Tell me about that. You were a part of that movement.

Before Chapleau can speak, though, Dunkin interjects: But only for a while. In 1882, Monsieur Tarte had a revelation. Chapleau became the source. (He smiles ironically.) It's said of Monsieur Tarte that he is the only politician who supported both sides of every conceivable question in Québec with equal brilliance. An interesting record.

Tarte: I'm capable of learning, Monsieur Dunkin, which is more than I can say of many others. But that's beside the point. In 1871, there was a political program drawn up that was called the Programme Catholique...

Dansereau intervenes somewhat sarcastically: These people ruined Cartier's Liberal-Conservative Party. We, the Bleus, didn't value extremism in politics, or in anything else for that matter. We were moderate democrats; we favoured the maintenance of our traditional institutions and way of life, and we did accept clerical authority as the chief upholder of social stability. We weren't interested in ecclesiastical dictates, however. But we were very, very attentive to the wishes of the bishops and the priests.

Tarte: If I may be permitted to continue. We, the Programmistes, favoured the Conservative party, because it was the only political association that offered any protection to the Church. However, our support was conditional on the party's willingness to always defend the religious interests of our people as expressed by the Church. We were prepared to put aside party discipline when the issue involved any aspect of Québec's religious life.

Labelle: You must tell your readers, Monsieur LaPierre, that the Programme came after the Guibord affair. As you well know, Joseph Guibord was excommunicated in 1869, because he didn't obey Bishop Bourget's order to leave the Institut Canadien. When he died in November of that year, he hadn't made his peace with the Church, so he couldn't be buried in the Catholic cemetery where he owned a plot. His widow sued the Church. . . . I see Monsieur Dunkin wants to speak.

Dunkin: The case attracted enormous attention. It raised important issues of clerical immunity, ecclesiastical prerogatives, and, above all, the separation of Church and State. If the Church won, it could mean that the Church was a state within a state—and independent of state control. That would have been hard to accept.

LP: Monsieur le curé, please finish with Guibord.

Labelle: Well, the case dragged on before the courts until late November 1874, when the Privy Council ordered Guibord to be buried in his plot, where his wife already was. The bishop and the parish priest refused, and the whole matter was sent back to the courts, while Guibord was carried back and forth, from the Protestant cemetery where he had been interred to the Catholic one. There were riots. The police and the army came out in force. Finally, the poor man was laid to rest beside his wife. But the bishop had the last word. He deconsecrated the place within the plot where Guibord was buried, while keeping Madame Guibord in consecrated ground. On that, I have no editorial comment to make.

Tarte: But there was more to the Programme Catholique than a rebuke to the Rouges.

Dunkin: There certainly was. That's what so pernicious about the Programme Catholique. You believed that the British North America Act had granted the Roman Catholic Church in Québec complete autonomy to govern itself in accordance with the canons of the Church. Consequently, all French-Canadian politicians were bound to frame any new legislation in accordance with the will of the Church—and to amend any existing laws accordingly. Good grief! You were opposed to the State having an independent say in the solemnization of marriage, education, and this silly pastime of the bishop of Montréal and the Sulpicians: the creation of parishes. It was a dangerous instrument in the hands of demagogues. I'm not saying you were a demagogue, Monsieur Tarte. You proved that when you left this clique of . . . whatever!

Dansereau: The Programme split our party, allowed direct clerical participation in the political process of both our country and our province, and made impossible the essential instrument we needed: we had to vote en bloc in order to protect our interests.

Dunkin: It also endangered Catholics outside Québec. Many were quite concerned that there would be a backlash against them. This is why Rome was so busy sending apostolic delegates to put the bishops and their priests in their place.

Labelle (smiling): It is interesting to note that the bishops of Québec were quite divided on the Programme issue. In fact, the majority didn't support it. They felt that the Programme Catholique—ultra-Catholic, as it was—was still a danger for the Church. In those days, the lay politician was at the service of the Church. He was subordinate. Now, with the Programme, he had the nerve to act in the name of the Church. That wasn't acceptable. They had therefore to reprimand the Programmistes and remind them of their place in the pecking order.

LP: You mean to tell me that the episcopacy and the clergy of Québec wanted people like our friends here to abide by their wishes or else face their wrath?

It is Dunkin who answers: There is no doubt whatsoever about that. And, by the way, where did that leave us, the Protestants? Or the English-speaking Catholics? There were many in Québec.

Dansereau: That's where we, the Bleus, came in. We made a distinction between the clergy as the guardian of our conscience and the clergy as the instrument to tell us for whom to vote. As such, there is no doubt that clerical authority was binding in those cases that involved moral and religious principles. But, in the ordinary political life of the Province . . . Non! The bishop, the priest: they were ordinary citizens in politics, like the rest of us. No special status!

Labelle: Even though the Programme wasn't accepted by the majority of the bishops, or even of the population, it had an appealing ingredient: it could be interpreted as a strong tool in the pursuit of our nationalism. Nationalism is founded on the equation of differences. Having a state religion in Québec, even one not established and official by law, constitutes la différence between us and the others. We can never be too detached from the importance of la différence in the pursuit of our French-Canadian national interests.

LP: If you permit, may we conclude this part of our discussion and turn our attention to the bringing of the majority of Québécois into one party? This one-party approach would constitute a bloc of votes to use in the pursuit of power and influence at the federal level. Or a coalition of "les forces vives de la nation" would achieve the same goal. I don't think, though, that either of these possibilities would work well at the provincial level. At least that's the conclusion I draw from the two such attempts made between 1872 and during the aftermath of the second Riel affair in 1885. Both of these attempts were disguised under the camouflage of a Parti National.

Dunkin: I think you're right. Coalition—or the pursuit of a substantial bloc of voters—doesn't work well at any level. Democracy operates on political division, and to the victor belong the spoils. A strong leader, like Cartier, is able to concentrate the votes around him. But he'll always have opposition within his own party and within the electorate. So our system works better when the leader is charismatic, when he can argue issues on broad principles, when he's able to make compromises, and undo quickly the harm to his political career he may have done himself by pursuing a policy that many oppose.

Dansereau: On the other hand, Christopher, there's strength in numbers. What we discovered after the Ultramontane stupidity was that the Bleu Party constituted a school, as it were. L'école de Cartier—and then, later, l'école de Chapleau—was a bloc within the general folds of the Conservative Party. We could use that to pursue our interests. We did, in fact. Laurier's victory in 1896—and many times thereafter—was because Monsieur Tarte here, aided by some of us, was able to bring that school into the fold of the Liberal Party.

Dunkin: I wouldn't know about that. I wasn't around.

I'm about to terminate our discussion, but Labelle asks me: Did we answer your question—or solve your riddle?

LP (Rather pompously, I think, I answer): You demonstrated that unanimity is difficult to achieve, given the scope and the freedom inherent in human nature, in the political process, and in the life of a nation, even an endangered one. The question I asked at the beginning was, What political measures should the French-speaking minority of Québec within Canada take to ensure its security, to decrease the apparent French-Canadian impotence, and to force the federal government to redress what they, the Canadiens, consider infringements of their rights? To that question, you have offered the following possible instruments: a strong, charismatic leadership; voting en bloc; coalition; and affirmation of la différence, in light of the fact that we are French-speaking Canadians and also that Québec isn't a province comme les autres. Am I on the right track?

Labelle: You have learned well, my son. However, there remains the pursuit of provincial autonomy.

LP: Can we do that another day? I have to walk Chazy. Mascou will be in touch soon. I thank you.

Labelle: We thank you. We look forward to seeing you and your creatures soon.

We all stand. We bow. Mascou ushers them out, and I go for a walk.

⚜

Québec didn't arrive in the new Canada empty-handed. From 1867 to 1920, Québec continued to make a substantial contribution to the general growth and welfare of our country.

Québec's land mass, though, was much smaller in 1867. At that time, the provincial authority controlled only the southern part of the province: there was no Québec sovereignty over the regions of Abitibi, New Québec or Ungava, and Labrador. (The border of Labrador was disputed until 1927, when the British Privy Council upheld Newfoundland's claims. Successive provincial governments, however, have questioned the validity of that settlement.) However, after Canada obtained the lands of the Hudson's Bay Company in 1869, Québec's territory was changed twice. In 1898, the federal government transferred the Abitibi region, and in 1912, Québec's frontiers were extended to Hudson Strait, thus including all the lands of New Québec or Ungava.

Three influential Québec historians—Paul-André Linteau, René Durocher, and Jean-Claude Robert—have stressed that Québec's boundaries "were imposed by outside governments, in London and Ottawa," leaving Québec with no authority whatsoever "over the formation of its territory." An interesting fact. But I have no evidence that it's remembered today, with the tiresome discussion about Québec's frontier, should the separatists achieve their goal.

Québec's land mass is now immense: 1,550,000 square kilometres. Like much of the rest of Canada, most of it (roughly 90 percent) is not inhabited.

In the first census taken after Confederation (1871), the population of

Québec was 1,191,516 (32.3 percent of the Canadian population), French-speaking Quebeckers constituted about 78 percent of the population of Québec, and French Canadians formed 31.1 percent of the total population of Canada. Fifty years later (1921), Québec had grown to 2,360,510 souls: 26.9 percent of Canada's total population. About 80 percent of the people then living in Québec were French-speaking, and 27.9 percent of the population of Canada was French-speaking. The balance was shifting.

Between 1871 and 1921, more people left Québec than entered it. However, the succeeding provincial governments, in spite of meagre resources, took steps to stop the haemorrhage by trying to find new sources of population, by enticing emigrants to return, by building better roads and railways to facilitate the transportation of goods and services, or by modernising agriculture. Many historians, though, have argued that these measures were either inadequate or they did the opposite of what they were meant to do. For instance, the modernisation of agriculture, good in itself, made many farm or rural labourers redundant, leaving them without readily available jobs due to the slow rate of industrialisation. Consequently, they had no choice but to emigrate.

Emigration, though, was not peculiar to Québec. One prominent Ontario politician once pointed out: "You cannot find one single solitary Canadian family which has not a son or a daughter or a brother or a sister or some near and dear relative now inhabiting the United States." (The brain drain in Canada isn't a new phenomenon—as some right-wing pundits would have us believe today.)

As for immigration, it is estimated that between 1846 and 1914 some sixty million people left Europe for the New World: 60 percent to the United States, 11 percent to Brazil, 8.7 percent to Canada. Québec received its share of those immigrants, but the vast majority of those who entered the province only did so for a while before moving on. In 1901, "foreign-born" Québécois totalled about 5 percent of the population; in 1931, it was over 8 percent, a slight growth. However, it did add variety to the Québec population landscape. Besides those who came from the British Isles and the United States, "others" (as they were referred to) began to arrive: in 1871, nearly eight thousand persons of German origin, 74 Jews, 539 Italians, and about three thousand of various other nationalities made for a total of 18,658. By 1931, that total had grown to 171,877. The most phenomenal increase was in the Jewish population, which jumped from 74 in 1871 to 60,987 in 1931.

The census of 1871 reported 6,988 Indians. By 1931, that population had doubled. (The Inuit weren't counted in 1871; the province then had no jurisdiction in the North, where they mostly lived. In 1931, the census lists their numbers at 1,159.) There were also 976 Métis in 1901. All these people had little contact with the provincial government—or with the general population of Québec. They "belonged" to the federal government. Even when, in 1912, the province agreed to negotiate with Aboriginal peoples regarding land claims, the provincial government did nothing. It wasn't until the 1970s that the authorities in Québec awakened.

The British North America Act had made immigration a joint federal-provincial responsibility, so Québec had a say in managing it. At the beginning, the province did try to recruit immigrants directly, but the financial crisis of the 1870s led to an abandonment of this policy, for the most part. (It would not be until the Trudeau era, in the 1960s and '70s, that Québec assumed more and more responsibility for attracting immigrants to the province.)

The result of all of this? Through massive emigration and a comparative trickle of immigration, Québec didn't grow as quickly as was hoped. In fact, had the fecundity rate not been so high, the population would have dropped drastically.

Historians Linteau, Durocher, and Robert reveal other interesting information. They write:

> By the 1840s and 1850s, the older areas of Québec could no longer absorb the French-Canadian surplus population, and French Canadians began to infiltrate the areas held by the British groups. By 1901, the Eastern Townships had a French-Canadian majority; so did the Outaouais, which had been an English/Irish region since 1880. Meanwhile, French Canadians also settled in the new regions that were beginning to open to colonisation: Saguenay–Lake St. John, Temiscamingue and the area north of

Montreal. In 1931, only three counties—Brome, Huntingdon and Pontiac—did not have French-Canadian majorities, and thirty-six of Québec's seventy-four counties were more than 95 percent French Canadian. Overall, Québec was Canada's most homogeneous province.

Which brings us naturally to the question of language. Québec is the most bilingual province in Canada. In 1931, close to 25 percent of the Quebeckers of British stock were bilingual, and slightly over 30 percent of Canadiens were. In the same year, about 14 percent spoke only English, 56 percent spoke only French, and 29.3 percent were bilingual. However . . . there are always "howevers". . . . Between the 1850s and the 1970s, the English language had a sort of privileged position in Québec. "Si tu parles pas Anglais, mon p'tit garçon," my mother told me, when she sent me, at twelve years of age, to St. Patrick's Academy in Sherbrooke, "t'auras pas d'ouvrage de bureau. Tu vas être comme ton père." Consequently, many of us who wanted "better jobs than our fathers" have had to learn English. That was true in my time—and in the time of my parents.

The geographer André Siegfried (1875–1959), when he visited Canada at the beginning of the last century, was shocked: "English is the speech of the managers and French of the menials." You could pass weeks in Montréal, he went on, without noticing that it was the home of a majority of inhabitants whose mother tongue was French. In Sherbrooke (in the Eastern Townships, now known as L'Estrie), where I lived in my youth, English was the language of work and even the language of civil administration. And the historian Michel Brunet has taught us that until 1925 the "cheques issued by the provincial government were in English only."

At the beginning of the 20th century, many associations came together to launch a counterattack, but they were often dismissed as "nationalist crackpots." Their aims weren't that bizarre: respect for the language of our ancestors; greater bilingualism at all levels of society, particularly in government; and the preservation of the language rights of the French-speaking minorities outside of Québec. Unfortunately for the country, idiocy prevailed, and they weren't very successful until the Trudeau era.

At Confederation, 85 percent of the population of Québec lived in rural areas. This situation changed dramatically in the years between 1867 and 1920. At the turn of the 20th century, over a third of Quebeckers lived in cities (an increase of 140.6 percent). And the trend continued: by 1911, over 44 percent resided in urban centres; and by 1921, a little more than half of the population of Québec lived in twenty-one municipalities with populations of more than 6,000. The major cities were and are Montréal, the metropolis of Canada, which was also a filthy city in 1867; Québec City, which was vegetating, as was Trois-Rivières; and Sorel, Sherbrooke, Valleyfield, and Hull, all of which were growing. This trend continued, except for the filth of Montréal, all through our period. The First World War contributed an enormous amount to the deruralisation of Québec, as it did everywhere else in Canada. By 1921, Montréal and the Island of Montréal had a population of over a million; Québec City and its suburbs, about 101,000; Sherbrooke had reached 23,515; Trois-Rivières, 22,167; and Hull, close to 30,000. All these people had discovered that the city was the place to be, if you wanted a job—and the prosperity that was supposed to go with it.

Where was Québec economically at the time of Confederation? Well, it had a good home market—and an extended market across Canada—in which to sell its goods, and its internal market grew rapidly as the population expanded. Between 1871 and 1901, Québec specialised its industries and its agriculture, expanded its markets, and developed the infrastructure necessary to maintain growth.

By the end of the 19th century, Québec had given itself important communication or transportation instruments. In 1867, Québec had slightly less than a thousand kilometres of track belonging to the Grand Trunk Railway and a few other small lines here and there. Montréal was the pivotal point. Confederation changed that less-than-satisfactory picture—the federal government built the Intercolonial and the Canadian Pacific Railways, and Québec profited from both of them. In addition, the province constructed railways of its own. At first the emphasis was on colonisation lines, which were meant to open up new areas of settlement in the province. The main accomplishment, though, was the Québec, Montréal, Ottawa and Occidental

(QMO&O), which was the result of the construction of two lines: the Montréal Colonisation Railway and the North Shore Railway. The former was the inspiration of le curé Labelle: he wanted a line between Montréal and Saint-Jérôme, to encourage colonisation and to bring the firewood of the Laurentian northland to the woodless citizens of Montréal. When the businessmen of Montréal got involved in it in the early 1870s, the line developed another mission: it would run from Montréal to Ottawa, along the north shore of the Ottawa River, and link with the Pacific Railway. To placate Labelle, a branch line would go to Saint-Jérôme. However, the Pacific Scandal and an economic depression delayed its construction.

As for the North Shore Railway, it was the inspiration of the élite of Québec City. It was to go from the provincial capital to Montréal, hugging the north shore of the St. Lawrence. Its construction was also delayed—the necessary capital couldn't be obtained on the London markets.

By 1874, the provincial government was determined to join the two lines and build the QMO&O railway. It would be the provincial masterpiece, and the people of Québec would pay for most of it. Three years later, the Montréal-Hull line was completed, and two years after that, the Montréal-Québec link was done. The province had spent fourteen million dollars and was the proud owner of 503 kilometres of rail.

When Chapleau became premier in 1880, he decided to sell it to private interests.

Building railways with taxpayers' money always led to scandals. The QMO&O was no exception.

⚜

Joseph-Israel Tarte and I are having tea. It is, of course, afternoon tea à l'anglaise. The others, who were to join us, have been detained somewhere en route. Mascou won't explain. Tarte is his affable self, and, as usual, most knowledgeable.

"The railway had cost a lost of money," he says, "and every year we had to find the 'argent' to pay for the repairs and the high interest costs. In the midst of an economic depression, that wasn't easy. It was obvious, therefore, that the best thing to do was to sell it and use the money for other worthwhile projects." He smiles and with a smirk he adds: "In my time, politicians never lacked worthwhile projects. At least, I never did. Do politicians of your day still have projects?"

"Oh yes. Lots." I eat, with relish, one of those thin cucumber sandwiches that only nuns can produce—at least in Canada. That duty finished, I say to Tarte: "You once described this railway as the most important property of the Québec people. But in 1880—a year after it's all completed—Chapleau decides to divide the railway and to sell half of it to the CPR and the other half to your and Chapleau's friend Louis-Adélard Sénécal, whom he had named general manager of the railway." I add with some sarcasm: "The people of Québec didn't enjoy their property for very long."

"Let's be reasonable, Monsieur LaPierre, the province had little money. The railway was in danger; it was marching rapidly towards bankruptcy. It was necessary to sell it. Chapleau wanted it sold to one consortium. But the company building the Canadian Pacific would only buy the link between Montréal and Ottawa for four million dollars. It was imperative, then, to find a buyer for the eastern section, that is, Montréal to Québec City. Sénécal was there and he came up with the money: another four million." Tarte is now enjoying the strawberries topped with chocolate. "By the way, Monsieur Sénécal wasn't my friend."

"Perhaps not at that time." More cucumber sandwiches for me—Tarte eats only the dessertish parts of the tea—and then I say, "Monsieur Tarte, you once described this sale to Sénécal as a theft."

"It was. Sénécal paid four million dollars and then, a few months after the contract was signed, he sold his shares to the Grand Trunk Railway, giving them a monopoly on the traffic between Montréal and Québec City; they had control of both sides of the St. Lawrence. We, in Québec City, didn't like that at all. Besides, I was then an Ultramontane, a Programmiste. I was opposed to Chapleau's policy, even though I understood quite well the implications of not selling." He finally swallows the strawberry he's been examining, before adding: "Sénécal made a lot of money. As for Chapleau, he wasn't pleased with me. He called me "une punaise qui s'appelle Israel"—and he told everyone that he would crush me. But, your friend Wilfrid Laurier understood what it was all about—if I may say so after the fact." Now, Tarte is relishing the choux à la crème. "We don't have many of these where I live now."

"You mean Laurier's famous article in *L'Électeur*, the Liberal newspaper of Québec City, in 1881?"

"Yes. That's it. It was called 'La caverne des 40 voleurs.'" Conspiratorially, Tarte tells me: " At first, no one knew who had written this libellous article consisting of accusations that showed a vast regime of corruption. It argued that Sénécal had erected robbery into a system; he was compared to the corrupt Bigot of New France. Angered and humiliated, Sénécal sued the newspaper for $100,000, and Laurier had to admit that he had written the article. Your Laurier felt sure of himself; he had accumulated an enormous amount of evidence to prove his case. Like everything else in Québec, the jury contained Bleus and Rouges. It was hopelessly divided. So the judge declared a mistrial and, afterwards, Sénécal took no other steps to re-open the issue." Tarte leans closer to me and adds: "Laurier settled his score with Sénécal!" And he goes back to his choux.

I know what he's talking about. Sénécal was instrumental in driving Laurier's newspaper, *Le Défricheur*, into bankruptcy. Sénécal also contributed the money needed to buy the votes necessary to bring about Laurier's defeat in Drummond-Arthabaska in 1877, shortly after Mackenzie had appointed him to the cabinet. Tarte leans closer to me again and whispers: "Laurier was loyal to a fault. But if you crossed him, he was merciless. A great man, nevertheless."

I won't go there. So, I come back to Tarte's turnaround: "Chapleau and Sénécal were your enemies before the summer of 1882; then, Chapleau entered the federal cabinet as Secretary of State. In October of that year, you left for Europe on the same ship as Sénécal, in the 'caravane de M. Sénécal,' said your political enemies. Monsieur Tarte, you came back from Europe as Sénécal's and Chapleau's devoted friend. There were many sceptics in your world who said you had been bought."

"Many nasty things were said against me, but I seldom paid attention. What my critics didn't understand was that it was better to make peace. I am by temperament a man who faces reality and adjusts to it. The reality was that Chapleau was in Ottawa; the railway was divided and sold; the incident was over. 'Let's go on,' I said to my readers."

I don't remind him that there was a prize for his conciliation: he was allowed to buy another newspaper, a newspaper more or less owned by Sénécal. Deals are deals—then, now, and forever. There was, however, a dénouement to this entire saga that's interesting to consider. I ask him about it and, very proud of himself, he tells me:

"In February 1884, the Québec cabinet formally asked the federal government for an increase in the per capita subsidy (all provinces depended upon this subsidy to meet their bills), and for some reimbursement for the cost of building the North Shore Railway. At the same time, Québec asked the CPR to buy the eastern section of the North Shore Railway. . . ." Tarte stops talking and asks: "You know about our railway?" In the usual way, I signify that I am quite aware of it. He continues.

"We wanted those requests met. Both refused. We had to do something to impose our will, show our determination. We certainly weren't prepared to be meek. We had our rights."

"So you rebelled?"

"Well, 'rebelled' is a big word." He smiles while deciding to re-open his conquest of the goodies on the pastry tray.

Satisfied, he continues: "But, in a way, we did. The French-Canadian Conservative members in the House of Commons decided to boycott the sittings until the federal cabinet granted our demands." He laughs. "The Québec members, the French-Canadian members that is, used to meet in room #8 in the Parliament Buildings. We went there and refused to move. Sir John A., realising that without the votes of Québec he wouldn't be able to push through a multi-million-dollar loan to the CPR syndicate, caved in. A wise man. He promised us a subsidy of $12,000 a mile for the North Shore Railway—and that he would look at increasing the per capita grants, which he did in the same session. As for the CPR: that came another day." He hesitates and adds with some relish: "I was the ringleader."

Tarte, then, sinks back in his chair, most satisfied with himself.

"And with this blackmail," I say sarcastically—I am, after all, a centrist—"you went back to Québec City and your members marched back dutifully into the House of Commons to vote in favour of lending $22,500,000 to the CPR."

Tarte nods in agreement and returns to his world. Sir John A. had the last word, though. The Québec members lost room #8 as their private domain.

⚜

Between 1896 and 1920, the Québec economy expanded considerably due to the development of hydroelectric power (the famous Shawinigan dam was started in 1898, and the Shawinigan aluminum smelter in 1901). A new economic upswing was starting in which prices began to rise, assisted by an increased demand for cheap consumer goods coming from the United States. All these factors prompted a new prosperity. This situation was fed by the development of the West, railway construction, and industrial growth in central Canada, particularly Ontario.

The new prosperity brought, in its wake, large foreign investment aided by Sir John A. Macdonald's national policy of protection for Canadian industries (most were American subsidiaries); a national policy that Sir Wilfrid Laurier, who was prime minister between 1896 and 1911, didn't change substantially. In 1900, foreign investment in Canada was considerable, 85 percent of which was coming from the United Kingdom. By 1920, this investment had almost quadrupled, but 44 percent was now coming from the United States. Ten years later, 61 percent was coming from the Americans.

The only cloudy economic period was in 1913, but the First World War quickly put an end to that.

In those days, there wasn't much concern about foreign ownership in Québec (or anywhere else, for that matter), even though the new economy favoured resources (rivers, minerals, trees on crown lands, etc.) owned by the people but administered by the province. But the succeeding provincial Liberal governments, which followed each other between 1897 and 1945, went out of their way to sell the publicly held resources. Progress, economic and social, meant jobs and jobs and jobs. "Who cares where the money comes from?" many said, and profoundly believed. And so, they fearlessly granted privileges of all sorts to large—mostly American—companies (monopolies) to encourage the exploitation of Québec's natural resources and the development of its industrial might. To encourage it even further, cabinet ministers acted as solicitors for large companies and sat on their boards of directors.

Where were the French-Canadian capitalists or investors in all of this? In hiding? In 1930, only 4.6 percent of the directors of large Canadian or Québec corporations were Canadiens. Les Anglais (meaning Americans) ruled the economy. But no one seemed to care. Oh, some nationalists questioned the turning over of the wealth of Québec's resources, in forestry and mining, to foreigners, and letting foreign capital develop our industries; but few paid attention to them. They were seen as Neanderthals, against progress, or worse, as favouring a "retour à la terre," the standard myth of the French-Canadian messianic nationalism.

Why weren't the French Canadians of Québec present at the birth of the great economy?

In 1945, a novel, written in English, spoke of the tensions between the French and les Anglais. *Two Solitudes* was written by John Hugh MacLennan

(1907–90), who is reputed to be the first major author writing in English to search for our national character. In his novel, published in 1945, he insisted that our stories were also worth telling in films and on television. In the novel, two English-speaking businessmen visit Saint-Marc, the home of Athanase Tallard, a sort of seigneur in the little town. In this passage, the visitors have just arrived by train; Tallard met them at the station:

> "I understand," [McQueen] said now, pronouncing each word carefully, "that there's a good waterfall on the river that runs just below the parish."
>
> Again Athanase allowed his face to show some surprise. "Yes, there is," he said. "When I was a young fellow, I used to fish in the pool just below the falls."
>
> "You can get a lot more out of a river than fish."
>
> "So you can." Athanase grinned. "Out of that particular river I get more than half my income. I've got a toll-bridge across it."
>
> McQueen shook his head from side to side. "The feudal system may be profitable, Tallard. But a power dam would be a lot more so."
>
> "What do we want with a dam in Saint-Marc?"
>
> McQueen's head was still now, and he stared out the window past Tallard's shoulder. "It would all depend on the body of water in the stream," he said. . . .
>
> "You know, Tallard," McQueen said, "if French-Canada doesn't develop her own resources, someone else is bound to do it for her. Bound to."
>
> "Someone else does so already, Mr. McQueen. Your business friends in Montréal. They've grown fat on us."

Tallard and the visitors go to see the falls, and after he has dropped them at the station, Tallard in his carriage ponders:

> McQueen was right. Unless they [the French Canadians] developed their own resources they would soon have none left to

develop. The English were taking them over one by one. If the process continued indefinitely the time would arrive when the French Canadians would be a race of employees. Perhaps, because they were a minority, perhaps because their education was not technical, they had no real share in the country's industry.

In some ways, MacLennan's appraisal of the tension between industrial development and the status quo has validity. Take, for instance, this quote from an eminent Québec theologian, spoken at a Saint-Jean-Baptiste ceremony in 1902:

> We are not only a civilised race, we are the pioneers of civilisation; we are not only a religious people, we are the messengers of the religious idea; we are not only submissive sons of the Church, we are, we ought to be, numbered among its zealots, its defenders, and its apostles. Our mission is less to manipulate capital than to change ideas; it consists less in lighting the fires of factories than in maintaining and radiating afar the hearth light of religion and thought.

Were French Canadians really educated so that they couldn't function in the economic order that arose after 1867 and particularly after 1896? The general answer seems to be yes.

In 1866, Québec's 3,589 primary schools enrolled 178,961 students. The secondary level consisted of some 237 educational facilities: 15 classical colleges, about the same number of industrial and commercial colleges, a few academies and special schools, largely for the handicapped, and three schools for the training of teachers. Close to 28,000 students attended these secondary and post-secondary institutions. (The "high school" existed only for Protestants.)

After Confederation, education remained nearly stagnant until the 1920s. This was largely due to the never-ending quarrels between the Catholics and the Protestants, and the determination of the clergy to control all of education in the province: the education of the young was the responsibility of parents, they said, and the Church was there to facilitate that. So, bishops, priests, brothers, and nuns had to run the system. God demanded it.

Consequently, Québec had no Department of Education from 1875 until 1964, when one was created during the Révolution tranquille. Moreover, the primary schools of the Canadiens were a jungle of decrees and regulations, structures and programs, and informal arrangements. In other words, there was no coherent system at that level—and no public system at all at the secondary level. The teachers were largely unqualified, unrecognised, and poorly paid; women were treated with little respect and earned much less than men; and too much emphasis was placed on religious observances, rituals, and what the priests judged to be suitable for good Catholic French-Canadian boys and girls about to become men and women in the world. Girls who didn't enter religious life were expected to become the mothers of many children and subject to their husbands. Boys were taught to adapt to the power of the Church and to their betters, to obey the will of God as expressed by those in authority, to avoid Protestants and Jews (after all, it was universal "knowledge" that the Jews had killed Christ—and many, according to the cardinal-archbishop of Québec, were natural Bolsheviks and so the enemies of God), and to guard "la langue, la race, et la foi," the elements of "la différence" between them and the others. In such a system, dedicated to keeping an entire people ignorant in the name of God, it's not surprising that the study of mathematics and the sciences didn't figure prominently in the educational equation. Furthermore, the economic conditions made it more or less necessary that most Catholic boys leave school when they turned ten or eleven, to take up employment. The girls weren't far behind.

It's no wonder that Québec had the highest rate of illiteracy in Canada.

However, in spite of the clerical establishment, some progress was made during those decades. More schools were established; more kids were "educated" or trained; teachers became more professional, particularly in the urban centres; and parents gradually began to develop the idea that education might be of value.

The Québec phenomenon of the classical colleges really constituted "higher education" in Québec. But these institutions were dedicated to a classical education that met the needs of the professional bourgeoisie. Such an education no doubt civilised the students to a degree far beyond students in other jurisdictions, but it made no businessmen or "entrepreneurs" out of them.

In spite of the furious opposition of the Church, succeeding provincial governments managed some reforms and established institutions that didn't fall under the control of the clerics. The École Polytechnique de Montréal was founded in 1873 to train engineers and, later, the École des Hautes Études Commerciales to prepare graduates for the world of commerce. In 1907, the government—again fighting clerical obscurantism—opened two technical schools "to provide our manufacturers with educated producers, highly skilled overseers, experienced foremen and élite workers." In the same year, a surveying school opened, and in 1910 one for forestry—both affiliated with Laval.

For most of this period, only the Université Laval (in Québec City) served the French-Canadian population. In Montréal, the largest city in Canada, there was only a branch of Laval. Why? Because the bishops wasted close to seventy years fighting, among themselves, about la question de l'université. The quarrel had nothing to do with education—it was all about prestige and money.

English-speaking Protestant youth fared much better. Their system was coherent, competent, and capable of adaptation. Above all, it had continuity—primary, secondary, post-secondary, crowned by McGill University, with an endowment of $6,720,896 in 1915. (Laval and its subsidiary in Montréal had $15,000 in its endowment fund.) Also, in Lennoxville (near Sherbrooke) a college had been founded in 1843 to educate English-speaking students, training some for the Anglican clergy. The college later became Bishop's University.

At Confederation, there were few Jews in Québec, but as the years went on, their numbers grew rapidly. At the beginning of the 1920s, about 40 percent of the students enrolled in Protestant schools were Jewish. This situation didn't please anyone: anti-Semitism was pretty general. And although there was a sort of separation of Church and State in Protestant education, many Jewish parents nevertheless felt that their offspring were being assimilated into a way of life they didn't approve of. So, in 1903, the Jewish community began to agitate to have its own schools. Shock waves ran through Québec, and the matter was taken up by the courts. Eventually, in 1928, the Judicial Committee of the Privy Council in London, the highest court for Canada, decreed that the Canadian Constitution didn't prevent the Québec government from establishing Jewish schools and diverting funds to them. Two years later, that decision resulted in a system.

If the world of "business" needed a skilled and well-educated managerial class with "entrepreneurship" or the spirit of it, then Québec youth were badly served by the clerical establishment and their allies, the professional bourgeoisie. The provincial governments, whose duty it was to establish the separation of Church and State, also betrayed them.

Back on the economic front, there is no simple explanation for the relatively low participation rate of French Canadians. Was French-Canadian capital available? The American takeover of Canadian resources and industrial might did not just happen in Québec. There was also the language issue: an established economic base, largely built on British foreign capital, was being kept on course by the imperialist sentiments that obsessed English-speaking Canadians all through this period. English-speaking "entrepreneurs" may also have had easier access to American capital than their French-Canadian counterparts.

But we shouldn't exaggerate the absence of French-Canadian entrepreneurial spirit. Banks were established, industries were fostered, securities were brokered, real estate was sold and developed, ships were built, and investors took a minority interest in many of the monopolies that existed. French-Canadian capital made all that possible. Furthermore, even though the position of the French-Canadian businessman may have been "nonexistent, microscopic, or modest," nevertheless, he was there. "The French-Canadian businessman," Québec historians tell us, "still had a solid local or regional economic base. He used provincial and municipal patronage to his advantage, and his economic base allowed him to exercise a degree of power with local or regional dimensions in the economic, political and social spheres."

As the industrial age expanded, working conditions became of some importance. In 1882, the Knights of Labor, though condemned by Rome until 1887, came to Québec from the United States. They would remain a force until the turn of the century.

Another organisation dedicated to the welfare of workers was the American Federation of Labor, among whose membership were craft unions, which had begun to represent workers in Québec as early as the 1860s. When the Federation was formally established in 1887, craft workers found a more hospitable home within its "international" union system than in that of the Knights. The essential work of the Knights of Labor—and of the international unions—was to resolve labour conflicts at a time when the union movement wasn't legalised—or even much recognised—and when the employer was a full-time god. However, the union movement also had other goals: safety, employment conditions of children under fifteen years of age, equal pay for men and women, and legal recognition of labour unions.

Before the beginning of the 20th century, the federal government undertook only two important actions to relieve the plight of the wage earner: one in 1872, when it took some cautious steps in the legalisation of labour unions; the other in 1886, with the establishment of the Royal Commission on the Relations of Labour and Capital. That Commission recorded abysmal abuses in the treatment of workers, and made significant recommendations that were not acted upon. As for the government of Québec, it did, in 1885, pass the Factories Act, which decreed that the work week for women and children would be sixty hours, seventy-two for men. But this law was observed more in its loopholes than in its spirit.

After 1896, there was a large expansion of the labour movement and a sharp increase in militancy. For instance, the 136 union locals in Québec in 1901 had tripled in number by 1916. These union locals, with quite varied membership lists, were largely international; but there were about seventy national unions and twenty-three Catholic ones. In Québec, as elsewhere in Canada, two factors contributed to the growth of the labour movement: the First World War with its massive industrialisation, and the Winnipeg General Strike in May 1919. This so-called Bolshevik strike was ruthlessly put down. In Québec, the clergy, whose members had never been too fond of workers organising in associations that weren't controlled by the Church, took notice of the strike. The Bolsheviks were at the gates of the heavenly city; it was, therefore, necessary to intervene. Thus, the Catholic Trade Union Movement was born, controlled, in every local, by the "chaplains" under the direction of the bishops. No Protestant could be a member of this holy crusade. By the end of the war, the Canadian Catholic Confederation of Labour had one-quarter of the unionized workers in Québec.

After its two attempts to deal with labour matters, the federal government abdicated in favour of the provinces. Fittingly, the first important Québec legislation dealt with accidents in the workplace, the Workmen's Compensation Act being enacted in 1909. It wasn't of great assistance, but no attempt to amend it was made until 1926. The province also created placement offices, reduced the weekly hours of work for women from sixty to fifty-five, and granted women some guarantee of a minimum wage. Attempts were also made to regulate child labour.

In Québec, the farmers were also organising themselves to protect their interests. They created co-operatives to give themselves fire insurance and to market their dairy products. They also developed political organisations to lobby governments. One of these was the Union des Cultivateurs de la Province de Québec.

In this period of economic growth, did people have a higher standard of living? Did they share equally in the blessings of the new economy?

No.

In rural Québec, poverty, disease, and lack of opportunities sent many to the cities, to increase the plight of the urban poor. The living conditions of rural Québec made a lie of the myth perpetuated by the clergy—that agriculture and colonisation were the "vocation" of the French-Canadian people. There were few financially secure peasants living off the bounties of the land, as the tenets of messianic nationalism would have us believe.

Life was even worse in the cities. There, a culture of poverty was digging itself deeply in the psyche of people. Landlords were exacting and vengeful; pollution drove many citizens to an early grave; diseases of all kinds (tuberculosis, influenza, measles) decimated the population; and the death rate, particularly among infants, was staggering (one child in three died before his/her first birthday). Governments were inactive, and the poor, the lame, widows, orphans, and the sick eked out a meagre existence through the charity of the Church, elegant ladies, and entrepreneurs buying as cheaply as they could a place in heaven. Historian Terry Copp estimated that, between 1897 and 1929, the majority of the working-class lived below the poverty line:

> A society conditioned to laissez-faire principles found pauperism an abhorrent idea; the concept of making one's way in the world was the very foundation stone of the social order. Yet, obstinately, the destitute insisted on being there. Fear of social disorder if the minimum needs of the poor were not met, as well as raw consciences, impelled the better classes to provide charity. But, in the laissez-faire context, it was necessarily stern charity, charity designed to be as uncomfortable and as demeaning as possible. Such a charitable system would meet the Christian duty of caring for real needs, while discouraging the vicious from seeking to make an easy life of pauperism.

In *The City Below the Hill*, published in 1897, the Montréal businessman, civic reformer, and politician Sir Herbert Brown Ames (1863–1954) laid out the living conditions of a working-class district of Montréal during the 1890s. Here are some of his descriptions of that neighbourhood:

> If one were to draw a line across the map of a portion of the city of Montréal . . . he would divide the south-western half of our city into two occupied districts, that to the west, is upon high ground; the other, that to the east, is in the main but little above the river level. The former region, for lack of a better name, we shall call '"the city above the hill," the latter, in contrast there from, "the city below the hill."
>
> . . . It will doubtless be unexpected information to many of the citizens of the upper city—where such a thing is unknown—to learn that the relic of rural conditions, that unsanitary abomination,

the out-of-door-pit-in-the-ground privy, is still to be found in the densely populated heart of our city. That the privy pit is a danger to public health and morals needs no demonstration, and yet in "the city below the hill" more than half the households are dependent entirely upon such accommodation. . . .

If we could imagine ten average families coming to settle within "the city below the hill" the division of accommodation among them may be expressed as follows: One family might secure an entire house to itself, but nine families must needs share theirs with another. Nine families might dwell facing the street, but one would have to live in the rear. Five families might have proper sanitary accommodation, but as many more would have to put up with the pit privy. Three families might have six rooms, four families might have five rooms, while the homes of the remaining three would contain four rooms. This, then, represents the home average for the dwellers of the west-end. There is still need for much effort before the home average can be brought up to the standard of the home ideal set forth in the introduction to this article.

. . .Think of it, a thousand persons living on an area but slightly larger than the upper part of Dominion Square. If the residents of this block stood in line, allowing twenty inches [fifty centimetres] to each person, they would form a solid row completely encasing the block on its four sides. Or let us express this condition in another way. In the part of the city familiar to us were the land divided equally among its inhabitants, each person would be entitled to about 100 square yards [84 square metres] as his share. If every person so provided stood in the centre of his plot of ground he would be about thirty feet [nine metres] from his next neighbour. But if he lived in this last mentioned block, 12 feet [3.7 metres] instead of 30 [9 metres] would intervene. Or yet again. The average city lot above accommodates three persons, in this block that lot would be required to accommodate at least nineteen persons. I have multiplied illustrations for it is very important that you should fully realise what a density of 300 persons to the acre means. In this locality, there are regions of considerable extent containing twenty times the population per acre to be found above Sherbrooke Street.

In "the city above the hill" are noble parks and numerous breathing places. Mount Royal is close at hand. By contrast look at this section, which lies between Mountain Street and the city limits, extending from CPR track to Notre Dame street. Here dwell 15,000 people, 5,000 of whom are children. One paltry plot of ground, scarce an acre in extent, dignified by the title of Richmond Square, is the only spot where green grass can be seen free of charge in all that district. I am far from being in favour of granting to corporations or individuals any of our city parks, but I would be willing to exchange some civic property not actually needed for an acre of land within the "Swamp" to be converted into a park for the relief of this congested district.

After such marked contrasts in the matter of density, of situation, of sanitary equipment and of breathing places, between the city above and the city below, shall we be surprised if we find that the natural law enunciated at the outset of this paper, be found to operate with relentless force?

In 1906, there were 167 cars in Québec and 1,176 in Ontario.
In 1920, Quebeckers drove 41,562 cars, Ontarians 177,561.
The blessings of an equal playing field.

⚜

It's a beautiful day. I'm in the park adjacent to my house, comfortably seated on a bench that the city fathers of Ottawa have so kindly put at the disposal of the lowly mortals who vote for them. I am contemplating where I am in this book—and how on earth I'm going to get to where I'm supposed to be. My eyes are closed, my mind meanders, and I let my imagination take me where it will.

With a start, I awaken when I hear a rather sharp voice say to me: "Like most men who write about the history of Québec, you haven't included many women in your book, at least the parts Mascou has been kind enough to show me."

I look at the woman who has appeared out of nowhere, and sits beside me. "Je suis Madame Marie Gérin-Lajoie."

She's a tall, aristocratic woman in her late seventies, dressed in black, her white hair tied tightly around her head, her eyes dark and small, and her mouth firm and somewhat severe. (Later, I find out that she was born in 1867 and died in 1945. She was a grande dame, a daughter of an eminent judge and the wife of an important member of the Québec bourgeoisie. She had firms views, and tried to put them in practice.)

"Women were around, but yet not there," I say, hoping to sound intelligent.

"We were there, all right—daughters who belonged to their families, wives burdened with a trunkful of duties, domestics severely exploited, girls doing hard jobs at an early age, unequal pay, and no rights."

"But, Madame, you were well off. Admired. Respected."

"That a small minority of women of my province had a high or medium standard of living didn't change our situation. We were all cramped in the status and the role that men, particularly men said to be of God, created for us. Some escaped into nunneries!" She hesitates before adding: "Unfortunately, they didn't get away from it all. Like us in the world, they too were always in the service of men."

"Did that make you angry?"

"It disappointed me." She opens her purse and brings out a notepad, which she studies before she says: "I once wrote some observations about the status of women in my society. Would you like me to read them to you?"

"Please."

She looks at her notepad again. "I'll summarise it. It's so

long you'll be on this bench until the end of your mortal existence." She reads to herself and then begins:

"In my time, and until the thirties and even beyond, a woman
was a person with no more rights and possibilities than a
minor." She looks at me and adds: "We could make a will; but that
was about all. A husband could get a separation on grounds of
adultery; but a woman didn't have the same privilege, unless she
could prove that her husband had brought his mistress into the
household. Think of that! As for financial capacity, she had
very little in her own right. Most of her financial dealings had
to be agreed to by her husband."

She looks at the children playing not too far from us. After
enjoying the moment, she turns towards me again and adds with
some sadness: "We were mothers. Our whole role and dignity were
defined in terms of our motherhood. But did you know that I
wasn't permitted to correct my children: I could only supervise
them. And I couldn't tutor my children without my husband's
consent." More bitterly than sadly, she adds: "It may have been
all nonsense. However, it was a profound injustice, an injustice
sanctioned by men, whether they belonged to God or the devil."

"What about Protestant women?"

"Insofar as the French civil law was applied . . ."

"Les coutumes de Paris?"

"Yes. In those aspects of the civil code, they had the same
status. However, the English tended to be more precocious in
this. By the turn of the century, women could attend the
Graduate School at McGill, and I think that by 1905 or so there
were maybe a dozen who were doctors. Whether they were practising or not is another matter. We weren't that lucky."

I think of Lady Aberdeen, the wife of the governor general. In
1893, she presided over the National Council of Women. "You
were a member of that organisation. By 1907, you even helped
found the Fédération Nationale Saint-Jean-Baptiste, to push
the cause of women."

"Yes. And a good thing too. We had to be cautious, though. And we had to spend much time on our knees to prove that all we did was in the name of God and in the tradition of the Church insofar as women are concerned. We even asked the archbishop of Montréal to draw up the rules that guided us."

"What did feminism mean to the archbishop?"

"He defined it as the zealous pursuit by a woman of all the noble causes in the sphere that Providence had assigned to us. We weren't, however, permitted to speak of the emancipation of women and of the low status of our rights; nor were we permitted even to think that we had been relegated to the sidelines, and we certainly were not about to be encouraged to storm the citadel of men."

Lost in some world of her own, she again looks at the children. Finally she admits: "Of course, the archbishop and the priests were to allow us a little bit of light . . ."

"And the prize you had to pay for that little bit of light was?"

"To let them control our movement completely."

"The right to vote? You fought for that?"

"Yes. However, we didn't much participate in what the English women had—the Montréal Suffrage Association—but not because we didn't want to. We had to be careful not to drive away the many women who were just awakening. During the war—I have seen two wars; I am here speaking of the first one—and shortly before the Conscription Crisis, the federal government allowed women who were army employees or who had close relatives in the army to vote. That was the beginning."

"Did the men of your class help you out?" I ask her as straightforwardly as I can.

She senses my doubt and laughs it off: "I know you're joking. We, their mothers, their wives, their daughters, all their women, became a threat to the social order and a danger to the Church. We were abandoning, so they said, the sacred mission of women. Our role was in the home, not on the hustings. We could, however, participate by entertaining, feeding, and looking after the men working tirelessly for our welfare. The arguments I liked the best—or which caused me fits of hysteria—were that I would become sullied; that I would divide my family; and that, as a woman, I didn't have the mental and physical abilities to participate in that arena. The nonsense men of good will can utter when pushed against the wall by the determination of the feeble sex."

"Please tell me, Madame, about Henri Bourassa and feminism." (Henri Bourassa [1868–1952] was a journalist, the founder of *Le Devoir* in 1910, a politician, and a fiery French-Canadian nationalist but not a separatist. He was the son of the great French-Canadian artist Napoléon Bourassa (1827–1916) and the grandson of Louis-Joseph Papineau of Rebellion fame. His nationalism was ferocious, and his Catholicism exclusive and domineering. His influence was great, and he played his cards well.)

She looks away and I feel that she is remembering many things she would prefer not to. Not looking at me, she finally says, "Monsieur Bourassa! And women! Monsieur Bourassa, man of religion, nationalist, and homme parfait as I was told he was, was nothing but a misogynist—a word that never crossed our lips. He was opposed to our gaining anything. French-Canadian nationalism at that time seemed to favour the domination and exclusion of women. He once said"—she searches in her notepad—"I've kept it all these years to remind me of the silly arguments of men. Here is what he argued: Sexual differences imply differences in sexual function, and differences in sexual function create differences in social function."

She looks at me and there is much sarcasm in her eyes. "The alleged 'right' to vote"—she practically spits out those words—"is only an aspect of the functions, the social responsibilities, that devolve on man as a result, perhaps, of his physical or mental structure but primarily of his position and duties as head of the family. End of quote!" She closes her notepad and puts it back in her purse. Looking at the trees surrounding us, she fixes her eyes on a large pine and she adds: "So biology determines our place in society and our rights in the order of life."

"In the elections of 1921, all Canadian adult women could vote in federal elections and, a year later, women were given the right to vote in provincial ones," I offer.

"Not in Québec. God help us. I tried to convince the bishops and the priests that by voting we would not be violating any of God's laws. I founded a committee to push the franchising of women and to convince politicians in the Assembly that we meant what we were saying. I got nowhere. The bishops organised their own groups of women to oppose us. Finally, I had no other recourse than to appeal to the Vatican." She laughs out loud and adds merrily: "In those days practically half of the bishops lived in Rome, permanently, to defend their cherished causes. I'm only being sarcastic. May God help me. Where was I? Oh yes. The Vatican! I went to Rome where the World Union of Catholic Women's Organizations was having a convention. Arguments and papers were presented ad nauseam. Finally the convention sanctioned women's suffrage; but the Pope added a proviso that suffrage could be exercised only with the consent of the bishops in each country—or in the case of Canada, in each province. We gained a little. And the struggle continued."

"Do you think the Pope had been influenced in his decision by Henri Bourassa?"

"I have absolutely no doubt about that. Bourassa had his contacts everywhere in the Vatican. And he was in Rome—just by chance!—during the meetings of the convention." She becomes silent and sad: "I lost, really lost, in Rome. I also lost in Québec. Before I went to Rome, a group of women and I met with the then premier of Québec. There was no way to convince him. 'As long as I am in power,' he thundered like a prophet of the Old Testament, 'you will never succeed.' In 1922, I felt beaten and I resigned. I was fifty-five years old. I had devoted over a quarter of my life to this cause. I failed."

I don't dare say a word. She stands, looks at me, at the children, at the trees, at the sun, and says: "God was kind. He gave us good women pour prendre la relève." She bows and walks away.

⚜

Other women followed Madame Gérin-Lajoie, particularly Thérèse Casgrain. She was a humanist, a mother of four children, a journalist, a woman of wealth and prestige, a reformer, and a senator. The campaign she led for Québec women to have the right to vote began, for her, in 1921—and ended in victory on April 25, 1940.

And it was not only in politics that women fought for their rights; they also did in education, in legal rights, and in many other areas. The struggle for emancipation was a long one, due largely to the coterie of misogynist clerics and laymen handicapped by their own importance.

Maria Chapdelaine is a classic French-Canadian novel. Written in the first part of the 20th century by Louis Hémon, and published in book form in 1916, it has appeared in 232 editions and in 23 countries. Hémon, a Frenchman who came to Montréal in 1911, went a year later to spend six months in northern Québec, where Maria Chapdelaine was born in his soul. He moved to Sudbury, and was killed by a train near Chapleau. Before his fatal accident, Hémon had sent his manuscript to *Le Temps*, a Paris journal, in which the novel was serialised. In 1916, it appeared in book form in Canada. In it, you discover what Québec was all about. Here is the conclusion of Hémon's masterpiece:

Maria looked at her father who was still asleep, his chin on his chest, as if meditating on death, and she remembered the simple songs he had taught the children almost every night.

À la claire fontaine
M'en allant promener . . .

In the American cities, even if you taught your children those songs, they would soon forget them!

The scattered clouds that a short while ago had marched across the moonlit sky had melted into an immense, thin layer of grey through which the light was strained. The snow, half melted, lay pallid on the ground, and between these two bright layers the black forest stretched like the front of an approaching army.

Maria shivered. The tender emotion she had felt faded away, and she once again said to herself:

"Just the same, it's a hard life here. Why should I stay?"

Then a voice stronger than the others made itself heard: the voice of the land of Québec, a mingling of a woman singing and a priest sermonising.

It came like a sound of bells, the noble clamour of an organ in the church, like a naïve lament and like the long, piercing cry exchanged by lumbermen in the bush. In fact, everything that makes up the province's soul was in this voice: the cherished solemnity of the ancient service, the sweetness of the ancient language jealously preserved, and the splendour and barbaric power of a new country where an ancient race had rediscovered its youth.

She thought: "We came here three hundred years ago, and we stayed. Those who brought us here could come back among us with pride, for while it may be true that we have learned little, we certainly have forgotten nothing.

"From overseas we had brought our prayers and songs. They have remained. In our breasts we had brought the strong hearts of our country's men, hard working and lively, as prompt to pity as to laugh, the most humane of all human hearts. That has not changed. We have set our mark on a great piece of the new continent, from the Gaspé to Montréal, from Saint-Jean d'Iberville to Ungava, saying here: Here, all the things we brought with us, our religion, our language, our virtues and even our weaknesses, become sacred and intangible things that must endure to the end.

"All around us strangers have come, we like to call them barbarians. They have taken most of the power and most of the money; but in this land of Québec nothing has changed. Nothing will change, because we are here to bear testimony to it. Concerning our destinies and ourselves we have fully understood nothing but that duty: to persevere, to survive. And we have survived, perhaps so that in several centuries the world may turn toward us and say: These people belong to a race than does not know how to die. We are a testimony to that.

"That is why we must stay in the province where our fathers stayed and live as they lived, in obedience to the unexpressed commandment written in their hearts and passed on to our own, and which we must hand down in our turn to our many children: In Québec nothing must die, nothing must change."

The immense layer of grey cloud had grown heavier, and suddenly the rain started again, bringing a little closer the blessed time of bare earth and ice-free rivers. Samuel Chapdelaine slept on, like an old man suddenly stricken by the fatigue of a long, hard life. The flames of the two candles flickered in the soft breeze, causing shadows to dance on the dead woman's face, so that her lips seemed to move in prayer or whispered secrets.

Maria Chapdelaine woke with a start, thinking: "So! It seems I'll be staying here!" The voices have spoken clearly and she felt that she must obey. Awareness of her other duties came back a little later, after a sigh of resignation . . . Her mother was dead and there had to be a woman in the house. But in fact it was the voices that had shown her the way.

The rain pattered on the shingle roof, and the world, happy to see the end of the winter, puffed at the open window sending little gusts of mild air like sighs of satisfaction. Through the night hours [she] remained motionless, her hands crossed in her lap, patient and devoid of bitterness, but dreaming, with a touch of pathetic regret, of the distant marvels she would never see, and her sad memories of this land in which it was ordained that she should live. And she thought of the warm flame that had caressed her heart and left her, and of the great, snow filled forest from which the young men, too daring, cannot return.

In May, Esdras and Da'Bè came down from the shanties, and their grief revived that of the others. But the earth was ready for seeding and no mourning could exempt them from their summer tasks.

Eutrope Gagnon came for a visit one evening. Perhaps it was when he stole a glance at Maria's face that he guessed her heart had changed, because he asked her, as soon as they were alone:

"Are you still figuring to leave, Maria?"

She shook her head, but without looking at him.

"Well . . . I know it's not the time to talk about it, but if you could tell me I have a chance for later on, I could stand the waiting better."

Maria replied:

"Yes. If you want, I'll marry you, as you asked, the spring after this, when the men come back from the bush for the seeding."

Sir Wilfrid Laurier dominated Québec's politics in this period. Through his speeches, it's possible to discover the most important debates that took place in Québec and Canada between the birth of Confederation and the end of the First World War—the role of the Church (that is, bishops and priests) in political affairs; the place of the French Canadians in Confederation; and Canada and foreign wars.

Wilfrid Laurier (1841–1919) is, along with Sir John A. Macdonald, the most important head of government we've had since Confederation. I know much about him, having written a biography of him a few years ago. I'm devoted to him. You understand: we were both born under the sign of Scorpio. Cooooool, as the young would say.

Laurier stated the following words in Québec City on June 26, 1877, as part of his remarkable speech on Canadian liberalism. It was a defining moment.

Je sais that in the eyes of a large number of my fellow countrymen, the Liberal Party is a party composed of men of perverse
doctrines and dangerous tendencies, pressing knowingly and
deliberately towards revolution.

Je sais that in the eyes of a portion of my fellow countrymen,
the Liberal Party is a party of men with upright intentions, perhaps, but victims and dupes of principles that are leading them
unconsciously but fatally towards revolution.

Je sais that in the eyes of another and not the least considerable
portion, perhaps, of our people, Liberalism is a new form of evil,
a heresy carrying with it its own condemnation.

⚜

"You should not make more of it than it was. It had some importance in the political life of my time; that I will grant you.
Beyond that . . . c'est une autre histore. It was also quite
frightening. I was young then." He was thirty-six.

I turn around and there he is at my door. He stands tall and
erect, with bountiful curly grey hair cut close to his head; his
well-shaved face is pale; his eyes are penetrating, with a kind-
ness and attention I've rarely encountered; and he is impeccably dressed in a grey, single-breasted morning coat. Underneath
it is a waistcoat, also single-breasted, covering a starched
white shirt with a butterfly collar and a long, black knotted
tie. His trousers are narrow and break over his black, polished,
and pointed boots, mostly hidden under grey-brownish spats. He
holds, in his right hand, a top hat.

"What shall we talk about?" he asks me, giving his hat to
Mascou. Before I answer, I watch him walk around the room,
staring at and studying the three or four pictures of him or
of his family that I have on the walls. Even the screen-saver
on my computer has his picture. Walking towards the wing
chair in the corner of the scriptorium, he says: "I certainly
am in evidence."

That voice, which so mesmerised his compatriots, is deep and beautifully modulated. He has a slight English accent when he speaks French, and an English one when he utters French words.

Mascou re-enters the room and places a glass of red wine on the table near Laurier's chair, and a plate of what appear to be tea biscuits. Mascou then sits on the sofa opposite Sir Wilfrid. Laurier thanks him and takes a sip of wine. "Excellent," he proclaims. "Full-bodied and rich. French, no doubt!"

"Canadian! From the Niagara Peninsula."

"Interesting. In my day, we made some wine in Québec. If truth be told, it was hardly drinkable." He drinks again, then adds: "Niagara! The Falls! Majestic! Like our country." He sets the glass down and tells me how he came to be at the Salle de musique, a public hall on Saint-Louis Street in Québec City, on that Tuesday night, two days after the feast of Saint-Jean-Baptiste in June 1877.

"For me, personally, it was a great occasion. A group of young Liberal men had invited me to speak on the meaning of the Liberalism I subscribed to. The room was filled. Even the Anglican archbishop of Québec! Many priests. Jesuits. Learned professors from the Université Laval. Journalists from far and wide. Political allies and too many foes. I was quite frightened. One of my friends reported to my wife, Zoë, that I was deadly pale—so pale that some people thought I was going to be sick. Perhaps. I certainly knew that my words would have some importance in the debate that raged about us and threatened our political life—and, if you permit me to say so, even our capacity to live as free citizens in the country of Canada."

He takes a deep breath, to gather his thoughts, no doubt. As he lifts his head, our eyes connect. I hope he finds a kindred spirit.

"Confederation," he says, "gave us, the French Canadians, practically a state of our own within our country, Canada. There was, therefore, a 'sentiment' that we could do what we wanted, insofar as being French-speaking and Catholic. That

255

situation did not escape the episcopacy and the clergy of Québec."

He waves his right hand to emphasise that outside of the Province of Québec, "it was another story . . . except, perhaps, in the diocese of Ottawa and in Saint-Boniface in Manitoba. You see, the 'Church,' as we called this holy institution created to help us save our immortal soul, held the view that the time had come to situate the position of the Church in Québec within the parameters of canon law. In other words, to them the separation of Church and State was incompatible with being a Catholic. They, therefore, decreed that in civil as well as religious affairs, the Church was paramount. It was called Ultramontanism, a political philosophy that many Conservatives in the province adhered to.

"I opposed this attitude: the Church, through her agents, might illuminate the conscience of the electorate, but she certainly could not impose her will. When she did, she engaged in 'influence indue,' which was against the law as the Supreme Court found in the 1870s.

"Most of the bishops and the vast majority of the clergy opposed my views, stating that I, along with my fellow Liberals, was engaged in the perverse tendency of 'le libéralisme catholique,' Catholic Liberalism, a political philosophy condemned by the Pope. It goes without saying that the electors could not, in good conscience, vote for the likes of me—or for the Liberal Party to which I adhered. I had to make the point that the English Liberalism I practised had little to do with the French or continental Catholic Liberalism. That was the situation when I made that speech."

"Why did you have to make it then, not earlier?"

"We, the Liberals, had been living with this sword of Damocles hanging over our heads since Confederation. We had lost many elections, having been branded enemies of the Church. In 1877, we had a chance to exercise power, both in Québec and in Canada.

It was imperative, in my view, to set the record straight. Some of my colleagues were not pleased with me; they were concerned that I was too radical to tackle such a sensitive subject."

I sense that he doesn't want to discuss what the clerics did to him during the greatest part of his career.

⚜

When Laurier moved to the Eastern Townships to edit a Liberal newspaper, practise law, and take care of his health, they made his life impossible. They bankrupted his newspaper, condemned him from the pulpit, and caused his defeat in the fall of 1877. Alexander Mackenzie, the second prime minister of Canada (and the first Liberal one) had invited Laurier into his cabinet. In those days, it was necessary for a newly appointed cabinet minister to face his electorate. When Laurier did that in his constituency of Arthabaska, he was branded a Liberal of the condemned kind, a friend of Garibaldi who had harmed the Pope and the interests of the Church, and an ally of the famous Guibord. No Catholic could vote for him and hope to go to heaven. He lost. He never forgot what had been done to him in the name of God. However, as we've seen, the episcopacy was divided, and Laurier was able to find a seat in the diocese of the more liberal archbishop of Québec, Elzéar-Alexandre Taschereau, whose brother was the chief justice of the Supreme Court of Canada. There, in the city of Champlain, Laurier was elected on November 28, 1877. He represented that constituency of Québec-Est for the rest of his political life.

⚜

"In light of all of that you've told me—and also of what you haven't—you had to make the distinction between your Canadian or English Liberalism and the Bishops' Catholic Liberalism. What was that distinction?"

"I am a Liberal. I am one of those who think that everywhere, in human beings, there are abuses to be reformed, new horizons to be opened up, new forces to be developed; and there is always room for the perfecting of our nature and for the attainment,

257

by a larger number, of an easier way of life. This is what constitutes the superiority of the Liberalism I am associated with. It is freedom. Catholic Liberalism, on the other hand, has been written in blood. It tends to enslave. It doesn't correct wrong. It has nothing to do with the political life of free men."

"What did you think the clergy were trying to do?"

"They wanted to organise all the Catholics into one party, without other bonds, without any other basis than a common religion. Had they been successful, they would have drawn our country into calamities, of which I could not foresee the consequences—except for one. If Catholics organised in one party, the Protestants would do the same. The peace and harmony needed for our country to survive would be gone, opening the door to war, a war of religion, the most terrible of wars."

"Did it ever cross your mind that you might be exaggerating?"

"Non!"

"Did the Church have a role in the political life of your compatriots? Or were the priests to be relegated to the sacristy?"

I see anger in his eyes; his lips become thinner; and he upbraids me. "In my time, no Liberal argued that the priest had no place in politics. If he wanted to take part, he had the perfect right. But that right is not unlimited. We have no absolute rights among us. The rights of each man, in our state and society, end precisely where they encroach upon the rights of others. The right of interference in politics ends at the point where it encroaches upon the electors' independence. That is what many of the episcopacy and clergy of my time did not understand."

"Did they understand it after your speech?"

"Not really. The Vatican intervened. The bishops wrote ambiguous mandements (episcopal letters) to clarify the situation. Some bishops acted in accordance with what they were ordered to do; others did not. They also issued directives to the clergy: to illuminate but not to dictate. Some obeyed. Many did not. It is not a perfect world!"

"But after 1877 it calmed down, only to start all over again in the elections of 1896."

"I suppose."

❦

In 1896, Laurier was leader of the Liberal party, having succeeded to that position in 1887. He had a good chance to become the first French-Canadian prime minister. Many in the Church, though, sought to deprive him of his victory. The issue was the Manitoba school controversy.

When the Province of Manitoba was created in 1870, the federal government granted the supervision of education to the province, with the proviso that the rights of "denominational schools which any class of persons have by law or practice in the province at the union" not be disturbed. If the minority ever felt deprived of its educational rights, it could appeal to the governor general in council for redress. The federal government also reserved for itself the authority to ask Parliament "to make remedial laws for the execution of the provision of this section" should the provincial legislature of Manitoba tamper in any way with this educational protection. Manitoba duly set up a dual school system, with a separate administration for the Roman Catholics of the province—and the necessary appropriations to support it.

Twenty years later, though, things had changed in the province. The Catholics were in a minority; the Protestants were strong and powerful, not to mention very interested in forcing every citizen into a beautiful Anglo mould. In the session of 1890, the Manitoba legislature replaced the school system created in 1870 with a non-denominational one. Roman Catholic schools could still operate, but as private schools with no subsidies from the Treasury. In addition, all citizens of Manitoba had to pay a school tax to support the new system.

And then the "fun" began.

Instead of disallowing the law, the federal government referred the matter to the courts. In February 1891, the Manitoba Court of Queen's Bench declared the law constitutional, a judgement that the Supreme Court of Canada reversed in October. The Manitoba government then lodged an appeal with the Judicial Committee of the Privy Council in

Great Britain, the court of last resort, which handed down its decision at the end of June 1892. It found the Manitoba school legislation to be *intra vires*; that is, constitutional.

Having been defeated in the courts, the French-speaking and Catholic minority of Manitoba had no other recourse than to appeal to the federal government for redress, as the Manitoba Act of 1870 gave them the right to do. There followed another judicial rigamarole: the federal government asked the Supreme Court if, in light of the Privy Council's decision, the government could act on behalf of the minority. On February 24, 1894, the Court said no. Lawyers had no alternative but to pack their bags and sail to London to ask Britain's House of Lords what to do. The Lords said yes to federal intervention, provided that the government didn't repeal the provincial legislation.

There was, after that, no way out; the federal government had to act. It issued a Remedial Order to Manitoba to restore the full rights of the Catholics of Manitoba. If the province failed to do so, the government promised to enact remedial legislation. On June 19, 1895, Manitoba declined to obey its federal masters. On February 11, 1896, after a cabinet crisis of some magnitude, the federal government initiated legislation that reintroduced the separate school system into the province, but with no financial provisions to pay for it.

⚜

"Did you tell your readers that, in the midst of all this mess, the Council of the North-West Territories abolished its own separate school system and limited the teaching of the French language in the schools? That was in 1892. The Council was encouraged by the Manitobans to commit this affront to the fundamental rights of the Catholic and French-speaking population in the Territories. Did you tell them that?"

"No, I didn't. Thank you for doing it."

"So, let us proceed." But he does not wait for my questions. And he speaks in the present tense, no doubt reliving the moments.

"It is the session of 1893. For the first time, I speak of this Manitoba school question, having no doubt whatsoever that in a country like ours we cannot permit ourselves to act the way the Manitoba legislature and the Council of the North-West Territories have. Their actions are arbitrary and without regard for national unity—which must always be our primary concern. There is no place in my Canada for the tyranny of the majority. We cannot afford it. Imagine what would happen if the Government of Québec limited the rights of the Protestant population?" He sighs, shaking his head, then tells me something I know too well: "There has always been a double standard in Canada: one for the English-speaking provinces and another one for Québec. I never can understand why this is so."

He sips some wine and continues holding the glass in his hand. "I also have no doubt that if the non-denominational system created by Manitoba is a de facto Protestant one, the federal Parliament must act. That is my view and I repeat it everywhere I go, particularly during my tour across Canada in 1894. National unity demands that the minority in Manitoba be allowed the privilege of teaching in their schools, to their children, their duties to God and man as they understand those duties, and as those duties are taught to them by their Church. But that objective cannot be achieved by imperious dictate and administrative coercion. It can only be done by conciliation. The successive governments that have replaced that of Sir John A. Macdonald do not understand that. They are their own worst enemies."

He puts down his glass. And from the tone of his voice, I know he's remembering the session of 1896, March 3 to be exact, when he entered the debate on the remedial legislation: "I do not wish that Parliament should proceed any further with this Bill. In asking that, I am quite certain that I am right; right for the minority in Manitoba and right for this young nation on which so many hopes are centred. I do this conscious that I am

261

threatened by the authorities of my own Church who desired
this legislation to become law. I am not bitter that these
threats are being made by the high dignitaries of the Church I
respect and love."

He stands and looks at the full portrait that I have of him
dominating the room. He moves towards it and continues repeating, word for word, what he said in the House of Commons on that
day in March: "So long as I have a seat in this House, so long as I
occupy the position I do now, whenever it shall be my duty to
take a stand upon any question whatever, that stand I will take,
not upon grounds of Roman Catholicism, not upon grounds of
Protestantism, but upon grounds which can appeal to the conscience of all men, irrespective of their particular faith, upon
ground which can be occupied by all men who love justice, freedom and toleration." He bows his head and goes back to his seat.
He drinks a little bit of the wine; puts his glass on the table, re-
adjusts his morning coat, crosses his legs and looks at me to ask:
"You know what happens after that? If so tell your readers."
     "Yes!"

⚜

The remedial bill was destined never to become law. It was too late in
the session and Parliament's life was running out. The governor general
prorogued it on April 23, 1896, and elections were called for June 23. Three
weeks later, the bishops, along with the archbishop of Ottawa, issued an
episcopal letter that condemned those who had rejected the remedial legislation as accepted by the bishops, who declared themselves to be the only
ones empowered by God to determine the best solution to repair the damage done to the Catholic minority of Manitoba. They, therefore, went on
to state categorically that the Catholic electors could only support or
endorse a candidate who would formally and solemnly promise to vote in
Parliament for a law endorsed by Their Excellencies. In a separate document to their clergy, they insisted on written declarations from the candidates to that effect. (All the Liberal candidates in Québec, save Laurier and

seven others, signed on the dotted lines. Moreover, in one diocese, no such written affirmation was demanded.)

⚜

"The bishops did not condemn the Liberal Party nor endorse the Conservatives," Laurier tells me. "That was a small blessing. However, everyone knew that if I became prime minister, there would be no such legislation. I was condemned. I had to be opposed. On the other hand, I would not oppose them. Often I wanted to rail at them. But I did not. I was not about to come down to their level. Only my wife knew how difficult my silence was."

Again that reverie!

⚜

Laurier, as everyone knows, beat the bishops at their own game. In spite of being condemned from many pulpits, of having his candidates threatened with the fires of hell, of being excommunicated, and of his partisans being refused the sacraments, Québec elected forty-nine Liberals and sixteen Conservatives. Then, on Saturday, July 11, 1896, Laurier became the first French-Canadian prime minister of Canada.

⚜

"My first task after forming my government," he tells me, "was to resolve the Manitoba schools question and to put an end to the interference of the episcopacy and clergy in political affairs. Please tell your readers about those two matters."

⚜

Laurier was able to negotiate what was called the Laurier-Greenway settlement. It didn't re-establish the separate school system as it had existed from 1867 to 1890. However, it permitted separate religious instruction, hiring of Catholic schoolteachers, and teaching in the French language—all under certain circumstances.

❧

"This settlement was not perfect; I had hoped to obtain more. But after six years of quarrels and a turbulence that bordered on civil war, it was not possible to obtain more. Then there is the principle of provincial autonomy. It is the cornerstone of Confederation. In a country like ours, a country of different creeds and races and languages, passions can easily be aroused. Only provincial autonomy can safeguard Confederation and the interests of the Province of Québec in particular."

"Do you mean to say," I ask, "that federal intervention should never be exercised?"

"Bien non. Je ne veux pas dire cela. What I want to say is that it can only be used as a last resort, when every other means has been exhausted, and when all hope of conciliation and of understanding with the provincial authorities has proved to be in vain." He waits to let that sink in before he adds: "Provincial autonomy and centralisation live side by side in Canada, and often do so in a state of antagonism. In provincial-federal controversies, there is a tendency not to keep in our hearts this one thought: Canada first, Canada forever, nothing but Canada. I wish we would!"

"As for Church-State relations, you knew that you would have no peace unless Rome intervened."

"What I wanted was for Rome to appoint a papal delegate who would come to Canada, investigate, consult, and redress."

❧

Laurier sent a couple of missions to Rome. The first one was a failure, but the second bore fruit on March 8, 1897, with the appointment of Monsignor Raphaël Merry Del Val—the thirty-two-year-old Spanish favourite of Pope Leo XIII—as papal legate. He spent three months in Canada.

❧

"He was a charming man and a most conciliatory prelate," Laurier says. "He was also quite firm. He was convinced that an injustice had been done to the Catholic population in Manitoba, and that the federal government had the power to redress the situation. However, Ottawa could not pass remedial legislation, regardless of what party was in power. Consequently, there was no other way but the sunny way of the Laurier-Greenway settlement."

❧

Del Val convinced the Pope of that situation and on Sunday, January 9, 1898, congregations in every Catholic church in Canada heard an encyclical that the Pope addressed to the Canadian episcopacy and the faithful.

❧

"It was called *Affari Vos*," says Laurier. "Do you know what it means?"

"Your Affairs," I answer with a little annoyance.

"Ah! They still teach Latin. No man can be educated without a thorough knowledge of Latin, Greek, and the classics. Canadians are lucky they can have it all in two languages," he laughs.

"The encyclical," I state, "asked the bishops to accept the Laurier-Greenway settlement as a beginning to the road of total redress, even though it was called 'defective, unsuitable, and insufficient.' Everyone, ordered the Pope, had to work within it and to derive from it as much benefit and advantage as possible. So you won!"

"I was satisfied. Even vindicated."

"But," I reply, "there was one tool remaining to nail down the coffin of episcopal and clerical pretensions."

"Please. Do not talk like that," he says. "Every citizen has the right to have political views and to express them. Above all, citizens also have the right to use politics to achieve their objectives.

That is democracy. So the bishops and the priests did what they had to do." He smiles kindly and adds: "They went too far."

"And Rome sent a permanent apostolic delegate to Canada in June 1899."

"Yes, Archbishop Diomedus Falconio. A fine prelate. We hardly had any trouble after that." He finishes the wine and stands up. "If you will excuse me, I need to speak to Mascou." They both leave me to tackle Louis Riel.

⚜

After the so-called first rebellion (1869–70), which coincided with the founding of Manitoba, Riel lived in the United States, then he returned to Canada and was elected as a member of Parliament (but never served), spent time in a Québec "mental" hospital, and then went back to the United States. In the summer of 1884, he returned to Canada again—this time to Batoche in Saskatchewan. He did so at the invitation of the Métis who had settled on the banks of the Saskatchewan River.

Why had they left Manitoba in the first place? The record provides the answer. They had not been able to live there harmoniously with the white population who came to Manitoba after the province was created in 1870. Often improvident, they allowed themselves to be robbed of their entitlement. Furthermore, they became a minority, a harassed minority, with their survival threatened. However, they didn't take up arms. Instead they fled. Some, too many, went to the United States, but a greater number found a haven of sorts along the banks of the meandering Saskatchewan River. There they squatted until they were displaced by the surveyors, the mounted policemen, the magistrates, and the white settlers who began to arrive in the late 1870s. And the struggle started all over again—a struggle involving entitlement to the land, and the security of their culture and way of life. They were once again rebuffed. They needed a saviour, and they went to Saint Paul, Minnesota, to find him. Riel returned to his native land, to his people who numbered 7,000 in the North-West Territories, but he wasn't able to convince Ottawa to act. On March 17, 1885, he formed a provisional government, naming himself "David" or "Exovede," which means "he was picked out of the flock." He was, by then, living in a world of his own, filled with delusions and God-given missions.

Eight days after the inauguration of Riel's government, the Métis engaged in their first battle. On May 15, it was all over. Riel surrendered to the "English general" whom Ottawa had sent to put down Riel's second rebellion. He was taken to Regina, where his trial was held, in which he was found guilty and condemned to death. After fruitless appeals for mercy, Louis Riel was hanged on November 16, 1885.

While in prison awaiting death, he wrote the following in his journal:

> Blessed be the judge who said to me: "If you obtain clemency, I will be the first to rejoice! But prepare yourself."
>
> My God! Through Jesus Christ, through the holy intercession of Mary, under the protective shield of Saint Joseph, inspire me with the most vivid conceptions of death; the most salutary, the most novel reflections; the most original and compelling meditations; the most dreadful thoughts about my last moments; so that I can profit as a Christian from the time I have yet to live.
>
> Death is not a phantom; she is a truth which I meet and whose force I will feel. She stands ahead of me as certainly as the road on which I set my foot.
>
> Death waits for me as the inkwell waits for my pen, to drench it in dark and sombre tears.
>
> Is my bed as useful to me as my coffin will be? The breathing which relaxes me and which takes place so easily in my heart and breast will stop one day and I will expire. Death, you will conquer me. You will put an end to my physical life. And my soul will be left with the moral life I have made for myself.

When the insurrection began, the people of Québec deplored it and wanted the government to put an end to it. However, as the army marched west with a battalion of Quebeckers, a story emerged of unanswered petitions, dismal poverty, and of a people despoiled of its lands and security. Slowly and gradually, the Canadiens claimed their role in the drama. Riel became "notre frère"; we were his family; our blood flowed in his veins. It was a "déchirement," a tearing apart. It intensified after Riel was in custody, and broke into a torrent of emotion after he was hanged. Many were convinced that it was not only Riel who was executed on that cold morning of November 1885; the French-Canadian "race" had also been on trial and was being executed. Unreasonable? Perhaps. But real, just the same.

Laurier was appalled at the execution. Morally, he felt that what Canada had done in the name of law and order was indefensible, because he knew in his heart that Riel wasn't hanged because he had caused a rebellion, but because some fifteen years before he had had an Ontarian, Thomas Scott, executed. To Laurier, it meant more division, as the old prejudices, the wounds, the slights came to the surface. Race and religion were, once again, about to dominate Canada's political life. Not the mercy, not the liberty, not the compassion he hoped for, but race and religion. And the villains were in Ottawa. He exposed that fact on Tuesday, March 16, 1886—in prose so glorious, so pertinent, and so full of humanity, that it continues to illuminate the souls of men and women a hundred and fifteen years later. Here are two extracts from that marvellous speech:

> I appeal now to my friends of liberty in this House; I appeal not only to the Liberals who sit beside me, but to any man who has a British heart in his breast, and I ask, when subjects of Her Majesty have been petitioning for years for their rights, and these rights have not only been ignored, but have been denied, and when these men take their lives in their hands and rebel, will any one in this House say that these men, when they got their rights, should not have saved their heads as well, and that the criminals, if criminals there were in this rebellion, are not those who fought and bled and died, but the men who sit on these Treasury benches?
>
> . . . Today, not to speak of those who have lost their lives, our prisons are full of men who, despairing ever to get justice by peace, sought to obtain it by war; who, despairing of ever being treated like free men, took their lives in their hands, rather than be treated as slaves. They have suffered a great deal, they are suffering still;

yet their sacrifices will not be without reward. Their leader is in the grave, they are in durance, but from their prisons they can see that that justice, that liberty which they sought in vain, and for which they fought not in vain, has at last dawned upon their country. . . ."

He then quoted from Byron's invocation to liberty, in the introduction to the "Prisoner of Chillon":

> Eternal Spirit of the chainless mind!
> Brightest in dungeons, Liberty thou art!
> For there thy habitation is the heart—
> The heart which love of thee alone can bind;
> And when thy sons to fetters are consigned—
> To fetters and the damp vault's dayless gloom,
> Their country conquers with their martyrdom.

Unfortunately, his rhetoric didn't win the day. In the middle of the night of May 14, 1886, Macdonald's government was sustained by a massive majority vote of 146 to 52. Twenty-four English-speaking Liberals supported it—over half of the caucus.

In time, Riel faded from the concerns of daily life, but remained quite alive in the consciousness of many. The country wasn't destroyed, nor did it self-abort. However, it was one more incident that raised doubts and caused much damage.

Since we never learn, we were soon repeating all. The fallout from the national crisis over Riel roused latent prejudices. In Dalton McCarthy, they found a nurturer. The scenario went like this. McCarthy was a racist, as well as a lawyer, a Conservative member for Simcoe North in Ontario, the founder of the Imperial League of Canada, the high priest of the Equal Rights Association, and an éminence grise behind the Orange Order. The mission McCarthy gave to himself was to abolish every vestige of the French language in Canada. His philosophy was simple: "One Québec is quite enough!" We were "the great danger to this Confederacy," and if bayonets were needed to curb "French nationalism," then he welcomed their use.

His campaign began in earnest with what was called the Jesuits' Estates Act, passed by the Government of Québec in 1888. It was meant to indemnify the Jesuits for the lands that they had received during the French regime and which the British overlords of Québec had confiscated. In 1867, these lands reverted to the province, leaving the government with a political dilemma of some magnitude. For twenty years, successive administrations attempted to indemnify the ecclesiastical establishment for the lands. Unfortunately, the bishops, the Jesuits, and everyone else couldn't agree as to the division of the indemnity. Honoré Mercier, who became the premier of Québec in 1887, decided to ask the Pope to be the arbitrator and put an end to controversy. Leo XIII did, and an Act to that effect was duly passed.

Mercier's settlement aroused the ire of the Protestants, and demands were made for the disallowance of the Act, on the grounds that a foreign power had supplanted the authority of the British Crown. There was a debate in Parliament, with the government winning the day. Laurier supported Macdonald. When Laurier rose to speak in the debate, he had come to realise the awful truth of McCarthy's campaign: to deprive the French Canadians of "everything which constitutes their distinct individuality in Canada." The war McCarthy was launching would take a long time to end, and would cause intolerable and, perhaps, irreparable damage to Canadian unity. "I denounce this policy as anti-Canadian," Laurier thundered in the House. "We are here a nation, or we want to be a nation." The danger to Canada's unity wasn't in the "duality of race" that was being represented as producing friction, and "that friction will produce danger." No, the danger to Canadian unity lay "in mutual forbearance and respect." In Québec, the people certainly listened, and Laurier began to appear as their saviour in the face of so much outrage and blackmail.

McCarthy lost over the Jesuits' Estates Act; however, he and his gang didn't forget, and they turned their attention to Manitoba. On August 9, 1889, Laurier was informed that the government there would move to abolish the separate schools and the French language in that province. We have already seen how Laurier dealt with that and, in effect, saved the day.

In the federal session of 1890, McCarthy introduced a bill to abolish the use of the French language in the legislature and courts of the North-West

Territories (in effect, what is now Saskatchewan, Alberta, and the North). The debate clearly showed that prejudice was just under the surface. A compromise was found, and McCarthy's bill was defeated. (However, as noted earlier, the Council of the North-West Territories did in 1892 what Manitoba had done two years earlier.)

The next language crisis occurred when Laurier, as prime minister, created the provinces of Saskatchewan and Alberta in 1905. In the proposed legislation, there was an article that became famous: Article 16. By it, Laurier meant to maintain separate schools in the new provinces. (In the reforms of 1892 and 1901, the Council of the North-West Territories had maintained separate schools and didn't force Catholic ratepayers to pay their school taxes to a non-denominational system.) He also didn't want a repeat of Manitoba; consequently, the Article went on to stipulate that section 93 of the British North America Act—the educational provisions—was to apply to the new provinces "as if, at the date upon this Act comes into force, the territory comprised therein were already a Province."

That stipulation didn't go down very well. Many in his government and party objected. With Henri Bourassa and his company of nationalists waiting on the sidelines, a crisis developed, and Laurier felt obliged to amend the law along the lines of the Laurier-Greenway settlement. In this compromise, he accepted the minimum for the minority, hoping that in time it could lead to something better. However, he had awakened the sleeping giant of Québec's nationalism. Was Canada our country? He hoped so, but he could hardly prove it.

We had to live through another language drama. This one took place in Ontario through the ignominious Regulation 17, which denied the Canadiens living in Ottawa the right to teach their children in the French language. The leader in this controversy was the Roman Catholic bishop of London, Ontario, whose name is not worth remembering. At first, Laurier didn't intervene, hoping that sanity would prevail. But it didn't, in spite of the courageous defiance of the law by the French-Canadian mothers of the capital. Laurier, in 1916, decided that the time had come to repair the injustice.

Ontarians of British extraction (and many in western Canada) were opposed to "granting greater privileges to the French." Canada wasn't a bilingual country, they argued. One language; one nation! It was, for them, the only way Canadians could be made out of the diverse linguistic, religious, and racial groups who were "taking over" the country. Added to this argument was the conviction that the "French" weren't doing their part in the war, which had begun in 1914. Bourassa's argument, in Québec, was that there was no need to participate in the war since Ontarians and too many Canadians, in depriving the French Canadians of their rights, were no better than the Germans.

On May 10, 1916, Laurier entered into a language debate once again. He wasn't there, he told the House, to teach the proponents of "one language and one language only" a lesson in British freedom. He was there "to plead before the people of Ontario, on behalf of His Majesty's subjects of French origin in that province," to let freedom ring. His petition fell on deaf ears; he lost by a majority of 107 to 60.

How many more times would we have to capitulate to survive? That question became more and more pertinent.

Between 1867 and 1918, Canadians participated in several military initiatives beyond our borders. For instance, between 1868 and 1870, over five hundred Canadiens enlisted in the Papal army to defend Rome from Italian troops, who wanted to bring about the unification of Italy. However, it was the Boer War and the First World War that again brought (what people used to call) "racial" tensions to the forefront of our national life.

On October 12, 1899, the British and the Boers went to war, with the Boers firing the first shot. It was heard all over Canada, precipitating a turbulence that was as dangerous, if not more so, than that caused by Riel, the schools issues, and the language controversies.

Here, in part, is what Laurier said in the House of Commons:

> The work of union and harmony between the chief races of this country is not yet complete. . . . But there is no bond of union so strong as the bond created by common dangers faced in common. Today there are men in South Africa representing the two branches of the Canadian family, fighting side by side for the

honour of Canada. Already some of them have fallen, giving to
their country the last full measure of devotion. Their remains
have been laid in the same grave, there to rest to the end of time
in that last fraternal embrace. Can we not hope that in that grave
shall be buried the last vestiges of our former antagonism? If
such shall be the result, if we can indulge in that hope, if we can
believe that in that grave shall be buried the former contentions,
the sending of contingents would be the greatest service ever ren-
dered Canada since Confederation.

⚜

There is a knock on the door and Laurier and Mascou walk in.

"Where were we?" asks Laurier, sitting down in his chair.

"The Boer War," I reply.

"Ah, the Boer War. How events befall us without our understanding the full impact of them. When we do, it is generally
too late."

"At first, Sir Wilfrid, you didn't want to intervene. But you
changed your mind. Why?"

Several seconds go by without an answer. "I did not know
whether anything was expected. Oh, the imperial government
asked for our help, but it did not seem proper to me to involve
Canada. After all, the security of our country was not threatened. I suppose I misjudged my compatriots. The descendants of
old England, those who identified themselves with the British
Empire, felt strongly that if Great Britain was at war, it was
the duty of Canada to help. So they wanted us to send a contin-
gent. On the other side of the precipice were Tarte and Bourassa,
who were both convinced that such a decision would constitute
a dangerous precedent. Canada would always have to participate
in British wars and what would that do to Québec? And so: what
to do to reconcile the irreconcilable? I could not call
Parliament, because the government would be defeated. The only
way was to find a compromise and garner as much support for it

as possible. We found it in equipping a force of one thousand volunteers and transporting them to South Africa. We did not recall Parliament; such a modest expenditure could not be regarded as a departure from the well-known principles of constitutional government and colonial practice, nor construed as a precedent for future action. Tarte was most helpful."

"Puisque le vin est tiré, il faut le Boer," I say with irreverence, quoting one of his ministers.

"Yes. Having poured the wine, we had to drink it." He smiles. "It does not sound the same in English." He shifts in the chair, before adding: "I think I could have gotten away with it had there not been riots in the streets of Montréal at the beginning of March 1900."

"The day the news of the deliverance of the British garrison at Ladysmith reached Canada."

"It provoked joy and enthusiasm in the hearts of many. But it went sour. The English students created havoc at the buildings housing French newspapers—and at City Hall. The French Canadians felt they had to retaliate. This enraged the English students, who arrived at the Montréal campus of Université Laval with guns, sticks, iron bars, and frozen potatoes. A melee ensued, and every window on the campus was broken. Drunk and exhausted, the students went home to lick their wounds. The next day, though, the newspapers picked up where the students had left off. I must say that they tended to be more irresponsible than the young people. There were more riots, more drunkenness, three or four days of it, if my memory serves me right."

"Then the debate moved into the House of Commons. You had a better time of it there."

"Perhaps. But such wounds go deep. I was not able to avoid that. What I did avoid, though, was the desecration of the very idea of this country. I spent all my life trying to prevent a split in the population along racial lines. A greater calamity could never take place in Canada. All I was concerned about was to try to promote unity, harmony and amity between the diverse elements of this country."

"Did you manage that during the First World War?"

He looks at me with those eyes that pierce you and leave you weak. "Like all the other cleavages we have had, that one was not necessary."

I want him to explain that statement, so I say, "In the first two years of the war, there don't seem to have been many complications and dangers to national unity."

"That is so. The war accelerated urbanisation and industrialisation. It added to our prosperity; it ended the economic slump that had prevailed earlier; and it gave jobs to thousands of men and women who had had none before. I heard somewhere that 'the army was a job.' I do not doubt that, and it accounts for the fact that recruitment was relatively easy during the two first years of the war."

He looks at Mascou and says: "I think I will need some wine. Please, my dear Mascou." Mascou leaves to fetch a decanter and a glass. Meanwhile, I point out to Laurier what we must never forget when discussing the First World War: "Most Canadians and Canadiens of military age never did volunteer, which is understandable to a certain degree insofar as the Canadiens are concerned. But the Canadians—and all that talk of sticking with the Empire come what may, and that Québec wasn't doing its part—was all hypocrisy!"

"Oh, do not be so severe, so judgemental. Your compatriots are your compatriots. They do what they have to do. They say what serves them best. But . . ."

Mascou comes in with the wine. He has brought a glass for me, too. When we've tasted the wine, I ask: "What were the feelings about the war effort at the beginning?"

"Feelings and opinions differed as to how best to help defend our two mother countries, Great Britain and France. How to be patriotic? When was enough, enough? It was natural that

English-speaking Canada wanted us to maximise the war effort.
And when Canadians were being slaughtered by the thousands,
their patriotism demanded conscription."

"Sir, isn't it a fact that those who cried the loudest for conscription were among those who were too old to go, who stood to
benefit and profit from the war effort, and those who were to
gain votes by it?"

"Perhaps. Certainly the vast majority of people who rushed at
me to remind me that I had to support conscription certainly
wouldn't have had the strength to carry a rifle. But we must
give everyone the benefit of the doubt. In their soul, they knew
that they had to sacrifice their sons in order to make the
future safe for all." He sips his wine slowly, pensively.

"What of Québec?"

"The people in my province were of the opinion that those who
wanted to go should go. Unfortunately, even though I begged and
begged them to enlist, many did not, giving me great grief. I
understand that no more than twenty thousand volunteers came
from Québec. Brave men. They did well on the various fields of
battle that this horrible war produced." He looks at the setting
sun and goes on: "We had to have one heart and one mind. We had
to be present at this slaughter. I wanted them, the boys whose
blood flowed in my own veins, to fight for the cause of the allied
nations. I was optimistic."

"But your optimism was misplaced?" I ask as gently as I can.

He leaves the setting sun for the anxiety in my eyes. I know he
was old, tired, and sad when all this happened. I also know that he
spared no effort to recruit the sons of Québec as well as those
elsewhere. I know that the Canadian people of that day sustained
an enormous war effort. Our sons were active on many fronts in
Europe as were our daughters. I know, too, the courage, the daring,
and the immense capacity to endure that the war demanded, not
only in Europe but also at home where women ran the factories, old
men worked the fields, and grandmothers knitted and minded the

young so their parents could do their part. It was a gallant effort. Nothing to be ashamed of there.

I also know that we endangered our economic security to fight that war, as the national debt and the cost of living skyrocketed. There was unbelievable corruption in the procuring and manufacturing of munitions. All this I know. I also know the burden of the casualties: the First World War killed 60,661 Canadians of all ethnicities, languages, shapes, and colours; it wounded another 172,950; it left 20,115 widows, orphans, and dependent parents and 77,967 disabled persons. For a country of our size—and even if you remove the size from the equation—it was an enormous effort, an unparalleled one. And yet it was not enough. I know all that. And so does he, sitting there looking at me as if to transfer to me all his anxiety, all his pain, and all his disappointment.

The inevitable was yet to come. However, before I venture further, I want to ask him why the young Canadiens didn't go. I don't, though. I know the explanation. Tradition, the low urban population, the small number of British-born residents, the general in charge in Québec who didn't speak a word of French, the Methodist minister in Montréal who was the chief recruiting officer, the oft-repeated pledge by the government that conscription wouldn't be imposed, and the effects of that misbegotten alliance between Bourassa and the Conservatives in 1911 to defeat Laurier. I know also that the war didn't have for us the same value that it had for English-speaking Canadians. Living here for centuries—and having little contact with France or Europe—we knew when enough was enough.

The young men of Québec and their parents, like Sir Wilfrid, didn't want conscription. They would do their part in Canada; they would encourage those who wanted to go to go; but they wouldn't be conscripted. Yet in spite of their protests, Parliament enacted conscription on July 24, 1917, by a vote of 102 to 44. The people of Québec became the easy targets of that policy.

"Conscription. Did it have to take place?"

"In my opinion, it was not necessary to so deeply divide the country. I was not about to help create such a cleavage, the consequences of which I knew too well. Also, I did not want to hand the province over to the nationalist extremists, who, roused by Monsieur Bourassa's empty rhetoric and the demagoguery of his partisans, and aided by the Jesuits, could do much damage."

"Civil war?"

"The talk of civil war in Québec was sheer nonsense. However, there was ample concern about violent uprisings. To arouse passion and prejudice may be the work of a moment; to quell a storm may be the work of years. I had to calm the storm. I did so by holding more recruitment meetings, speaking at them, encouraging the young to enlist, and protecting Québec from abuse." He waits a moment, then says with sadness: "If the truth be known, I did not think conscription would be that helpful."

He was right. Of the 125,750 draft-age men in Ontario, 118,128, or 94 percent, sought exemptions, only 4 percent less than in Québec. Everywhere across Canada, high exemptions were the norm, except in the Yukon. I tell him that.

"Those numbers tell the story of why it was done."

"What do you mean?"

"Conscription had little to do with the war. It had much to do with putting Québec in its place, as it were. Riots ensued, martial law was proclaimed, protesters were shot, a whole people was attacked and reviled"—he bows his head—"and all for naught. All they achieved, those who wanted to put us in our place, was to sow the seeds of discord and disunion. Conscription was an obstacle and a barrier to the hope that this country would attain the aims Canadiens had when Confederation was effected."

"The riots in Québec City, just before Easter, in 1918 . . ." I don't finish the question.

"The riots were not only against conscription, but also against the high cost of living and the constant arrests by the military police of those who were suspected of avoiding the draft, a vigilance far greater than in the rest of Canada. Four civilians were killed by the police, ten soldiers were wounded, as were many residents of the city, and fifty-two persons were arrested. Violence. Almost desired." Again he goes back to his time, reliving it all. "If the law had been applied in such a way as to respect the rights of the people and applied fairly all across the land, it would not have been resisted, and the violence could have been avoided. But they chose not to do so. For their own reasons."

"Canada wasn't finished, though."

"Canada was severely wounded, but I had no doubt that it would survive. We had been near the precipice. Now we had to rebuild."

"How?"

"By allowing Canada to be the inspiration of our life." He stands and walks to the door, followed by Mascou. "Au revoir, Monsieur LaPierre."

Mascou opens the door and they disappear.

⚜

VI

Plus ça change, plus c'est pareil 1920–1959

❧

*T*he nearer history comes to the present, the more it defies history per se. Consequently, I need to concentrate on particular events that speak of recent times: the nationalism of the twenties, of the Depression, the Second World War, and of the workings of the man we know as "Le Chef," especially through the Asbestos Strike of 1949, an event that brings in one of the great figures of our Canada, Pierre Elliott Trudeau.

The events being so near, I wonder if Mascou can work his magic. However, I've learned never to underestimate him.

In *The French Canadians, 1760–1945*, Mason Wade devotes two chapters to the period from 1920 to 1939. The first one is called "Nationhood and Internationalism"; the second one, "Industrialization and Laurentianism." He tends to be severe in his analysis, but it remains valid to a large extent.

Laurier had been right in his assessment of the impact of the language and conscription issues that plagued the country between 1885 and 1920. These thirty-five years of national crises severely tested the value of Canadian diversity, which was, to Laurier, the cornerstone of the country's existence, as was his vision of the Canadian people as a people devoted to compromise, compassion, and the acceptance of the duality of Canada. In fact, his vision was left in a shambles. (So was, by the way, Henri Bourassa's vision of a bilingual Canada.) By the end of the First World War, no one had yet fully grasped the impact of the immigrants of neither French nor British origin on the evolution of Canada.

Laurier's view of diversity didn't favour the creation of a melting pot à l'américaine—the minting of Canadians in the image promoted by the Canada First Movement, the Orange Order, the Imperialist League, and the Equal Rights Association—a view shared by the British establishment of western Canada. Diversity wasn't a word in their vocabulary.

It wasn't in Québec's either: immigrants were frowned upon because they accepted the English language as their primary language. Accordingly, they identified with, or became part of, les Anglais. In that way, they participated in the numbers game between "us" and "them." We had, therefore, to be vigilant. But how? French Canadians had no intention of absorbing the immigrants or shaping them in their own image. On the other hand, French Canadians didn't accept either the notion or the reality of diversity any more than did their English-speaking counterparts. Everyone understood that a Canadien-Québécois–pure laine was the birthright of those who entered the world via the birth canal.

If diversity wasn't acceptable, what then of the Canadiens?

Laurier felt that the British North America Act didn't protect the French language across the land, except in those places where it was specifically stated. He hoped that through the systems of Catholic schools, which Confederation had initiated, the language would be preserved outside of Québec. However, as we've seen, even these constitutional arrangements could be arbitrarily put aside. Alors? Time and good will was his answer. (Given recent developments, he was more right than wrong.)

Mason Wade gives another answer: according to him, the French Canadians retreated "into a narrow provincialism." Perhaps they did, but it wasn't totally their doing. Rather, it was the legacy of the racism and indifference of the English—Anglais pure laine—who traumatized "new Canadians" into accepting what they considered to be a "proper" Canadian identity. Thus were the values of Canada distorted. That's what led to the "ethnic cleavage" that prevailed, a cleavage Laurier had predicted. The questioning of French-Canadian rights and influence would, Laurier pointed out, "predispose French Canada toward a more rigid isolationism in the postwar world than otherwise probably would have prevailed." Consequently, the French Canadians of Québec looked upon Canada's increasing involvement in international affairs—and the greater economic dependence upon the United States that followed the First World War—with suspicion, for both "represented a threat to French-Canadian cultural survival, and hence reinforced Québec's tendency to turn inward upon itself. . . ."

And Wade goes on to express a point of view with which it's difficult to disagree: "French Canada's long conditioning against imperialism resulted in some postwar years of battling against a British political imperialism that was fast dying, while the lack of an economic point of view among most humanistically educated élite long blinded French-Canadian spokesmen to the new American economic imperialism, which offered an even greater challenge to a minority determined to maintain its separate way of life." However, there was a dilemma. With American "economic imperialism" came a culture, a foreign culture, made up of gadgets, consumer goods, toys, greater industrialization, a higher standard of living, and all the rest of it that the people welcomed and much desired. This reality forced the élites to become more and more concerned. After all, they had to redeem the soul of French Canada, for it was on its way to perdition.

Furthermore, about the postwar era, Wade states that "it was a new and different Quebec which faced a new and different situation in that postwar Canada of 1920." Its population wasn't growing as fast as the rest of Canada's, and emigration to the United States continued to deplete the French-Canadian pool. In 1921, the census recognised that Québec was indeed an urban province; rural parishes were sending more and more of their sons and daughters to the cities of Canada or those of the United States. The province's industrial output was slightly less than Ontario's, and it had increased considerably during the war. The result of this economic situation was that Québec was the province least affected by the depression of 1921. It had a huge labour force demanding jobs, and a good standard of living.

Since Québec's industrial development was largely paid for by Americans, British, and the Anglais, it was inevitable that Quebec's "traditional way of life and the nature of French-Canadian nationalism" would be "radically altered." Furthermore, the postwar economic development accentuated the perpetual ethnic rivalries and chicanes—more of "them"; fewer of "us." According to Wade, "the French Canadians were left behind in business and industry, for they lacked both capital and training in economics, engineering, and the physical sciences." The result was that they "found themselves no longer masters in their own house." Instead of questioning their lack of qualifications, they attributed that marginality to ethnic discrimination. As for those who lived in rural Québec—not to mention their sons and daughters exiled in the cities—they blamed the Anglais who controlled everything and wouldn't adjust or make concessions to the French-Canadian way of life. And everyone became irritated with the Jews.

Where could the French Canadians turn, then?

As we've seen, the value of Confederation had decreased considerably in the French-Canadian psyche. More and more, the conviction grew that there wasn't much hope in that direction. So French Canadians had to find a new home—or so many thought.

If we were dominated economically (in 1934, Americans owned one-third of Québec's industrial capital), that domination could be countered through a French-Canadian economic nationalism, with all the institutions that went with it—labour unions, caisses populaires (credit unions), co-operatives, banks, etc. Sad to say, it was in retrenchment that we found security.

To my way of thinking, we should have stormed the barricades, adapted our culture and way of life to the new reality confronting us, and created alliances with our compatriots to bring about a Laurier-type Canadian nationalism.

We didn't, any more than we do today.

Nationalism is the outcome of the consciousness of a national identity. New France sowed the seeds for Canadiens and Canadiennes. Thus,

French-Canadian nationalism (and its modern manifestation: Québécois nationalism) is close to three hundred years old. During that time, it has undergone many metamorphoses. Its recurring theme, however, has always been la survivance.

In his own way, Sir Wilfrid Laurier was a French-Canadian nationalist, and it was natural for him to want to protect French Canada and ensure its survival. To achieve his goal, he had to make severe accommodations. But he hoped that, in time, the Canada that he saw so clearly would cease questioning the presence of the French Canadians, and would find in that dual national existence a source of strength and identity. Diversity, the cornerstone of Canada's being, is rooted in the defence of the duality of Canadian life.

A large number of his compatriots, however, didn't welcome Laurier's compromises to effect a reconciliation with les autres. Many felt that his compromises encouraged British imperialism, with all its negative attitudes towards the existence of the French language, education in French, and the French Canadians themselves.

One who agreed with that assessment was Henri Bourassa. Beginning with the Boer War, he felt pushed around by the impérialistes. This feeling became a conviction with the educational and language crises of the first decade of the new century. He found refuge in a different kind of nationalism from Laurier's; however, Bourassa wasn't about to retrench within the walls of Québec as many have suggested. Prepared to use French-Canadian nationalism to attract many to his cause, he was no isolationist and no separatist. He was a pan-Canadian, French-Canadian nationalist. He preached a Canada consisting of two societies existing in the bosom of a single state. Equality was his battle cry. That, however, couldn't be achieved unless the government of Québec was a faithful ally and unless the French Canadians were powerful at the federal level. Which meant finding accommodating allies. Rejecting Laurier's Liberal Party, Bourassa tied his political caravan to that of the Conservatives. It didn't work.

In the years after the First World War, the Liberals, provincial and federal, dominated the political life of Québec. Liberals of that time can be described as practical nationalists: they tended to stress the need for economic accommodation if Québec, and the French Canadians, were to survive. National rhetoric wasn't for them.

Where then were the more ardent nationalists to go? The Liberal Party was out of their reach. Since Laurier had absorbed the Cartier-Chapleau wing of the Conservative Party and since the other element of it, the Ultramontanes, had self-destructed, there was no hope there either. They had, therefore, to improvise. In 1917 they founded a magazine, *L'Action française*, which became a movement called Action française, an offshoot of the Ligue des droits du français, which some clerical and lay nationalists had founded in 1913 to protect the French language, wherever it was spoken in Canada, against les Anglais.

L'Action française, a monthly, was the catalyst for an organization known as the Ligue d'Action française, which was founded in 1921. The magazine also published the annual *Almanach de la langue française*; ran a publishing house, a book shop, and a library; organized public lectures and writing contests (all over Québec and elsewhere in Canada) on historical and nationalist themes; and lent its prestige and good offices to novelists, playwrights, and essayists whose works encouraged a prise de conscience for la survivance. It was clearly understood that "quand notre peuple aura acquis l'esprit de race et la fierté de race, il voudra constituer son intégrité française et catholique" (When our people have acquired the pride of being French Canadian, the people will regain their French and Catholic integrity).

Those connected with the Ligue d'action française had a hero to emulate and call upon: Dollard Des Ormeaux (1635–60). He was also the "hero" of my childhood, imposed, I might add, by the nuns who taught at the Couvent de Disraëli in the Eastern Townships, where I went to elementary school as a border. We used to celebrate Dollard's exploits with epic poems and plays that we wrote or the nuns did. Many were doing the same thing in schools and colleges across the province. We were told that he had saved our French-Canadian and Catholic civilization.

⚜

While I am daydreaming, Mascou enters softly. "Come," he says, "I have something to show you." As usual, I close my eyes, and when I reopen them, I am at the end of the Island of Montréal, not far from where the Rivière des Outaouais meets the St. Lawrence—we're at the Long Sault Rapids. I stand on the shore with Mascou. Across the water, there is a little incline and an abandoned fort, rudely made. There are soldiers and Indians standing around. Mascou points out who they are.

"Over there, to your left, are about forty Hurons. Having heard that the French were planning to intercept Iroquois canoes loaded with furs, they followed. They arrived yesterday."

"What do you mean: they arrived yesterday? I thought they came with the French soldiers."

"They did not. Had they left Montréal with the French on the 20th of April, Dollard and his people would have arrived here much sooner." He smiles—at least what looks like a smile. "You see the rapids? These are not dangerous and treacherous rapids. They are quite simple to navigate. Yet, it took Dollard and his people eight days to conquer them."

"Why?"

"No one in the French party knows how to handle a canoe properly."

"You haven't taught them?"

He's smiling in that way again. "I did not have to. They think they know."

"And the other Indians?"

"Four Algonquins." His eyes scan the faces on the other side. "I have not met the Hurons or the Algonquins."

"You know the Frenchmen? I read somewhere that some have been in Canada for about seven years, others about two or three. Is that right?"

"As far as I know, yes. Your people spend much time admiring these men and arguing among yourselves about their courage, their purpose, and their glory. It seems to me a waste of time. How the loyalty of the white man operates is a mystery to me. You never talk about my people, except to say that they run away, or betray, or steal." He goes closer to the water as more soldiers appear, coming from the surrounding woods, carrying logs. "If you have read about this expedition, you know that there are seventeen Frenchmen, soldiers—because no one can be just a settler—who asked to come here to ambush the Iroquois returning from their hunting grounds. They have to pass here on their way to their land. Everyone knows that."

"Why the Long Sault?"

"The Iroquois will have to go through the rapids in single file. This is what makes them vulnerable."

I want to know the names of the seventeen. Dollard Des Ormeaux, who is in command, is well known to a Canadien like me. On the other side of the rapids, he stands tall in the middle of a small group. He is twenty-five, and he's the garrison commander at Fort Ville-Marie in Montréal. He's known to be a pleasant man of good background, and courageous. Like his companions, he's unmarried. "Who are the soldiers with Des Ormeaux?"

"To his right are Jacques Brassier and François Cusson—we call him "Pilote"—and Alonie Delestre, who, at thirty-one, is the oldest. Turn your eyes now to the left of Des Ormeaux. There you see a group of four, unpacking supplies. They are René Doussin—he's also a miller; Christophe Augier; Jean Lecompte—a digger and woodcutter; Louis Martin—at twenty-one, he's the youngest—he herds cows, and . . ."

"He herds cows? Why is that important?"

"Well, somebody has to herd the cows." He points to two soldiers by the canoes handling the guns: "Le Sieur Jean Tavernier is the armourer, and helping him is Simon Grenet."

"And those coming out of the woods with the logs?"

"The group is led by the locksmith Nicholas Tiblemont, and the others are Nicolas Josselin; Jean Valets, who is a ploughman; Robert Jurie, Étienne Robin, and Jacques Boisseau. Missing is Roland Hébert." He looks for him. "Ah! There he comes. Out of the water over there. He likes to fish."

"Why the logs?"

"The fort was built a long time ago. It is falling apart. With the help of the Indians, they will try to build a palisade."

We watch them, in silence, working away at different tasks. There is no mingling of the Indians and the Frenchmen. "I understand," I say, "that before their departure from Montréal—or Ville-Marie, as it is called in your time—Dollard's men all went to confession, to Mass, and received Holy Communion. They also made their wills, since they swore not to flinch before the enemy, even if it meant death."

"The stories you people make up. The facts are they did perform their religious duties, a normal procedure; only two men out of the seventeen, Tavernier and Valets, made wills; as for the oath your history books and some enthusiastic authors make much of, it was not really an oath. What they agreed to, among themselves, was that under no circumstances would they ask for mercy should they be captured. Our people do that all the time. We swear on our honour to fulfil our mission, to do it to the best of our ability, and to help one another. The French and the Canadiens also do it frequently. They have learned it from us. Dollard and his men did not write anything down, nor did they sign any document. It was, as one of your more intelligent historians has said, a verbal contract of partnership."

"Where did you find that"

"From one of your professors at your Université Laval. He wrote honestly about Dollard and this expedition. His name is André Vachon." Mascou looks sheepish: "I helped him."

I am astounded. Never has Mascou spoken at such length about anything in the whole time I've known him. "There is much controversy among historians as to why Dollard is here," I mention. "Some—most of them, in fact—tell us that there is an Iroquois army being made ready to invade New France. To stop them, Dollard came here. Others argue differently."

Mascou looks at me briefly before he casts his eyes on his moccasins. "Those who argue differently, as you say, are right." He drinks some water from his pouch. "You have read the letters of Mère Marie de l'Incarnation. Remember?" I nod my head in agreement. "Then you must recall that she talked about this supposed army; but she says clearly that she and the entire colony did not see or believe that this would happen. There is your answer."

"So these seventeen men didn't know about an army." I should have remembered that! In Dollard's mind, the Iroquois who would pass here were not the vanguard of a powerful army. They were just hunters returning home. Marie de l'Incarnation confirmed this, I suddenly recall. I look across the river and the men, helped by the Indians this time, are still working away. "You're right, of course. She also wrote to someone in France that around May 15, 1660, it was announced that an Indian army was approaching. It surprised her and everyone else."

"And by May 15, our friend Dollard and his companions were all dead."

The men in front of me, readying themselves to meet the Iroquois at Long Sault, don't know they are preparing for their death. I look at them and then at Mascou. "Then what the hell are they doing here?" I ask Mascou.

"Their duty. What else would they be doing here?" He walks to the river and looks around, anticipating something. Not finding what he's looking for, he comes back and sits beside me. "This is a normal 'petite guerre'—the name the French give to a raid like this one. The authorities at Ville-Marie know that the Iroquois are returning. As I have said before, they have to go through the rapids. This place is therefore a good place to attack them so that they will not do any mischief on their way home. And, with luck, Dollard will take their furs. To the victor belongs the spoils. It is as simple as that." He waits a moment before adding: "Dollard is expecting a relatively small band of Iroquois." He stands and says: "Today is Saturday, May 1, 1660. Tomorrow will be Sunday. Let us go back to your house and I will tell, as best I can, the rest of this story."

In my house, Mascou continues the saga of Dollard Des Ormeaux and his band. "On Sunday, May 2, Dollard's scouts saw some Iroquois lurking about, but the Iroquois also saw the French, and returned in haste to the main group of hunters. A couple of hours later, two or three hundred Onondagas, with hatchets in their belts, paddles in their hands, and muskets at the prows of their canoes, appeared, taking the seventeen French, who were having their midday meal, totally by surprise."

Mascou goes on to relate that there were many more Iroquois than Dollard had anticipated. When I ask him why that was so, he replies: "The Iroquois are planning to attack New France. There are five hundred of them on the Richelieu River, awaiting the arrival of the Onondaga hunters who are now at the Long Sault." He looks out the window of the living room, and while patting Chazy, he continues. "The battle begins but the Onondagas are rebuffed. They quickly send a canoe to the Richelieu to bring back reinforcements, who arrive five days later, about May 7. Meanwhile, the battle rages around the fort we saw earlier. There are roughly sixty men inside; there is not much hope. Dollard is running out of food and water; some of his men are wounded or dead; it is cold; the stench is overpowering; and they can hardly swallow the thick flour or the sagamite they are accustomed to eating on such missions."

Mascou turns around to continue his tale: "The rest is predictable. The powerful Iroquois army arrives. There is talk of a truce. Some Hurons, between twenty and thirty, cross the barricades and join the Iroquois. Dollard tries various ways of harming the enemy, but he is not successful. In despair, the French ignite a barrel of powder and throw it over the palisade at their foes, but it hits a branch and falls back into the fort, exploding."

He sighs: "It is over. There are only a few able-bodied men in the fort. One of them takes his axe and kills the wounded so they will not fall into the hands of the victors. When the Iroquois enter the fort, they find five Frenchmen and four Hurons alive. The battle, begun on Sunday, May 2, ends seven days later. The Hurons are adopted, as is the custom. The five Frenchmen are killed—one at the fort itself, the other four later." Again that long sigh: "Thus ends the tale of Dollard Des Ormeaux." And Mascou disappears.

He doesn't tell me if it was all worth the effort. He doesn't confirm if, indeed, Dollard and his men saved New France in the spring of 1660.

⚜

For the zealots of the Ligue d'Action française, Dollard became the embodiment of the religious zeal, the courage, the bravery, and the dedication that we should all emulate as we lived our lives dedicated to la race, la langue, et la foi. Since then, we have found out that Dollard was an adventurer and a fur trader whom the Iroquois caught by surprise. He appears not to have been a hero-martyr to our cause. Or so it is said now.

L'Action française and the Ligue were opposed to the vast sellout of Québec's resources to the Americans and wanted to increase the stature and role of the French Canadians in the economic life of the province. However, there was ambiguity. Here is Mason Wade again:

> The criticism advanced by *L'Action française* was a natural concomitant of its entire attitude to economics. That attitude was moralistic and intellectual and revealed the contemporary distaste for materialism and the fear of the assimilative power of the industrial world. It led *L'Action française* to stress the dangers of industrialization even while recognising the importance of industrial and commercial ventures for the survival of French Canada.

291

Where were Québec's economic aims to be achieved? In agriculture, of course—agriculture was best suited to the French-Canadian way of life and to its economic survival. But the group's preaching got it nowhere.

The Ligue's nationalists extolled the virtues of the rural village and emphasized the evils lurking in every street and ally of the cities—prostitution, exploitation, anarchy, alcoholism, women not remembering the place God had given them, fathers abandoning their children. There was also the great evil of the cinema, which corrupted the young, Americanised them, anglicised them, weakened their moral fibre, made criminals out of them, and left them to wander in a desert bereft of ideas, ideals, and the gentle prodding of faith. "Dans un pays que l'on dit catholique, l'on laisse ouverte, à côté de l'église et de l'école catholique, une vaste école de démoralisation." In essence, next to Catholic churches and schools can be found schools teaching moral turpitude.

To the spiritual dangers of the cinema was added a physical one: on a Sunday in January 1927, the Laurier Palace became engulfed in flames, and seventy-eight children lost their lives. Something had to be done. And in time, the government initiated censorship laws and forbade children to go to the cinema unless accompanied by an adult.

The evil of the city was incarnated in—who else?—the Jew. *L'Action* stated clearly that the Jew was dedicated to the making of money and the control of the world. The Jew was everywhere, "infecting" the neighbourhoods. The Jew was an important obstacle to the realisation of the French-Canadian dream. The Jew had to be unmasked. To that end, the *Almanach* published a list "of Jewish businesses hiding behind French names."

We can conclude, with Professor Susan Mann Trofimenkoff, that "the entire reaction of the *L'Action française* to the city suggests a fundamental pessimism about the compatibility of French Canada and urban society, and the function of moral watchdog suggests a rather dismal view of the majority of the French Canadians . . . The somewhat wistful determination to trace the causes of moral temptation to external factors shrouded the fear that the city might be the death-knell of French Canada."

The Ligue was also caught in another contradiction when it dealt with the protection of the French language across Canada—and it toyed with the idea of separatism between 1922 and 1927. The participants in the Ligue were convinced that an independent French state in North America, namely Québec, was possible and desirable. Confederation had had its day. Furthermore, it was the plot of les Anglais to put an end to the French-Canadian nation by destroying its soul. Only an independent state would prevent that. At the head of that state would be "le chef," the incarnation of the virtues and the mission of the French Canadians. When western French-speaking Canadians pointed out that they would be left isolated, the eminent preachers of separatism argued that an independent French state on the banks of the St. Lawrence would create a forceful solidarity that would permit survival—or redemption—for all co-religionists and compatriots. It's fortunate that hardly anybody in the 1920s was willing "to follow the lead of a group that was morally repelled by politics but intellectually fascinated by the political world and that offered two political myths—le chef and the separate state—as the solution to French Canada's problems." We were not out of our minds!

In January 1928, *L'Action française* was dissolved. It couldn't survive the antagonism of the provincial government, the doubts of Rome and of the Québec episcopacy, and the internal dissensions that had plagued it all its life.

Lionel-Adolphe Groulx (1878–1967) was a historian, a priest, and the nationalist evangelist of the twenties. He has also been described as the spiritual father of modern Québec. As le chef of the Ligue d'action française; as a popular historian, lecturer, and novelist throughout his life; as a dedicated teacher and professor; and as a holy priest of the Church, he inspired many young people to be proud of who they were, to be intimately linked with their "glorious" past, and to be dedicated to Québec's future. He also made anti-Semites of many of them. His influence is hardly present today, but there is no denying that for close to seventy years Abbé Groulx was important in almost every aspect of Québec's life. When he died in 1967, the government of Québec gave him the first state funeral in the province's history.

In her *Variations on a Nationalist Theme*, Susan Mann Trofimenkoff has published the most important articles written by Groulx. Here are some excerpts:

... The future shall be theirs, who keep the past
Who keep their unremorseful memories whole
And stay near tombs of glory to the last
To mingle with the dead their living soul.

The future shall be theirs whose proudest goal
Is the retention of their mother tongue:
This epic music where their father's soul
Vibrates in prayer as though a hymn were sung.

[From *L'Action française*]: The most serious implication in all this is that peace does not exist in our country—it has gone forever. Behind this struggle to crush the French language lies such contempt for what is right and equitable, such pride in sheer power that no part of our political constitution is secure.

 ... But who could seriously challenge the importance of this struggle? We sometimes complain of being misunderstood by foreigners; we deplore the fact that so many of our relatives from France have to rediscover us each year; we are distressed that so few people believe in our survival and that in certain places we are already considered a race threatened with extinction. What are we complaining about? How could strangers travelling in our province or in our cities not believe in our abdication and our disappearance when so many French Canadians hide their French origins behind English signs, when railroad companies spread the network of their English geography over the French countryside? What tourist, for example, could have guessed the existence of a French city at the mouth of the St. Maurice River when, not so long ago, all he could see at the station was the English name "Three Rivers"? Can we really pretend to be a vigorous French race when we accept notices and advertisements from transport and other companies in English only with the sole exception of Défense de fumer and Défense de cracher, when we tolerate English as the sole language of business with clients, when we invariably ask for a telephone number in English or accept from our public utility companies letters written in English only, when we consult only English menus in our restaurants and cafés? Do you think many other nations, proud of their origins and determined to live, would tolerate such a situation for any length of time?

[On French-Canadian nationalism]: The essence of our being can be expressed in two words, French and Catholic. French and Catholic we have been, not merely since our arrival in America, but for the past thousand years since and even before Tolbiac and the birth of the Frankish nation. Our rights go back far enough to inspire respect, and surely we are of quite respectable lineage as well. We are the direct descendants of the French people who left France around 1660–1680 when she was the leading nation in the world. Moreover, our faith teaches us that as Catholics we are, through our spiritual birth, of a stock that is more princely than any on earth. We are of a divine race, we are the sons of God.

. . . Here then, in its entirety, you have the ideological and emotional substance of French Canadian Nationalism. Of all the colonial nations that are branches of modern Europe, there may be some which are richer materially; but how many could boast of greater spiritual wealth?

. . . In our present atmosphere we must shun the sort of bilingualism that would mean being unable to speak our mother tongue better than the other, and that might introduce confusion as to which language should receive our strongest emotional attachment.

. . . Our strongest and most pressing danger from the outside arises from the fact of our being a minority group, a minority in nine provinces, a minority in the whole of Canada. That is the terrible situation in which we have been placed by Confederation. It gave us the immense advantage of reconstituting Quebec into an autonomous state. On the other hand it transformed us into a minority throughout the country and at the federal level. Before 1867 we had never been a political minority, not even under the Union which had given equal parliamentary representation to Upper and Lower Canada. We have now been condemned to the role of a political minority for 82 years. Have our representatives in Ottawa during that time succeeded in finding the exact synthesis, the fair balance between what is due to the Federal government and what is due to the country, the Province, the nationality, the party—as would have been done by the English, the Irish, or the Jews? Who would dare claim that they have? There is the dark blot on our record.

[On having a French state]: Whether one likes it or not *we shall have our French state!* We shall have a young, strong, beautiful, radiant home, a spiritual, dynamic centre for the whole of French America. We shall have a country with its French nature stamped upon its visible features.

Groulx wasn't always well received. Here is an excerpt from an article of October 21, 1927, in *Le Soleil*, an important newspaper of Québec City: "To judge by its writings, *L'Action française* has the most impressive collection of narrow minds in the country. . . . [It is] an ingenious device to let people prattle and prate, adopting positively Olympian attitudes, interpreting the secret designs of Providence itself, governing the whole of mankind, doing everything except that which requires simple common sense." Three days later, the paper attacked again: "Utopian fantasy! Is *L'Action française* anything else? While these men are busy fluttering around the question of an independent French state on the banks of the Saint Lawrence . . . the world goes on without them, and in spite of them."

When, in 1937, the rumour circulated that the abbé might accept in principle the idea of becoming prime minister of French Canada, another newspaper asked: "What are Abbé Groulx's chances of success?" Not much, the editor claimed: "Until now this racist leader has been able to count on the support of a few directors of some young people's associations. People who are over thirty-five and less susceptible to thoughtless enthusiasms are almost solidly against any exploitation of regional nationalism. They simply refuse to be fenced in."

On the other hand, when Groulx died in 1967, Claude Ryan, the editor of *Le Devoir*, the newspaper that Henri Bourassa founded in 1910, wrote that Groulx had played a decisive role in the evolution of modern Québec, even though he was much less influential between 1940 and 1960. Why?

In the same article of May 24, 1967, Ryan gave the major reason for this eclipse. The generation that emerged between the end of the Depression and the beginning of the Révolution tranquille of the 1960s came to believe that "nothing more could be expected from traditional nationalism, that the ways of the future had to be sought in entirely new paths." It was in this period that "movements of Catholic Action developed, strongly universal and social in nature, severing thereby the traditional alliance between nationalism and religion."

In passing, let it be said that Groulx was the precursor of the Catholic Action movement, a movement that tended to bring together laymen with the social activism of the clergy, particularly in urban areas. For instance, it was Groulx who founded the Association catholique de la jeunesse canadienne-française, in 1903–04. From it sprung a powerful, dynamic, and socially involved force grouped in varied organisations, such as the Jeunesse ouvrière catholique, Jeunesse étudiante catholique, and Jeunesse rurale catholique.

Perhaps the last world on Abbé Groulx should be given to Claude Ryan: "Yet without ever engaging in partisan politics, without ever abandoning the spiritual perspective which colours his entire work, Groulx had a decisive influence on the temporal destiny of his people. He was, in brief, the spiritual father of modern Quebec. Everything noteworthy, everything novel on the Quebec scene has carried the imprint of Groulx's thought."

I once described the Depression as the twelfth most important event in the history of Canada. It all began dramatically enough; but few thought it would last as long as it did. Here is how the *Canadian Annual Review of Public Affairs, 1929–30* described the beginning of this great human tragedy:

The Crash in the Canadian Stock Exchanges during the latter part of October and the first half of November, which reached proportions never attained hitherto in the history of these Exchanges, was the outstanding event in the financial history of Canada during the year 1929, as it was indeed in that of the United States and several other countries where the Stock Exchange plays an important and sometimes a dominating part in financial operations. For several days, conditions both in Canada and New York reached what was generally termed a "panic," during which stocks were cast overboard without regard to existing prices, and the market crashed to low levels with each succeeding outburst of selling, until it seemed at times as if nothing could stem the frantic tide and re-establish prices on anything like a firm and stable basis. The losses incurred by holders of stocks, whether of the investor or speculator type, were simply terrific, as the declines were greater than had ever taken place before in the history either of the New York or Canadian Exchanges, just as the torrent of selling had been preceded by a bull market whose proportions and bubbling spirits had never before been equalled in Exchange history.

. . . On the morning of Friday, Oct. 25, 1929, a large heading was spread across the top of the front page of *The Globe*, in bold type: "Speculators Shaken in Wild Day of Panic."

. . . This, however, was only a fairly substantial index of what was to follow. On the succeeding Monday, Oct. 29, a new panic set in, following a short-lived rally, and a new record of liquidation, both in New York and on the Canadian Exchanges, was established.

Thus it began, this drama that was to last between October 1929 until the beginning of the Second World War, this tragedy that marked all of us who lived as participants in it. Between 1929 and 1933, the effects were severe but uneven; there was a short recovery thereafter. But in 1937 and 1938, Canadians and Canadiens were hit again with a force they could hardly sustain. The only relief came with the war. It was therefore welcomed, since it gave us hope that all would be well. As someone put it, "It was the mocking irony of our economic system," because the war became "the ultimate moral Christian solution for unemployment." Many said over and over again: "Maybe there will be a war and we'll get paid to fight."

In talking about the Depression with my parents, my relatives, and my acquaintances—and in reading the various historical surveys of it—I have no doubt that Confederation failed us. Or was it those in power? Perhaps. There seems to have been no pity anywhere—from God, from Churches, from governments, from nature, from relief agencies. There seems to have been only a conspiracy—of governments, the police, and the "trusts"—to destroy our pride in ourselves, to make us impotent and dependent, and to impede the only instrument that could possibly help us: the labour-union movement. What is one to conclude when every relief program was inadequate, temporary, and subject to changing rules as the crisis deepened? What is one to conclude when in the spring of 1932, at a time when the unemployment rate was more than 25 percent, governments and relief agencies decreed that it was wrong for people to expect that they—the governments and the business machines—could find jobs for everyone unemployed? What is one to conclude when the unemployed, particularly the men—and the younger ones, at that—were "transients, lazy bums, and parasites, who only wanted to live on the dole"—the dole being the instrument that killed initiative and enterprise, especially in the young, according to the holy ones? What is one to think when the police—citizens like us, but paid ones—became the instruments of brutal repression, so that law and order could be maintained? What is one to think when the prime minister of one's country invited Canadians and Canadiens to show their patriotism by beating all those who dared argue that all was not well?

The federal government had immense powers, and there is no doubt that, for a long time, it refused to use them. The Conservative government of the times didn't really begin to act until 1935. However, the Bennett New Deal—as the relief legislation was called in honour of the prime minister of the times: Richard Bedford Bennett (1870–1947)—was declared unconstitutional. Only the provinces, it was decreed, were empowered to bring relief to the people of Canada. But the provinces were mostly bankrupt themselves. In their misery, my parents threw out Bennett and replaced him with William Lyon Mackenzie King. Unfortunately, for my parents and the rest of us, he wasn't useful either. He did manage, though, to establish a Royal Commission to find out how we had gotten into this mess. And then, the war came to save him.

As for Québec, it finally got rid of the Liberals, who had ruled the province since the end of the 19th century, and brought in Maurice Le Noblet Duplessis, as we shall see later.

Francis Reginald Scott (1899–1985) is a favourite of mine; during my days at McGill University, I knew him well. Scott was an eminent professor of constitutional law, a founder of Canada's socialist movement, and a poet. His wife, Marian Dale Scott, was a fine artist. In 1935, he wrote about the "efficiency" of the capitalist system in a poem titled "Efficiency," about the irony of the Depression:

> The efficiency of the capitalist system
> Is rightly admired by important people.
> Our huge steel mills
> Operating at 25% of capacity
> Are the last word in organization.
> The new grain elevators
> Stored with superfluous wheat
> Can load a grain-boat in two hours.
> Marvellous card-sorting machines
> Make it easy to keep track of the unemployed.
> There is not one unnecessary worker
> In these textile plants
> That require a 75% tariff protection.
> And when our closed shoe-factories re-open
> They will produce more footwear than we can possibly buy.
> So don't let us start experimenting with socialism
> Which everyone knows means inefficiency and waste.

❧

It's pouring rain and cold when Mascou transports me to a church basement somewhere in Montréal. On the way there, he tells me that the parish priest is interviewing applicants who are gathering at his church to determine whether they are worthy of relief. He explains "worthy": "It means that, in allocating money or food or services, the priest and his relief advisor must determine whether those soliciting the help of the Church are good Catholics, whether they have tried to find work, whether they have children or other dependants, etc. The people, you see, have to be worthy of relief because the rich who donate would not want their charitable offerings to go to the undesirables and the lazy."

There's hardly any light and, I'm certain, no heat at all in the church. People are standing in the darkness around the walls, shivering, and in the middle of the room, under a single bare light bulb, there is a table where the priest in his overcoat, a biretta on his head, is sitting, and next to him is the relief advisor in a thick sweater.

The priest calls the first applicant, who is an elderly lady. She stands humbly in front of him and after having made the sign of the Cross, she says: "I need help. My daughter-in-law is ill. She lives with me. Her children too. There are five of them."

"Do you work?" asks the priest, not unkindly.

"I'm a laundress for a rich family in what they call Westmount. Three days a week: Monday, Wednesday, and Friday."

"How much do you earn?"

"A dollar a day." She counts on her fingers: "It makes three dollars a week."

"We can count. Thank you," says the relief worker irritably. "Does your employer pay your carfare?"

"Oui, Monsieur!"

The two men look at one another, and she reads their decision in their eyes. The priest looks down at his pile of papers and, without looking at the old lady in front of him, he says: "I don't know if there's anything we can do for you. You have employment. You're lucky. You should keep it."

"But I can't," the old lady replies, crying. "My daughter-in-law is ill. She can't work. And the children? What am I to do with the children? They're too young to work." Desperately she looks around the room for help: "I'm all alone."

"Where is her husband and yours?"

"I'm a widow. Her husband has gone away. We don't know where." She takes the priest's hand and adds: "Please help me. I pray. I go to Mass. I light candles. Please help me."

The priest pushes her hand away and says: "We can only help those who have no employment. Find comfort in God, my child." He blesses her before he says: "Go with God, my child." He removes her hand, and calls for the next supplicant.

Disoriented, the old lady leaves.

The relief worker hands a piece of paper to a young woman and says: "Can you read?"

"Non, Monsieur."

He takes the paper away from her, stands up, and says loudly: "Pay attention, all of you. Here are the rules for food allowances and menus for one week for a family of five." He brandishes the paper, and with authority and in a firm voice he says: "This means that with the money you receive for food, here's what you have to do . . ." He brings the paper he's holding close to his eyes and reads:

"1. Each child under the age of two must have 3 teaspoons of cod-liver oil daily.

2. Tomatoes, fresh or canned, may be used in place of oranges.

3. Always use the water in which vegetables have been cooked for mild soup, soup stock or stews.

4. Day-old bread is better for children than fresh bread and costs less.
5. Buy food in bulk, instead of in boxes or packages; it is cheaper.
6. Milk, fruit, vegetables, whole wheat bread, and cereals are essential to health."

He looks around the room before adding: "Tea is not included as it has no food value. This does not imply that its use by adults is discouraged. You should also reduce cereals and sugars to buy cocoa, seasonings, baking powder, etc." He sits down. The woman standing in front of him takes the paper and leaves.

I ask Mascou to return me to my time.

⚜

I am rereading the testimony of many who described their plight in Barry Broadfoot's *Ten Lost Years, 1929-1939:*

My mother operated a sewing machine factory in the East End of Montreal . . .

If you went to the bathroom more than twice in a shift you were docked and there were just two toilets for those hundred women and they ate lunch at their machines because there was no washroom or lunchroom. No fire escapes. No sprinklers. No ladders. Windows sealed tight. There was no union. If you even thought union, it was out. Out! Out! Ask for a raise? Out! Take two days off sick. Out! Think. Out!

. . . In those days the church was my wife's life, they would make all of it better. She'd light the stove and put in the bread at 5:30 in the morning to be ready for breakfast when she comes home again, and she'd tie her boots by the strings together and put them around her neck and walk four miles [six kilometres] for early mass. Not when there is snow, she's not that crazy, you know, but every other time. Every day.

Just her. Sometimes on bad days maybe, only she is at mass, but she makes that priest say mass. The priest charged her 50 cents a week to say mass. You know, that is his charge, like my grocery store charges 60 cents for a pack of smokes. To this guy mass is a business. To my wife it is going to end the bad days, that life we had, you know of salt pork and beans. The kids, we had 10, would get cod liver oil again, you know.

I am sorry. I forgot to say. The reason my wife wore boots around her neck, you know, she did not want to wear them out. At the church, she would sit on the steps and put them on like that.

. . . Oh God, don't tell me about those days. They were some days, eh! There were 17 in my family, and while today that is a very big family it was not so big in those times. My mother's sister, Marie, she had 21 and they were all alive. Yes, all alive. That may be a rarity but it was not a miracle.

. . . When I was 13 my mother says no more foolishness. I can read and write okay, can't I? Okay, you go to work. School is fine as far as you are concerned, ma petite, and in a French Canadian house you might think the husband is boss but he is not, it is the woman, and it is my mother who says what is for me. I have four older sisters and four older brothers and they are all working making garments, in the textile plants run by these Jews and I get it. Yes, I sure get it. I get ten hours a day and six days a week and I get four dollars when I am 13, and if you don't smile nice at those damned foremen they can make you out of work right there.

Then, to depress me even more, I read a couple of letters that were sent to the prime minister of Canada, begging for his help. I find one from a man living then in Tancredia in the Province of Québec and written to Bennett in 1934:

I had hoped to get work this winter in the camps usually operated near here, by J.R. Booth and Gillies, but there are none this winter because Taschereau refused to come to an understanding with these companies. Consequently we married men are obliged to remain at home thinking of what will become of us this winter. I worked this summer for the farmers for 25 cents per day and my board. You can see this was a starvation wage and that it was impossible for me to feed and clothe six small children and my wife . . .

Here's another one from a woman of Angliers, who wrote in 1935:

I am the wife of a return soldier who has served 4 years overseas under the Canadian army and I am a mother of 5 children living. On the 6 of Jan 1934 I took very sick as I was in a family way suffering from so many diseases I started to lose my eyesight. And which the Doctor told my husband it was through weakness. So finally on the 16 of Jan when my baby girl was born I was in real darkness I wasn't able to see no one around my bed. And I stayed in bed 3 month Jan Feb & March without no treatment whatever because my husband was without work and which he has been for several years. So the first part of April I started to get up for the first time. On which I wasn't able to see nothing with very little food in the house & 6 children it was very hard for me to get better so on the 11th of June my baby got a bad cold and she died . . . we had no money . . . please have mercy on me as I'm only a young mother age 32 and the condition I am I cannot attend my housework.

In *Canada My Canada, What Happened?* I related what the Depression meant to me. Here is what I lived in the dirty thirties and what I continue to have inside of me:

My family was then living in Lac Mégantic, a small town in the Eastern Townships of Québec, where I was born on November 21, 1929. My father was a lumberjack for Cliche Lumber, where he worked twelve hours a day for eighty cents. My mother looked after their five children and did odd jobs as a cleaning woman for the most affluent families in our community.

Two images of those moments stick in my memory, their vividness undimmed by the many years since. First: for years during the Depression we had meat only on Sundays. The rest of the week we ate bread and molasses and sometimes vegetables, if our relatives in a nearby village brought us some. On Sundays my mother cooked *boeuf haché*, ground beef cooked in brown sauce with onions and potatoes. My parents never ate with us on Sundays, saying that they did not like beef. Instead they scraped what little gravy was left after we were finished. Much later in life I realized that both of them really liked beef, but that they had gone without so that their children could be relatively healthy.

Second: At one point my parents could not pay the instalments on the furniture they had bought. The sheriff came and repossessed everything, except a rocking chair for my mother, who was then pregnant, and a little wagonette my elder brother had hid under the verandah. After they left, my mother sat in her chair for a long time, rocking and weeping.

Shortly afterwards she went to work in a hotel as a cook, and we children were packed off to a convent in Disraeli, where we stayed for the full school year, even during the Christmas holidays. In the summer, she rented a cottage for a couple of months, but we did not have a permanent home again until we moved to Sherbrooke in 1939.

Of all the events of my life, the Depression marked me most. I remain in awe of mother's courage, her devotion, and her love. Remembering my father, this once proud man, I know what humiliation is. Looking into myself, I understand my fear of poverty. In that, I'm not any different from all those who've lived through the dirty thirties.

The Depression had a particular effect in Québec that wasn't found in the rest of Canada. A sort of French-Canadian nationalism grew—fierce and radical, and it became quite widespread. It arose because someone, something, had to be blamed for all that misery. The criminal was easily identified: foreign capital. Foreign capital meant les Anglais. Consequently, the antagonism between what is now known as the two founding nations grew. It found itself in the media, in slogans of all sorts like "Le Québec pour les Canadiens français," in Catholic unions, in political affiliations, and in the revival of the movement "achat chez nous"—buying what one needs from French-Canadian firms and stores.

Much involved in this anti-foreign movement were a group of twenty university students who, in 1932, founded an organization called Jeune-Canada. They dedicated it to the protection of French-Canadian rights across Canada and to the maintaining of Québec as a rural, agricultural, French, and Catholic community. The group's traditional nationalism led naturally to talk of an economic and politically independent Québec. In addition, they also attacked the trusts, foreign capital, immigrants, and, particularly, the Jews. The Jews were an easy target: they owned the corner stores frequented by French Canadians.

In their anti-Semitism, the students were aided by a rag called *Le Goglu*, which had no purpose other than to promote French-Canadian hatred against the Jews. Hating the Jews became part of one's patriotism. *Le Goglu* argued that Québec had been handed over to the Jews. Therefore, the time had come to regain Québec by showing "them" that French Canadians were the masters on the sacred soil of their ancestors.

This anti-Semitic madness went on and on, encouraged as it was by the most educated citizens and many in the highest echelons of Québec's society, including the Church. In 1934, for instance, the interns at Montréal's Catholic Notre-Dame hospital went on strike because a Jewish intern had been hired—Samuel Rabinovitch, a young graduate of the medical faculty of the Université de Montréal. To explain their strike, the interns argued that the Catholic patients of the hospital found it repugnant to be treated by a Jew, while they, the other interns, certainly didn't want to spend a year closeted avec un Juif. And the list of the outrages perpetrated against the Jews in Québec could go on and on. It is said, though, that Québec wasn't much different from the other provinces in the ferocity of its anti-Semitism.

It doesn't appear that Jeune-Canada protested too much, if at all. In 1938, as economic conditions improved—or the young students grew older—the movement ceased to exist. In time, its members became eminent Canadians, well respected and well employed.

I wonder if, in their adult years, they ever thought of the harm they had done in the name of la race, la langue, et la foi. Perhaps. Or, maybe they attributed their antics to des folies de jeunesse.

Between 1935 and 1939 and due to the deteriorating international situation, Mackenzie King's government increased defence spending considerably. Eleven members of his caucus, from Québec, objected and voted against the increase—an indication of things to come

On August 25, 1939, in anticipation of the war, the War Measures Act was invoked, giving almost absolute powers to the government.

Seven days after Great Britain declared war on Germany, Canada followed suit—on September 10. As soon as this decision was taken, the lines were drawn. On the one hand were, according to the popular parlance of the day, the Anglais (everybody who wasn't French Canadian) or the impérialistes (favouring Canada's participation in each and every war of the British); and, on the other hand, the French Canadians (who were in favour of a great war effort as long as it was for the defence of Canada but who were also opposed to all forms of compulsory service overseas).

Fourteen days later, in an act typical of his demagoguery, Duplessis called a provincial election, only three years into his mandate. The election was fought on the slogan that a vote for him was a vote against Canada's participation in the war and against conscription. With substantial support from federal Liberals, the provincial wing robbed Duplessis of his victory, and on October 24, a Liberal government took over in Québec. They had garnered seventy-one seats in the legislature; Duplessis had elected fourteen members. However, the Liberal victory was accompanied by a solemn commitment: the Liberals in Ottawa, who had assured the Liberal victory in Québec, promised that they would never be part of a government that tried to conscript Canadians and Canadiens.

In the federal elections the following March, Mackenzie King was returned to power with an increased majority, which included sixty-four Liberals from Québec. King had a mandate to run the war as he saw fit. By the end of May, over 25,000 men had been sent to Great Britain. (When war had been declared, Canada had only 4,000 reservists.)

April 25, 1940, was a great day for the women of Québec. They were "permitted" to vote in provincial elections. There was much opposition. The Church wasn't pleased. "We are opposed . . ." yelled the cardinal-archbishop of Québec. Why? The usual silly reasons.

In June 1940, the federal government passed the National Resources Mobilization Act, which required all Canadians to place their person, their services, and their property in the service of the war effort. The Act included the proviso that persons were not required "to serve in the military, naval or air forces outside of Canada and the territorial waters thereof." That law was accepted in Québec without much opposition. What followed it, though, was more complicated.

In mid-August 1940, the federal government ordered that every man and woman between the ages of fourteen and sixty had to register in order to be placed wherever they would be more useful to the country. In other words, conscription for service in Canada. Everyone had to be in possession of the registration card at all times, under pain of severe fines. Without the card, as well, no one could obtain a job or ration tickets. It was also decreed at that time that single men between the ages of nineteen and forty-five had to serve in the military as well as all those married after July 15, 1940. The first conscript soldiers, young Québécois, were sent to Valcartier for their training.

Although 1941 was a relatively quiet year, three important events took place. In July, five thousand workers at the Aluminum Company of Canada, the most important war factory in Canada, walked out. Due to the War Measures Act, the strike was illegal. The army was called in, and five days after beginning the strike, the workers were back at their jobs.

On November 26, 1941, Ernest Lapointe (1876–1941) died in Montréal. As a politician, minister of justice, Mackenzie King's right-hand man and his lieutenant in Québec, Lapointe had used his presence and prestige to ensure Québec's participation in the war effort. He did promise, however, that there would be no conscription for overseas service.

Less than two weeks after Lapointe's death, the Japanese attacked Pearl Harbor, and the United States formally entered the war.

In the first years of the war, French Canadians did what they had promised: to do everything possible for the defense of Canada. The Régiment de Maisonneuve was the first Canadian unit to draw a full complement of volunteers for overseas service. By January 1, 1941, fifty thousand French Canadians were in uniform. One-third of the sailors in the Royal Canadian Navy were French Canadians. As for the Air Force, many enlisted and most of them served in the French-Canadian fighter squadron, Les Allouettes, formed in June 1942. In addition, many of the men and women of Québec were employed in the war industries and related activities. (My mother ran a boarding house in Sherbrooke and served over seventy-five meals a day to workers of the textile industries near our home.) Agricultural output also increased considerably, but there was a shortage of workers. French Canadians also contributed generously to war loans, and there often were over-subscriptions.

But even all that wasn't enough for the impérialistes. They were upset that French Canadians enlisted less for overseas service than the "good British." To many from Québec, what was important was to defend Canada, not to engage in "overseas adventures." And so, from 1942 until the end of the war, bonne entente was hard to find.

Georges Verreault was born in April 1920, in what is known as Saint-Henri in Montréal. Seven years later, his family moved to Verdun. In 1939, Georges became a linesman for the Bell Telephone Co., and two years later he enlisted in the army as a signalman. Six months later, he was with the Royal Rifles of Canada (a Québec regiment in which many French Canadians served) and was sent to Hong Kong where he was attached to the brigade headquarters. His fighting days, which began on December 7, 1941, ended on Christmas Day, when the British forces in Hong Kong capitulated.

Georges became a prisoner of war, spending some time in Hong Kong and then being transferred to Japan. Over the four years of his incarceration, he would live in camps in Yokohama, Shinagawa, and Ohasi. Freed in August 1945, he returned to Montréal in October, went back to Bell, married, and settled in Cap-de-la-Madeleine. He was forty-six when he died in 1966. His body was that of an eighty-year-old man. The Japanese had done that to him.

310

Georges Verreault was able to survive because of his diary. He started it on October 29, 1941, while on the ship to Hong Kong. He ended it on Sunday, September 16, 1945, when he was again on a ship, "un destroyer léger et en pleine mer." The final, short paragraph ended with a few simple words, so full of hope: "Je commence une nouvelle vie!!!" (I begin a new life!)

On Wednesday, December 24, 1941, he had noted in his diary that, even though a rain of bullets and bombs fell all about him, he was not harmed. "Je ne suis pas tuable!" (I am not killable!) But he was horribly hungry. He spent Christmas Eve attending "une messe de bombes" (a Mass of bombs) instead of the Midnight Mass he was accustomed to back home.

The next entry is for December 26: "Jour de NOËL! Four o'clock in the afternoon, we have capitulated!" They had no more ammunition; the exhausted soldiers could hardly stand up, but they were angry at having to lay down their arms. Many lives had been "sacrifiées" for nothing; his comrades "dead for nothing." He couldn't describe what he felt in his heart. His solace was to call his captors every name under the sun.

His *Journal d'un prisonnier de guerre au Japon, 1941–1945* was published in 1993. In a postscript, "Hommage à Georges Verreault," his son, Michel, wrote that his father lived his life with an exemplary courage, inhabiting a body that was all broken up. Not once had his father complained of the pain he had to endure to survive. He had transformed his lourd secret (heavy secret) into a great affection for his family and so many others.

"Georges Verreault mérite cet hommage." George Verreault deserves this tribute.

The deterioration of the relations between Canada's two principal groups really took hold with the plebiscite of January 1942, which asked Canadians and Canadiens to free the government from its promise not to impose conscription for service overseas. The campaign, lasting from January until the end of April, was ferociously fought in Québec, where, no surprise, the opposition was almost total. The reasons were obvious: a yes vote would mean that Mackenzie King's government would be free to impose conscription for service overseas; the impérialistes would see to that. Very few accepted the government's argument that the plebiscite was not for or against conscription—it was merely to permit the Canadian authorities to consider imposing conscription should it become necessary in the pursuit of the war effort.

"Non!" was the cry, "Cent fois non!"

To those who demanded a greater effort and sacrifice, Canadiens retorted that Canada was doing the best it could; it had taxed its resources to the limit; in fact, it had done more than most of Britain's allies. Enough was enough. And lurking behind the arguments was the perceived anti-French-Canadian feeling that animated so many English-speaking Canadians: "The goddamn frogs are at it again!" It wasn't the war effort that demanded overseas conscription; it was the urge, the desire, the determination to put Québec in its place. The refrains had all been heard before, but now they were sung more often.

There is little doubt that Québec's isolation would leave national unity in tatters. The circumstances, as was proven in 1945, didn't demand taking such a chance. In 1942, the anxiety was real: Canada was about "to forge the nails which will serve to seal the coffin . . . of Confederation." And conscription would awaken the ghost of separatism. "We are not separatists," it was rightly said, "but let us not be forced to become separatists. We wish indeed to dwell in the same house, but the house must be habitable for all." A promise was a promise. A pledge was a pledge.

The Québec organization in favour of the Non was the Ligue pour la défense du Canada. The newspaper *Le Devoir* was its official vehicle, and the radio station CKAC popularised the cause. Its principal leaders were Chanoine Groulx; Jean Drapeau, the future mayor of Montréal; Michel Chartrand, a labour leader; Maxime Raymond, a federal member of Parliament; and André Laurendeau, who was to co-chair the 1963 Royal Commission on Bilingualism and Biculturalism.

The Ligue did its work very well: on April 27, 1942, 72 percent of Québécois voted Non. In the other provinces, the Yes side won by a vote of 80 percent.

Less than a month later, on May 11, Mackenzie King, confident that the citizens had freed him from his pledge, and pushed by the Conservatives and many in his own caucus, introduced Bill 80. The bill allowed the government to introduce conscription for overseas service if necessary; but "it was not necessary at the present moment and perhaps never will be"—in other words, the famous "not necessarily conscription, but conscription if necessary."

Following the discord of the plebiscite and its aftermath, another disaster occurred—the Dieppe Raid of August 19, code-named "Jubilee." French Canadians participated in that battle, it was said, with courage and valour. Unfortunately, the English press in Canada, always eager to slander the Canadiens, attributed the failure of the raid to the French Canadians, who were bad soldiers and "zombies."

It was also in 1942 that a new nationalist party was born in Québec: the Bloc populaire, which was dedicated to the defence of provincial autonomy and of the rights of the French Canadians in Ottawa. Its motto: "Canada to the Canadians, Québec to the Québécois." By 1944, the Bloc had elected five members to the legislature. It also had a presence in Ottawa, where it favoured the United Nations but not NATO because "it is an armaments race." The Bloc didn't contest the provincial elections of 1948, and in the spring of 1949, it ceased to exist.

The year 1943 brought strikes, the fall of Benito Mussolini, the election of a Communist to the House of Commons, and the Québec Conference (Churchill, Roosevelt, and Mackenzie King). It was also the year of Paul Triquet of the Royal 22e Régiment.

"Paul Triquet was born at Cabano, in the Rimouski Country, Québec, on April 2, 1910," reported the *London Gazette* on March 6, 1944. "He attended Cabano Academy and later took six years of night school in Québec City. While at school, he was a member of the Cabano Cadet Corps which his father organised and trained, so he was keenly interested in military training from an early age. He enlisted as a private in the Royal 22é Régiment on November 3, 1927, and received rapid promotion. The action which won him the Victoria Cross has been described as a 'magnificent flash of greatness.'" He was also awarded a French decoration—Chevalier of the Legion of Honour—for the same action.

The Gazette quoted the citation at the award ceremony:

> For determined leadership and example.
>
> The capture of the key road junction on the main Ortona-Orsogna lateral was entirely dependent on securing the hamlet of Casa Berardi. Both this and a gully in front of it had been turned

by the Germans into a formidable strong point defended by infantry and tanks.

On December 14, 1943, Captain Triquet's company of the Royal 22e Régiment with the support of a squadron of a Canadian Armoured Regiment was given the task of crossing the gully and securing Casa Berardi. Difficulties were encountered from the outset. The gully was held in strength and on approaching it the force came under heavy fire from machine-guns and mortars. All the company officers and 50 percent of the men were killed or wounded. Showing superb contempt for the enemy, Captain Triquet went round reorganizing the remainder and encouraging them with the words, "never mind them, they can't shoot." Finally when enemy infiltration was observed on all sides shouting, "There are enemy in front of us, behind us and on our flanks, there is only one safe place—that is on the objective," he dashed forward and with his men following him broke through the enemy resistance. In this action four tanks were destroyed and several enemy machine-gun posts silenced.

Against bitter and determined defence and under heavy fire, Captain Triquet and his company, in close co-operation with the tanks, forced their way on until a position was reached on the outskirts of Casa Berardi. By this time the strength of the company was reduced to 2 sergeants and 15 men. In expectation of a counter-attack Captain Triquet at once set about organizing his handful of men into a defensive perimeter around the remaining tanks and passed the mot d'ordre, "ils ne passeront pas." A German counter-attack supported by tanks developed almost immediately. Captain Triquet, ignoring the heavy fire, was everywhere encouraging his men and directing the defence and by using whatever weapons were to hand personally accounted for several of the enemy. This and subsequent attacks were beaten off with heavy losses, and Captain Triquet and his small force held out against overwhelming odds until the remainder of the battalion took Casa Berardi and relieved them the next day.

On January 24, 1944, Lord Halifax, the British ambassador to the United States, made a speech in Toronto, advocating the creation after the war of a central imperial government in London for all the Commonwealth countries. The French-Canadian press was not amused.

The following events also happened in 1944: May 7: the military police shot a young French-Canadian deserter in Saint-Lambert de Lévis.

June 5: The Montreal *Gazette* reported a brawl between sailors and "zoot-suiters" that had taken place the previous Saturday in Verdun, in the bars, nightclubs, dancehalls, restaurants and on the streets of central Montréal, as well as in Parc Lafontaine. Zoot-suiters were thought to be French Canadians opposed to the war effort.

June 6: The Allies invaded France, which was liberated on August 25.

August 8: Maurice Duplessis was returned to power in Québec.

November 23: Mackenzie King's government issued an order-in-council, which sent 16,000 conscripted soldiers to the battlefields of Europe.

At that time, in Canadian training camps,there were 4,100 deserters: 450 Ontarians, 1,000 from the Prairies, 100 from the Maritimes, and 150 from the Pacific Command. In Québec, there were over 2,000 deserters.

On November 27, Charles Gavan "Chubby" Power, a veteran of the First World War, in which he was seriously wounded and was awarded the Military Cross for gallantry, resigned as minister of national defence for air. He was opposed to "conscription" for overseas service. Since Power was an English-speaking Liberal from Québec, he knew Québec and her people better than anyone else among his English-speaking compatriots. Parts of his speech are worth quoting:

> I do not believe such a policy to be necessary at this time, nor will it save one single Canadian casualty.
>
> . . . Conscription may be justified in moments of national crisis and in defence of one's country; and in the discussion of Bill 80 of 1942 I said so. It might have been justified at certain periods and phases of this war when we were on brink of almost certain defeat. It might have been justified if D-Day had

been a smashing catastrophe instead of a brilliant success. But these days are now past. We have no right to tear this country asunder at this stage, and in this state of the war.

. . . A word as to the consequences of this controversy. Millions of honest, decent people in all parts of Canada and of all shades of opinion are in the process of hating and reviling one another. Reason and sincere conviction have given way to hysteria on both sides. Cleavage between classes and between races has been driven deeper and deeper. The most tragic thing of all is the weakening faith and confidence in public men—not only by the people of one province, but in all provinces; not only amongst those who hold one view, but in men and women of all sides in this unfortunate debate.

As to the cleavages to which I refer, I cherish and hold fast to the ideas of the chieftain under whose aegis I entered this house, Sir Wilfrid Laurier. He could not and would not believe that as a Canadian he could belong to a party of one province only. With him, I cannot and will not subscribe to a purely isolationist provincial standpoint. . . .

My hope, my prayer is that there will be no such outcome, and that with the advent of external victory and peace, peace and understanding may come within our own country.

On November 29, 1944, a crowd of two thousand young men marched in the financial district of Montréal, breaking windows. A few days earlier, the Union Jack had been burned in Chicoutimi and in Rimouski. In Québec City, youths broke the windows of the *Chronicle-Telegraph* and at the home of the federal justice minister.

And the following events marked 1945:

January 3: The first conscripted men went to the Front.

February 24: A battle raged in Drummondville between the military police and a group of young people whose papers weren't in order.

May 8: The war ended in Europe.

June 11: Mackenzie King won the federal elections, but with a reduced majority.

August 6: An atomic bomb fell on Hiroshima.

August 9: An atomic bomb fell on Nagasaki.

August 14: The Japanese capitulated; the Second World War ended.

During the Second World War, nearly 42,000 Canadian men and women died; 53,000 were wounded or reported missing in action.

During the Second World War, 12,908 men were conscripted for overseas service after the order-in-council of November 23, 1944, which had authorised the conscription of 16,000. It was judged that since circumstances were changing in Europe, the full complement did not need to be sent.

What are we to say to all of this? Conscription for overseas service wasn't necessary. The Conservative Party, the party of the maudits Anglais and of the impérialistes, was prepared to put King's government on the defensive and tear the country apart for its own political advantage.

Then, there was Maurice Le Noblet Duplessis, Conservative, founder of the Union nationale and premier of Québec from 1936 to 1939 and from 1944 to his death in 1959.

Opinions about Duplessis vary; many are not complimentary. I was too young to be interested in politics in his first term, and I left Québec in 1948 and didn't return until the early days of the Révolution tranquille.

His niece said that he had one major flaw: in the presence of "intellectuals," he generally became sarcastic and cruel. She added that he was fond of revenge. On the other hand, she found him intelligent and a synthesizer of great skill.

Apparently, he could remember almost anything he wanted to, and he was loyal, generous, and kind. And he didn't care about money. Others speak of his charm and of his sincerity, which he displayed only in the security of his office.

However, Duplessis never left anyone indifferent: one either admired or detested him. Sure of himself and of his ability to work hard, he never doubted his capacity to deal with whatever came his way. Naturally, he was always right. He hated to travel and seldom took any holidays—watching baseball games, especially the playoffs, was his favourite entertainment.

He was opposed to the granting of the vote to women, because his mother didn't vote and never asked for it: a woman was, above all, a mother and the guardian of the home. These were her Catholic duties, in addition to bearing many children. She had no time to meddle in politics; therefore, she mustn't be given the opportunity to fail in the duties that biology, God, and the Church imposed upon her.

Duplessis' political allies and opponents considered him the best Québec politician of the century. At the beginning of his political career, though, he was more of a playboy. But, as he grew up, he came to rule Québec with an iron hand, buying anyone who would let him, including the clergy, whom he courted shamelessly. "Every project was blessed; the parish priests called him 'Dieu-le-Père'; I even saw a bishop kissing his hands," related one of his Liberal opponents. He could speak for hours without saying anything of any value.

His cheval de bataille, of course, was provincial autonomy, which he considered sacred and not negotiable. This is why he refused federal assistance to Québec universities and objected to family allowances, another federal program. However, outside of the Tremblay Commission (on constitutional problems) and the creation of a provincial income tax, he did little to bolster provincial autonomy.

Another horse he liked to whip was Communism, because therein lay sedition—and all those who opposed him or his policies could be Communists, on the verge of revolution. That is why he didn't trust intellectuals and journalists, professors, labour leaders, and women's-rights activists. With their non-traditional thinking, these people would endanger the Church, and place law and order in jeopardy. And his tactics were notorious: his way of handling patronage, of buying votes, and of turning over the natural resources of the province to foreigners. To protect the people, and at the invitation of the cardinal-archbishop of Québec, he prepared a law, passed in the legislature in 1937, called "La loi du cadenas." It prohibited the distribution of any materials in favour of Communism, and the attorney general, who was Duplessis, could affix a padlock—cadenas—on any

Communist establishment. He had the support of the Church and of the more traditional nationalists for this anti-democratic law.

However, he did create jobs.

Duplessis's Union nationale party was founded to contest the provincial elections of 1935. It was made up of the remnants of the provincial Conservative Party and of the membership of the Action libérale nationale, an organization of young and disenchanted Liberals who favoured social, economic, and political reforms. The Action abandoned Duplessis when they realized that he had outmanoeuvred them and that he had no intention of implementing their program.

The Union nationale existed mainly to realise Duplessis's agenda. As such, it favoured the traditional nationalism of Québec; it rejected separatism; it fought for a strict adherence to the British North America Act in matters of provincial powers; and it supported a workable accommodation with the trusts and foreign investors for the development of Québec's economy. Its support came from rural voters, small- and medium-size businesses, unorganized workers—and priests, bishops, and devoted Catholics. The English-speaking voters distrusted it, even though large English-speaking companies filled the Union's electoral coffers.

However, with such shaky foundations, the party hardly survived Duplessis's death. His successor, Joseph-Mignault-Paul Sauvé (1907–60), governed for only four months, dying suddenly in 1960. Yet, it was Sauvé, with his famous "Désormais" (henceforth), who ushered in an era of immense change in the political and social fabric of Québec. The Révolution tranquille of the 1960s arose out of that Désormais. The Union nationale lost the elections of 1960 to the Liberals, but it regained power in 1966 under Daniel Johnson. Unfortunately, he too died suddenly. Upon his death, Jean-Jacques Bertrand (1916–73) led the government and the party until the elections of 1970, when the Liberals, under Robert Bourassa, won. After that, the Union nationale was no longer a force in provincial politics.

Two issues illustrate Duplessis' understanding of his role in the society of which he was le chef: the Roncarelli affair of 1946 and the Asbestos Strike of 1949.

Frank Roncarelli was a Montréal restaurateur with a liquor licence. He was also a Jehovah's Witness. This sect became quite active in Québec in 1944. Without permits, they distributed their tracts up and down the streets of Montréal, attacking the Catholic Church, and proselytising, to the horror of the clergy and of Duplessis. When Witnesses were arrested, Roncarelli generally paid their bail. For obscure reasons, the police, many churchmen and politicians, and other "nice" people became convinced that Roncarelli was the leader of the sect and, therefore, responsible for all the tension between the Jehovah's Witnesses and the Catholics. Duplessis, who was attorney general and premier, saw Roncarelli as a public menace. In 1946, he ordered the chairman of the Liquor Commission to revoke Roncarelli's liquor licence, thus ruining his business. Roncarelli had never been charged with obstruction of justice, or of proselytising, or even of encouraging the distribution of pamphlets.

Duplessis admitted that he had given the order because he considered Roncarelli a traitor to, and a slanderer of, the province. It was his duty, Duplessis insisted, to annul the permit for good. Roncarelli sued for redress. The case went all the way to the Supreme Court, which, on January 27, 1959, declared that Duplessis had committed a public wrong and ordered him to pay damages personally.

What of Quebeckers in all of this? Most applauded Duplessis; they were quite hostile to the Jehovah's Witnesses.

Ten years before the Supreme Court's decision, Duplessis had been caught in another situation that demonstrated his lack of appreciation of human rights. On February 14, 1949, five thousand asbestos miners went on an illegal strike. (The most important asbestos mines in Québec were, and are, situated in the town of Asbestos, 63 kilometres north of Sherbrooke, and in Thetford Mines, 107 kilometres south of Québec City.) The miners were members of the Canadian Catholic Confederation of Labour (CCCL). For the next 120 working days in Asbestos (114 days in Thetford Mines), the strike paralysed the towns and challenged the authority of the Church, the State, and the English bosses. It also affected the entire labour movement, and it had a profound impact on Quebeckers. As well, it led to a prise de conscience, which, no doubt, forced Québec's episcopacy to reconsider the foundations of French-Canadian nationalism.

Jean-Charles Falardeau, a sociologist at Université Laval, noted that the strike was one of the rites of passage "by which the French-Canadian trade-union movement has gradually reached adulthood." That adulthood consisted in being recognised, in being heard. But, to achieve that adulthood, the labour-union movement had to demonstrate that it had power and that it could use it.

Before that strike, Falardeau reminds us, "Every labour dispute of any importance involving the Catholic trade unions was originally defined and ultimately settled (officially and unofficially) by the trinity of management, government, and Church." In Asbestos and Thetford Mines, the miners broke this pattern: they decided to speak for themselves through their labour union. In that decision, the entire labour movement of Québec and of Canada closed ranks. "The CCCL emptied its treasury and asked its members for supplementary dues. Cheques and truckloads of foodstuffs began to arrive [in the region of the strike] from unions affiliated with the Trades and Labour Congress or with the Canadian Congress of Labour."

Pierre Elliott Trudeau was an active defender of the strikers. In *Québec at the Time of the Strike*, he wrote:

> In 1949, the memorable asbestos strike occurred because the industrial workers of Quebec were suffocating in a society burdened with inadequate ideologies and oppressive institutions; because the national importance of the working class was out of all proportion to its low prestige; because its economic gains as a class were accompanied by a loss of social status . . . because our moral and political philosophy of labour did not take enough notice of the fact that we had become an industrialized people.

What did the workers want? They wanted a salary increase of fifteen cents an hour, some form of social security, obligatory deduction of union dues, and the elimination of the asbestos dust. The Johns Manville Company offered five cents an hour and nothing else. Because the miners didn't go to arbitration, their strike was illegal. The company engaged "scabs," who were protected by the provincial police whose members were paid an additional fifty dollars a week by the company. Clashes ensued, many strikers were wounded, as were policemen and strike breakers. A few were arrested.

The Church was not indifferent to the plight of the workers. Many bishops warned Duplessis that they weren't about to sacrifice Catholic workers on the altar of capitalism. To the bishops, the strike was illegal but "juste." They ordered collections in all the churches to assist the miners ($170,000 was collected). The archbishop of Québec helped negotiate the settlement and he forced both the government and the company to face their responsibilities. Other bishops intervened with sincerity and clarity. The archbishop of Montréal, Joseph Charbonneau, was fired by the Vatican because of his part in the conflict. He was critical of the government, particularly Duplessis. Many conservative clerics, along with Duplessis and his cabinet, felt that Charbonneau had crossed the line into the political arena. When the strike was over, the papal representative in Canada summoned Charbonneau to Ottawa and asked him, for the good of the Church, to resign. As an obedient servant of the Church, he accepted his fate and exiled himself to Victoria, British Columbia, where he died.

What of Duplessis? He was a man of law and order, trained to obey lawful authority. There was a law in place: it had to be obeyed. Those who didn't obey had to be punished. It was as simple as that. The miners flouted the law, so, he argued, he had no other choice but to do all in his power to break the strike. Had Duplessis acted wisely and contented himself with upholding the law, violence might have been avoided, and less hardship suffered. Using that domineering way that was his trademark, le chef would be obeyed. He and his ministers criticized every union position and upheld the company at every opportunity; he berated the labour leaders; and, above all, he allowed "his" police to act brutally and without restraint. It was no wonder that the strikers looked upon the arbitration process as partial, unsympathetic to their plight and goals.

Terrible hardships resulted in Asbestos, a small town of 8,000 people who were directly affected by the strike—the mine was the only place where work could be found. As the magazine *Cité Libre*, which Trudeau, Gérard Pelletier, and a few others founded in 1950, remarked: "It was something which took possession of the city, brought people together, and entered into the minds of all . . ." As the strike continued, it became painful to bear: "Men no longer ate more than one meal a day. Rents went unpaid; the tradesmen, laden with a heavy burden of credit, were close to bankruptcy. Scabs, recruited in the surrounding towns, arrived in the morning and left again in the evening, under Provincial Police escort." So discouraged did the strikers become that towards the end of April, they "gave up all their demands, and insisted only on a single guarantee: that when the return to work occurred, nobody would suffer reprisals." That simple request was refused.

In May 1951, a man by the name of René Rocque, who was the CCCL's assistant director of organisation, found himself in prison. He had been found guilty of "conspiring, between May 1 and 6, 1949, to prevent certain people from doing what they had the right to do by the use of violence or the threat of violence." What he had done was to try to stop the scabs along the road coming into Asbestos and talk to them.

Trudeau ends his book about the asbestos strike with the following words:

> At the present conjuncture of events in Quebec, however, we're clearly aware of the fact that the only powerful medium of renewal is industrialization; we are also aware that this medium will not provide us with liberty and justice unless it is subject to the forces of an enlightened and powerful trade union movement. Who will reproach us because we still believe, with the labour movement as a whole, in the promise: Blessed are those who hunger and thirst for righteousness, for they shall be satisfied.

Something quite spectacular happened in Québec in 1950. In a letter to the Catholics of the province, the bishops called on French Canadians to adopt a new vocation: an urban one that would go hand in hand with the rural and agricultural one the faithful already had. That urban vocation was meant to

323

develop an economic and social regime based on the dignity of the worker. The bishops admitted that city life was less "protective of human values"; nevertheless, it wasn't the destroyer of souls. City life and industrial work "are not outside God's plan and do not lead fatally to materialism and the loss of Christian values."

What the bishops said, in effect, was that living in a city and working in a plant were accepted forms of human activity and that French-Canadian nationalism should see itself in that light as well. That was revolutionary—at least for the bishops. The people already knew that they could as easily go to heaven from a city as from a village.

Maurice Le Noblet Duplessis died of a massive stroke on September 7, 1959, at Schefferville in northern Québec.

During his terms as premier, private and public investment in Québec—some from Canada, but most from elsewhere—increased to twenty billion dollars. The standard of living also went up: in 1945 the total revenue of individuals was two billion dollars; in 1960, six billion. Duplessis built 4,000 schools; increased the number of beds available in the hospitals by about 30,000; gave Québécois their first autoroute and thousands of kilometres of secondary roads, over which 2,400 new bridges were constructed; developed electric power by constructing twenty-five new hydro facilities; and electrified 96 percent of the farms of Québec.

With his death, another era in the history of Canadiens—and of Canada—had come to an end.

VII

Vive le Québec libre
1960–1980

*O*n October 5, 1970, Pierre Elliott Trudeau is the Liberal prime minister of Canada; Robert Bourassa is the Liberal premier ministre de la province de Québec; René Lévesque, of the Parti québécois, is the leader of Her Majesty's Loyal Opposition in the Assemblée nationale; and Jean Drapeau is the mayor of Montréal.

On October 5, 1970, two armed men enter the residence of the senior British trade commissioner, on Redpath Crescent in Westmount, a wealthy anglophone area in the centre of Montréal. A few minutes later, they emerge with the commissioner, James Cross, between them. They take him away in a taxi.

On October 5, 1970, the nightmare that was to last until the end of that year begins.

On October 5, 1970, it is said that Canadians and Canadiens lost their innocence!

❦

I'm back at that place that is not here and at a time that is not now, on the Internet site known as <u>explor'.ca</u>. Mascou takes me to the chat room reserved for the stories of Canada between the end of the Second World War and the day before today. He tells me the rules of engagement: "All participants are incognito, nothing can be attributed to anyone, and you can do what you want with what you hear." I log in, and Mascou, who seems to be in charge of the room, assigns me the colour silver. There is only one other participant present, colour green. "Where are the others?" I ask Mascou.

"I have assigned them to other rooms. You only need to speak with this person."

"Bonjour," the green colour says, "Mascou indicated to me that you wish to discuss the Révolution tranquille. How is that Révolution important to you?"

"It's part of my life."

"Why?"

❦

Why indeed! The difficulty is knowing where to begin. I'm a child of the Depression. I felt the pain of the poverty and vulnerability of my parents. But what has that to do with the Révolution? In the 1960s, there was perhaps some residual anger—it seemed that no one could do anything to make our lives easier. As I look back now, I ask myself, Was the Quiet Revolution important to me because I was a witness to our impotence?

Or was it the Second World War that opened me to the world? Even though I was only fifteen when it ended, I was hearing about societies quite different from mine and that men and women in my milieu were discovering in the 1950s through television. One of those people, who returned safe and sound, initiated me into a world of knowledge and personal possibilities that left me troubled and, at the same time, excited. Did that have anything to do with the Révolution?

Vive le Québec libre (1960-1980)

I became a man during the regime of Duplessis. I certainly rejected what he stood for. Did the Révolution tranquille orchestrated by Jean Lesage, René Lévesque, Eric Kierans, and so many others coincide with my own?

⚜

I type in silver on the screen: "All I know is that to me and to everyone I knew in Québec, the Révolution was imperative."

"Do you mean to say that circumstances had made it so? Or that you were ready for it?"

"Both." For several minutes I type words and sentences and paragraphs furiously. Whoever is green erases much of what I write. When I look at what remains, I find the following: "Between 1945 and 1960, the vast majority of us, who were now living in urban centres, had means of communication we'd never had before. Sitting in our living rooms, a magical screen projected pictures from all over the world; we saw and learned things we had never been told about; we experienced theatre and music that left us spellbound; we travelled faster and farther; and we wondered where the hell we had been. In darkness. We had to have light. And the light would only come if, with courage and no parti-pris, we entered the frightening, but challenging, world of modernity. We had to change. We needed democratic instruments that we ourselves chose—instead of having them imposed in the name of la race, la langue, et la foi by a power-crazy élite of clerics and bishops and a parasitical bourgeoisie. They had been entrenched in a regime they had created for their own good; they were determined to preserve it. We needed the economic tools to lessen our dependence on les Anglais. We needed social tools that would free us from the clerical agenda that had entombed us. We didn't want their charity any more. We wanted to live off our own resources, our own talent, and that openness that had made coureurs de bois of the vast majority of our ancestors. No more hand-me-downs; we wanted to acquire what we needed—ourselves. We were convinced of that. Our governments were corrupt and abusive of our rights; our economy was dependent on the superiority of others; our natural resources had been sold to foreigners for a song and without our consent; we had the highest rate of illiteracy in the western world; we controlled nothing except our incapacity to act; we had allowed ourselves to be polluted in order to have jobs; and, to end this litany, our social instruments, like education and social services, were in the hands of men and women who had little interest in change—it would destroy their power. We were a downtrodden people with a limited future."

"How did this Révolution begin?"

"After the death of Duplessis, the new premier uttered the word 'Désormais,' a marvellous word. What it meant exactly, we had no idea. It was the promise of a new beginning, but Sauvé died too soon to realise his dream. However, when the Liberals arrived in 1960 under the leadership of Jean Lesage, we hoped the dream and the promise would become one."

"Did it happen?"

"In time. And up to a point. Rome wasn't built in a day."

"Did you know this Jean Lesage?"

"I met him once and interviewed him once. Before you ask, I wasn't impressed. To be fair, we wanted him to do so much. All he was interested in was good government—to curb patronage, do things for people, and put some order in federal-provincial relations by abandoning Duplessis' sterile attitude." I wait for a sign of interest from my green interlocutor. When none comes, I go on: "He was a conservative at heart. If the word 'revolution' was in his vocabulary, it had to be a quiet one." I emphasise the word "quiet." "On the other hand and to be fair to him, I don't think he fully grasped what was demanded of him. Later, when the Révolution took hold, with repercussions nobody had foreseen, I suspect he asked himself, What have I unleashed?"

"You were disappointed?"

"At first, I think many were disappointed. Lesage was a bright man; he was handsome; he had a beautiful voice and he was full of energy. But he was also pompous, his self-confidence often sounded like arrogance. However, I don't think it was in his nature to seize the day. That was disappointing." I laugh—and I type the sign for that.

"What's the joke?"

"We had a premier in Newfoundland, Joey Smallwood. He once said, either to me or in public, 'I've met De Gaulle and Jean Lesage; if truth be known, De Gaulle is a very humble man.'"

There is no laugher at the other end. "The first time I met Lesage," I write, "was during a party convention, in Montréal. A committee I was on had decided to recommend that the Legislative Council, that remnant of colonialism, be abolished. More important, we wanted, desperately, a ministère de l'éducation. That, in our view, had to be the beginning of the renewal of a people. We were summoned to Lesage's suite and lined up as if waiting for the Queen. He came in, walked up the line, and shook our hands. Then someone in our group told him of our two resolutions. His reply paraphrased a Churchill quote: 'I will not become the prime minister of Québec to dismantle the system of education we now have.' Then he looked at us and said, 'Thank you, gentlemen.' As we were being ushered out, I turned to him and said, 'Vous n'aurez pas le choix.' His handlers looked at me as if I had gone mad. He just smiled and said: 'Merci bien.'"

"Did he have a choice?"

"Non. A year or so after coming to power, he named a Royal Commission on Education. Its report was favourable, and the ministry was created in 1964. It wasn't easy for him. The bishops were up in arms. But having made up his mind, he cajoled and charmed his way through, and he made many compromises."

"Like what?" the colour green asks.

"Well, the private collèges classiques, run by the Church,

remained intact." I bang my fingers on the keys to make a point:
"These bloody privileged private schools have always blocked
access to university for the majority of Québec students. The
bastards! I'm telling you, whoever you are, that if they don't
become part of the system, the important reforms made by the
Lesage government will have no lasting influence.

"In time, they became part of the system, did they not?" When
I don't reply, the following appears on the screen: "Sir, remember that the ministère de l'éducation was created and that the
minister of education kept intact his co-ordinating powers.
Surely you had what you wanted." When I don't respond to that,
the message continues: "Were there not other educational
reforms at the time, like a comprehensive public secondary system? You never had that before—and free education at all levels, compulsory education extended from fourteen to sixteen
years of age, and free textbooks. Surely, that was a good beginning." There's another pause and then I read: "Your Monsieur
Lesage did not tackle the problem of confessionality. Did you
expect him to?"

I'm not surprised that my green friend knows so much. After
all, Mascou wouldn't send me someone who wasn't knowledgeable.
I answer the question: "I knew that everything couldn't happen
that fast."

"But we were on our way."

"Yes." I find the words "we" and "our" interesting. "Who are
you?" I ask.

"You know the rules." We both wait. Then: "You said you
interviewed Lesage. When was that?"

"In 1963. It coincided with the assassination of President
Kennedy. It was a sad day." I stop typing, remembering. We had
just interviewed Lesage, and the crew and I were sitting in
the bar at the Château Frontenac in Québec City when the
television showed the news from Dallas. People kept talking
and laughing, then someone yelled for quiet. There it was on

our screen, the replay of a dreadful moment. There wasn't much conversation after that.

My Web friend waits in silence. Finally, I type that by the time of the interview, my attitude had changed towards Lesage. I had come to respect him and appreciate what he had done and was doing. I give my friend a list of the reforms: "Under Lesage, we began the reconquête of our economy. To that end, the government created the Société générale de financement, the Québec Council of Economic Reorientation, the Industrial Research Council, and the Société de développement industriel, not to mention the Régime épargne-action and the Caisse de dépot et placement to marshal the immense sums delivered by the Québec Pension Plan. The private electric power utilities were nationalised as Hydro-Québec, and the immense hydro-electric development on the Manicouagan River was begun. That dam became the symbol of our technological coming of age. In addition there was a steel complex, largely owned and operated by Québec. We gave ourselves free medicare and secularised private social institutions such as hospitals. We tried to enrich our culture, not by practising 'state interventionism,' but rather by co-ordinating the activities of organisations working for the expansion of Québec's culture."

Before I can continue with my list, green text reappears with "This cultural reform was aimed, was it not, at creating a climate to facilitate the blossoming of the arts?"

"These were the very words Monsieur Lesage used in the Assembly." Again I need to ask: "Who are you?"

The reply is the same as before: "You know the rules." A few moments later: "Tell me more."

"Non." I type. "You tell me more."

"Let's see. Reforms were made to the municipal system; the opting-out formula was encouraged; and thus was Confederation reformed and a balance returned to the division of powers between the federal and the provincial governments . . . "

"It was the decentralisation of powers."

Nothing happens for a while, then: "The reform of our constitutional system had to go via decentralisation." Another
moment, then, "I almost forgot. We took our first steps on the
international scene. Imagine that. It felt good!" The screen
goes blank again, then the green comes back: "Before I go,
this Révolution was no catching-up, as so many said at that
time. What the people of Québec did with the government's
assistance and encouragement and the brain power of so many
capable ministers was to make a collective effort to reassess
their individual and collective values, their institutions,
their national creed, their way of life, and their relationship with other Canadians, the world and their God. French
and English—all the people of the Province of Québec—did
that. It was a marvellous effort."

I feel whoever the green colour belongs to is in the same room
with me. I know him, I tell myself. However, I won't ask again
who the person behind the colour is. Before I can start the conversation again, I read: "Au revoir, Monsieur LaPierre. I liked
the interview you did."

I liked all the words he wrote. Did the green colour belong
to . . .

I leave it at that.

⚜

So, in the 1960s, Québec and its governments gave themselves goals: "A
radical reconstruction of education; the improvement of living standards;
the creation of a viable economy in which public and private ownership
could flourish; a sharp break with the patronage-plagued political morality
of the past; the development of a French-speaking managerial class that
could take its place in the business community of Canada and of the world; a
complete reappraisal of the relations between Church and State; the elabo-
ration of a coherent social welfare program; increased assistance to those
Canadiens living beyond the borders of Québec; the emergence of a new
type of French-speaking politician in Ottawa in whom rested most of the

responsibility for creating a truly bilingual and multicultural Canada; the nourishing of French culture by closer association with the French-speaking community of the world; and, ultimately, the realisation of the dream that Canadiens could really be equal partners in Confederation.

Jean Lesage fought three elections: in 1960, which he won; in 1962, which was a sort of referendum on the nationalisation of electricity under the slogan "Maîtres chez nous," which he won handsomely; and in 1966, which he lost to a revitalised Union nationale under Daniel Johnson. After that, he remained leader of the Liberal Party until his resignation in 1970. He had served in that capacity for about twelve years.

He knew he had moved too quickly and that he had failed to explain adequately the reforms undertaken, hence the 1966 backlash. But he had stayed the course. He knew perhaps better than anyone else that, as Dale Thomson writes in his biography of Lesage, "For French Canadians, life in North America was a constant challenge that could only be met through a high level of initiative and competence." That was all.

How successful was Lesage's Révolution? That's a difficult question. Its immediate effects were tangible, useful, and worth building on. The long-term effects, on the other hand, are more complicated to assess. The state apparatus that the Révolution created became, as René Lévesque described it, "a monster," practically out of control, while Jacques Parizeau saw it as a jungle of red tape that paralysed Québec. The young became disenchanted with it, and they began to seek a solution to their problems and ambitions elsewhere, particularly in a Québec nationalism that included independence, sovereignty, and separatism. The last word, however, should be left to Professor Thomson:

> Perhaps the most far-reaching change brought about by the Quiet Revolution concerned French-Canadian values. With the disintegration of traditional structures and the freer exchange of ideas, the former relative homogeneity of French-Canadian society gave way to increasing diversity. The final years of the Lesage government were marked by increasing social conflict; succeeding governments faced even greater challenges to their

333

authority. The Parti Québécois sought to rally the population around an updated version of the collectivist ideal, but in vain; its sovereignty-association option never rallied a majority of the population. Rejecting claims that the Parti Québécois government was carrying on the Quiet Revolution, two CEGEP professors argued that, on the contrary, the Quiet Revolution had set Quebec on the path towards a society based on the primacy of the individual, not of the collectivity. Québecers, they maintained, had passed from "a society that we could describe as organic and in which the general will is considered the national will to a liberal society in which the general will is considered to be the result of agreement among individuals."

However, Québec society couldn't be transformed from the top down without giving rise to antagonism and to the tearing apart of nationalism.

In late 1962, the USSR, which had been awarded the right to hold an International Exhibition, informed the bureau in charge that it had to cancel its plans. Immediately, the Canadian government renewed its proposal to hold such an exhibition in Montréal, to coincide with the hundredth anniversary of Confederation. The bureau agreed—it even elevated Montréal's exhibition to "first-category status." Such an exhibition had never been held in North America. It meant that Expo 67, as it came to be called, would have to cover the whole range of human endeavours.

Late in 1962, the various levels of government passed enabling legislation, which stipulated that the federal government would pay 50 percent of the cost, Québec 37.5 percent, and the City of Montréal 12.5 percent. A conference of educators, poets, professors, and artists created the theme: La Terre des Hommes—Man and His World—a theme based on a book by French poet and aviator Antoine de Saint-Exupéry. Work then began on a master plan, which was completed in late 1963.

The most taxing problem was where to put this exhibition. After much discussion—and with the clock ticking—planners agreed that it would be on an island in the St. Lawrence River. Île Sainte-Hélène, a beautiful park in the middle of the river, linked to Montréal by the Jacques-Cartier Bridge, would be the focus, and land reclamation would considerably expand the island. A new island was also created, Île Notre-Dame. When dredging couldn't reclaim enough land, the earth from the tunnels dug for the Métro was used. All of this was done in the space of a year. Eventually, the area was divided into four main parts: the entrance was at Mackay Pier, a part of the Port of Montréal, and it became known as the Cité du Havre; the second part was on the western section of the enlarged Île Sainte-Hélène, connected to the city by a new bridge across the St. Lawrence, Concordia; the third area was Île Notre-Dame; and the fourth, called La Ronde—a superb amusement park—was situated at the eastern end of Île Sainte-Hélène.

The Queen duly opened Expo 67, and Canadians and Canadiens came by the thousands to discover themselves and the world. Hundreds of countries and states and institutions participated as well, learning about us, a confident northern people. We were proud. We had arrived.

Few incidents disrupted the joy of the moment—except for the visit of the president of France, Charles André Joseph Marie de Gaulle, known simply as Général De Gaulle.

He arrived in Québec City on July 23, 1967, on France's largest warship, the *Colbert*. When he was met at the Anse-au-Foulon (where James Wolfe had landed his army to conquer Québec in 1759), the governor general, Roland Michener, was royally booed by a mob of separatists who didn't relish the few bars of "God Save the Queen." De Gaulle, then, took the premier, Daniel Johnson, with him in the presidential car. Along the route to Québec City Hall, one could easily count the Canadian flags. On the other hand, the French and Québec flags were countless. When De Gaulle spoke to the crowd, he said: "Vive le Québec, vive le Canada-français, vive la Nouvelle-France, vive la France." Then, Canadiens, some fifty thousand of them, sang "La Marseillaise" proudly and in unison—to the great delight of the correspondent of *Le Monde*.

To De Gaulle, we, the six million Canadiens, were still French men and French women. (He arrogantly ignored the fact that the cowardice of the French army forced our abandonment: we were considered so unworthy by his predecessors that they exchanged our land for some insignificant islands.)

He called us, "les Français d'ici"—and, like the colonials we were supposed to be, we lapped it up.

On the next day De Gaulle began his pilgrimage from Québec to Montréal, a voyage of some 290 kilometres along the north shore of the St. Lawrence. In his honour, the highway was rechristened "Le Chemin du Roy." To De Gaulle and many others, it became "Le Chemin de la liberté." Everywhere his motorcade passed, delirious crowds greeted him triumphantly. From Pointe-aux-Trembles, his point of entry into the territory of Montréal, to the city hall on Notre-Dame Street, close to half a million people welcomed him.

Towards the end of the day, he finally got to his destination, where over 15,000 people were packed in front of the building and in the adjoining Champ-de-Mars. We are told that for the liberator of France, it was the happiest day of his life since his march up the Champs-Élysées after the liberation of Paris in 1944.

With difficulty he managed to leave his car and to climb the many stairs leading to the entrance of the building. People were calling his name, and often he turned to acknowledge them. As he was about to enter the building, a band played the national anthem of Canada. The crowd, preferring "La Marseillaise," didn't welcome Calixa Lavallée's hymn in honour of our country, and their cries of protest drowned out "O Canada." No sooner had de Gaulle entered the great hall than the cry "On veut De Gaulle" came from thousands of throats.

A few minutes after his entrance, De Gaulle appeared on the balcony of the City Hall. The people below him chanted over and over again, and more loudly each time: "Un discours! Un discours." They wanted a speech. Mayor Jean Drapeau didn't think it possible—or perhaps wise—for De Gaulle to speak. But Drapeau was overruled, and a microphone was quickly found and hooked up. The general came forward and the crowd became eerily silent. He opened his mouth and in his sonorous voice he declared: "C'est une immense émotion qui remplit mon coeur en voyant devant moi la ville de Montréal française. Au nom du vieux pays, au nom de la France, je vous salue de tout cœur."

Silence. Then: "Ce soir, ici, et tout le long de ma route, je me suis trouvé dans une atmosphère du même genre que celle de la Libération."

All hell broke loose. In an instant, Québec became a liberated country! De Gaulle added a few sentences and then ended with the usual: "Vive Montréal! Vive le Québec!" And he stopped. He looked around at the people below him, where he saw hundreds of placards proclaiming "France libre, Québec libre," "Le Québec aux Québécois," "Notre État français, nous l'aurons." The crowd became silent again. The general pulled himself up to an even greater height and he yelled out: "Vive le Québec libre!" accentuating the word "libre."

Drapeau was stupefied. The crowd was silent for a moment, then cries of joy erupted. Hardly anyone heard the "Vive le Canada français! Et vive la France!"

What did it mean, this "Vive le Québec libre"? To the English-speaking press and to the indépendantistes, there could only be one meaning: "Vive l'indépendance du Québec!" As for the Québec journalists, they weren't that dramatic. It would be foolish, they wrote, to see De Gaulle's words as an endorsement of separatism.

The federal government was astounded. Québec was not the France of Nazi occupation. It didn't need to be liberated. And, furthermore, De Gaulle was interfering in the affairs of a sovereign country. On July 25, the day that had been set aside to celebrate the presence of France at Expo, De Gaulle went through his routine, but there was no "libre" rhetoric. On that day as well, Canada's prime minister, Lester B. Pearson, declared his disapproval and censure publicly. Faced with that, De Gaulle refused to visit Ottawa, and left for Paris.

Here are a few newspaper headlines of July 25, 1967:

The Gazette: De Gaulle Tells Quebec "Become Your Master."

The Montreal Star: Protocol Takes a Tumble—De Gaulle Speech Stirs Storm; French Leader Openly Backs Separatism.

La Presse: De Gaulle déclenche de vives réactions en s'écriant: "Vive Le Québec Libre!" Ottawa est consterné—Réunion extraordinaire du cabinet fédéral demain.

Le Soleil: De Gaulle: "Vive Le Québec Libre," cependant, à l'Expo, il déclare : "Vive le Canada, vive le Québec."

Young people marched in the streets, chanting, "Québec libre, oui, oui, oui! Québec libre, de Gaulle l'a dit." They went at it all night.

René Lévesque was nearby, "among the guests, waiting patiently on a large terrace." When De Gaulle began to speak, "in one instinctive movement we drew closer to the [TV] screen, crouched low so as not to block other people's view." Then he goes on to say in his *Memoirs*:

> It was in this posture that his "Vive le Québec [pause] libre!" held us paralysed a few instants. Then, hearing the deathly silence that reigned behind us, we turned around to face the rest of the guests. It is rare to have such an opportunity to see the two Montreals so clearly. In a state of shock, frozen in a fury that as yet was only emitting a few anticipatory rumblings, stood the Anglophone city. As for French Montreal, except for those constrained by office or acquaintance to reserve, they did not hide broad, complicit smiles, or even, in the background, gestures more discreet but just as enthusiastic as those of the crowd in the street.

Later on, he adds, when thinking about "De Gaulle l'a dit," that "it did not seem to me at all advisable to have recourse to some external authority, no matter how prestigious." He was therefore ready "to bide our time and let the dust settle." And he added in the same paragraph:

> In this country dominated by an Anglophone majority, the emancipation of our minority people would have to be the result of a purely indigenous movement, or nothing. In the same way that a conceded liberty is often illusory, a liberation that has to count on others to help it get started stands every chance of never getting off the ground. Consequently, we must neither take nor seem to take our inspiration from sources outside the country. When the day comes, it would be up to Québécois alone to decide, to seize their fate with a firm hand, and on that basis go forward, already free.

It took him a year, he tells us "to become definitely convinced that the future lay in that direction and, in attempting to move from dream to reality, to succeed finally in drawing a coherent project to follow."

The time has come, therefore, to speak of the coming of the Parti Québécois and of the living with it.

The story of the Parti Québécois is the story of René Lévesque.

René Lévesque (1922–87) was a journalist of great ability, a war correspondent, a television host of the famous program *Point de mire*. He was probably the most influential television commentator Québec ever had. He was also an articulate, energetic, and popular minister in the Lesage governments, the founder of the Parti Québécois, and the premier of Québec from 1976 to 1985.

Lévesque's day came on September 18, 1967, when he declared at a meeting of his constituency:

> . . . There are key moments in the existence of a nation when boldness and quiet courage become the only form of prudence that can be applied.
>
> If the nation does not then accept the calculated risk of major steps it can lose its destiny forever, exactly like a man who is afraid of life.
>
> Nevertheless, on the road to guaranteed survival and permanent progress on which no nation can be allowed to stop, we have been moving for some time towards a crucial crossroads. It is up to us to choose the political status which suits us best; that is to say, the road which permits us the most sure and efficient way to accomplish the necessary steps.

Those necessary steps were to him, the abandonment of the constitutional status quo, "the full control of each and every one of [Québec's] principle collective decisions," Québec becoming a sovereign state, and the maintaining of "an association" with our neighbours and partners in "English Canada." In conclusion, he added:

Such an association seems to us tailored to permit us, without the encumbrance of constitutional rigidities, to make common cause with permanent consultations, flexible adjustments and appropriate mechanisms which our common economic interest requires: monetary union, a common tariff and co-ordination of fiscal policies. Nothing would prevent us—to the degree that we learn to understand each other better and to co-operate better in the context—from freely adding other areas where the same common action would seem mutually advantageous.

In short, we would have a regime within which two nations, one whose homeland would be Quebec, the other arranging the rest of the country to suit itself, would associate themselves in a new adaptation of the current formula of the common markets to form a new entity which could, for example, call itself the "Canadian Union."

Thus was la nation québécoise born.

Lévesque repeated his solution to Québec's future in a book, *An Option for Quebec*, published in 1968. First he established who "we," the French-speaking people of Québec, were: "We are *Québécois*," and that meant "first and foremost—and if need be all that it means—is that we are attached to this one corner of the earth where we can be completely ourselves: this Quebec, the only place we have the unmistakable feeling that 'here we can really be at home.'" The way to maintain that and, at the same time, the way to the future was "a sovereign Quebec." There was no way out of that because: "for our own good, we must dare to seize for ourselves complete liberty in Quebec, the right to all essential components of independence, i.e., the complete mastery of every last area of basic collective decision-making." That meant that "Quebec must become sovereign as soon as possible." Added to this sovereignty, but not limiting it, would be a New Canadian Union in which Québec would be an associate and a partner of Canada in a common enterprise.

As for Jean Lesage's Liberal Party, it too had a "national, constitutional imperative." In a paper designed to counteract the souveraineté-association thesis, it held the following to be self-evident:

It [the Liberal Party of Québec] believes nevertheless that a new Canadian constitution, including special status and increased powers for Quebec through a new division between the federal Parliament and that of Quebec, can best serve the political, economic, cultural, and social interests of the French Canadians;

It thus rejects separatism in all its forms, for it would run counter to the higher interests of Quebec and the French-Canadian nation, would be achieved at the expense of the young, the workers, and the farmers, and could do injury to the policy of "Maîtres chez nous" [the policy that Jean Lesage had devised];

It earnestly calls for a new Canadian constitution based on formal recognition of the presence of two nations in Canada and on the clearly demonstrated will to make French Canadians full members of a new Canadian confederation;

The new constitution of Canada should, among other things, make provision for the establishment of a true constitutional court and for a declaration of the collective rights of minorities and majorities in Canada.

Unable to get the Liberal Party to accept his constitutional position, Lévesque resigned in November 1967. After discussions with séparatistes or indépendantistes groups in Québec, he formed with them the Mouvement souveraineté-association in the same month. A year later, the Mouvement ceased to exist and the Parti Québécois was born. The next two years were spent organising the party and publicising its program. Time was also set aside to harangue les Anglais.

In 1969, Lévesque attacked what he called "a wealthy, influential" English-speaking Montréal minority "who don't want to let go of their privileges and prerogatives." As the *Canadian Annual Review* of 1969 (University of Toronto Press) indicated, he accused them—and those not so wealthy and influential—of "raising spectres, spreading delusions, and engaging in 'mental terrorism' by systematically labelling as 'separatist' everything under the heading of violence, activism, terrorism, etc."

When asked what would happen to those "others" who weren't of his language group, Lévesque generally replied, "Nothing!" However, he would add after a long, pregnant pause, "But I will insist that they speak French."

By this time, a precarious situation had developed among the peoples of Québec, those whose mother tongue was French and those others, les autres. "Are we part of this new nation, this nation québécoise?" many of les Anglais asked themselves, while a few courageous souls publicly demanded to know. The tendency was to let them stew.

It doesn't appear that those "others" in Québec were much in touch with the so-called Québécois fact that had developed since the Second World War. This is understandable, as it hardly penetrated their lives. The language of commerce, business, and work was largely English and English-speaking Quebeckers had extensive educational and social institutions that operated most of the time in English. Also, many took pride in not speaking French, while the Canadiens (or the Québécois, as we were being called more and more) had to be bilingual to assume even marginal positions in the economic hierarchy. By the time René Lévesque developed his option for sovereignty, discontent among "the French"—the preferred expression of les Anglais to describe us—had grown. They demanded that French be the dominant language in a society that wanted desperately to be master of its own house.

McGill University had become the symbol of the malaise. Situated at the centre of a large cosmopolitan city, full of diversity, and surrounded by all of us who were Francophones (the "French"), McGill was the bastion and the guardian of "English" power and presence in Québec. Yet it remained almost totally unaware of the fact that Montréal was in Québec. When the Québécois revolution arrived at its doors, the university had "to be carried kicking and screaming into the new world."

On the other hand, times weren't easy for McGill and the English-speaking population of Québec, which included most of the immigrants of other language groups. What was happening can be simply stated: the uncomfortable feeling of being a minority grew. It hurt. Yet a large number of those "others," particularly at McGill, attempted to understand that if you lived *in* Québec, you had to be *of* Québec. But this message fell on deaf ears.

Moreover, the excessive emphasis on exclusivity that the new Québec élite preached and its paranoia were certainly not conducive to harmony. Many English-speaking Quebeckers, who had lived in Québec for decades, and even centuries, became fearful and anxious. They cut their ties and left.

It took three elections to bring the Parti Québécois to power. In the provincial elections of 1970, the PQ won 23.2 percent of the vote, with Lévesque being defeated in the riding of Laurier on the island of Montréal. The Liberals elected 72 members, the Parti Québécois, 7; the Union nationale, 17; and the Ralliement créditiste, 12. After a close analysis of the results, constituency by constituency, the *Canadian Annual Review* of the year concluded:

> Never before in modern Quebec's history had the line between many French Canadians and the non-French Canadians been so firmly and clearly drawn, unless it was the provincial election of 1939. The conflicts over separatism, and perhaps equally over language and educational policy, had born fruit. The issue was personalised and results more bitter on election night when it was clear that the Italian-Canadian voters of Laurier had deserted Lévesque and refused to give their support to an Italian UN candidate to vote solidly Liberal, and that in the constituency of Ahuntsic, non-French Canadians had narrowly defeated Jacques Parizeau.

The elections included foreboding incidents. The *Canadian Annual Review* of 1970 reported that an important Montréal brokerage firm advised its clients to move their securities out of Québec, and a trust company "openly sent a shipload of securities out of the province in nine Brinks trucks." These gestures weren't destined to usher in harmony.

In an interview given after the elections and published in the *Ottawa Citizen* on August 22, 1970, Lévesque made several points that intensified the situation:

> Q: How do you interpret the election results? Some saw massive approval for federalism in the election.

A: First a fact that is terribly flagrant. It's that 95 percent of the Anglophone bloc—I studied enough polls, including Laurier—voted Liberal . . . Even little old ladies on stretchers were hauled out in the end-of-régime panic, as if it were the end of the Roman Empire. They got them out and they manipulated them to the hilt . . . I don't have to draw pictures for you. It can become very grave . . . in other countries this kind of thing provokes explosions. I was brought up half in English and half in French and have lived in English as much as I have lived in French. Yet I have never experienced such disgust . . . as the disgust I experienced because of the way information was manipulated in the Anglo-Saxon Establishment at Montreal with its propaganda media, its disrespect for a population which they treated like "natives."

Q: Can the independence of Quebec really be achieved democratically? Considering the makeup of the population and the electoral map, it seems that the answer is no.

A: It's possible eventually that the answer will be no. It's possible only we can't accept it . . . I think that the last democratic chance will be in the next election . . . And if there is the same manipulation of elections—and I'm talking more about manipulation of the minds than of the electoral system—it's obvious that the conscious minority . . . is going to have the almost irresistible temptation to blow up the institutions. But I honestly believe there still is a chance.

Then, as if to prove him right, came the October Crisis, but the violence that marked this shameful month, which began on October 5, 1970, had antecedents that for seven years had been swept under the carpet.

The Front de libération du Québec (the infamous FLQ) was founded in 1963 to terrorise Québécois into accepting the independence of Québec.

Between 1963 and 1970, the FLQ carried out 200 bombings, in which a few people were killed, some wounded, and many terrorised. Yet, oddly enough, the population remained relatively passive, while the politicians and the police did what they thought was necessary to put an end to it all.

Why was the population so passive? Many reasons can be alleged—from fear of being involved to a belief that it was just a passing phase, a sort of rite of passage, that didn't involve many. To me, the answer is otherwise. It lies in the fact that the repeated terrorist acts were largely directed at les Anglais—a group that included federal institutions and those whom the FLQ considered Québécois collaborators; that is, those in high finance or in politics. Furthermore, we were told not to worry, that it was only the work of a few hotheads without any credentials.

What follows is a sort of diary of the period between October 5 and December 28, 1970. It consists of a series of recognised facts, listed with no commentary. However, I have added certain explanations where I thought they might help. (This diary is based on John Saywell's book *Quebec 1970, a Documentary Narrative*.)

⚜

October 5, 1970, at 8:15 a.m.:

James Cross, the senior British trade commissioner, is kidnapped. On the same day, a communiqué is sent to the provincial and federal governments.

October 6, 1970, at 9:30 a.m.:

The communiqué is broadcast in its entirety. It acknowledges the FLQ's responsibility in the kidnapping of James Cross, and insists that the governments involved "must see to it that the repressive police forces do not commit the monstrous error of attempting to jeopardise the success of the operation by conducting searches, investigations, raids, arrests by any other means," should they want to "save the life of the representative of the ancient racist and colonialist British system." In addition, the FLQ manifesto "must appear in full on the front page

345

of all the principal newspapers in Québec." It must also be "read in full ... during a programme ... to be televised live or pre-recorded between 8 and 11 p.m. on Radio-Canada and its affiliated stations in the province."

There are also other demands: ordering the release of "political prisoners," a plane to take them away with their families, and a "voluntary tax of $500,000 in gold bullion" to be placed on the plane. The governments concerned have forty-eight hours to meet the conditions enunciated in the communiqué.

During the evening of the same day, the federal government, after consultation with the Québec and British authorities, rejects the demands of the FLQ.

October 8, in the evening:

Radio-Canada, having received instructions from the federal authorities, broadcasts the FLQ manifesto. Gaston Montreuil takes thirteen minutes to read it. Here is, in part, the FLQ's manifesto:

> The Front de libération du Québec wants the total independence of all Québécois, united in a free society, purged forever of the clique of voracious sharks, the patronising "big bosses" and their henchmen who have made Quebec their hunting preserve for "cheap labour and unscrupulous exploitation."
>
> ... We have had our fill of Canadian federalism ....
>
> ... We have had our fill of taxes which the Ottawa representative to Quebec wants to give to the Anglophone bosses to encourage them to speak French, old boy, to negotiate in French: Repeat after me: "Cheap labour means manpower in a healthy market."
>
> ... We have had our fill of promises of jobs and prosperity while we always remain the cowering servants and boot-lickers of the big shots who live in

Westmount, Town of Mount Royal, Hampstead and Outremont . . . .

. . . We live in a society of terrorised slaves, terrorised by the big bosses like Steinberg, Clark, Bronfman, Smith, Geoffrion, J.L. Lévesque, Hershorn, Thompson, Nesbitt, Desmarais, Kierans. Compared to them Rémi Popol, the lousy no-good Drapeau the Dog, Bourassa the lackey of the Simards, and Trudeau the fairy are peanuts.

. . . We are terrorised by the capital Roman church. . . .

. . . The number of those who realise the oppression of this terrorist society are growing, and the day will come when all the Westmounts of Quebec will disappear from the map.

. . . We must fight, not singly, but together. We must fight until victory is ours with all the means at our disposal as did the patriots of 1837–38 (those whom our sacred Mother church excommunicated to sell out to the British interests).

In the four corners of Quebec, may those who have been contemptuously called lousy French and alcoholics start fighting their best against the enemies of liberty and justice and prevent all the professional swindlers and robbers, the bankers, the businessmen, the judges, and the sold-out politicators from causing harm.

We are the workers of Quebec and we will continue to the bitter end. We want to replace the slave society with a free society, functioning by itself and for itself; a society open to the world.

Our struggle can only lead to victory. You cannot hold an awakening people in misery and contempt indefinitely. Long live Free Quebec!

Long live our imprisoned political comrades.

Long live the Quebec revolution!
Long live the Front de libération du Québec.

October 10 at 6:00 p.m.:

Pierre Laporte, the forty-nine-year-old minister of labour and of immigration in the provincial Liberal cabinet, is kidnapped as he plays football with his son and his nephew.

October 15 at 3:07 p.m.:

Premier Robert Bourassa informs the National Assembly that he has asked Ottawa for military support. A few hours later, more than one thousand soldiers reach Montréal. More are to follow in the days to come.

October 16 at 3:00 a.m.:

Prime Minister Pierre Elliott Trudeau receives letters from the premier of Québec, the mayor of Montréal, and the director of the provincial police asking for emergency powers to deal with what is described as a deteriorating situation.

On the same day, at 5:17 a.m.: The prime minister's office issues a formal statement that the War Measures Act has been proclaimed. (The War Measures Act, passed in 1914, confers emergency powers to the federal cabinet that permit it to govern by decree, when Canada is deemed to be in a state of war, invasion, and real or apprehended insurrection. This is the first time in our history that it has been used in a domestic crisis.)

On the same day, just before nightfall: Two hundred and fifty suspected members of the FLQ are detained.

October 17 at 7:00 p.m.:

The FLQ informs a reporter at the Montréal radio station CKAC that the body of Pierre Laporte can be found in an abandoned car near the Saint-Hubert airfield.

October 18 at 12:25 a.m.:

Police open the trunk of the abandoned car and find the body of a murdered person, who is identified as Pierre Laporte.

On the same day at 3:00 a.m.: Prime Minister Trudeau addresses the nation on television:

> It is with shock and consternation I believe that all Canadians have learned of the death of Mr. Pierre Laporte, who was so cowardly assassinated by a band of murderers, and I can't help feeling as a Canadian, a deep sense of shame that this cruel and senseless act should have been conceived in cold blood and executed in like manner.
>
> I want to express to Mrs. Laporte and Mr. Laporte's family the very deep regret of the Canadian people and of the Canadian government and our desire as Canadians to stick together in this very sorry moment of our history.

On the same day: Throughout the day, the police continue their searches and more FLQ suspects are detained.

November 2:

The federal government introduces the Public Order Temporary Measures Act into the House of Commons to replace the War Measures Act, as promised earlier by the government. (The new Act maintains many of the regulations found in the War Measures Act but limits their application to the FLQ. It also reduces the "presumptions of affiliation with the illegal association," adds some legal safeguards for those arrested, and makes April 30, 1971, the expiry date for the application of the Act.)

November 5:

Twenty-four persons detained since the imposition of the War

Measures Act appear before a judge. All are remanded until
January 1971.

December 1:

The bill introduced on November 2 is adopted 174 to 31.

December 3:

By 8:30 a.m. the police and the army are surrounding an
apartment at 10945 rue des Récollets; the street is cordoned off,
schools are closed, and the inhabitants are evacuated. Fire
trucks and army canteens are set up, and a medical team arrives.
The Cuban embassy is alerted, and the Canadian pavilion at Man
and His World becomes an extension of the embassy.

At 11:00 a.m., a negotiator, the Montréal lawyer Bernard
Mergler, enters the apartment to negotiate with the FLQ members
present in the building. (They are the members of the FLQ cell
that have kidnapped James Cross.)

At 12:55 a.m., a 1962 Chrysler, surrounded by motorcycles and
police cars and carrying three of the kidnappers, who are armed
with six sticks of dynamite and two M1 semi-automatic rifles
and a pistol, begins its journey to the Canadian pavilion.

At 8:00 p.m., the kidnappers, along with the wife and child of
one of them and two of their associates arrested earlier, are on
their way to Cuba.

December 4 at 1:07 a.m.:

The three kidnappers, along with the four others, are admitted to Cuba.

On the same day, James Cross is freed.

December 23:

The prime minister of Canada and the premier of Québec agree
that all military personnel, with the exception of some body-
guards, will be removed from Québec by January 4, 1971. (By

that time, most of the 7,500 troops stationed in Québec had already left.)

December 27 at 8:40 p.m.:

The police, suspecting that the alleged murderers and kidnappers of Pierre Laporte are at a farm house on L'Acadie Street in the village of Saint-Luc, thirty-two kilometres southwest of Montréal, surround the property. The farmhouse is owned by an FLQ sympathiser. They proceed, with the owner, to a concrete building and, when the basement floor is lifted, they discover a six-metre tunnel. The owner knocks on the bricks and calls the name of a person, who answers "Oui!" The man with the police then says: "If you want to die, I will die with you. But that's wrong. Our cause is a good one . . . You are still needed." The police invite a prominent doctor and writer, Jacques Ferron, to negotiate.

December 28 at dawn:

The man in the bunker surrenders.

⚜

By the end of the crisis, of the 468 persons arrested and held, 408 had been released without charges. And thirty years after the FLQ crisis, controversy continues to plague the assessment of the principal actors in the drama: Why was the support for the FLQ manifesto among the Canadiens of Québec so widespread? Why didn't public pressure force the governments to negotiate after Pierre Laporte's abduction? Did the nationalism of the séparatistes, the indépendantistes, the souverainistes, lead inevitably to the violence of 1970? Was Québec really in a state of "apprehended insurrection"?

Most of the answers to these questions haven't satisfied inquiring minds.

And what of René Lévesque and the Parti Québécois in all of this?

His position was always clear: violence is not our way; this is the way of rats. When a house is on fire, he understood, you don't let the people burn, saving the furniture, so concentrate on Cross, not the prestige of the state.

Consequently, he condemned the violence and he advocated negotiation with the kidnappers of James Cross. On October 14, he called fifteen men to a meeting at the Holiday Inn in Montréal to prepare a statement to that effect. Here, in part, is what it said:

> The Cross-Laporte affair is primarily a Quebec drama. One of the two hostages is a citizen of Quebec, the other a diplomat whose functions made him a temporary citizen with the same rights to respect for his life and to his dignity as a man as us all.
>
> . . . This is why, forgetting the difference of opinion we have on a number of subjects, solely conscious for the moment of being Québécois and therefore totally involved, we wish to give our complete support to the intention announced Sunday evening by the Bourassa government, which means basically our strongest support for negotiating an exchange of the two hostages for the political prisoners. This must be accomplished despite and against all obstruction from outside Quebec, which necessarily implies the positive co-operation of the federal government.

In his *Memoirs*, he recorded his feelings when he heard the FLQ manifesto being read on Radio-Canada:

> On Thursday, October 8, when the manifesto hit the airwaves, a multitude of Québécois found themselves implicated. They certainly had no sympathy for the call, in coarse language, for a revolution to "strip their power to harm from the professionals of holdups and fraud: bankers, businessmen, judges, and sold-out politicians . . . " But on the other hand, the long list of grievances that preceded this conclusion was far from unfounded.

Lévesque went on to decry the mention of his name and that of the Parti Québécois in the manifesto, in which the kidnappers stated clearly that they were supporters of both. That caused Lévesque and his party great harm: "Our adversaries wasted no time in transforming the allegation into a certainty and then into a slanderous slogan which, travelling from mouth to mouth and chalked up on the walls, for several months did us incalculable harm: 'PQ=FLQ! PQ=FLQ!'"

When the War Measures Act was invoked, Lévesque was furious. In a lengthy statement, he expressed his views and his philosophy:

> Quebec no longer has a government.
>
> The bit of country over which we had any control has been swept away by the first hard blow. The Bourassa cabinet has stepped down and is no longer anything but a puppet in the hands of the federal leaders.
>
> ... Nor can we help thinking and saying that this degradation of Quebec was intended—quite consciously by some and instinctively by others.
>
> The guiding factors have taken two extreme forms.
>
> Firstly there is the thoroughly official, legally recognised federal establishment, backed by economic and other forces. It was from here that the first murmur was heard of the likelihood of resorting to all means including a military force to contain Quebec, and, if need be, putting her in her place.
>
> At the other extreme let us hope that those very people who threw themselves body and soul into a career of subversion and terrorism—both of which are so tragically contrary to the best interests of our people—may at last realize now that they have in fact been the forerunners of the military regime thereby endangering the basic rights of all Québécois.
>
> Finally, we do not know how large the revolutionary army is or was, nor the extent of their power to create disorder and anarchy. Until we receive proof to the contrary—and every responsible citizen should demand this proof and be given it as soon possible if it exists or the contrary—we will believe that such a minute, numerically unimportant fraction is involved, that rushing into the enforcement of the War Measures Act was a panicky and altogether excessive reaction, especially when you

353

think of the inordinate length of time they wanted to maintain
this regime.

. . . In view of the extremes which have for all practical purposes caused the destruction of our government, Quebec's
democrats must overcome their differences of opinion immediately and find the means or the organisations for building the
moral power necessary to defend our basic liberties and, at the
same time, all our hopes for the future.

How clear was his position?

The electors of Pierre Laporte's riding had the opportunity to express
their view on the matter; for, on February 8, 1971, there was a by-election in
Chambly. After the election, the *Canadian Annual Review* of 1971 reported:
"In the 1970 election, 85 percent of the voters had turned out, 48.5 percent
voting Liberal and 27.2 Péquiste. On February 8 only 66 percent turned out
with Cournoyer [the Liberal candidate] receiving 22,647 votes and Marois
[the PQ candidate] 11,452."

Lévesque was able to turn the defeat of his party into a victory. He argued
that the results in Chambly "told all of Canada that political independence
has not lost ground in these nine months, but gained it."

In some ways, the *Canadian Annual Review* agreed with him:
"Undoubtedly Chambly had helped the Parti Québécois consolidate its position as a viable and legitimate political party. And as the Bourassa government faced one crisis after another—none of which strengthened its political
appeal—and as neither the selection of Gabriel Loubier as the leader of the
Union nationale nor its change of name to Unité-Québec promised miracu-
lously to enhance its popularity, the PQ undoubtedly emerged as the most
serious threat to the Liberals at the next election."

What conclusions can we draw from the FLQ crisis of 1970? There is no
doubt that many in Canada—and I was one of them—lost whatever illusions we might have had about Canada. In the pursuit of a just society, we
agreed to suspend our liberties, and let our governments rule by decree and
despoil many of our rights. We haven't come to grips with that yet.

The events of October 1970 also led us to a fundamental conclusion:

Québec nationalism could not be free of violence; repression was bound to follow. Is that still so today?

Finally, as Professor Saywell so aptly says in *The Rise of the Parti Québécois*:

> Whatever the future of the FLQ, the October crisis was a turn-ing point in Canadian history. Superficially, it forced a re-examination of Quebec nationalism, and the relations between Quebec and the rest of Canada. Far more important, however, it forced a re-examination of fundamental attitudes, beliefs, and values. The nationalism of the FLQ might be limited and con-tained; its radicalism brought Canada fully into the last half of the century, for it challenged less the existence of the nation-state than the nature of the society within it.

Lévesque called the years between 1971 and 1976 "the long march." It took him sixty-five months—some 2,000 days—to achieve his goal of bringing his party to power so that he could advance the cause of Québec's independence.

During this long march, the PQ lost again in 1973, electing only six mem-bers—one fewer than in 1970. Lévesque was defeated in Dorion, but his party increased its popular vote by seven percentage points and became the official opposition. The Liberals elected 102 members.

Losing the election was a particular blow to Lévesque. At the PQ's con-vention the preceding February, he had clarified several issues that tended to divide the party. One of these was the place of the English-speaking (and the immigrant) minority in the new Québec he was trying to build. As he was a civilised man, he was determined that the treatment of Québec's minorities should be fair. The French language had to be the only official language of the new nation and it had, as well, to be the dominant language in the work-place. English schools had to be retained, but there could be adjustments as to the number of students in those schools. As for new immigrants, they would have to be educated solely in French schools and, in the new Québec, they would have to show competence in the French language before they could be granted a permanent visa or citizenship.

In that February 1970 meeting, the question of how independence would be achieved was tackled and the convention agreed that the process would begin as soon as the National Assembly proclaimed the independence of Québec; the transfer of all powers exercised by the federal government and affecting Québec would immediately begin and would be completed within seven months; meanwhile, there would be a referendum "in order to solidify this independence"; discussions would be held with Ottawa regarding the division of assets, etc.; Québec would seek admission in the United Nations and recognition from other states; international treaties would be respected; and Québec's frontiers (even extending them to the "Arctic lands and islands") would be reaffirmed and defended.

As far as the PQ was concerned, Lévesque, with his personality, his rhetoric, his easiness with people, his sense of values, and his credibility, was the key to winning the elections. Yet, according to the *Canadian Annual Review* of that year, "confusion continued to remain, if not reign, here and there." However, the party attempted to mitigate the confusion by being more forthright in its publicity. It also had powerful allies in the labour-union movement and many national organizations. In the final analysis, though, it was René Lévesque who would make or break the elections. Or so it was thought.

The Liberals were not idle. The economy was quite good and the labour front was quiet. In their political manifesto, they reaffirmed their position: "on a priority basis . . . to obtain a fiscal division which will enable Quebec to fully assume its constitutional responsibilities." Regarding what was called "la question nationale," the party stated categorically that "Canadian unity is absolutely essential to the development of Quebec society and to the improvement of the quality of life of its citizens. *The option of the Liberal party of Quebec is clear and specific; it is that of Canadian federalism.*"

The Quebec electorate chose federalism. Lévesque took his defeat gracefully: "Thousands of Quebeckers understood what the PQ offers . . . and one day we will penetrate the last fears and complexes which prevent so many from seeing how beautiful and fruitful life as a nation would be."

The elections were followed by an examination of all the factors that led to such a defeat. In the middle of November, in Québec City, the council of the PQ met to iron things out. Not much was resolved, though, and

Lévesque refused to seek a by-election. Instead he would help found and keep alive a newspaper to be called *Le Jour*.

In his *Memoirs*, he wrote of his personal position in those years:

> As for my own performance over this period, it seems to me to have been a saw-toothed affair. Beaten, then beaten again in the elections, asking myself every six months what I was still doing in this madhouse, I had finally consented, reluctantly, to accept a modest salary as one of the party's permanent staff. As a result, besides being hard up, I found myself in the abominable position of the man who is the employee of the people he is leading. Certain critics did not hesitate to rub this in, and I often became so ill-humoured I reached the stage where one realises that one is quite hateful.

In May 1974, René Lévesque made it clear that he would remain at the head of the party should the November meeting of its National Council confirm him. However, there were many in the party who argued that Lévesque's time was over. Some pointed out that the electors of two constituencies had refused to endorse him and unless he could re-enter the legislature before the next elections, he should resign as party leader.

Lévesque fought back. He had faults, he agreed; his leadership wasn't perfect; the party organisation—though a necessity, "is not a panacea and above all not an absolute"—needed improvements; the divisions in the party had to be removed; and a clear position on independence had to be stated unequivocally, along with a strong and attractive political program that would achieve the independence of Québec. After much discussion—the Parti Québécois loved to discuss—it was left to the National Council that was to meet in November to "redefine the process of attaining independence." Was independence to come suddenly after a referendum or would a separation occur by stages? That was the question. The Council decided, on Lévesque's advice, to stay the course.

In 1975, more squabbles arose between the party's moderates and hardliners. Then came the elections of 1976.

Since the elections of 1973, which saw Bourassa returned to power, nothing had seemed to go right for the Liberals. The government had to deal with escalating inflation; the costs of the 1976 Montréal Olympics had risen from a quarter of a billion dollars to 1.5 billion; unemployment was high; the mood of the electors was disenchanted; labour relations were pathetic, with Québec accounting for 41 percent of all work stoppages in the country; labour leaders and unions were in open rebellion; farmers weren't too happy; and the teachers were agitated. To make matters worse, no one seemed to be satisfied with the language law, Bill 22, which the government had adopted in 1974 and which made French the language of civic administration, services, and the workplace; it also stipulated that children of immigrants had to take tests to prove their proficiency in English before they could attend English schools.

In passing, here is what Lévesque had to say about Bill 22 in his *Memoirs*:

> Big surprise! In May the Bourassa government at last decided to make a move on the linguistic front. It immediately drew fire from both sides. For Anglophones, Bill 22 was a horror. . . . So tests were imposed on little shavers, six and seven years old, isolated from their parents who were boiling mad at the whole business. . . . One thing is certain, my reaction was not the same as that of the hardliners . . . which boils down to one word: betrayal.
>
> If one . . . recalls the fact that the Liberals are the "English party" and that Bourassa's government reflects this amply, I consider that for once the Premier showed real courage.

A poll taken in the spring of 1976 revealed that the dissatisfaction with the Liberal government was at 66 percent, while 29 percent of Quebeckers endorsed René Lévesque as the leader best able to meet the aspirations of the people. Had an election been held on the day the poll was taken, 41 percent (the number was higher among the French-speaking residents of Québec, especially those living outside of Montréal) of the voters would have voted for the Parti Québécois and 28 percent for the Liberals.

The PQ's electoral plans had been determined well before Bourassa called the election on October 18. The campaign was to be fought on the government's record. The alternative to that government was, naturally, the Parti Québécois. Furthermore, as the *Canadian Annual Review* of 1976 pointed out, "The promise of a referendum would defuse the question of independence, and allow non-separatist Quebeckers to vote Péquiste." There would be little attention paid to the PQ platform so as not to give the Liberals a chance to attack. Finally as the *Review* noted, "the election would be fought at the local level, riding by riding."

As far as the question of independence was concerned, Lévesque explained the procedure to arrive at that goal in an article he wrote for the July 1976 edition of *Foreign Affairs*:

> The way we see it, it would have to go somewhat like this. There is a new Québec government which is totally dedicated to political independence. But this same Québec, for the time being, is still very much a component of federal Canada, with its quite legitimate body of elected representatives in Ottawa. This calls, first of all, for at least a try at negotiation. . . . Obviously there would have to be the referendum which the Parti Québécois proposed in order to get the decisive yes-or-no answer to the tired question: What does Québec want? . . . If the answer should be no, then there's nothing to do but wait for the momentum of change to keep on working until the answer is yes, oui, then the pressure is on Ottawa. . . .
>
> Fully confident of the basic integrity of Canadian democracy, and just as conscious that any silliness would be very costly for both sides, we firmly believe that the matter would then be brought to a negotiated settlement.

The Liberals, on the other hand, also had a program, the centrepiece of which was stated over and over again, especially in their last full-page ad in the newspapers on Saturday, November 13:

> . . . We mustn't fool ourselves.
> We mustn't let anyone else fool us.

On Monday, it's not a simple choice between parties. . . . On Monday, we must not trigger the separation process.

Really our choice is obvious: Either we set Quebec adrift—towards inevitable separation from Canada . . . or else vote for *the only party* that can give us *stability* and *security* while pledging itself to respond even better to the needs of all citizens.

It's either *one* or *the other*.

Think about it.

On Monday, let's not gamble everything we've won.

On Monday, let's not break up Canada.

Let's vote *Liberal*.

On Monday, November 15, 1976, the Parti Québécois of René Lévesque won 41 percent of the popular vote, with seventy-one seats. Lévesque himself was elected in Taillon with a vast majority. The Liberals elected twenty-six members (they had elected 102 in 1973) with 33.8 percent of the popular vote.

In its assessment of that victory, the editors of the *Canadian Annual Review* concluded: "Clearly the two step approach to independence allowed some federalists to vote for the Parti Québécois. But it was also clear, though not statistically, that separatism had ceased to frighten the voter." Furthermore, the PQ had been able to dissociate independence from violence and it had, as well, "neutralised the extremists on the nationalist and socialist front." The province had therefore taken a "giant step towards independence; for the first time it was clear that independence was regarded as one of the rational and legitimate options open to the Québécois. Neither the province nor the country could ever be quite the same again."

On that fateful night of November 15, 1976, Lévesque found words that he described as, "words that were truly new, words that weren't my usual style at all and that must have come from beyond my own thoughts, or most probably were dictated by that collective unconsciousness palpitating out there before me." Whatever the process was, he said: "I've never been so proud to be a Québécois! We're not a little people, we're closer to something like a great people."

A month later, on December 13, he was in Ottawa attending a federal-provincial conference of first ministers. According to his *Memoirs*, the rules of the new game, were, he told his colleagues, as follows:

> We have stated clearly, and I wish to repeat it, that we do not claim to see this vote as a mandate for Quebec's independence. Our commitments are clear on this point: when the time comes, it will be up to the public, and to them alone, to decide the issue in a referendum.
>
> . . . We believe that Canada and English-speaking Canadians are capable of accepting such a perspective that would make it possible in a different setting not to isolate ourselves from each other, not to continue to harass each other with artificial issues like bilingualism, but rather to differentiate political institutions which should be different, while maintaining and even expanding all types of co-operation and exchanges that are mutually beneficial to us. We are certain that the development of Quebec, like that of Canada, clearly depends on this.

But before the referendum could take place, the Lévesque government had to govern in such a way as to satisfy the principles and agendas of Lévesque, of his ministers, and of the members of his party. Many of the reforms his government introduced and passed were long overdue: an Auto Insurance Act establishing state-run property damage insurance and no-fault compensation, a new Civil Code, a massive reform of family law and of management of Québec's public lands, etc. The centrepiece of the reforms was the Charte de la langue française, the now famous—or infamous—Bill 101, passed in 1977. French became the only official language of Québec, to be made dominant in the workplace, in business, and in commerce. English was banned from billboards, government forms, and even restaurant menus, not to mention stop signs and in the names of towns, roads, streets, rivers, and mountains. A sort of language police was created to enforce the application of the Charter. In schools, all the children of Québec were to be educated in French at the primary and secondary levels (that is, until CEGEP) except for those whose parents had gone to an English-speaking school in Québec. Those who immigrated to the province either from inside or outside Canada also had to pursue their primary and secondary education in French.

With the pieces in place—a popular demonstration that Lévesque, his government, and his party were good governors and had the ear of the people—the time came to hold the referendum on Québec's future.

The date was set for May 20, 1980. The question was as follows:

> The government of Quebec has made public its proposal to negotiate a new agreement with the rest of Canada, based on the equality of nations;
>
> this agreement would enable Quebec to acquire the exclusive power to make its laws, levy its taxes and establish relations abroad—in other words, sovereignty—and at the same time to maintain with Canada an economic association including a common currency;
>
> no change in political status resulting from these negotiations will be effected without approval by the people through another referendum; on these terms do you give the Government of Quebec the mandate to negotiate the proposed agreement between Quebec and Canada?

In his *Memoirs*, Lévesque admitted that the question was "rather long and heavy." However, he insisted that it was "transparent" because "in three short paragraphs and some hundred words the essence was there for anyone who knew how to read."

At the beginning of the referendum campaign, the Oui side (the provincial government) was doing well, even better than the Non side, the one held by the provincial Liberals and the federal government. Two months before the vote, in all of Québec, 46 percent of the population was for the Oui and 43 percent for the Non. Among French Canadians, a majority, 55 percent, were in favour of sovereignty association, while 46 percent still wanted to renew federalism. The young, between the ages of eighteen and twenty-four, were 69 percent for the Yes side, those between twenty-five and fifty-four showed various degrees of support. Those over fifty-five were opposed, in large numbers.

Then, a few days after the above poll was taken, came a disaster. Here is how Lévesque described it in his *Memoirs*:

> One day in March in a modest meeting that would normally have sunk quietly beneath the sands of time, Lise Payette [a cabinet minister and a popular television personality] got caught up in one of those feminist declarations prompted by her job as Minister of the Status of Women. In the most logical way imaginable she had set about exposing a school text presenting two great incarnations of traditional sexism—little Guy, future champion and perfect macho, and little Yvette, model miniature housewife, broken in to be perfectly submissive. So far so good. But carried away by her subject and "pushed by some devil," our colleague dropped a remark to the effect that Québec women would have to learn to sit up and sit still if ever Claude Ryan [the leader of the Québec Liberal Party and a former editor of the newspaper *Le Devoir*] took power because he was married to a protracted "Yvette." This was not only in poor taste but untrue and Lise Payette soon heard about it, for several journalists made a point of enumerating Madame Ryan's exceptional accomplishments and made it a duty to execute the guilty party in the public square.

This incident reinvigorated the Non campaign.

Forty days after that, 60 percent of the people of Québec said Non to that "rather long and heavy" question that the government of Québec had asked. Lévesque had lost.

"To this day," he wrote in his *Memoirs*, "no one knows if our two-fifths vote for the 'oui' represented 49 or 51 percent of French Quebec that night. On the other hand, the three-fifths vote for the 'non' was sadly incontestable."

❧

I close my eyes and Mascou brings me to the evening of May 20, 1980. Standing near him on a high beam of the Paul Sauvé Arena, I look down on the crowd below me. There are over 5,000 people gathered on what is usually the hockey rink. Many are in tears; some hold their infant children in their arms; lovers cling to each other; friends hold hands; and those not connected to anyone in particular are soon enveloped in the arms of perfect strangers. Journalists and cameramen and photographers are everywhere, and most of them appear to sense the great emotional drama that is being lived out on the cement floor of the arena. René Lévesque's wife is at the back of the platform on the verge of tears. Beside her, all in black, is Lise Payette. We wait.

Suddenly, from the wings, he comes. All crumpled up in his clothes. His head down. His expression downcast. He walks to the microphone slowly, painfully, it appears to me. His sadness is palpable. You can feel it all over the hall and certainly up where I stand, unafraid of the height.

Only when he is at the microphone does he lift up his head to acknowledge the cheers that come his way and the immense love that flows towards him at the same time. When he speaks, his voice is calm and not shaky. However, one can sense the effort that is being demanded of him. He talks and, later, I will remember only that he told those before him—and particularly the young—that there will be another day. And when that day comes, "we will be here to greet it." He waits for his words to be felt as they should. A moment of hope in the vast pool of despair around him. A moment of comfort to ease so much pain. Then: "But I must admit that tonight I would be hard pressed to tell you when or how." Again another moment is followed by a word of caution: "In the meantime we must live together."

He moves his feet a little. From where I am standing, he seems to shrink into himself. Either he has no more words or he wishes to put an end to them, for he starts singing the first words of Gilles Vigneault's beautiful hymn. Even though he is terribly off-key, his "Gens du pays" is softly sung, and all those in front and around him pick it up—and in one voice the words of the unofficial national anthem of the people of Québec come alive.

When the song dies down, he bows his head. A moment later, he lifts it. A faint and shy smile illuminates his face. He turns slightly towards the wings. As he does so, he says, "À la prochaine."

His shoulders sink a little. He walks away. And Mascou brings me home.

⚜

René Lévesque did not call a referendum during the life of his second government, 1981–85.

The Search Continues

✣

*T*he question "What does Québec want?" has always masked an underlying mind-set: "Why can't these people ever be satisfied with what they've got!" Obviously, that attitude doesn't make for constructive harmony, but it also betrays a blindness. British Columbia has been bitching since 1871, when it entered Confederation. No one asks, "What do those crazy people want?" The West has been alienated since Macdonald and Cartier created Manitoba in 1870 and since Laurier did the same for Saskatchewan and Alberta in 1905—Alberta has complained constantly, Saskatchewan and Manitoba tend to threaten less. But again, no one asks: "What the hell do these farmers and cowboys want?" As for Atlantic Canada, it has been complaining ever since Nova Scotia ceased being a "have" province ten years after Confederation. During the federal election of 2000, those alienations were expressed loudly and often, not just by a particular political party that the alienated of Western Canada had created.

Since Macdonald's national policy of the late 1870s, Ontario has steadily grown in wealth and importance. A visiting Martian might conclude that the province has been so busy making money on the backs of the rest of us that they haven't been much inclined to talk of alienation. Indeed, Ontarians are well aware that what they want they will get. After all, it has become a maxim of Canadian faith that to the degree that Ontario is rich, the rest can eat a few times a week.

"What does Québec want? is not our question," the people of Québec will tell you today, as they have for centuries. When you react in astonishment, they will say: "We know what we want." Then, they will shrug their shoulders à la René Lévesque and, with that Cheshire-cat smile of his, they will add apologetically, "We don't always agree as to the means to get what we want. That's probably what confuses you!"

The last twenty years of the 20th century were dominated by attempts to address what was generally understood to be Québec's wish list: a revision of the Canadian Constitution in order to increase the power base of the Québec government.

Trudeau was one of the few who really understood that Québec's wish list wasn't about power grabbing, even when couched in the loftiest of language. He also realised what the Reform-Alliance takes for granted: many provincial politicians jump on Québec's bandwagon only to satisfy their own demands, without necessarily sympathising with Québec. Trudeau was convinced that the single most important element on the Québec wish list was simply to be allowed to be. How one interpreted the "to be" is the key to understanding the puzzle of Canada.

After the 1980 referendum, Lévesque and the PQ lived in what he called "some painless purgatory." The defeat stung, but what was more hurtful was the "heavy curtain" that had fallen and closed off "the horizon." For Lévesque, Québec had missed the moment: "For the first time, during those few hours of May 20, our people had had a say in their own destiny, the same people who had been so pushed around by history, from the French regime to the English occupation, from the beginning of self-government to the Union, and to Confederation. How many people are there in the world who have refused such a chance to acquire full powers for themselves peacefully and democratically?" He feared that, having lost, "our development would be whittled down."

Yet, the Parti Québécois won the election of 1981. Surprise! In 1976, the party had elected seventy-one members; in 1981 it obtained eighty-two seats (with 49 percent of the vote)—after the easiest campaign of the seven Lévesque had been through. The people were satisfied with what he accomplished in his first mandate. The results surprised and pleased him. "It seems to me," he wrote, "when looking back on the four years that followed, that politically that was my last night [election night] of unmixed joy. We felt the euphoria of the resurrected."

The same cannot be said of the 1985 election. The policies didn't work as smoothly; the recession had hit with great force—the "economic collapse," Lévesque called it; the constitutional agenda took enormous time and energy and was filled with recriminations and "crises"; and the party was again divided on the question of sovereignty-association: sovereignty tout court, independence, and separation—one form not being synonymous with another. As for Canadians, they were beginning to have their fill of nationalism. Times were hard. Constitutional revival wasn't an issue for the majority of the electorate, and they were becoming annoyed at a government being whirled away like straws in the wind.

In 1984, Lévesque announced that the PQ should set aside temporarily the souveraineté-association issue. At a congress in January 1985, the party supported him, but the decision caused a rift with many cabinet ministers, and others left. Discouraged and spent, Lévesque resigned as party leader and premier in June. His successor was Pierre-Marc Johnson, the elder son of the former Union nationale premier of Québec, Daniel Johnson, who had served between 1966 and his untimely death in 1968. Johnson (fils) didn't have much time to revitalise the party and give it new direction between Lévesque's resignation and the December 1985 election.

On the other hand, the Liberals had been able to resurrect themselves. After the demise of the party in the election of 1976, Robert Bourassa, the then premier, resigned in 1978 and was followed by Claude Ryan, the well-known and respected editor of *Le Devoir*. Ryan served at *Le Devoir* between 1964 and his election to the leadership of the Liberal Party, a position he held until 1982. A year later, the party elected Robert Bourassa as its leader, in one of the most fascinating comebacks in the history of Canada's political life.

In the 1985 election, the Parti Québécois won only twenty-four seats. Johnson stayed on, but unable to bring new life to the party, he resigned in November 1987, a week after René Lévesque's death. Jacques Parizeau then became leader, only to lose the 1989 election (returning only twenty-nine members with 40 percent of the popular vote) to Bourassa.

It was in this way that Robert Bourassa and the Liberals inherited the constitutional agenda.

A year before his death—almost to the day—René Lévesque wrote in his diary: "'Thoughts take wing,' writes Julien Green, 'but words travel by foot.' It's midnight. The wing droops, the words crawl. I've almost no more paper and no time left at all."

It was Lévesque's last entry. He died on November 1, 1987.

Since Confederation, three issues have appeared on the Canadian constitutional agenda: provincial autonomy (the division of powers between the federal and provincial governments and the "exclusive autonomy" of the provinces in the exercise of those powers); "patriation"—a word peculiar to us–of the Constitution (the British North America Act of 1867, a statute of the British Parliament); and the place of Québec within Canada.

Little separates these three issues; the difficulty is deciding where to begin.

Every political party in Québec has, since Confederation, insisted on provincial autonomy to preserve the special character of the province and to protect its distinct identity in North America. Over the years that meant largely no federal interference in the powers that the BNA Act assigned to the provinces. And various proposals have included a devolution of power, an opting-out formula, a veto power, equality or independence, and souveraineté-association.

Patriation of the Constitution—never as important in Québec as it was to others—began with the Balfour Report of 1926, when the self-governing dominions, including Canada, obtained full autonomy. At first, Canadians

were occupied by finding a suitable amending formula, but in the 1960s
Québec insisted that no amending formula was acceptable—and therefore no
patriation—unless the process included a redistribution of powers favouring
the provinces. It therefore rejected the Fulton-Favreau amending formula in
1964 on the grounds that the other provinces could prevent Québec from
obtaining changes to the distribution of powers.

Daniel Johnson initiated the option "égalité ou indépendance" in 1965. It
meant equality between the "two founding peoples" of Canada—those who
spoke English and those who spoke French. No great advance had been made
by the time of Johnson's death in 1968. However, he left a province much
divided between a militant and, at times, a violent, separatist movement on
the one hand and the bulk of the population on the other. His successor, Jean-
Jacques Bertrand, took up the torch, and the endless debate for a constitutional position, more powers, more money continued.

When Robert Bourassa came to power in 1970, violence had already entered
the debate. The terrorist organisation known as the Réseau de résistance was
followed by the Front de libération du Québec. At the command of these two
organisations, bombs were planted in Montréal's radio stations, military estab-
lishments, RCMP barracks, the central Post Office building, and mailboxes in
residential Westmount. A bomb was also found in the Legion Hall in Saint-
Jean, not too far from Montréal. Important national monuments and federal
buildings were defaced with slogans, and an attempt was made to derail a train
carrying the prime minister of Canada. There were hundreds of demonstrations and marches, the most violent of which took place during the visit of the
Queen to Québec City in 1964. Incidents continued after that, the three most
terrifying being the pelting of the prime minister with stones at the Saint-Jean-
Baptiste parade of 1968, the kidnapping of James Cross, and the kidnapping
and murder of Pierre Laporte in 1970.

In January 1971, to regain some form of peace, Bourassa demanded whatever constitutional change was necessary so Québec would have primary
responsibility in all social-policy sectors, through the necessary devolution
of powers along with financial allocations to make it possible. What did that
mean? many asked. Would Bourassa's demands lead to a much decentralised
federalism? Or asymmetrical federalism? Or a special status for Québec?

The answer came from Victoria, B.C., when, in the middle of the night of June 16, 1971, the first ministers meeting there accepted the Victoria Constitutional Charter.

Under the terms of this charter, the Canadian Constitution was to be patriated with a formula for amending it, along with a sort of Charter of Rights and Freedoms and a veto for Québec. In addition, language rights were to be enshrined at the federal level and three of the nine judges of the Supreme Court were always to come from Québec. Finally, the federal government became bound to consult the provinces prior to enacting social legislation and to accept opting-out with financial compensation.

It was a good deal—but not good enough for Québec, even though Bourassa signed it along with his colleagues. However, when ministers in his cabinet and others pointed out that he had forgotten the constitutional control over family allowances, he tried to obtain that at the last hour, but he failed. He then withdrew Québec's consent—the second time in less than a decade. A Québec signature on a document was quickly losing credibility.

Between 1971 and the referendum merry-go-round of 1980, constitutional reform filled the days of the chattering classes. During 1975 and until Lévesque defeated him in 1976, Bourassa was ever present with various solutions. One was that Québec (and the other provinces) should have full control over all cultural matters, and should receive, as well, new powers of taxation. However, his demands fell on deaf ears in Ottawa, and with Lévesque's coming to power, the Québec agenda changed from a mere reorientation of federal-provincial powers to the far-reaching sovereignty-association.

However, this didn't mean that Lévesque was out of tune with the provinces in demanding more powers. At a provincial conference of first ministers in the summer of 1978, he and all his provincial colleagues endorsed the 1975 Bourassa position in what has been called the Saskatchewan Charter. That, too, went nowhere. Canada was, therefore, back at the starting gate: what was needed to keep Québec in Confederation and how far would the "other" Canada be prepared to go? And pacifying Québec meant that the other provinces would be the beneficiaries.

Another attempt to solve the problem was made when the Pepin-Robarts constitutional task force, appointed in 1977, reported in 1979. We were then told that Canada lived under a federalism that had two parts. The first part was a union of diverse provinces and territories that were sovereign and united under one constitution. The second part was a federation of two founding nations. The task force also warned us that if Québec wasn't recognised as a "distinct society"—with the primary responsibility to promote the "French" fact within the province and with all the powers and financial resources that mandate implied—Canada would cease to exist. Thus was "asymmetrical federalism" introduced into our constitutional vocabulary. If true, it applied, of course, to all the provinces, but the proposers of this solution were certain that only Québec would avail itself, obtaining in the process a special status, if not de jure at least de facto.

In dealing with other matters, the task force pronounced the provinces equal and asked that they be allowed a voice in appointments to the Supreme Court and other federal bodies; proposed the abolition of the Senate and its replacement by a Council of the Federation, the members of which would be named by the provincial governments; and recommended the incorporation in the Canadian Constitution of a Charter of Rights and Freedoms dealing with individual and collective rights.

Not waiting for the task force's report, Prime Minister Trudeau seized the initiative. In the new Canadian federation he wanted, there would be a new division of powers between the federal and provincial governments, in favour of the provinces; increased provincial representation on federal institutions and boards; a Council of the Federation to replace the abolished Senate—half of the members of that Council would be named by the Legislative Assembly of each province and the other half by the House of Commons; an amending formula; a Canadian Charter of Rights and Freedoms; and the patriation of the Constitution.

After that, the whole question degenerated into a circus. From every corner of the land came a deluge of constitutional proposals that went nowhere. It was obvious that nothing could be done until Québec held its referendum in May 1980. When that was defeated, with its sovereignty-association option, there was no alternative but to produce "the new Canada." To achieve that, though, there had to be a consensus among the constitutional players.

In the summer of 1980, Trudeau offered to patriate the Constitution and entrench in it a Charter of Rights and Freedoms. Lévesque was not pleased. He considered the Charter "an instrument to reduce the powers of Québec." He wrote in his *Memoirs* that Trudeau's proposals "had the singular virtue of giving everybody the goose pimples." The other provinces didn't like the idea of the Charter either, because, according to Lévesque, "this kind of American-style Bill of Rights [was] completely foreign to the unwritten tradition of British institutions." In September, at a constitutional conference, the Trudeau plan was rejected. Following that contretemps, Trudeau announced, in October 1980, that he would proceed unilaterally. He hoped to have the Canadian Parliament do the deed before Christmas.

Again Lévesque was incensed and called upon Québec's Assemblée nationale to issue a protest. The Québec Liberals, under Claude Ryan, refused to accept Lévesque's wording and, instead, proposed a version of their own that proclaimed Québec's attachment to federalism and its advantages, thus rejecting sovereignty-association. Lévesque couldn't accept that. "I begged Ryan," he wrote, "not to push us to the wall like this. I asked him to put himself in my place. A little more and I would have gone down on my knees to him." Ryan was unconciliatory, "quite content to let me stew in my own juice." The Assembly, failing to reach unanimity, was obliged to record a divided vote "that sadly undermined our position."

Meanwhile, the provinces were organising themselves to fight Trudeau's proposal. At first, Québec, Alberta, Manitoba, Prince Edward Island, Newfoundland, and British Columbia—the Gang of Six, as they were called— challenged the federal plan in the courts. (By September 1981, the Gang of Six had become the Gang of Eight when Saskatchewan and Nova Scotia joined the group.) In February 1981, the Manitoba Court of Appeal found in favour of Ottawa as did the Québec Superior Court of Appeal in April, but the Supreme Court of Newfoundland condemned the federal proposal as illegal. With no alternative at hand, Ottawa, in April, referred the whole matter to the Supreme Court of Canada, seeking answers to three questions: Would the federal proposal affect the powers of the provinces? Was there a constitutional convention that obliged the federal government to consult the provinces? Was the consent of the provinces necessary?

In April, three days after he had won a second term, with an increased majority, Lévesque was meeting with the Gang of Eight in Ottawa. He allowed that the reference to the Supreme Court enabled them all to "breathe a little more." It was at that meeting (Trudeau refused to join them) that the so-called April Accord was signed by the eight provinces, an accord that called only for an amending formula, which had no specific veto for Québec in it. It was also at this meeting that Lévesque, no doubt in return for his compromise regarding the veto, had the seven provinces present give their word of honour that they wouldn't shatter their unity by agreeing to a separate deal, either individually or collectively.

Why did Lévesque abandon the traditional demand of Québec: a veto power? Here is how he explained it: "I should perhaps admit that this old obsession has never turned me on. A veto can be an obstacle to development as much as an instrument of defence. If Quebec had it, Ontario and perhaps other provinces would surely ask for it, too. And, as in Victoria in 1971, it would be possible to block change and in protecting oneself paralyse others, leaving everyone way ahead . . . or behind." What mattered to him was the right to opt out, which was, in his mind, "a much superior weapon, at one and the same time more flexible and more dynamic."

On September 28, 1981, the Supreme Court of Canada answered the questions it had been asked. The judges agreed unanimously that the federal proposal affected the powers of the provinces. Did there exist a constitutional convention whereby the provinces had to consent to any changes to the Canadian Constitution? By 6-3, their lordships said yes. Was that consent necessary? Yes (6-3) according to convention; no (7-2) according to law. There was nothing else to do but to have another constitutional conference. This one, called "the one last meeting," convened in Ottawa on November 2, 1981.

In summary, this four-day gathering of first ministers was filled with proposals, discussions, compromises, forming and breaking alliances, and deals. Trudeau had three objectives: patriation, an amending formula, and a Charter of Rights. During the conference, the idea of a referendum took some prominence, but, privately, Saskatchewan, B.C., Alberta, and Newfoundland put together an amending formula and a clause to limit the effect of the Charter.

Lévesque, who only learned of this on the final morning, failed to persuade Trudeau to use the referendum option and, therefore, refused to sign the accord. Here now is how René Lévesque remembered it all.

As usual, the opening session was a series of carefully prepared solo performances. Trudeau began by stating his three objectives again: repatriation, an amending formula, and his inseparable Charter of Rights. He also took the opportunity to attack the right of opting out, saying that in his opinion, it constituted a permanent negation of "National will," since a single province would be able to oppose a consensus of the others, and go off in its own direction. He was looking straight ahead as he talked, but it was obvious who and what he meant. [Ontario's Bill] Davis followed with his habitual "noble father" patter, the sole aim of which was to reinforce a federal position a little.

Then it was my turn, according to the rule that gives the floor to "First Ministers" in order of the seniority of their provinces. I didn't mince my words. Stressing the fact that Trudeau had no mandate to act unilaterally, I defied him to put his plan to the voters. Forgetting [New Brunswick's Richard] Hatfield, who was simply a ventriloquist's dummy, I next listened to our seven counterparts with the strictest attention. None failed to underline the unconstitutional character of the federal project, but first [B.C.'s Bill] Bennett, then naturally, [Saskatchewan's Allan] Blakeney, started mixing discreet advances in with their well-justified reproaches. They seemed to be saying to Trudeau: "Find something or other, if you possibly can, to let us reach a compromise." The common front was decidedly beginning to crack.

The next day, Tuesday, it fell to Bill Davis, who adored posing as the honest mediator, to launch the decisive phase of the discussions. He tabled a compromise motion. If Trudeau would accept the "Vancouver formula," couldn't the eight dissidents resign themselves to put up with this Charter? For us there was no question of endorsing this hypocritical verbiage essentially aimed at wresting from Quebec its sovereign authority in education. Without taking such an absolute stand, several other provinces also had strong reservations. Reminding the meeting that England had done very well without any such legalistic yoke and nonetheless had not suppressed its citizens' human rights, our Anglo-Canadian fellows were leery of this "government by judges" that was to be installed above parliament. I shared this point of view.

Seeing his precious Charter so fiercely attacked, Trudeau, it appears, spent a good part of the night bringing up his big guns. As for us, all we could do was touch wood, knowing that we could expect the worst.

The following morning, at a breakfast meeting, one didn't have to be very perceptive to see that now there were only seven of us left. Blakeney had drawn up a "new" formula whose sole originality was that it purely and simply eliminated the opting-out clause. Since this treachery was backed by a thick document, it was certainly not the fruit of nocturnal inspiration. On top of this, as I realized shortly after, our Chairman, Bill Bennett, was not standing exactly square on his feet. I had given him the text of the statement we had prepared for the public meeting, but he had simply mislaid it—"So sorry!"—and didn't seem to be in any great hurry to find it again. Whereupon I had only to pick out around the table several other pairs of averted eyes to conclude that the Gang of Eight had decidedly had its day.

It was then that Trudeau, toward the end of the morning when there was scarcely any time left for explanations, pulled the rabbit out of the hat. If there was no agreement, he announced, he would settle for repatriation alone, and then we would have two years more to reach agreement on the Charter and the amending formula. After which, if the impasse persisted, the litigious question would be submitted to a pan-Canadian referendum.

Trudeau had put on his exacerbated air, clearly implying that this time he had reached his limit. Our ex-allies drew back a step, almost in horror. They didn't want a referendum any more than a charter of rights, less, in fact, because they were scared stiff of having to oppose something Trudeau was sure of passing off as being as virtuous as apple pie.

As for me, I was trying to weigh the pros and cons. Our common front was a dead issue. For the time being, then, we didn't have much to lose, and two years down the road . . . who could tell? Besides, if the whole population had a chance to vote on such a fundamental subject, wouldn't that be democratically more respectable than all this intrigue that ended up poisoning the atmosphere?

In an insinuating and provocative tone, Trudeau pushed me to the wall. "You, the great democrat," he said, "don't tell me you're afraid to fight . . ."

At the time he really seemed sincere.

"All right," I said.

After lunch, however, we were to discover that in reality it was a politician's trick of a rather repugnant kind. An "explanatory" text had been distributed that squirmed with almost incomprehensible subtleties, but its underlying import was as clear as day. Before a referendum could take place, consent would have to be obtained from each and every province! Behind his Oriental impassivity one could feel Trudeau literally rejoicing. He had put one over on us. To reach his own concept of democracy. In his concept, from the word "go" the end justified the means. He had just given us one more proof of that.

At any rate, his manœuvre served to drive a last nail in the coffin of the late common front. I couldn't even be bothered wondering who'd look after the burial.

Just the same, before going back to the the Hôtel de la Chaudière on the Quebec side of the river, Claude Morin and I took the precaution, as a formality, of giving our telephone number to two or three of the others who, as usual, were staying in Ottawa.

"If anything new comes up, don't forget to call us."

"No problem," they replied, but they had trouble looking us in the eye.

We had been reproached since for staying in Hull that night. Did they expect us to snoop around the corridors of the Château Laurier, listening at keyholes perhaps?

Towards one in the morning, since no one had called except to remind us of the frightful breakfast at eight-thirty, I turned in.

Reliving the adventure that had absorbed us since Spring and that was now drawing ineluctably to its close, I had some trouble getting to sleep.

Thursday, November 5, 1981. Because we had to cross the river in the middle of rush hour, I got there late. Brian Peckford [Newfoundland], who had been chosen to bell the cat, said, showing me a sheet of paper that had been put beside my plate, "We've put together a final proposition. It's very short, it only takes a couple of minutes to read."

It was short all right, but no less clear for all that.

They had taken advantage of our absence to eliminate the most crucial of our demands, that is, the right to financial compensation in case of opting out. It was the stab in the dark.

For giving their consent, the others had managed to wring concessions from the federal government that seriously weakened several dispositions of the Charter. In short, all this shady dealing, presided over in some kitchen apparently by the Chrétien-[Roy] McMurtry-[Roy] Romanow trio, had resulted in a dish that was basically mediocre in which Trudeau's initial designs had been considerably diluted. It was said, for that matter, that he was furious to have to put so much water in his wine. He was even more so, I am sure, when he found himself obliged to make partial amends for the unspeakable wrong he had done us, to give Quebec back its right to financial compensation in the fields of education and culture.

Fruit of a great deal of trickery, palmed off on a country that once again the authorities had not deigned to consult openly on

the question, this constitutional monument was already beginning
to show foundation cracks and wouldn't last eternally. The only
thing that seriously bothered us was that Ottawa would now have
the power to reduce the scope of Bill 101 to the benefit of Anglo-
Québécois, though this would in no way put our basic positions
in danger.

It was the procedure much more than the content that was
intolerable. May 20, 1980, had been an infinitely sad day of
mourning. November 5, 1981, was the day of anger and shame.

We had been betrayed, in secret, by men who hadn't hesitated
to tear up their own signatures, and without their even taking the
trouble to warn us. We knew that for them it had gone against the
grain to accept certain of our conditions in April. But they had
put their signatures to it. For us that was as good as a signed contract. But for them . . . one could see now that it had been nothing
but a simple instrument used to pressure the federal government.
Their signatures had never had the weight we gave ours. As I
have read somewhere, although the Englishman may seem to be
impeccably scrupulous in private life, one should always keep a
close eye on him when it comes to public issues. I therefore swore
that . . . but a little later . . .

Tricked by Trudeau, dropped by the others, all we could do
was tell them briefly our way of looking at things before returning to Quebec. All around the big conference table, except at our
place, it was congratulations and hearty laughter, some even
going so far as to toast this doubtful victory.

"I am infinitely sorry," I told them, "to see Quebec back in the
place the federal regime has traditionally reserved for us: once
again Quebec is all alone. It will be up to our own people to draw
what conclusions they can. When they have done that, I think
you may feel a little less joyful than you seem to be now."

On April 17, 1982, Queen Elizabeth II came to Ottawa to put her signature on our newest constitutional document: Constitution Act, 1982. It

included the Canadian Charter of Rights and Freedoms and an amending formula.

All the provinces and territories signed on. The Province of Québec did not.

"The night of the long knives," as the constitutional episode of November 1981 was called, met with fury and bitterness in Québec, for it was a "most despicable betrayal." And beyond it there seemed to be no hope! Claude Morin, the Québec Intergovernmental Affairs minister, emphasised this when he said in the Assemblée nationale that all that remained to be done was for the Anglophone-dominated federal government and the nine Anglo-Canadian provinces to ask London, another no less Anglophone government, "to diminish, without consent, the integrity and jurisdiction of the only French-language government in North America."

To this day, in the Province of Québec, there is no escaping the feeling that the Québécois were betrayed in the middle of that night.

Five years later, in April 1987, another attempt was made to bring Québec into the "constitutional family of Canada." By that time Brian Mulroney was prime minister, having been elected in 1984, and Robert Bourassa had been premier since 1985. Both leaders were determined to end Québec's isolation (although the province was legally bound by the provisions of the Constitution Act of 1982).

In May 1985, Bourassa had established a set of five proposals that would enable Québec to "resume a full role in the constitutional councils of Canada." Among these proposals were the following: Québec would be recognised as a distinct society within Canada, the Chartre québécoise des droits et libertés would have primacy over the Canadian Charter of Rights and Freedoms, Québec would receive a veto over changes to federal institutions and the creation of new provinces, and the federal and provincial governments would enter into a redistribution of powers between them. This set of proposals became the basis of the Meech Lake Constitutional Accord of 1987.

After negotiations, Ottawa and the provinces and territories unanimously agreed to meet Québec's demands and to recognise that Québec would have the primary responsibility to protect and promote its distinct character. The other provinces and the federal government would have the duty to protect the "fundamental characteristic" of Canada—a Canada that speaks French concentrated in but not limited to Québec and a Canada that speaks English concentrated in the rest of the country but also present in Québec. The first ministers were in agreement, as well, that future judges of the Supreme Court of Canada, and senators, would be chosen from lists prepared by the provinces, that the provinces could have recourse to an opting-out formula with full compensation, and that all provinces were equal.

The first ministers initialled the agreement and had three years (until June 1990) to have their respective legislative bodies ratify the accord. It would then become part of the Canadian Constitution. Two years later, the Parliament of Canada and seven provinces had ratified it. There remained New Brunswick, Manitoba, and Newfoundland.

At the last minute, New Brunswick's Legislative Assembly ratified it, but in Manitoba, an election in 1988, in which the accord was the central issue, resulted in the defeat of the New Democratic government that had initialled it. The new minority government reassessed it and, eventually, presented it to the Legislative Assembly for ratification. However, Elijah Harper, a Native chief, angry that the accord had not mentioned Aboriginal peoples, their rights and their issues, delayed the proceedings until time ran out. Then, in Newfoundland, a newly elected (1989) Liberal government, headed by Clyde Wells, disapproved of the distinct-society clause. Wells went on to become the chief architect of its demise, as he rallied his province and many outside of it to his point of view. But Ottawa intervened and Wells finally agreed to refer it to his legislature. However, when the accord died on the order paper in Manitoba, he withdrew it, because, by then, Meech was dead.

However, Québec was probably the main instrument of the demise of the accord. In December 1988, the Supreme Court of Canada had declared unconstitutional Québec's determination to outlaw English on commercial signs. To silence the uproar, Bourassa invoked the "notwithstanding" clause of the Constitution Act of 1982 to overrule the Supreme Court. Bill 178, a fascist legislation, required that all outdoor commercial signs be in French, but permitted bilingual ones indoors, provided that the part of the sign in French be much larger and more visible than the English portion. As Bourassa admitted, the legislation trampled the individual rights of the English-speaking residents of Québec, but according to him it was in the national interest that this be so.

Bill 178 infuriated the rest of Canada and no doubt gave a splendid opportunity for governments and citizens to review the distinct-society clause. Did it give new powers to Québec? A special status? Would it be used to undermine the Charter of Rights and Freedoms? Would it create two Canadas? However, Québec was still not a member of the "constitutional family of Canada."

As I wrote in *Canada My Canada, What Happened?*

Both the content and élitist process of the [Meech Lake] accord struck me as harmful to Canada and to me as a citizen. I felt that Meech altered my relationship with the national institutions that governed me by introducing a provincial middle-man in nominations to the Senate and the Supreme Court. To me it was an opening for provincialism to become the dominant force to the detriment of national paramountcy. The accord also placed the Constitution of 1982 in a strait-jacket by making future changes, particularly in the matters of rights for women and Native people, sexual orientation, and the creation of new provinces, practically impossible. And the mammoth changes proposed in the accord were to be imposed on Canadians without proper and direct consultations with them. I dismissed the discussions in the provincial legislatures and in the House of Commons as inconsequential: after all, these bodies were the creatures of the signatories to the accord.

The only point in the Meech Lake accord I agreed with was the statement that Québec was a distinct society. It is. It has been since 1608, and it will be always. And that fact should be recognised. It need not confer any additional rights or powers to

Québec, nor arm it with a capacity to thwart the national will. If Meech confirmed the fact of Québec's distinct status, it also laid down an obligation: that distinctness must be protected. And I believe that it is the responsibility of all Canadians, through a constitutional statement, not only to protect it but to guarantee it. Québec cannot be left alone with that responsibility.

Across the chasm of our so-called Canadian disunity, we didn't call each other too many names and we certainly didn't shoot at each other. However, all Canadians and many Canadiens were made to feel responsible for the "failure" of Meech and guilty of having, once again, betrayed Québec. Forgetting that close to 92 percent of Canadians and Canadiens had, through their elected representatives, endorsed the accord, we, nevertheless, assumed the guilt.

And we would have to try again to find a way to bring Québec into the "constitutional family of Canada."

Oka is a small village in the beautiful hills of Québec, just west of Montréal, not far from the Mohawk reserve of Kanehsatake. In the summer of 1990, the mayor and council of Oka were in the process of taking over land adjoining the burial ground of the Mohawks so that rich white men would be able to play eighteen holes of golf instead of nine. To defend their honour and that of their ancestors, the Mohawks set up a blockade. The Sûreté du Québec stormed the blockade, during which an officer was killed. The Canadian Armed Forces were called in, for the second time in less than a generation, to restore order among the people of Québec.

The attitudes and behaviour of many during the Oka crisis provide more than enough evidence of the moral vacuum of that period.

The Abenaki artist Alanis Obomsawin wrote and produced a series of films about that event, the most important of which is *Kanehsatake: 270 Years of Resistance.*

To bring the people into the constitutional discussions and assess their views as to the vitality of Confederation, Canadians and Canadiens were consulted, perhaps, ad nauseam. Within Québec, there was the Allaire Committee and the Bélanger-Campeau Committee. In addition, Ottawa had the pan-Canadian Beaudoin-Edwards Committee and the Citizen's Forum on Canada's Future—the Spicer Commission. Then, in September 1991, the federal government followed with a comprehensive document called *Shaping Canada's Future Together*, which was entrusted to a joint parliamentary (Castonguay-Dobbie) committee, to elicit the views of the peoples of Canada. Unfortunately for the cause of Confederation, we remained rather silent, no doubt bored to tears.

Faced with the non-participatory attitude of citizens, the government thought it wise to convene five constitutional conferences in January and February 1992. Having forgotten the First Peoples, the government announced a sixth constitutional conference. All of this culminated in a federal document called *A Renewed Canada*, which led to the Charlottetown Accord in September 1992 negotiated by the federal government, the provincial and territorial governments, the Assembly of First Nations, the Native Council of Canada, the Inuit Tapirisat of Canada, and the Métis National Council. By that time, many provincial governments had determined that no constitutional changes would be made without a referendum, and Québec had given notice that if "Canada" wasn't able to come up with an acceptable offer to Québec by October 1992, a referendum on sovereignty would be held. Prime Minister Mulroney called a national referendum for October 26, 1992. On that day 75 percent of eligible voters went to the polls. Six provinces (Nova Scotia, Québec, Manitoba, Saskatchewan, and British Columbia) and one territory (Yukon) rejected the Charlottetown Accord. On that day, 44.8 percent of the voters endorsed the accord, 54.2 percent rejected it.

To this day, Québec is not part of the "constitutional family of Canada."

In 1993, Robert Bourassa resigned and was succeeded by Daniel Johnson, another son of the former premier of Québec. In the elections of September 1994, Jacques Parizeau, who had succeeded Pierre-Marc Johnson as leader of the Parti Québécois in 1987, defeated the Liberals.

By that time, the federal Liberals under Jean Chrétien were firmly entrenched in Ottawa, having won a majority in the elections of 1993.

Across the aisle was an opposition fractured along regional lines. The Conservatives were hardly alive; the New Democratic Party barely breathing; western Canada was largely represented by the Reform Party; and Her Majesty's Loyal Opposition was the separatist Bloc Québécois. (The Bloc was founded in June 1991, and Lucien Bouchard became its leader. In the federal elections of 1993, the Bloc elected 54 members in Québec with 49.3 percent of the popular vote.)

Parizeau, to fulfil an electoral promise made in the elections of '94, decided to hold a referendum on Québec's future on October 30, 1995, when Québécois and Quebeckers would be asked the following question: "Do you agree that Québec should become sovereign, after having made a formal offer to Canada for a new economic and political partnership, within the scope of the Bill respecting the future of Québec and of the agreement signed on June 12, 1995?"

Referendum questions in Québec are never simple. The Bill referred to is Bill 1—an Act respecting the future of Québec, along with a preamble that praises the glories and benefits of sovereignty. As for the "agreement signed on June 12, 1995," the co-signators were Parizeau, Bouchard, and Mario Dumont, the leader of the Action démocratique du Québec.

At first, the Non had it in the polls, but after Bouchard replaced Parizeau as the leader of the Oui side, matters improved greatly for those favouring sovereignty. The campaign was controversial and emotional, with rallies and slogans and intimidation—as well as promises. The most important of those was from Jean Chrétien, who, during the final days of the campaign, promised to take the necessary steps to recognise Québec's "distinct society" and to guarantee the province a veto over constitutional changes. Whether this intervention helped or not is moot; on October 30, 1995, the Non side won with a razor-thin 50.56 percent. (Subsequently, there was alleged interference by the Oui side, when a large number of voters on the Non side saw their votes declared void, and it is doubtful that the enumeration was done properly.)

Three federal initiatives came out of the 1995 referendum. The first was a recognition by Parliament of the distinct-society status of Québec; that is, a society characterised by the French language, a unique culture, and a civil law system. The second initiative was to grant a veto to the western region, the Atlantic region, Ontario, and Québec over all future constitutional changes. (Later, British Columbia was added to this long list of vetoers.) The third contribution to national peace was that the federal government would hand over to the provinces its role in training workers in the labour market, apprenticeship and co-operative education programs, and workplace-based training.

These federal resolutions addressed some of the difficulties, but certainly did little to make federalists out of separatists. Monsieur Parizeau had to resign after the referendum because of a racist remark that he had made in his speech following the vote. Lucien Bouchard succeeded him, until his resignation in January 2001. His deputy premier, Bernard Landry, a fervent separatist, will probably replace him.

Now that we are in new century, Québec has still not joined the "constitutional family of Canada."

And so we come to the end of this highly personal recounting of the tale of Québec. Often, in telling this tale, I have emphasised what I love about Québec: the passion and the roller-coaster emotions of the people; their feeling sorry for themselves and their honest search for an honourable way to be themselves; their sense of adventure, which has taken them all over the planet, and yet, too often, their withdrawal into themselves; their love of life and their way of finding themselves in the stories they tell, the songs they sing, the gigues they dance in the pursuit of a god that has tended to be harsh and, from time to time, a source of compelling strength.

These people opened a continent to a civilisation that has much nobility in it, and they introduced a new language to North America. These people made a home in Canada and they intend to keep it by protecting it and embellishing it. These people have experienced the value of diversity, even at the risk of their collective life. These people have often tried to self-destruct, but they have had the skills to pull back and reinvent the tools necessary to become themselves. These people have great courage and a zest for life that many ought to emulate. They are a good people and sometimes a great people.

Thus ends my tale.

❧

Mascou enters. "Come," he says, "we will go for a walk."

"Not in the park, I hope. I go there often enough."

"No," he replies. "We will go where you sat by the fire with Prince Domagaya, the son of the King of Canada, Donnacona."

I'm happy with that.

"Come," he adds, "Chazy and Champa are waiting."

I close my eyes.

❧

Bibliographical Notes

✣

*I*n writing this book, Katherine Keefler, Doris Cowley, and I used many fine books and articles written by scholars who have described and assessed the life and times of the province of Québec.

Among those I should mention in particular are two important research tools to which I frequently referred for information: one is the *Dictionary of Canadian Biography/Dictionnaire biographique du Canada*, vols. I to VII (University of Toronto Press/Les Presse de l'université Laval, 1966–1990) and the other is *The 2000 Canadian Encyclopedia World Edition/2000 L'Encyclopédie Canadienne Edition Bilingue* (McClelland & Stewart) on CDRom.

In addition, the reader may want to consult *The Canadian Centenary Series: A History of Canada*, edited by Ramsay Cook (Toronto: McClelland & Stewart). For the purposes of this book I used vol. 1, *Early Voyages and Northern Approaches 1000–1632*, by Tryggvi Oleson (Toronto, 1963); vol. 2, *The Beginnings of New France 1524-1663*, by Marcel Trudel (Toronto, 1973);

vol. 3, *Canada under Louis XIV 1669–1701*, by W.J. Eccles (Toronto, 1964); vol. 4, *New France 1701–1744*, *"A Supplement to Europe,"* by Dale Miquelon (Toronto, 1987); vol. 5, *New France 1744–1760*, by G.F.G. Stanley (Toronto, 1968); vol. 6, *Quebec: The Revolutionary Age: 1760–1791*, by Hilda Neatby (Toronto. c. 1966); and vol. 8, *Lower Canada 1792–1840*, by Fernand Ouellet, trans. Patricia Claxton (Toronto, 1980). Also there is Gustave Lanctot's three-volume *A History of Canada* (Clark, Irwin, 1973).

I also referred to the excellent series on video, *Epopée en Amerique—Une Histoire Populaire du Québec*, directed by Gilles Carle, narrated by Jacques Lacoursière and produced by Imadission. This is a truly marvellous work, and I believe every province should have its history so aptly recorded.

For Samuel de Champlain, see Samuel de Champlain, *Oeuvres de Champlain*, 6 vols. (Québec: C.H. Laverdière, 1870); H.P. Biggar, *Samuel de Champlain Works* (Champlain Society) or Narcisse Eutrope Dionne, *Samuel Champlain*, 2 vols. (Québec, 1891–1906). For Marie de l'Incarnation, please consult Claude Martin, ed., *La vie de la Vénérable Mère Marie de l'incarnation, première supérieure des Ursulines de la Nouvelle-France, tirée de ses lettres et de ses écrits* (Paris, 1677).

Then we move into a list of specialized works of interest and books from which I have quoted extensively:

Broadfoot, Barry. *Ten Lost Years 1929–1939: Memories of Canadians Who Survived the Depression*. Toronto: Doubleday, 1973.

Chapais, Thomas. *Cours d'histoire du Canada*. Trois-Rivières: Boréal Express, 1972.

Colombo, John Robert, ed. *The 1999 Canadian Global Almanac*. Toronto: Macmillan, 1999.

Garneau, François Xavier. *Histoire du Canada*, 9 vols. Montréal: Les éditions de l'arbre, 1944.

Gélinas, Gratien. *Tit-Coq*, trans. Kenneth Johnstone. Toronto: Clarke, Irwin and Co. Ltd., 1967.

Hémon, Louis. *Maria Chapedelaine*. Caen: Laurence Olivier Four, 1982.

Hopkins, J. Castell. *Chronology of Canadian History, from confederation in 1867 up to the end of 1900*. Toronto: Annual Review Publishing Co., 1905.

Horn, Michiel, ed. *The Dirty Thirties, Canadians in the Great Depression.* Canada: Copp Clark, 1972.

Kalm, Pehr. *The America of 1750: Peter Kalm's Travels in North America*, ed. A.B. Benson. 1927; reprint 1966.

LaPierre, Laurier L. *Canada My Canada, What Happened?* Toronto: McClelland & Stewart, 1992.

———. *1759 The Battle for Canada.* Toronto: McClelland & Stewart, 1990.

———. *Sir Wilfrid Laurier and the Romance of Canada.* Toronto: Stoddart, 1996.

Lévesque, René. *Memoirs*, trans. Philip Stratford. Toronto: McClelland & Stewart, 1986.

Linteau, Paul-André, René Durocher and Jean-Claude Robert. *Quebec: A History 1867–1929*, trans. Robert Chodos. Toronto: J. Lorimer, 1983.

Saywell, John. *Quebec 70.* Toronto: University of Toronto Press, 1971

———. *The Rise of the Parti Québécois, 1967–1976.* Toronto: University of Toronto Press, 1977.

Scott, F.R. *Selected Poems.* Toronto: Oxford University Press, 1966.

Thompson, Dale. *Jean Lesage and the Quiet Revolution.* Montreal: Editions Quebec/Amerique, 1986. Translated by McClelland & Stewart, 1986.

Wade, Mason. *The French Canadians (1760–1945).* Toronto: Macmillan, 1956.

Any casual reader will realise that this bibliography is far from being exhaustive. The reason is that in its preparation, I was only interested in listing books that can readily be found in ordinary Canadian libraries. Should the reader be interested in further materials, he can look in any library catalogue under *Québec*. In the text, I have also referred to certain authors. Most of their works are easily accessible.

Acknowledgements

*T*his book has occupied part of my life over the past three years, as it was delayed by the liberation of my prostate and the heartbreaking illness of my grandchild, Alex LaPierre, daughter of Dominic and Laura. I thank her for choosing the light. I also thank her parents for living in the light!

In the writing of this book, I have incurred several debts of gratitude and I owe heartfelt thanks to many.

I say, "Thank you!":

to those who lived the story of Québec and shared it in their memoirs and diaries, in their novels and poems and essays, in their paintings and sculptures, and in the buildings they designed;

to those who came to visit me in my time to relate the part they played in the story of Québec;

to the professional historians and scholars, journalists and commentators, artists and onlookers who have told the story of Québec before me;

to the personnel of the libraries and archives and my researchers,

Katherine Keefler and Doris Cowley.

Without the intelligence, engagement, skill, and compassion of Katherine (Kathy) Keefler, who researched most of it, I would not have been able to write this book.

At Penguin, there are several to whom much is owed: Cynthia Good, the president and publisher, who thought I could make the tale of Québec interesting, especially if Mascou was around; Barbara Berson, the editor, is a paragon of diplomacy and patience, good humour and intelligence; Dennis Mills, the copyeditor, knows where every word and punctuation mark belongs, has a compassionate disdain for sloppy writing, and is obsessed with sources and bibliographical notes; and Cathy MacLean the illustrator, who designed the cover and the book to be attractive enough for potential readers to buy it.

At my house, there is Lucie Wilson, who promised to be nice to me for two weeks. She kept her promise even though I went away for one of those two weeks. She owes me one. There is also Michel (Mitch) Miller, who is kind and generous with his time and solicitude. Then, in and out, is Doris Cowley who researches, types, organises this and that, runs the office of Telefilm Canada in Ottawa, is recording secretary for the Heritage Fairs program, and finds time for her family, not to mention mine. It's difficult for me to find words that match what I owe them.

In Vancouver, where my soul really is, Jeto Sengara gives me a home and her precious love, while Sandy Logan and Larry Beasley, Arthur Erickson, Lois Milson, Vicki Gabereau and Tom Rowe, Daryl and Anne-Marie Duke, Don Shiota and Denis Lim contribute such an enormous amount to my well-being.

In Toronto, Mary Joyal offers her hospitality and care. It was in her kitchen that Charles Aubert de la Chesnaye came to see me.

I miss my agent, Bruce Westwood, of Westwood Creative Artists. He does more than what he needs to do to make it all happen.

To Harvey Slack, I owe the tranquility of mind and heart—but not so much of place—that is needed to perform the exacting task of writing a book. His comforting presence and participation in my life creates an adventure lived at many levels.

Acknowledgements

Chazy, the dog, and Champa, the cat, give affection endlessly. I appreciate that.

And Mascou comes and goes.

Index